Scu

GENERAL EDITOR

- Penelope Curtis

SECTION EDITORS

- Matthew Withey
- Jon Wood
- Victoria Worsley
- Denise Raine

PROJECT COORDINATOR

- Jackie Howson

Sculpture in 20th-century Britain

Volume I Identity, Infrastructures, Aesthetics, Display, Reception

Henry Moore Institute

Published in 2003 by the Henry Moore Institute
74 The Headrow Leeds LS1 3AH

ISBN 1 900081 98 9

The Henry Moore Institute is part of the Henry Moore Foundation

www.henry-moore-fdn.co.uk

EDITORS Penelope Curtis, Denise Raine, Matthew Withey, Jon Wood, Victoria Worsley
PROJECT COORDINATOR Jackie Howson

PROJECT MANAGER Paul Manning
COPY-EDITORS Fiona Sewell, Stephanie Richards
PROOFREADER Elizabeth Teague
INDEXER Rosemary Dear

DESIGN & PRODUCTION Groundwork, Skipton
PRINT & REPRO Triangle, Leeds

The twenty authors writing in this book represent some of the more significant scholarship in the field of British sculpture studies. Some are established scholars, some have just begun to make their mark on the area, while others would not even think of themselves as working in this field. All this is deliberate: we hope this book will help to take the history of sculpture into the history of art, which has itself long since moved to embrace a much wider cultural history. We are grateful to our contributors for taking on an unconventional project, and for agreeing to write to the titles for which they were commissioned, rather than the essays which they might themselves have chosen to deliver.

This book is the companion to *Volume II: A Guide to Sculptors in the Leeds Collections*, which is both a catalogue and a collection of short monographic essays. That volume has specific relation to Leeds – in terms of documentating relevant material held in the collections of Leeds Museums and Galleries and the Henry Moore Institute – whereas this volume is freed of that responsibility. We wanted it to stand as a 'survey' of sculpture in 20th-century Britain, while at the same time allowing our authors to present new and original insights gathered as a result of their own archival research or of their own direct experience in the field.

In 1981 the Whitechapel Art Gallery published *British Sculpture in the Twentieth Century*, a point of departure for our own publications over twenty years later. Over and above the fact that it is more possible to assess a century's sculpture once that century is finished, our own publications both follow and depart from the Whitechapel's model. Our publications, like the Whitechapel's, accompany an exhibition, but are designed to have a much longer life. (The Whitechapel's exhibition was shown in two parts, the first, *Image and Form 1901–50*, the second, *Symbol and Imagination 1951–80*; our own exhibition is *Other Criteria.*) Unlike the Whitechapel, we have deliberately eschewed the category 'British sculpture' in favour of 'sculpture in Britain', and sought to provide a framework which, though chronological, is not preconceived.

Other Criteria is drawn from our own collections and connects with the specific details provided in Volume II. The brief for this volume, however, was much wider, and ambitious in a different way. We asked ourselves how best to present a new 'history' of British sculpture, and we asked many colleagues to join us in that debate. Once again, we looked at the Whitechapel's *British Sculpture in the Twentieth Century* with the aim of assessing how scholarly interpretation had evolved since 1981. We looked at other catalogues too, but the more recent (and largely foreign) exhibitions devoted to the subject rarely went any further than, or even as far as, the Whitechapel's collection of essays.

Two workshops, held in 2000 and 2001, helped to confirm some of our initial instincts about the way forward, and also to define the framework within which we wanted our authors to work. The rather neutral division of the century into four quarters goes some way towards avoiding the standard chronological breakdown of British sculpture. We wanted our authors to think outside those predetermined categories (New Sculpture, direct carving, continental modernism, the 'geometry of fear', the New Generation, the New British Sculpture) and to bring to their periods new, different and more personal lines of enquiry.

Having decided to quarter the century, it followed that we assign each quarter to one of our curatorial team, with Matthew Withey taking the first, Jon Wood the second, Victoria Worsley the third and Denise Raine the last. Each of them has been responsible for editing the five essays within their period (as well as for an equivalent section of essays in Volume II) and for compiling its timeline. Each section takes in the five themes – Identity, Infrastructures, Aesthetics, Display and Reception – on which we settled as revealing of the ways in which sculpture was practised and understood, and of the ways in which recent scholarship was tending.

The short bibliography compiled by Denise Raine – the Institute's librarian – takes its point of departure as 1981, building on the more comprehensive listing to be found in the Whitechapel catalogue. We hope that the present publications stand the test of time as successfully, and play their part in changing perceptions of the history of British sculpture so that its study continues to become more sophisticated.

Penelope Curtis
Curator, Henry Moore Institute

Contents

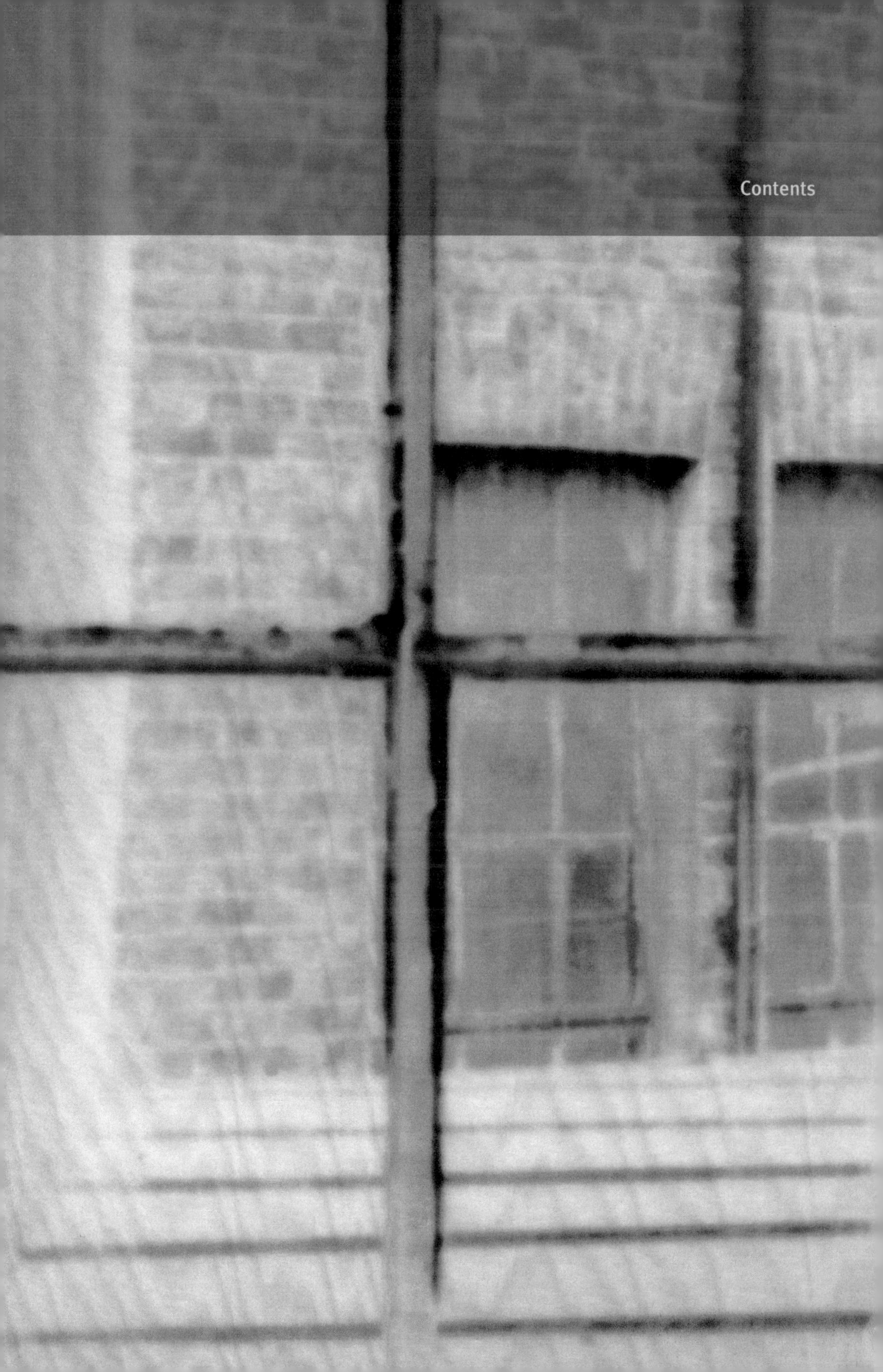

Section essays

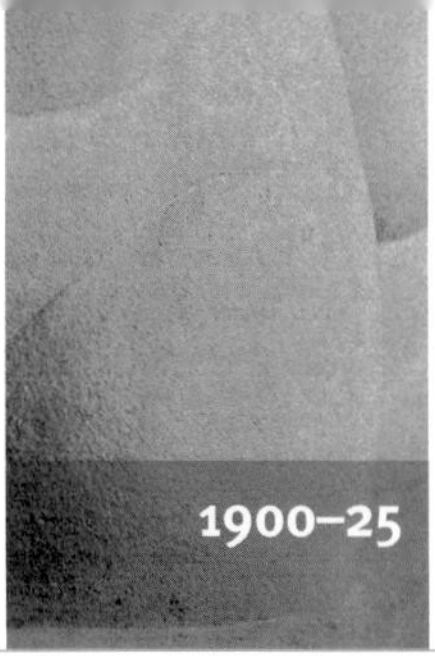
1900–25

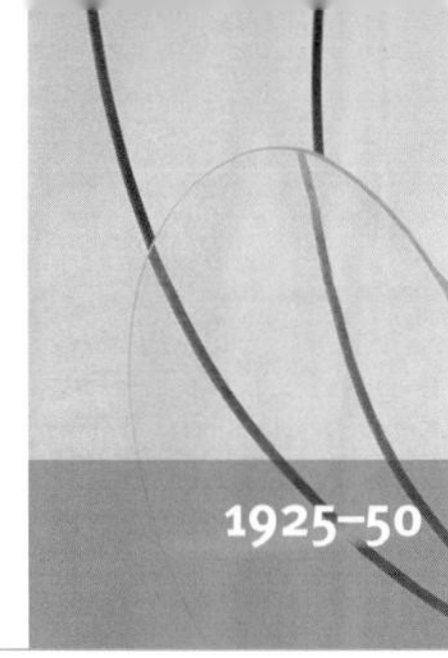
1925–50

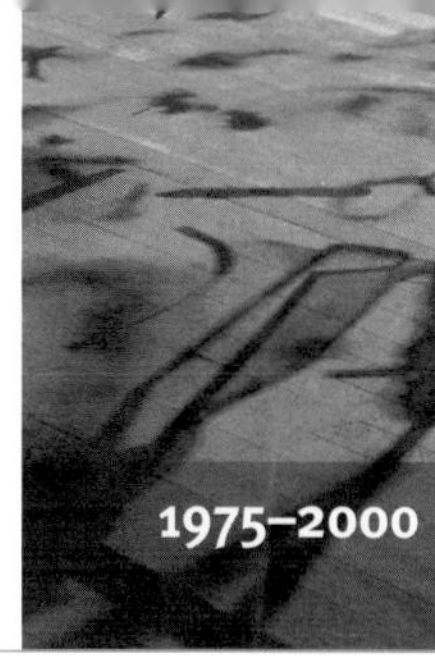
1975–2000

All items illustrated in the Timelines are drawn from the Leeds Collections

1900

- *Exposition Universelle*, Paris – exhibiting British sculptors include Charles John Allen, Gilbert Bayes, Alfred Drury, Edward Onslow Ford, George Frampton, William Goscombe John, Andrea Lucchesi, Frank Lynn-Jenkins and William Hamo Thornycroft
- Edouard Lantéri becomes the first professor of modelling at South Kensington Art Schools
- Alfred Gilbert appointed professor of sculpture at the Royal Academy Schools
- Sculpture scheme for Kelvingrove Art Gallery and Museum completed in Glasgow, having been overseen by George Frampton
- Thomas Brock completes his monument to Frederic Leighton for St Paul's Cathedral, London

1901

- Alfred Gilbert goes into exile in Belgium
- Edward Onslow Ford dies – his monument to Queen Victoria is completed in Manchester
- Work begins on the Victoria memorial for the Mall in London, overseen by Thomas Brock
- George Frampton and Frank Lynn-Jenkins finish work on the sculpture scheme for Lloyd's Registry of Shipping on Fenchurch Street, London
- M. H. Spielmann publishes *British Sculpture and Sculptors of To-day*
- Memorial to Dean Hook by Frederick William Pomeroy erected in City Square, Leeds
- Francis Derwent Wood settles in London after leaving his post as a modelling master at Glasgow School of Art
- William Hamo Thornycroft completes his memorial to King Alfred at Winchester

1902

- Edouard Lantéri publishes the first volume of his *Modelling: A Guide for Teachers and Students*
- George Frampton becomes master of the Art Workers' Guild
- Thomas Brock's equestrian statue 'The Black Prince' erected in City Square, Leeds
- George Frederick Watts accepts the Order of Merit
- Alfred Drury's Queen Victoria memorial erected in Bradford
- Alfred Turner's memorial to Queen Victoria completed at Tynemouth
- Auguste Rodin's 'St John the Baptist' purchased by public subscription in England, and presented to the South Kensington Museum

1903

- Theodore Spicer-Simson produces his first medals
- Alfred Gilbert settles permanently in Bruges, though his reredos for St Albans Cathedral is still being completed in England
- Eric Gill takes up stone-carving

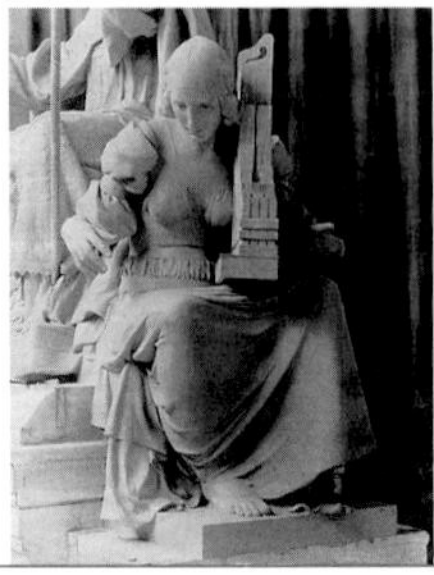

'Music' by George Frampton for the facade of Kelvingrove Art Gallery and Museum, Glasgow

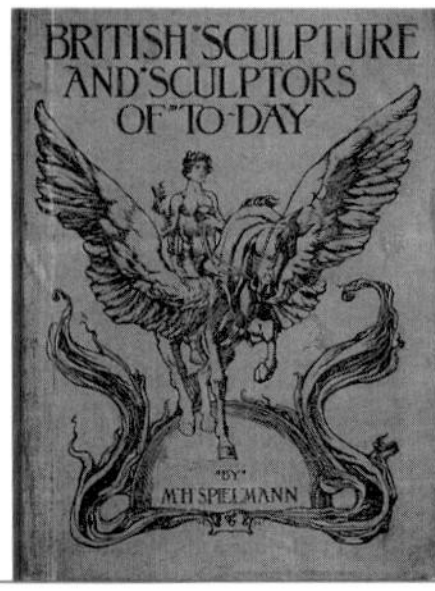

Cover of M. H. Spielmann's *British Sculpture and Sculptors of To-day*

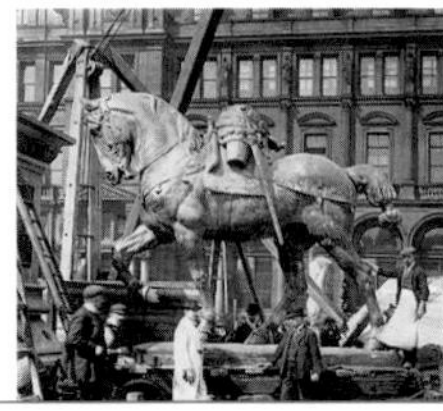

'The Black Prince' by Thomas Brock unveiled at City Square, Leeds

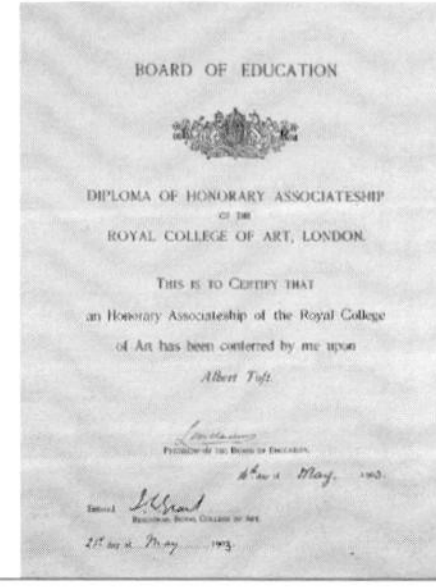

Albert Toft's certificate from the Royal College of Art

1904

- Alfred Drury receives a commission to complete the sculpture scheme for the War Office in Whitehall, London
- George Frederick Watts dies
- Royal Society of British Sculptors founded – founder members include George Frampton, William Silver Frith, Frank Lynn-Jenkins, Thomas Stirling Lee, William Reynolds-Stephens and Francis Derwent Wood – Thomas Brock becomes the first president
- Auguste Rodin's 'The Thinker' exhibited in London, and later in Oxford – the sculptor is nominated *honoris causa*

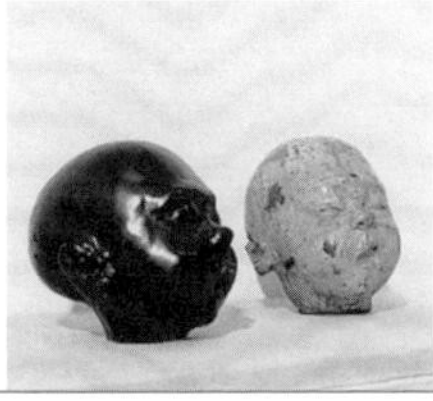

'Baby Asleep' by Jacob Epstein

1905

- Jacob Epstein destroys the contents of his studio in Paris and moves to London
- Charles John Allen completes the Queen Victoria memorial in Liverpool
- Benjamin Creswick's memorial to the men of Huddersfield completed in the town's Greenhead Park
- William Goscombe John completes his memorial to the King's Regiment in Liverpool
- Frederick William Pomeroy completes four colossal bronze figures for the Vauxhall Bridge in London
- William Hamo Thornycroft completes his Gladstone memorial for the Strand, London
- Albert Toft completes his memorial to Queen Victoria for Nottingham

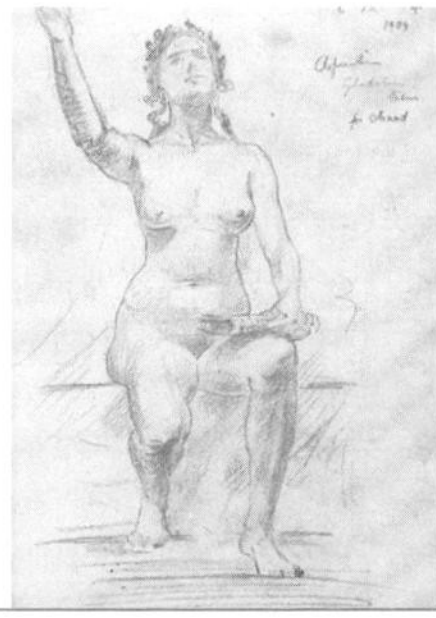

Page from one of William Hamo Thornycroft's sketchbooks for the Gladstone memorial, London

1906

- Gilbert Bayes begins teaching at Camberwell Art School
- Eric Gill takes his first apprentice – Joseph Cribb
- Auguste Rodin receives an honorary degree from the University of Glasgow

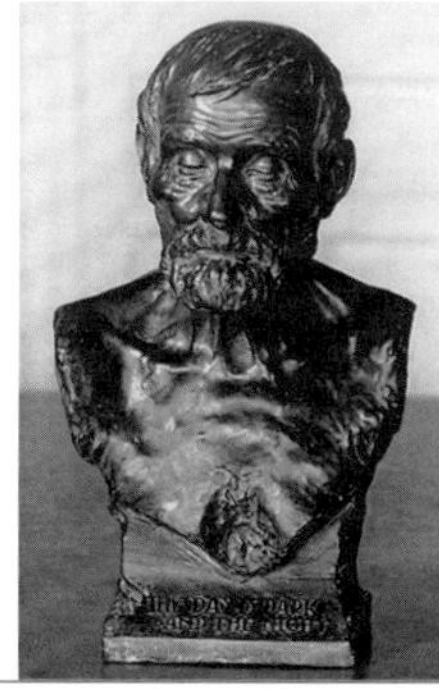

'The Day is Dark and the Night' by Edward Caldwell Spruce

1907

- Completion of the sculpture scheme for the Victoria & Albert Museum, London
- Mary Grant dies
- Edward Roscoe Mullins dies
- Jacob Epstein invited to execute the sculpture scheme for the new headquarters of the British Medical Association on the Strand, London
- William Robert Colton appointed professor of sculpture at the Royal Academy Schools
- Henri Gaudier-Brzeska wins a scholarship to study English at the Merchant Venturers' College, Bristol
- Alfred Gilbert exhibits 'Mors Janua Vitae' at the Royal Academy – he will not show there again until 1932
- Eric Gill resigns as a member of the Fabian Society and the Art Workers' Guild
- Auguste Rodin receives an honorary degree from the University of Oxford

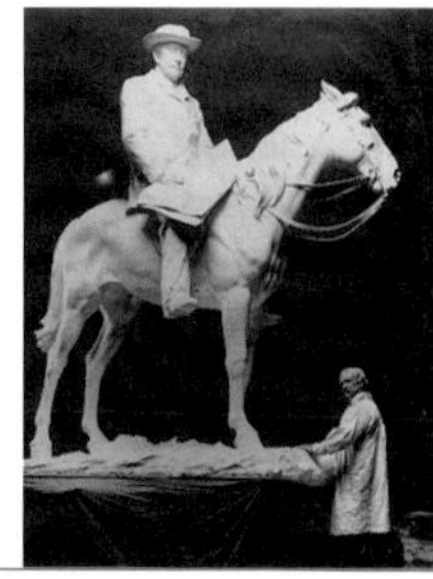

William Hamo Thornycroft with the equestrian statue for his memorial to Cecil Rhodes in Kimberley, South Africa

1908

- Jacob Epstein's British Medical Association sculptures unveiled
- George Frampton knighted
- Frederick William Pomeroy becomes master of the Art Workers' Guild
- William Reynolds-Stephens completes his 'The Scout of War' equestrian statue for the town of East London, South Africa
- Albert Toft completes the pulpit for the Congregational Church on Palatine Road, Manchester
- One-man show of Reginald Fairfax Wells' statuettes opens at the Carfax Gallery, London
- Alfred Gilbert fails to complete his commission of a 'Victory' for the Duke of Rutland's Boer War memorial

1909

- Alfred Drury completes four colossal bronze figures for the Vauxhall Bridge, London
- Albert Toft completes the monument to Edward VII for Highgate Park in Birmingham, the South African war memorial for Cannon Hill Park in Birmingham and the Welsh national memorial for Cathays Park in Cardiff

1910

- George Frampton's 'Peter Pan' erected in Kensington Gardens, London
- William Robert Colton's Royal Artillery memorial unveiled on the Mall, London
- William Hamo Thornycroft completes his Curzon memorial for Calcutta
- John Macallan Swan dies
- Eric Gill makes his first sculptures

1911

- Thomas Brock and William Goscombe John knighted
- Henri Gaudier-Brzeska moves to London
- Gwendolen Williams leaves England for Rome
- Eric Gill has his first exhibition of figure carvings at the Chenil Gallery, London
- Jacob Epstein naturalised as a British subject

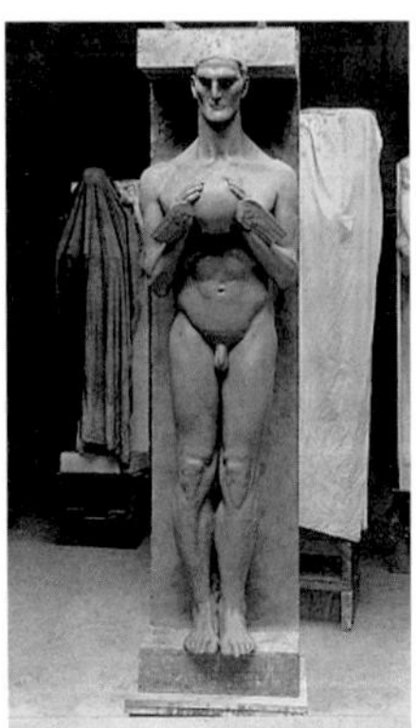

Colossal figure by Jacob Epstein for the facade of the British Medical Association, London

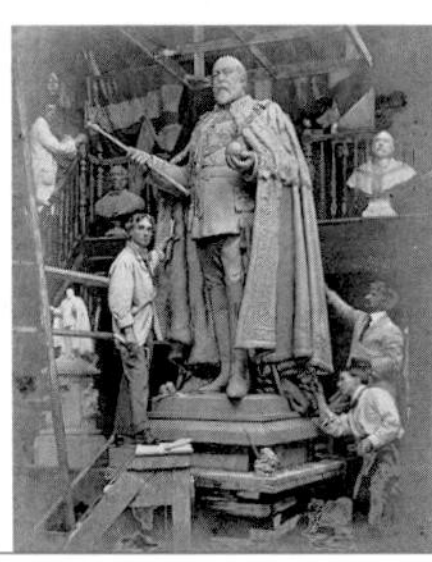

Albert Toft and his assistants with the clay model for his monument to Edward VII

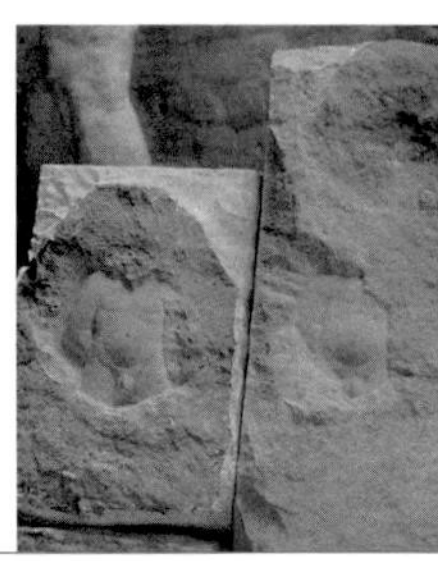

'Cocky Kid' – an early figure carving by Eric Gill

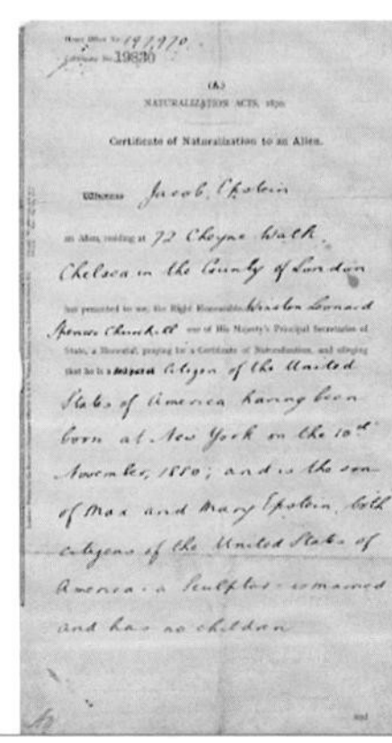

NATURALIZATION ACTS, 1870

Certificate of Naturalization to an Alien.

Whereas Jacob Epstein

an Alien, residing at 72 Cheyne Walk, Chelsea in the County of London

has presented to me, the Right Honourable Winston Leonard Spencer Churchill one of His Majesty's Principal Secretaries of State, a Memorial, praying for a Certificate of Naturalization, and alleging that he is a Citizen of the United States of America having been born at New York on the 10th November, 1880; and is the son of Max and Mary Epstein, both citizens of the United States of America; a Sculptor; is married and has no children

Jacob Epstein's official naturalisation papers

1912

■ John Tweed completes the equestrian statue for Alfred Stevens' Wellington monument in London, commissioned fifty-six years earlier

1913

■ Jacob Epstein's first solo exhibition, at Twenty-One Gallery, London

1914

■ Rebel Art Centre founded by Wyndham Lewis at 38 Great Ormond Street, London
■ Theodore Spicer-Simson publishes *Portraits and Medals in Relation to Life and Art*
■ Paul Montford completes his figure groups for Kelvin Way Bridge, Glasgow
■ Charles Sargeant Jagger gives up the Prix de Rome to enlist in the British Army
■ Alfred Gilbert completes a monumental chimney-piece for the Leeds industrialist Sam Wilson
■ Jacob Epstein completes his monumental tomb for Oscar Wilde, installed at the Père-Lachaise Cemetery in Paris – while there he meets Constantin Brancusi, Henri Gaudier-Brzeska, Amedeo Modigliani and Pablo Picasso
■ Jacob Epstein also contibutes two illustrations to the first issue of *Blast*
■ Henri Gaudier-Brzeska contributes an article entitled 'Vortex Gaudier-Brzeska' to *Blast 2*. He then enlists in the French army

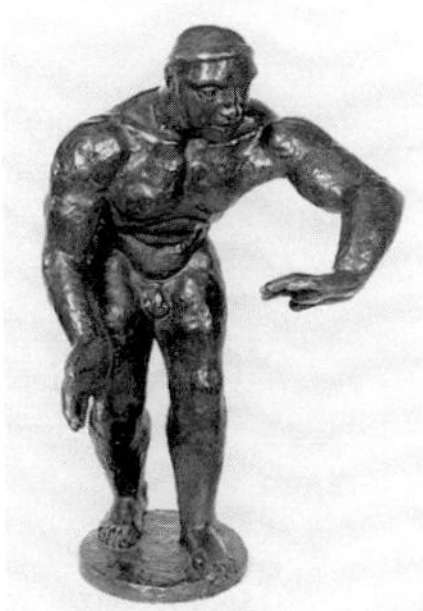

'The Wrestler' by Henri Gaudier-Brzeska

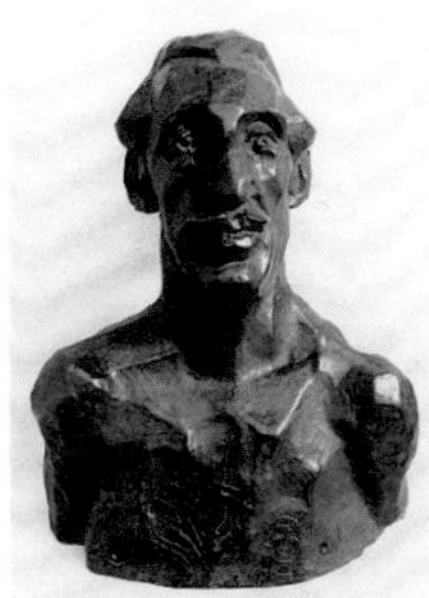

'Bust of Horace Brodzky' by Henri Gaudier-Brzeska

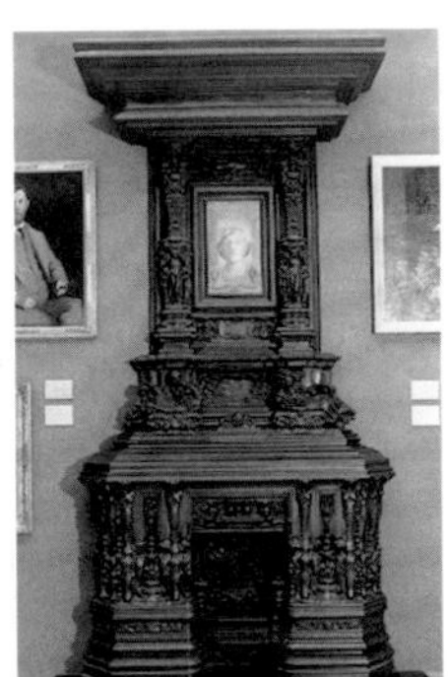

Alfred Gilbert's chimneypiece for the Leeds industrialist Sam Wilson

1915

■ Henri Gaudier-Brzeska killed in action on 5 June
■ 'Vortex Gaudier-Brzeska (Written from the Trenches)' published posthumously in *Blast 2*
■ Jacob Epstein's 'Rock Drill' exhibited for the first time, at the London Group Show
■ Lawrence Atkinson publishes *Aura*
■ James Havard Thomas appointed the Slade School's first professor of sculpture
■ Ivan Meštrović settles for a brief spell in London. His first major British exhibition is held at the Victoria & Albert Museum

1916

■ Ezra Pound publishes *Gaudier-Brzeska: A Memoir by Ezra Pound*
■ Lord Ronald Gower dies
■ Thomas Stirling Lee dies
■ Henry Moore carves his first 'sculpture': a wooden Roll of Honour commemorating Castleford High School pupils enlisted in the British army
■ Gilbert Bayes completes his sculpture scheme for the Art Gallery of New South Wales, Australia
■ William Goscombe John completes his 'St David' for Cardiff City Hall
■ Francis Derwent Wood loses out to Alfred Drury in a competition to design the statue of Joshua Reynolds for the front of the Royal Academy

1917

■ Auguste Rodin and Edouard Lantéri die
■ William Hamo Thornycroft knighted
■ Frank Lynn-Jenkins moves to New York City
■ Eric Kennington made an official war artist
■ Jacob Epstein fails to get a similar appointment, but he does sell £1,600 worth of bronzes at his first Leicester Galleries show in London
■ Eric Gill commissioned to produce the Leeds University war memorial

1918

■ Albert Hodge dies
■ Francis Derwent Wood succeeds Edouard Lantéri as professor of sculpture at the Royal College of Art
■ Memorial exhibition of Henri Gaudier-Brzeska's work held at the Leicester Galleries, London

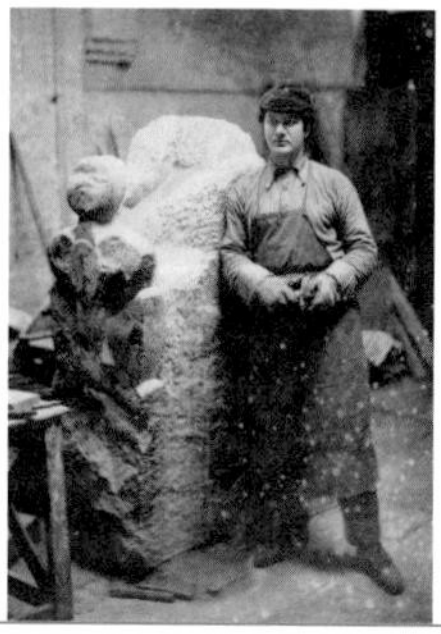

Jacob Epstein in his studio with 'Mother and Child', c.1915

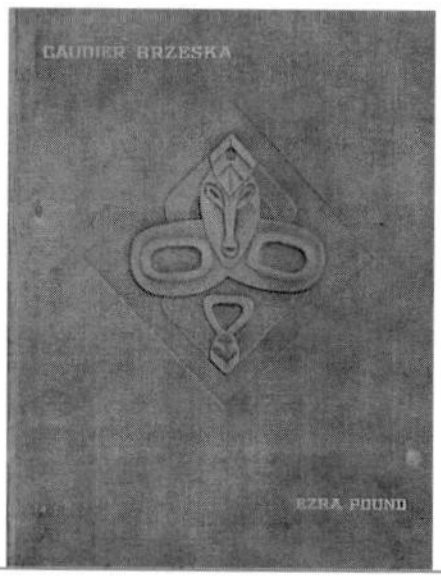

Cover of *Gaudier-Brzeska: A Memoir by Ezra Pound*

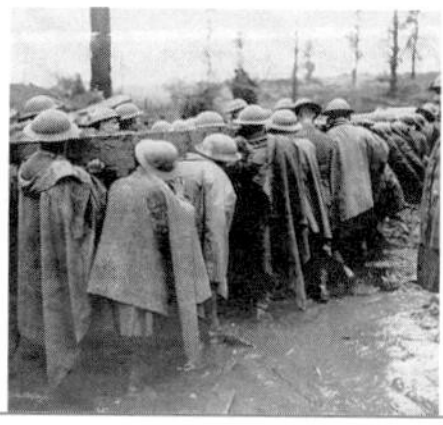

Photograph taken in 1917 at the battle of Flanders, belonging formerly to Gilbert Ledward

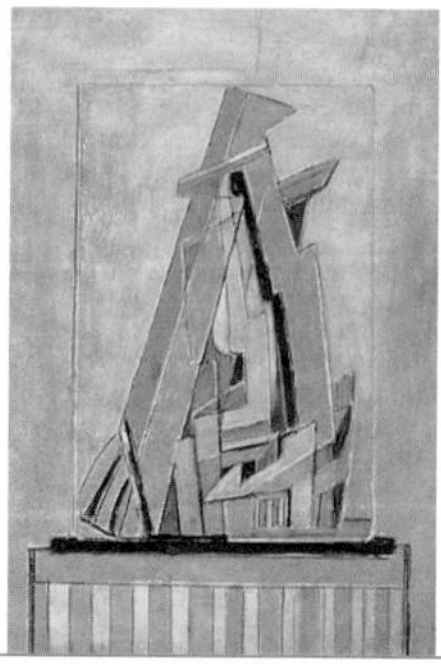

'Abstract Composition No. 1' by Lawrence Atkinson

1919

- Hermon Cawthra works for a short time with Paul Montford
- Charles Sargeant Jagger begins work on 'No Man's Land' while convalescing from his war wounds

1920

- Bertram Mackennal completes his equestrian statue of Edward VII for Waterloo Place, London
- Leon Underwood wins the Prix de Rome, but decides not to go, instead joining the Royal Academy staff as an assistant life drawing teacher

1921

- Bertram Mackennal knighted
- Paul Montford emigrates to Australia
- William Robert Colton dies
- Leon Underwood opens the Brook Green School in London
- Jacob Epstein's work is discussed in *Sculpture of To-day* by Kineton Parkes and attacked for what Lorado Taft call its 'crudities' in *Modern Tendencies in Sculpture*
- Charles Sargeant Jagger commissioned by the Royal Artillery War Commemoration Fund to produce the Royal Artillery memorial at Hyde Park Corner, London

1922

- Thomas Brock dies
- Rayner Hoff wins a scholarship to British School at Rome
- The first Lord Leverhulme founds the Lady Lever Art Gallery at Port Sunlight
- Leon Underwood has his first exhibition, at the Chenil Gallery, London
- Jacob Epstein commissioned to execute the W. H. Hudson memorial
- Charles Sargeant Jagger begins work on the Anglo-Belgian memorial at Brussels

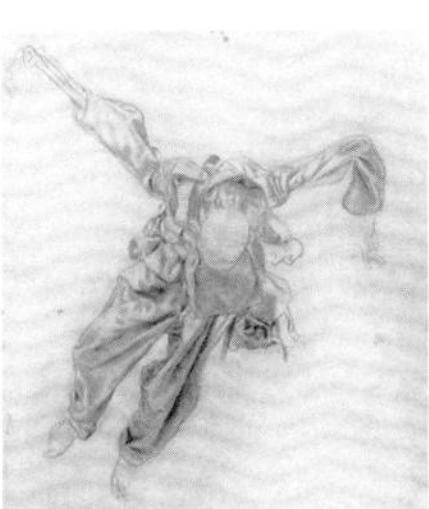

Sketch drawing for 'No Man's Land' by Charles Sargeant Jagger

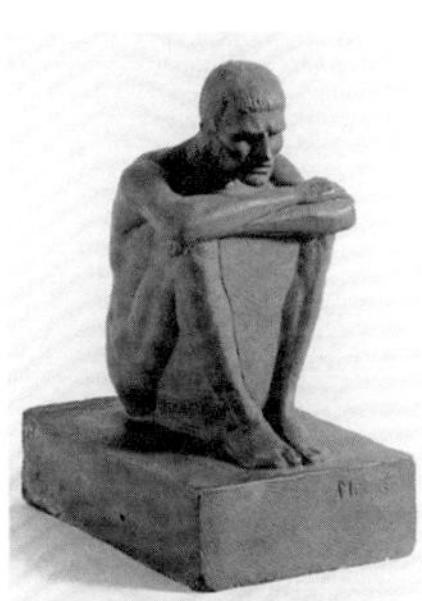

'Seated Nude Man' by Henry Moore

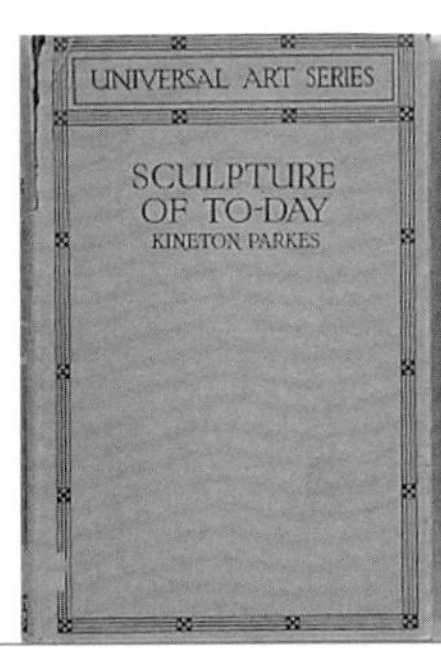

Cover of *Sculpture of To-day* by Kineton Parkes

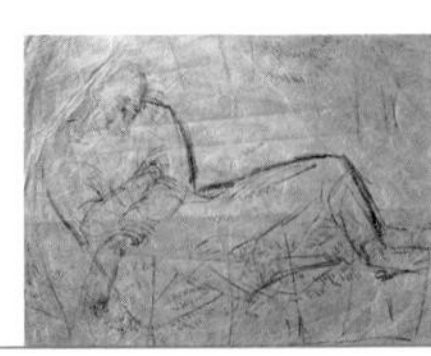

Sketch drawing for the memorial in Hyde Park to W. H. Hudson by Jacob Epstein

1923

- Rayner Hoff emigrates to Australia, where he becomes head teacher of the sculpture department at East Sydney Technical College
- Gilbert Bayes begins designing and modelling polychrome stoneware decorations for Royal Doulton
- Francis Derwent Wood leaves his job as professor of sculpture at the Royal College of Art

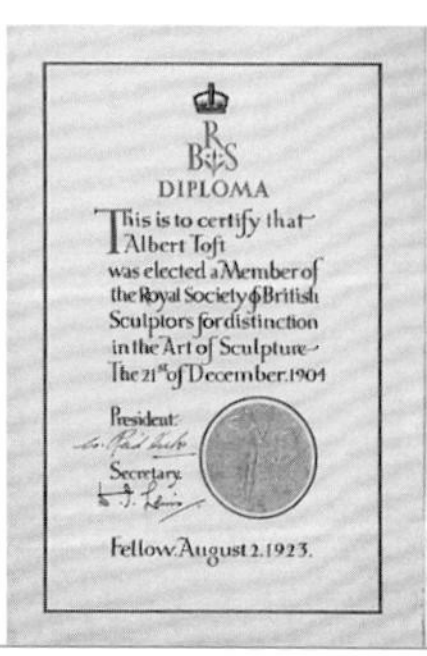

Albert Toft's certificate from the Royal Society of British Sculptors

1924

- Roger Fry attacks Epstein's work in the 26 January edition of the *New Statesman*
- Jacob Epstein rejected as a candidate for the job as professor of sculpture at the Royal College of Art
- Eric Kennington completes his first major work of sculpture: the war memorial to the 24th Allied Forces in Battersea Park, London
- Work completed on the Victoria memorial on the Mall, London
- *British Empire Exhibition* at Wembley in London features sculpture by Gilbert Bayes, Frank Dobson and Albert Toft
- Albert Bruce-Joy dies
- Frederick William Pomeroy dies
- William Silver Frith dies
- John Skeaping wins the Rome Scholarship, seeing off the challenge of his future wife Barbara Hepworth

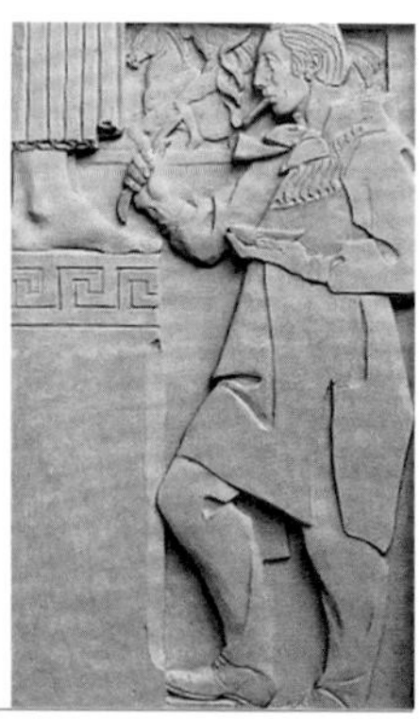

Gilbert Bayes' relief carving of 'Sculpture' for the *British Empire Exhibition* at Wembley

Punks and professionals

The first decades of the 20th century saw an increasing competition between two different, yet related, definitions of the sculptor. Both established professional sculptors – sometimes referred to in derisory fashion as 'gentlemen artists' – and younger, less conventionally trained artists shaped sculpture in these years. One cannot adequately understand the complex range of sculptural options in the early 20th century without taking both these 'professionals' and these young 'punks' seriously, for the members of each group constructed their identities in relation to the other.

Professionals

Beginning in the late 1870s and early 1880s, a new set of parameters for sculptural practice and theory developed in Britain. This modernising movement, which would in 1894 become dubbed the 'New Sculpture', reconsidered the foundations of sculptural tradition and re-evaluated the roles played by sculpture in both public and private.[1] After gaining momentum in the 1880s, the New Sculpture style came to dominate sculpture in Britain, and by the Edwardian period many of its major players were firmly established.

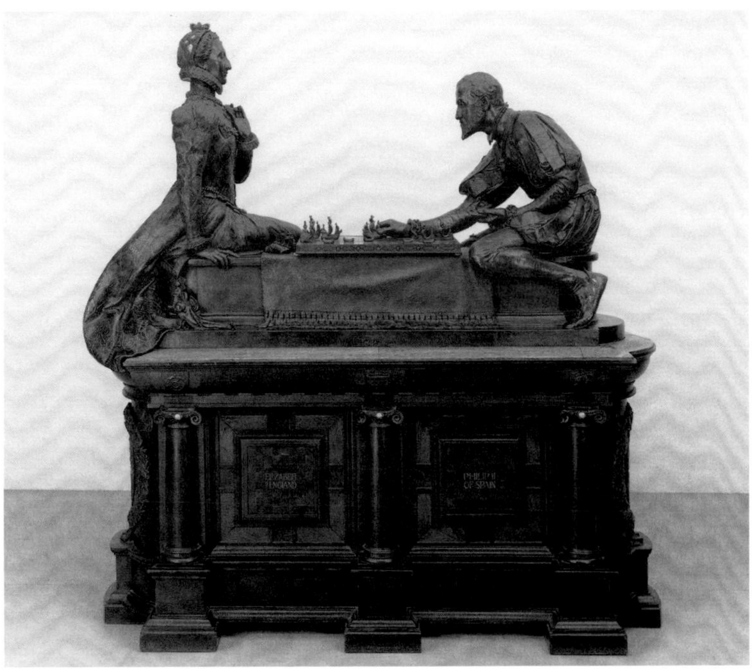

1 Williams Reynolds-Stephens, 'A Royal Game', 1906–11

2 William Goscombe John, 'Memorial to the Engine Room Heroes', 1916

3 Kathleen Scott, 'These Had Most to Give', 1923–4

4 Charles Sargeant Jagger, 'No Man's Land', 1919–20

Broadly, a predominant theme in the many manifestations of the New Sculpture movement was its renewed concern with how viewers and publics engaged with sculptural objects. Artists strove to activate the encounter with sculpture, and reconsidered its place in the gallery, in the streets and in the home. The particularities of the style grew out of, on the one hand, the infusion of a greater degree of verisimilitude into the traditions and ideals of sculpture and, on the other, the investigation of the processes and materiality of sculpture as a means to activate these naturalistically rendered forms. Rather than an unchanging and eternal conception of sculpture as the image of the classical ideal, they engaged upon the vexed pursuit of updating or renovating the function and format of sculpture. The New Sculpture was distinct from other versions of modern sculpture being formulated in Europe at that time because of the degree of this dual commitment to naturalism as a manifestation of a new sculptural ideal and to the literal sculptural object as the site of the viewer's engagement.

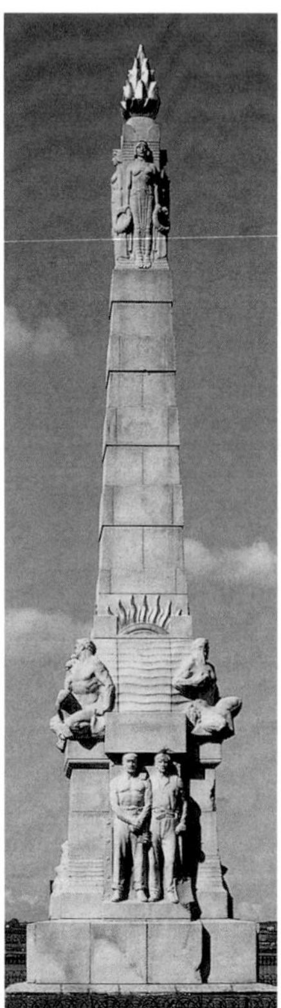

The New Sculpture was developed by a host of artists working from the 1880s and continuing through the 1920s and 1930s. The tenor of the New Sculpture undoubtedly changed as the 20th century began. Many of its important exponents, such as Edward Onslow Ford, Harry Bates and Frederic Leighton, had died (in 1901, 1899 and 1896, respectively). In 1903, Alfred Gilbert went into self-imposed exile in Bruges, only returning to England in 1926. Of those who remained, William Hamo Thornycroft – who had been crucial in the definition of the New Sculpture in the early 1880s – had steadily grown less innovative and less experimental as the 1890s wore on. By the 20th century, he had become the kind of establishment sculptor he longed to overthrow in his youth. For instance, he was instrumental in blocking James Havard Thomas' work from the Royal Academy, instigating the embarrassing 'Lycidas' scandal of 1905.[2] More public than Thornycroft was George Frampton, who became one of the most prominent sculptors of the first quarter of the century as well as a vocal opponent of modernist sculpture in England.

It would, however, be a mistake to look on the later New Sculpture as a jealous hold-over from the 19th century.[3] The movement evolved and developed new priorities and concerns. The conditions of sculptural production had undoubtedly changed. At the beginning of the 20th century, the death of Queen Victoria and the embarrassment of the Boer War concluded the 'statuemania' that had fuelled the New Sculptors and their annual innovations for the Royal Academy exhibitions. Even

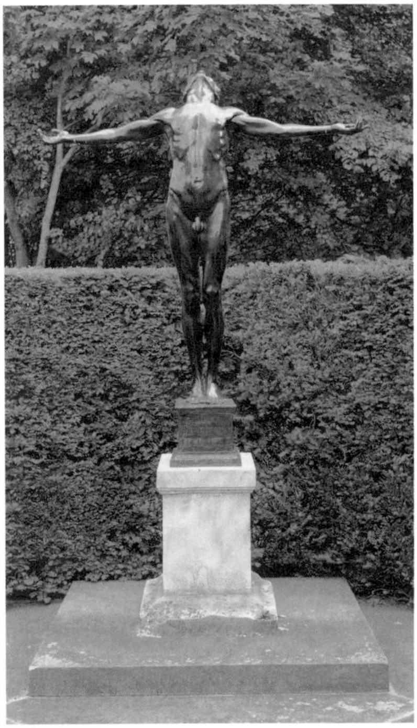

though the production of monuments went on in the 20th century, there emerged far fewer opportunities than previously (a situation that would continue until after World War I).

The New Sculpture adapted to new conditions and reconfigured its general commitment to verisimilitude. William Reynolds-Stephens, for instance, became increasingly critical of the conventional emphasis on statuary; in his own work he productively cross-bred sculpture and decorative art (Fig.1) to create complex and often unexpected works (thus providing a prototype for emerging artists such as Gilbert Bayes).[4] Reynolds-Stephens even went so far as to advocate a break with the emphasis on the body that was central to the New Sculpture, seeing a more productive avenue in the hybridity of sculpture and decorative object.[5] A crucial figure in the second wave of the New Sculpture, William Goscombe John (Fig. 2) proved himself to be catholic in his stylistic choices, attempting to assimilate aspects of modernist sculpture throughout his 20th-century career.[6] Artists such as Bertram Mackennal and Kathleen Scott (Fig. 3) engaged in sophisticated attempts to update the New Sculpture's concerns with naturalism, contemporaneity and the address to the viewer.[7] Even Frampton incorporated aspects of modern stylisation and formal reductiveness in a work like his Cavell monument of 1915–20,[8] and sculptors such as Charles Sargeant Jagger (Fig. 4) compellingly built upon the New Sculpture style and concerns to capture the terrible drama of World War I.

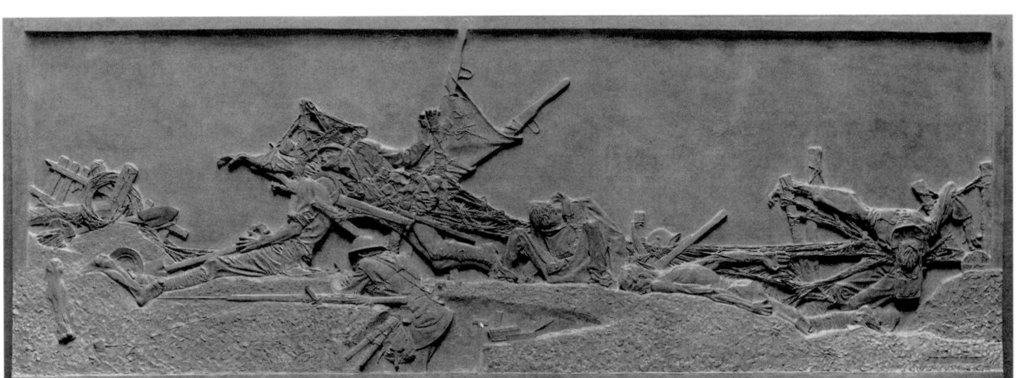

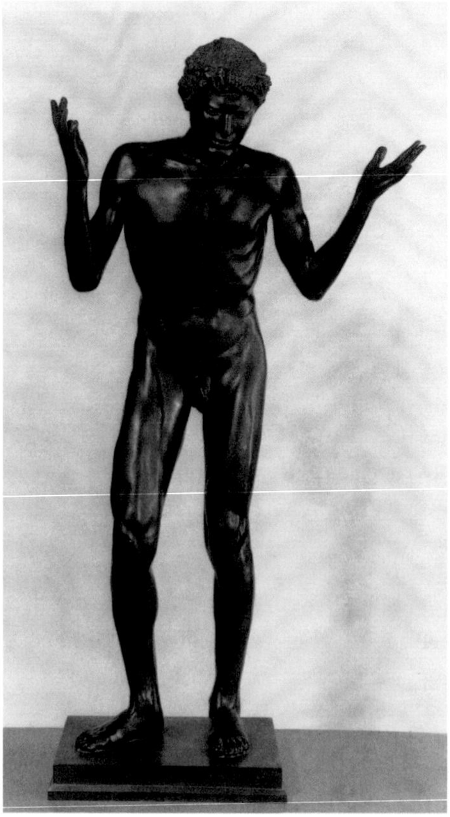

In the first decades of the 20th century, the professional sculptor still had a major role to play. Despite the reduced demand for monuments and commemorations of the kind obsessively encouraged in the late Victorian era, there remained a body of professional sculptors who contributed to building and civic projects. The two decades of the New Sculpture in the 19th century and its emphasis on the contribution of sculpture to a variety of public and private spaces both fed off and fed into the Arts and Crafts movement. Consequently, there emerged an increasingly varied production of a range of objects integrating art and design.[9] At the same time, alternatives to the innovations of the 19th century began to emerge within the framework of professional sculpture. Most significantly, after the 'Lycidas' scandal (Fig. 5), Havard Thomas, who remained an outsider to the RA throughout his career, was appointed as professor of sculpture at the Slade School of Fine Art in 1911. Though critical of the RA and its methods, he and his students nevertheless operated within and contributed to the mode of the professional sculptor in the early 20th century.

A core set of traits characterised what I am calling the professional sculptor in this period. Generally, these artists worked within existing institutions for the production and consumption of sculpture (training academies, established exhibitions and commissioning committees) and understood their training in the traditions and techniques of sculpture to qualify them for participation in civic life. The professional sculptor was considered primarily a creator of public monuments, building on the celebrity status Royal Academicians enjoyed in the Victorian era. Throughout history, sculpture has played an important civic role in western societies. The most durable and permanent of media, sculpture has been used by various constituencies in and out of power to consolidate and illustrate a set of ideals for that group. Consequently, sculpture (even that intended for the gallery) labours under an expectation of exemplarity. It is this underlying assumption that fuels the virulent and recurring debates about the propriety of public sculpture. At the same time, this assumption guaranteed for the sculptor a discrete place in polite society during this

5 James Havard Thomas, 'Lycidas', 1905

period. Even among the competitive versions of professional sculpture represented by artists such as Thornycroft at the RA, Reynolds-Stephens and the later Arts and Crafts movement, and Havard Thomas at the Slade, such professionalism (rooted in tradition and a body of technical education) was taken to be the starting point for a sculptor's individual efforts and contributions.

Many professional sculptors in early 20th-century Britain (in contrast with the last quarter of the 19th century) responded to the new climate for sculpture by reaffirming established stylistic choices and art-theoretical concerns, and it was this retrenchment that became the target for so many modernist attacks. The active competition on art-theoretical terms that characterised the first decades of the New Sculpture gave way to a more restrained and cautious environment. It is in such a climate that the work of Havard Thomas, Reynolds-Stephens, Goscombe John, Scott and Jagger stands out for its commitment to the definitions of professional sculpture and for its continued efforts to work within these parameters in the face of a vibrant and burgeoning modernism. We should be aware that the innovations of most professional sculptors in this period are not readily discernible, in marked contrast with those of more deliberately oppositional artists. Within the realm of art theory, the work of these sculptors proved to be sophisticated and compelling, while still meeting the expectations of the institutions underwriting their position as 'professionals' in society.

Punks

The constellation of tradition, training and received societal values was targeted and rejected with the emergence of the modernist sculptor. This type of individual would often pride himself on working outside and against the established norms and networks for sculpture. Instead, he appealed to a new, specialised audience, one aggressively pursuing novelty and modernity.

In the art-historical narratives of subsequent decades, modernist art came to overshadow other, concurrent forms of aesthetic production. Not only for Britain, but in accounts of 20th-century art generally, the celebration of avant-garde values and ideals has structured the way earlier historical periods have been characterised and remembered. This is especially problematic when considering the co-existent strands of modernising sculpture – the New Sculpture *and* more self-consciously modernist art – during the early 20th century. Crucially, what has been overlooked is the symbiotic relationships across the range of possible positions and groups.

The rhetoric surrounding modernist art (in Britain and elsewhere) is, at base, a negative proposition defined by rejection and repudiation, though more recent studies of modern art across Europe have begun to take seriously the more fundamental and often fraught engagements with conventions and traditions that form the basis for these disagreements and rejections. British modernism, however, is often reductively characterised as autogenic or merely imported. This is especially the case with modern sculpture in Britain, often believed to be born almost fully formed from the 1908 scandal surrounding Jacob Epstein's British Medical Association sculptures.[10]

In the brief yet volatile years before World War I, artists such as Epstein, Henri Gaudier-Brzeska and Eric Gill moved sculptural representation beyond 'plausibility,' as Ezra Pound argued.[11] Convincing and recognisable mimesis waned as a priority in favour of increasing emphasis on formal arrangements and their material determinants. Critics such as Pound and T. E. Hulme ardently defended these new forms of sculpture. They argued that illusionism and veristic representation were disingenuous aims for sculpture and saw in the stylised carvings of the modernists a more direct and authentic purpose. In the developing rhetoric of sculptural modernism, it was direct carving (Fig. 6) that gradually came to overshadow other elements in the newly expanded range of sculptural options. Reinforced by the likes of Henry Moore in the 1930s, direct carving became simplistically equated with modernist sculpture, and work that did not fit into that equation (such as Epstein and Gaudier-Brzeska's modelled figures) was dismissed or ignored.[12] In fact, a survey of the sculptures produced by Epstein, Gaudier-Brzeska, Frank Dobson, J. D. Fergusson and Gill discovers significant instances of morphological similarity between works by these modernist sculptors and the 'professionals'.

Beyond these resemblances, it should be noted that terms through which modernist sculpture was articulated and defended in early 20th century Britain shared core concerns with the earlier modernising theories of the New Sculpture (most notably, an activation of materiality and a concern for its productive interplay with the figural image).[13] One needs to have some common ground as the basis for a disagreement, and the 'punks' often took on their 'professional' predecessors on their own terms. Pound, for instance, attacked the 'caressability' of the Greek tradition, correctly discerning (and strategically inverting) the New Sculptors' emphasis on the corporeal fusion between sculptural image and object.[14] There was substantial antagonism (and much misunderstanding), but there were also shared assumptions and beliefs.

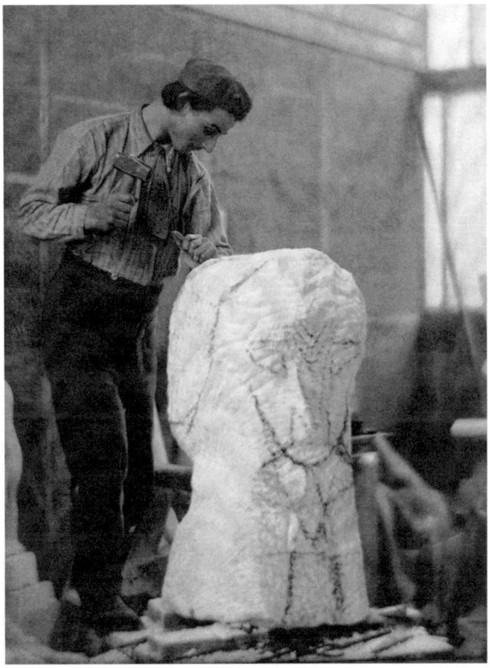

Overall, given that the rhetoric around sculpture was so passionate on both sides, one must question the received presumption that the established and the oppositional were wholly alien to each other. The overlapping webs of engagements and dependencies amongst sculptors and critics at that time have, subsequently, gone undiscussed in the story of British sculpture.

Beyond the level of sculpture theory, the public identities these sculptors espoused were also inextricably linked. In order for 'modernism' to define itself as a movement, as a group and as an identity, the 'establishment' had to be consolidated and caricatured into a relatively stable stereotype, thus making it easier to reject. This is not to deny the value of modernist innovations but rather to acknowledge that they, like the sculptors themselves, did not operate in a vacuum. Modernism in early 20th-century Britain was, to all intents and purposes, a distinct subculture that defined itself through critique and opposition. Consequently, these young 'punks' who thumbed their noses at tradition needed the very 'professionals' they purported to reject. The groups formed their identities through mutual conflict.

In his classic study of the punks and teddy-boys of post-World War II Britain, Dick Hebdige defined subculture as a style which 'signals a Refusal'.[15] A style, like an identity, is constituted through the repeated and shared use of elements which, in turn, come to act as signifiers *of* that style.[16] Modernist sculpture in Britain (and indeed modernisms in other locales as well) came into being through such a process of style-formation. Subculture, Hebdige reminds us, is articulated in direct opposition to established ideologies and institutions. Even if not overtly critical or revolutionary, subculture is nevertheless based on a partial exclusion and refusal. Appropriating this definition, we can begin to re-evaluate the accepted narratives of modernist sculpture in Britain. Without losing the critical and oppositional basis of modernism that is often simplified and heroised as 'avant-garde', this concept provides the basis for an understanding of the actual historical complexities of the period in which punks and professionals worked in tandem.

6 Henri Gaudier-Brzeska carving the 'Hieratic Head of Ezra Pound'

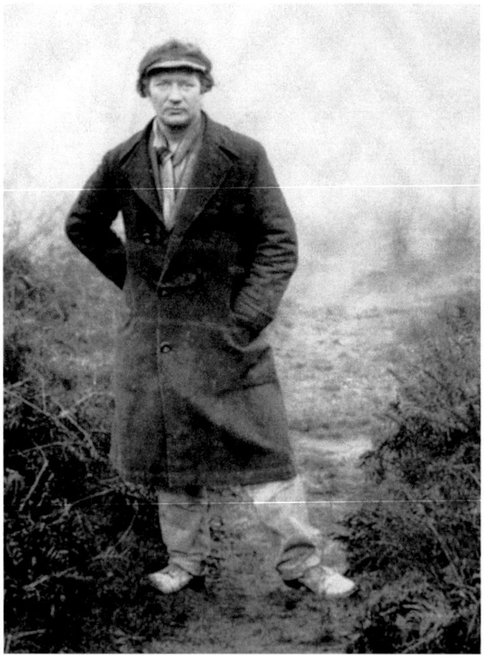

A central component of Hebdige's analysis is the concept of *bricolage*, borrowed from Claude Lévi-Strauss. The 'do-it-yourself' recombination of received concepts, commodities and signs, *bricolage* as used by Hebdige referred to the active appropriation and subversive transformation of tradition and convention. An example, he states, was the mods, who 'could be said to be functioning as *bricoleurs* when they appropriated another range of commodities by placing them in a symbolic ensemble which served to erase or subvert their original straight meaning'.[17] Though I risk over-simplifying both Hebdige's argument and the complex concept of *bricolage*, it seems that his argument about the formation of subcultures illuminates the historical situation of British art in the first decades of the 20th century.

Bricolage transforms commodities into oppositional signs (which, of course, may in turn become commodified). What is significant about Hebdige's argument, however, is his stress on aesthetic commodities such as style, fashion and attitude (Fig. 7). Just as the punks and mods constituted new, subversive messages through dress, fashion and music, so too did the bohemian circles advocating modernism recombine aspects of received tradition and convention to articulate an oppositional (but nevertheless dependent) subculture. Lisa Tickner has recently put forth a compelling account of modernism in Britain that stresses the importance of these subcultural formations and the bohemian (but, importantly, not working-class) society of artists and patrons in the years before World War I.[18] The many autobiographical (and often gossipy) accounts of the period take as a given the existence of a group of collectors and viewers who fuelled the fad for modernism and to whom the affectations of Wyndham Lewis, Pound, Epstein or Gaudier-Brzeska appealed.[19]

According to Hebdige, this subculture was – like that of the punks of later decades – decidedly not an autogenic break with convention but a savvy and strategic appropriation and subversion of norms and conventions. New ideals were put in place and new networks of patrons developed to support them. This fad for the modern fed

7 Jacob Epstein in Epping Forest, 1924

8 Jacob Epstein, 'Bust of Mary McEvoy', 1910

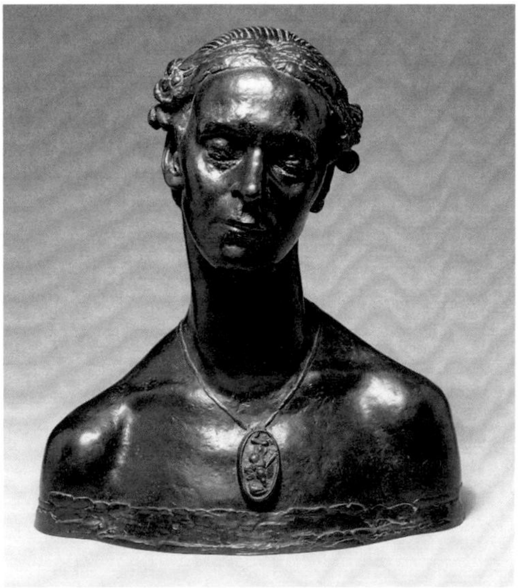

directly off mainstream culture, gaining its cachet from its defiance. This may at first seem like a simple point, but it is essential to remember this symbiotic relationship between mainstream and subculture, for it has frequently been overlooked in the accounts of modern art in Britain. Too often commentators have simply repeated the rhetorical assertions of the modernists, and their story has become a history not of the vital and contentious culture of art but of the insular story of the modernists themselves. Understanding early 20th-century modernism as a subculture allows us to move beyond the simplistic – and still determining – myths of the break, the rupture and the revolution of modernism.

Pushing the concept of *bricolage* further, we can also begin to expand the scope of a history of modern art in Britain. The modernists were *bricoleurs* in that they adapted and appropriated elements of mainstream sculpture theory, aesthetics and forms in order to subvert them and articulate an alternative. That is, the innovations of the modernists can only be adequately understood if one grasps the conventions they were defying and, quite substantially, adapting. The professionals, in such an account, are equally important, and any story of modern art that reduces the formation of modernist subculture to a wilful and complete rupture with the past overlooks the actual historical complexity and, more fundamentally, the deeper art-theoretical questions.

The story of modernist sculpture in Britain begins to look different, and ultimately more complex, with this interdependent relationship in mind. For instance, we can take more seriously the formative roles played by sculptors such as George Gray Barnard and Havard Thomas in the early development of Epstein (which he downplayed in his much later autobiography), as well as begin to acknowledge the significant morphological and art-theoretical affinities of his work with the New Sculpture as practised in the Edwardian period (Fig. 8). After coming to England, he sought out sculptors such as Havard Thomas, and his apprehension of the terms of Edwardian sculpture provided the basis for his gradual development of new attitudes. Gill contributed to many diverse projects, and even Gaudier-Brzeska hints in his writings and artworks at a greater awareness of Victorian sculpture than is usually assumed.

Additionally, the ostensibly 'traditional' works by the likes of Goscombe John or Scott can be re-evaluated in the light of modernist sculpture theory. In addition, those disavowed bronzes of Epstein and Gaudier-Brzeska can be more adequately discussed if we conceive of modernism as a nuanced subcultural recombination of convention and tradition. A problem in the heroic accounts of modernism in Britain has been its fundamental eclecticism. All the artists involved experimented in a range of styles, yet the non-carved work of Epstein, for instance, has been relegated to an uncomfortable footnote in the story of modern-sculpture-as-direct-carving (based on the writings of Pound and R. H. Wilenski). There are many such works that do not fit, and in striving to defend modernism in Britain in relation to its contemporary formulations in Europe, art historians have omitted these works from the story.[20] A further example is the hotly contested legacy of Gaudier-Brzeska, over whose work debates raged for decades, speculating on what path – direct carving or modelling – he would have ultimately pursued had he lived.

The answer to these dilemmas lies in reconsidering the rhetoric of modernism to account for the complex range of affinities, contestations, dependencies and parallels that existed as present options for both the punks and the professionals in the first decades of the 20th century. The historical complexity that has proven so resolutely unassimilable to the received rhetoric of modernism is exactly what is significant and compelling about sculpture in Britain in these years. In other words, we – like the artists themselves – need to be aware of the identities of both the punk and the professional in order to begin to understand the historical situation of sculpture in Britain and argue for the wider relevance of its conceptual concerns.

David J. Getsy

Notes

1 See S. Beattie, *The New Sculpture*, New Haven, CT, and London, Yale University Press, 1983, and B. Read, *Victorian Sculpture*, New Haven, CT, and London, Yale University Press, 1982, pp. 273–386.

2 See D. Getsy, 'The *Lycidas* "scandal" of 1905: James Havard Thomas at the crux of modern sculpture in Britain', in D. Getsy (ed.), *Sculpture and the Pursuit of a Modern Ideal in Britain, c.1880–1930*, Aldershot, Ashgate, forthcoming 2004. An expanded account of this incident will also be a chapter of my forthcoming *Body Doubles: Encountering Modern Sculpture in Britain, 1877–1905.*

3 For commentary, see B. Read, 'Whatever happened to the New Sculpture?', in J. Glaves-Smith (ed.), *Reverie, Myth, Sensuality: Sculpture in Britain 1880–1910* (exhibition catalogue), Stoke-on-Trent, Stoke-on-Trent City Museum and Art Gallery, 1992, pp. 21–5.

4 See L. Irvine and P. Atterbury, *Gilbert Bayes: Sculptor 1872–1953* (exhibition catalogue), London, Richard Dennis and Fine Art Society, 1998.

5 W. Reynolds-Stephens, 'A plea for the nationalisation of our sculpture', *The Nineteenth Century and After*, vol. 69, no. 407, January 1911, pp. 160–8.

6 See F. Pearson, *Goscombe John* (exhibition catalogue), Cardiff, National Museum of Wales, 1979.

7 See M. Stocker, '"My masculine models": The sculpture of Kathleen Scott', *Apollo*, vol. 150, no. 451, 1999, pp. 47–54.

8 See S. Malvern, '"For King and Country": George Frampton's *Edith Cavell* (1915–20) and the writing of gender in memorials to the Great War', in D. Getsy (ed.), *Sculpture and the Pursuit of a Modern Ideal in Britain, c.1880–1930.*

9 See S. Tillyard, *The Impact of Modernism 1900–1920: Early Modernism and the Arts and Crafts Movement in Edwardian England*, London, Routledge, 1988.

10 For a discussion of the events of 1908, see R. Cork, *Art Beyond the Gallery in Early 20th Century England*, New Haven, CT, Yale University Press, 1985, pp. 9–60.

11 E. Pound, 'The New Sculpture', *Egoist*, 16 February 1914, p. 68; reprinted in H. Zinnes (ed.), *Ezra Pound and the Visual Arts*, New York, New Directions, 1980, p. 181.

12 For a discussion of this development, see P. Curtis, 'Barbara Hepworth and the avant garde of the 1920s', in P. Curtis and A. Wilkinson, *Barbara Hepworth: A Retrospective* (exhibition catalogue), Liverpool, Tate Gallery, 1994, pp. 11–28; and P. Curtis, 'How direct carving stole the idea of modern British sculpture', in D. Getsy (ed.), *Sculpture and the Pursuit of a Modern Ideal in Britain, c.1880–1930.*

13 For an example of this concern from the 1890s, see D. Getsy, '"Hard realism": the thanatic corporeality of Edward Onslow Ford's *Shelley Memorial*', *Visual Culture in Britain*, Spring 2002, vol. 3, no. 1, pp. 53–76.

14 There are many instances, but in particular see E. Pound, 'The Caressability of the Greeks,' *Egoist*, 16 March 1914, reprinted in Zinnes (ed.), *Ezra Pound and the Visual Arts*, pp. 184–6.

15 D. Hebdige, *Subculture: The Meaning of Style*, London, Methuen, 1979, p. 3.

16 My use of 'style' in reference to Hebdige should be distinguished from the multifarious concept of style in art-historical narratives. The literature on style – individual, group, period, etc. – is vast. For a methodological prolegomenon for its usage, see Whitney Davis, 'Style and history in art history', in W. Davis and R. W. Quinn (eds), *Replications: Archaeology, Art History, Psychoanalysis*, University Park, Pennsylvania State University Press, 1996, pp. 171–98.

17 Hebdige, *Subculture*, p. 104.

18 L. Tickner, *Modern Life and Modern Subjects: British Art in the Early Twentieth Century*, New Haven, CT, Yale University Press, 2000. See also Cork, *Art Beyond the Gallery*.

19 There are too many autobiographical accounts to cite here. A discussion of the bohemian scene can be found in W. Wees, *Vorticism and the English Avant-Garde*, Toronto, University of Toronto Press, which largely tells the history of Vorticism as a story of these social networks.

20 A highly visible example was the 1996 exhibition at the Galerie Nationale du Jeu de Paume, Paris, *Un Siècle de Sculpture Anglaise*. For commentary, see A. Sleeman, 'In the Queen's Parlour, inspired by tea and made of gentlemen: British sculpture in the twentieth century as "sculpture Anglaise"', *Sculpture Journal*, 1997, vol. 1, pp. 72–9.

'Infrastructure' is a term encompassing the networks and businesses that form the context in which art is practised. It may also be seen as the interface between the studio and the wider world or the means by which art is made public. The focus of this essay is to map connections between groups of artists in the first quarter of the 20th century, thus gaining an overview of how sculptors worked together to practise their craft. The dominant history of sculptural practice in the 20th century has created a divide between the modernists and the mainstream. Integrating these separate strands is beyond the scope of this short study, but to counter tendencies of earlier histories this essay emphasises the experience and activities of the mainstream majority. Drawing this map is not a simple task. Networks are by nature fugitive and evidence of their existence or significance is often elusive. However, by examining letters and other documents alongside the records of a variety of institutions, societies, clubs, art schools and exhibitions, it is possible to start uncovering how networks were established, how they operated, who were the influential figures and why.

Fundamental to the level of contact between sculptors and their identity as a group was the demographics of those practising this art. Liverpool, a rich city with a lively art scene, supported just three sculptors (Charles John Allen, Herbert Tyson Smith and Edward Carter Preston), while London, predictably, was home to a much larger number. A provisional estimate of practising sculptors across the country can be drawn from membership records of the Royal Society of British Sculptors (RBS) and the Chelsea Arts Club. Of the 194 sculptors registered between 1900 and 1925, 149 (76 per cent) lived or worked primarily in London, compared with 27 (about 14 per cent) living outside London and another 18 (around 9 per cent) whose addresses are unknown. Further RBS records suggest there were just under half this total number of sculptors active at any one time.[1] These low figures fit with statistics on sculpture students at leading London art schools. From 1900 to 1925, an average of three sculpture students enrolled at the Royal Academy Schools each year. Between 1907 and 1924, only thirty-one students listing sculpture as their intended profession left the Royal College of Art, an average of two per year if an adjustment is made for the temporary closure of the school during World War I. As students, sculptors found themselves outnumbered – five painters for each sculptor at the RA Schools – a pattern repeated in similar or less favourable proportions as practising artists.[2]

The sculptors holding positions of influence within this small network formed a tiny elite. A study of the tenure of senior offices on committees

– such as the council of the RBS, the sculpture faculty of the British School at Rome, the Royal Fine Art Commission, the selection panels for the *International Exhibition* in Rome of 1911 and the *British Empire Exhibition* of 1924 – reveals the same names recurring; we also find that the majority of these sculptors were academicians. It is notable that almost any committee led by a sculptor was chaired by one of three academicians elected prior to 1903: William Hamo Thornycroft, Thomas Brock or George Frampton. Furthermore, the rank and file of committee members were typically drawn from the seven academicians elected between 1909 and 1922: William Goscombe John, Alfred Drury, Frederick William Pomeroy, William Robert Colton, Francis Derwent Wood, Henry Pegram and Bertram Mackennal. The only non-academician to achieve any notable position was William Reynolds-Stephens, who became president of the RBS and of the Imperial Arts League. The dominance of academicians affirmed the power of the RA. This arose from its wealth, its semi-public status and the pre-eminence of the Summer Exhibition. The RA controlled trusts benefiting indigent artists and the Chantrey and Leighton funds for purchasing works of art, adding further pressure for artists to secure access to its network. The Academy's position was also strengthened by royal patronage. Among the many privileges this brought was an annual audience with the king, at which the business of the year was submitted for approval and he signed diplomas for newly elected academicians. This association lent weight to the Academy's position as the assumed voice of the sector. A further measure of the significance of access to the court circle is evidenced by the strenuous efforts of groups such as the Incorporated Society of British Sculptors (as the RBS was initially entitled) to acquire such connections. In the early years of the RBS, entire council meetings were devoted to selecting gifts and writing loyal addresses to the royal family. A strong sense of having 'arrived' accompanied George V's decision to grant the Society its royal charter in 1912.

The annual dinner was the visible means by which the RA courted people with influence. There were usually about 260 guests. Of these, only a quarter were members, the majority being royals, peers, bishops, diplomats, MPs, baronets, art patrons, government officials, university vice-chancellors and other prominent persons.[3] An instance of the dinner being used to promote sculptors' interests occurred in 1922 when the Royal Fine Art Commission was under discussion. That year, Viscount Esher was seated between Brock and Frampton instead of in his usual place among the other peers. Esher was a trustee of various museums and chairman of the commissioners of the 1851 Exhibition.

He had been a close adviser to the royal family for nearly thirty years and was also friends with politicians from all parties. Evidently this discreet lobbying of Esher was successful, one result being Frampton's appointment to represent the interests of sculptors when the Royal Fine Art Commission was formed a year later. Surveys of the RA dinner guest-lists over many years provide a barometer of those in power. Fabian Ware and Sir Lionel Earle, for example, were invited from 1918, when their respective positions at the War Graves Commission and Office of Works made them useful contacts. It is also interesting to see who was *not* invited. The *British Empire Exhibition* of 1924 included some 1,130 living artists and was the most important showcase for the arts in London in the immediate postwar period. Yet none of the organising team was invited to the dinner apart from the duke of Devonshire, who, as a peer, was on the guest-list anyway.

Networking and lobbying within the membership was at least as important as developing external connections, because almost all Academy business was conducted via a voting system. Sculptors formed one of many pressure groups within the Academy and their interests were safeguarded by ensuring enough of their supporters were elected to influence voting. This was made easier in 1917 when a resolution was passed stating that there should be no fewer than six sculptor academicians and five sculptor associates.[4] For those seeking to gain membership of the Academy, internal support was essential, as nominations had to come from within the organisation. Elections were held about three times a year and involved a three-tier voting system. In the first round there might be as many as twenty-two names. Those getting four or more 'scratches' would go forward into the second round, from which the two who received the most votes would be placed head to head. Inevitably, alliances were formed either to secure or to block certain individuals. These alliances were an integral part of the process and candidates could appear many times on the list. Some eventually succeeded in securing membership. Others did not. The fact that a number of those given membership, such as Eric Gill (ARA 1937), did not seek election while others, such as Walter Marsden, actively desired admission but failed, not only affirms the Academy's elitism but offers a measure of the acceptability of membership across the entire range of practitioners. This was not true of all 'establishment' organisations. Taking Gill again as an example, he was elected onto the faculty of the British School at Rome in November 1931 but soon resigned to disociate himself from its policies.

Undoubtedly, the Academy was powerful, but as sculptors' interests had to compete with those of painters and architects, even senior academicians acknowledged it could not meet the aspirations of the entire profession. To fill this gap, the RBS was formed in 1904 with the object of protecting 'the interests of British Sculptors and the consolidation in Great Britain of the profession of sculpture'.[5] This agenda also reflected a trend that had been growing since 1880 for many professional groups, from writers to chartered accountants, to create networks that would establish a clear identity for a sector, safeguard common interests and enhance status.[6] Although the RBS never challenged the Academy as the pre-eminent voice for the profession, its records show that membership was sought by aspiring and established sculptors alike.

Under its first two presidents, Brock (1905–9) and Charles Lawes-Wittewronge (1909–11), the RBS adopted an assertive stance on issues of professional identity. Thomas Stirling Lee drafted rules for running sculpture competitions aimed at ensuring that a sculptor was always among the judges, and that competitors were paid fees.[7] In addition, an adjudication service for disagreements over commissions was set up and model contracts were written.[8] Reynolds-Stephens emerged as the principal watchdog for the profession on the RBS council. Among the points he raised was the need for sculptors to establish the size of an edition before a work was sold, and to be wary about the risk of donating works to charitable causes, as these works were often sold below market price.[9] The RBS council put pressure on the government regarding wider issues such as changes to copyright law (1909), the cost of railway transport for sculpture (1913) and the introduction of a luxury tax (1918).[10] The Society also launched a campaign to improve the display of sculpture in provincial museums. Manchester City Art Gallery was among the institutions that responded sympathetically to this initiative, including a sculpture gallery in plans to rebuild the museum in 1910. The Walker Art Gallery, Liverpool, on the other hand, reacted with hostility to requests from the RBS in 1905 to include a sculptor on the Autumn Exhibition hanging committee and achieve the 'more effective and efficient exhibition of works'.[11] In retaliation, Brock adopted trade union tactics and directed RBS members to withdraw from exhibiting in Liverpool. The intransigence of Brock and Lawes-Wittewronge on the one hand and the Walker on the other resulted in this embargo lasting seven years. The membership appears to have been largely loyal to RBS policy, although some, notably Allen who as a resident of Liverpool had the Walker and its allies on his doorstep, were put in a very difficult position. The dispute was finally settled in 1912 by Frampton, whose conciliatory approach resulted in an agreement with the Walker on terms originally sought by the RBS.[12]

Collaboration and cooperation coexisted with rivalry in the RBS, as members inevitably competed for commissions. The RBS provided an information service on sculpture competitions, including opportunities throughout the empire and, in the early 1920s, for war memorials. Sometimes the president of the RBS, or his nominee, was invited to be an assessor in a competition. The aim was to ensure a fair process of adjudication and the selection of a professional artist, but maintaining impartiality could be difficult. Indeed, in 1913–14 the selection of sculptors for a scheme at Cardiff City Hall caused a major split in the RBS council with lasting consequences. The patron, Lord Rhondda, originally proposed a competition, but then directed the RBS representative, James Havard Thomas, to select by invitation. Havard Thomas put himself forward and also chose T. Crook, Ernest Gillick, Goscombe John, David McGill, Pegram, Pomeroy, Henry Poole, Alfred Turner and John Tweed. Half of this list were members of the RBS council. In response, four council members who were not selected (Derwent Wood, Albert Hodge, Frank Lynn-Jenkins and Paul Montford) accused Havard Thomas and the president, Frampton, of changing the terms of the selection process without proper consultation. An uproarious extraordinary general meeting took place in early 1914, with the result that three senior academicians – Frampton, Goscombe John and Pomeroy – together with Gillick, McGill and Havard Thomas, left the RBS.[13] There were now no academicians on the council and so important was this link considered to be that Brock, the retired president, was persuaded to resume his role. Following so soon after the dispute with the Walker, this affair gave the RBS a reputation for being quarrelsome. In order to unite the organisation, succeeding presidents Colton (1914–21) and Reynolds-Stephens (1922–32) pursued a more conciliatory path, but the effectiveness of the Society as a networking organisation and voice of the sector was significantly undermined.

Exhibiting was the principal means whereby artists made contact with patrons, but few sculptors had the connections necessary to get solo exposure. Interestingly it was the 'outsider' Jacob Epstein who was unusually successful in this regard. The overwhelming majority of sculptors were reliant on exhibiting at the RA Summer Exhibition. In itself, this was dependent on gaining the approval of a few senior academicians. Up to 1920, there was only one sculptor on the selection committee. Between 1900 and 1915, this was either Alfred Gilbert (who resigned from the Academy in 1908), Frampton, Brock or Thornycroft. A slight change occurred after 1916 when the three academicians elected since 1903 began to serve: Drury, Goscombe John and Pomeroy. In 1919 the selection committee was enlarged, allowing two sculptors to be elected thereafter. Associates became eligible and members served a maximum term of two years on the committee.[14] Despite these reforms, the Summer Exhibition retained its exclusive image because works by members dominated the show.[15] In 1901–2 there were fewer than three sculptures by non-members for every one by a member. Under pressure, the RA gradually improved this situation, so that by 1913 the ratio had grown to eight to one, but this did not last. By 1925, the proportion was back down to four to one.[16] The Academy responded to criticism of selection methods (falling visitor numbers also caused concern) by introducing various reforms, including altering rules for Academy elections. However, pressure to change the Summer Exhibition was ultimately limited by a lack of competition – no other venue exhibited anywhere close to the RA's average of 214 sculptures a year.

In any case, exhibiting outside the Academy structure was predicated on belonging to a society or group. Many of the societies set up to challenge the hegemony of the Academy were primarily for painters, though alliances with individual sculptors were sometimes formed – Havard Thomas, for instance, was a founder-member and secretary of the New English Art Club. The International Society of Sculptors, Painters and Gravers (ISSPG) was rare in that it represented all the major art forms and maintained a scope which was international. The absence of academicians on its governing council also made the ISSPG unusual (in the period before World War I the council members were Edouard Lantéri, Stirling Lee, Havard Thomas and Harry Wilson).[17] In 1905 the ISSPG affirmed its international commitment by electing Auguste Rodin as president. This enhanced the position of sculptors in the ISSPG, and from then until the war they achieved near equality on the Society's exhibition selection panel. In the same period, the number of sculptures exhibited by the ISSPG rose to an unusually high level: around one sculpture for every seven paintings. After the war, this dropped back to one sculpture per twenty-nine paintings, but even this was a more favourable ratio than those achieved by many other exhibiting societies.[18] The RBS was the only organisation that attempted to mount exhibitions devoted solely to sculpture. In 1905–6 the RBS council worked energetically to organise a large-scale group show, with members using business contacts to find empty commercial premises. Unfortunately, even with Lawes-Wittewronge's extensive city connections, no suitable property could be found, and the project eventually failed. The price of mounting such a show was another difficulty. Advice was taken from the eminent RA, Sir William Richmond, who considered that the Society lacked the network of wealthy patrons to raise the necessary £2,000–3,000.[19] Thereafter the RBS adopted a more collaborative strategy, working to enhance the representation of sculpture at international exhibitions – the major ones being the 1911 *International Exhibition* in Rome and the *British Empire Exhibition* of 1924. Members also combined forces with societies such as the Institute of Painters in Oil, as well as putting together small shows on a semi-commercial basis, as at Waring and Gillow (1915) and the Fine Art Society (1920).

Less structured social networks existed in parallel with formal art institutions. The majority of sculptors resident in London lived and worked either in St John's Wood and its environs or in the Chelsea/Fulham area. Those living in the north of the city tended to be the older, more established sculptors, though Thornycroft's residence in Kensington was an eminent exception. Unlike most of their generation, younger artists such as Gilbert Bayes and William Reid Dick opted for St John's Wood. Reid Dick used his proximity to the older sculptors to cultivate connections. For instance, he became very friendly with Frampton, succeeding him as an academician in 1928. Chelsea, with its bohemian reputation and cheaper rents, attracted the younger, less established sculptors. Its streets harboured sculptor enclaves such as Glebe Place, home to Derwent Wood, Conrad Dressler, George Gordon, W. B. Fagan, Basil Gotto and, on a more temporary basis, F. J. Wilcoxson, William McMillan and Sidney and Vernon March. Networks could form around studios either by shared occupancy or by tenancy passing from one artist to another. For instance, 14a Cheyne Row was occupied variously by Albert Bruce Joy, Gillick, Gilbert Ledward, McMillan, Henry Carr and C. W. Dyson Smith. Place of residence was linked to other sorts of social circle too. The academicians of St John's Wood were more likely to be members of the Arts Club, conveniently sited close to the Academy in Dover Street, whereas the west London set and other, less established artists congregated at the Chelsea Arts Club. Derwent Wood seems to have been the only sculptor academician who avoided Dover Street and remained a committed Chelsea Arts Club patron. Sculptors had played a key role in founding the Chelsea Arts Club; it grew out of gatherings at Stirling Lee's studio in 1890 and he, Lynn-Jenkins, Adrian Jones, Gotto and Henry Poole all held the office of chairman between 1900 and 1915.[20] Sixty-five sculptors joined the Club between 1900 and 1925. One of its many attractions was the possibility of forging connections with the architects, who equalled sculptors as a proportion of its membership. The balls organised by the Chelsea Arts Club, from 1908 onwards, became an established feature of the social season, demonstrating London society's wish to mix with artists. Here networking was of the most informal kind as music and spectacle were the chief attractions.

Aspiring sculptors usually made their first contacts at art school, either horizontally through peers or vertically through tutors. As many students attended more than one college, and the more successful of these completed their studies at the Royal College of Art or the Royal Academy Schools, these networks crossed institutional boundaries. The RCA occupied a particularly strong position as the primary teacher-training centre in Britain. Within this, Lantéri's status as a master of modelling was almost legendary. He worked at the RCA for nearly forty years, training generation upon generation of sculpture tutors. Through their positions in provincial art schools, these new tutors formed a national network, and in turn sent star students back to the RCA. Among this younger generation were the sculptors: Ledward, Herman Cawthra, Harold Youngman, Charles Sargeant Jagger, McMillan, Alfred Hardiman, Charles Wheeler, Walter Marsden and James Woodford, who would later become the academicians and adjudicators of the 1920s and 1930s. Lantéri's reputation also brought a number of professional contacts to the RCA. These included Goscombe John, who in 1913 set up a competition for students to design a seal for the committee of the King Edward National Memorial for Wales. Goscombe John also helped RCA students by employing them as assistants, extending his support to one such protégé, Youngman, by purchasing two of his works.

In some situations, older sculptors were willing to learn from the younger generation. An example of this occurred in the sculpture faculty of the British School at Rome (BSR). Frampton, as chairman from 1922 to 1928, invited certain ex-scholars onto the committee, encouraging them to advise upon and improve the scheme. This situation was mutually beneficial as it brought Ledward, Jagger and Hardiman (scholars of 1913, 1914 and 1920 respectively) into contact with the most senior representatives of their profession, together with VIPs on the BSR council and executive committees. Many of these VIPs, through a wish to ensure the success of the BSR, were active in their support of the ex-scholars. Viscount Esher, Alfred Mond and

Stephen Courtauld, for example, all purchased or commissioned work from Hardiman, Jagger, Winifred Knights, Ledward, Tom Monnington and H. Wilson Parker. The effective operation of the BSR network was entirely due, meanwhile, to the efforts of the secretary, Evelyn Shaw, who befriended students, eminent artists and public figures on the committees, treating them all with diplomacy and tact.[21] While only a tiny number of sculptors benefited from scholarships – the scheme started in 1913, no awards were made between 1915 and 1919, and there was no award in 1921 – the assistance given to those fortunate few was vital. Ledward and Jagger, whose scholarships were paid in 1915, while the latter was in the army, were given a year's support in 1919 to make work. This helped them bridge the gap between military service and professional practice. Hardiman was allowed to stay in Rome for an extra year, and though he did not receive a stipend, he was given other kinds of financial assistance. The BSR also gave Hardiman advice and support in 1928 when a sculpture commission for Imperial Chemical House, Millbank, resulted in litigation. In 1936, furthermore, Shaw and D. Y. Cameron persuaded Patrick Duff at the Office of Works to obtain a grant of £2,000 from the Treasury when the cost of completing the Haig memorial threatened to push Hardiman into bankruptcy.[22] For other scholars, the connections forged in Rome provided mutual support. An example of this occurred in 1932 when the Rome scholars of 1925 – the architect Charles Minoprio, the painter Edward Halliday and the sculptor Woodford – collaborated on the refurbishment of the Good Intent restaurant in the King's Road, London. The scholars were not the only ones to benefit from an association with the BSR; the various committees provided a uniquely inclusive and regular point of contact for professional artists, patrons and government representatives. Even the Royal Academy had no equivalent of this.

Networking was not exclusively about attaining a position or status. It was also directed at supporting those in need. The chief agency was the Artists' General Benevolent Institution (AGBI), based at Burlington House and closely allied to the Royal Academy. Art societies, such as the RBS from 1916, appointed a steward whose job it was to raise funds among members and present them at the AGBI annual dinner. Accessing these funds was often assisted by contacts, a poignant example of this being the case of Emile Jacot, a Rome scholar in 1925. In his second year at Rome, Jacot fell ill with what appeared to be pneumonia (though it later turned out to be tuberculosis, contracted while on active service in World War I). Initially, the BSR paid his stipend while he was in a sanatorium in Switzerland, but after six months the faculty could not justify a continuation. Jacot's wife appealed to the BSR for other forms of support, and eventually Goscombe John and Jagger managed to obtain a grant from the AGBI. Tragically the money arrived after Jacot's death, but it did help his widow settle the inevitable doctor's fees.[23] Many other societies (including the ISSPG) listed a benevolent fund amongst their aims, but lacked the means or patrons to establish one. Nevertheless, the aspiration is evidence of the uncertainty attached to the profession, and it is telling that the more successful artists felt obliged to assist those less fortunate than themselves.

This study is too brief to be fully inclusive – its limitations in regard to the experience of modernist sculptors have already been noted. Among the other interesting topics that would repay research are the ways in which women sculptors negotiated their position within the male-dominated societies and institutions. There would also be value in making analyses of networks generated by wartime service and the impact of changing economic conditions. Above all, an investigation of the relations between sculptors and the various craftspeople supporting their practice – stonemasons, *formatori*, *practiciens*, models, foundry workers, and so forth – is long overdue. If the emphasis of this text is on sources and approach rather than on context and conclusions, it is nevertheless clear that continuity and stability characterised the mainstream establishment of sculptural endeavour. Rather than challenging existing structures, the changes that did occur – the establishment of the Rome scholarships and the RBS's efforts at encouraging professionalism, to name but two – were absorbed and eventually used to further the interests of the establishment.

Ann Compton

Notes

Conversations with Sarah Crellin enhanced the planning and research of this essay while the writing was aided by Adam Sigerson. Warm thanks are due to Dennis Wardleworth for researching the archive of the International Society of Sculptors, Painters and Gravers on my behalf. Much gratitude also goes to the British School at Rome and the Royal Society of British Sculptors for generously allowing me access to their archives.

1 See the election records of the Chelsea Arts Club, 1904–25, Kensington and Chelsea Reference Library, London, and M. Hayes, 'A chronological list of RBS members' and 'Voting papers for the election of 25 Fellows', July 1923, RBS Archive, London.

2 For records of enrolments in the Royal Academy Schools see *Royal Academy of Arts Annual Report*, 1900–25, Archive, Royal Academy of Arts, London, and *Register of Royal College of Arts Students*, 1907–24, Archive, Royal College of Arts, London.

3 'Royal Academy of Arts annual dinner plan of tables', 1900, 1902–14, 1919–20, 1922–25, Archive, Royal Academy of Arts, London. There was no dinner in 1901, as a mark of respect following the death of Queen Victoria; nor were there any during World War I and the dinner was cancelled in 1921 because of a coal strike.

4 *Royal Academy of Arts Annual Report*, 1917, p. 6, Archive, Royal Academy of Arts, London.

5 Letter sent to prospective members of the RBS and quoted in *Royal Society of British Sculptors Council Minutes*, 10 January 1905, Archive, RBS, London.

6 H. Perkin, *The Rise of Professional Society: England Since 1880*, London, Routledge, 1990, p. 86.

7 *Royal Society of British Sculptors Council Minutes*, 5 November and 3 December 1906, Archive, RBS, London.

8 *Royal Society of British Sculptors Council Minutes*, 11 October and 1 November 1920, Archive, RBS, London.

9 *Royal Society of British Sculptors Council Minutes*, 17 January 1916 and 15 January 1917, Archive, RBS, London.

10 For copyright law, see *Royal Society of British Sculptors Council Minutes*, 5 April, 7 June and 1 November 1909 and 16 October 1911; for railway transport costs, ibid., 20 January, 17 February, 19 May, 20 October, 17 November and 15 December 1913; for luxury tax, ibid., 30 April and 29 May 1918, Archive, RBS, London.

11 *Royal Society of British Sculptors Council Minutes*, 3 July 1905, Archive, RBS, London.

12 There are numerous references to this dispute, but see especially *Royal Society of British Sculptors Council Minutes*, 3 July and 21 September 1905, 2 November 1908 and 20 May 1912, Archive, RBS, London.

13 *Royal Society of British Sculptors Council Minutes*, 19 May and 15 December 1913, 12 January and 20 April 1914, Archive, RBS, London. There is also a valuable account of this dispute in F. Pearson, *Goscombe John at the National Museum of Wales*, Cardiff, National Museum of Wales, 1979, p. 15.

14 *Royal Academy of Arts Annual Report*, 1919, pp. 35–7, Archive, Royal Academy of Arts, London.

15 Members of the Academy were allowed to submit six works and non-members three. The proportion of members to non-members is based on sixteen sculptor RAs and ARAs in this period compared to 194 sculptors registered as members of the RBS and the Chelsea Arts Club (see n. 1).

16 Figures drawn from the Reports on the Summer Exhibition in *Royal Academy of Arts Annual Report*, 1900–25, Archive, Royal Academy of Arts, London.

17 F. Howard, *Scrapbook*, p. 28, TGA 738.10, Hyman Kreitman Research Centre, Tate Britain.

18 International Society of Sculptors, Painters and Gravers Exhibition Catalogues, Box 1, LON-INT, Hyman Kreitman Research Centre, Tate Britain.

19 See especially *Royal Society of British Sculptors Council Minutes*, 24 July 1905 and 2 July 1906, Archive, RBS, London.

20 T. Cross, *Artists and Bohemians: One Hundred Years with the Chelsea Arts Club*, London, Quiller Press, 1992, pp. 8–9 and 158.

21 For a general history of the BSR, see A. Wallace-Hadrill, *The British School at Rome: One Hundred Years*, Rome, British School at Rome, 2001.

22 Alfred Hardiman, Rome scholar 1920, Artist File, Archive, British School at Rome, Rome.

23 Emile Jacot, Rome scholar 1925, Artist File, Archive, British School at Rome, Rome.

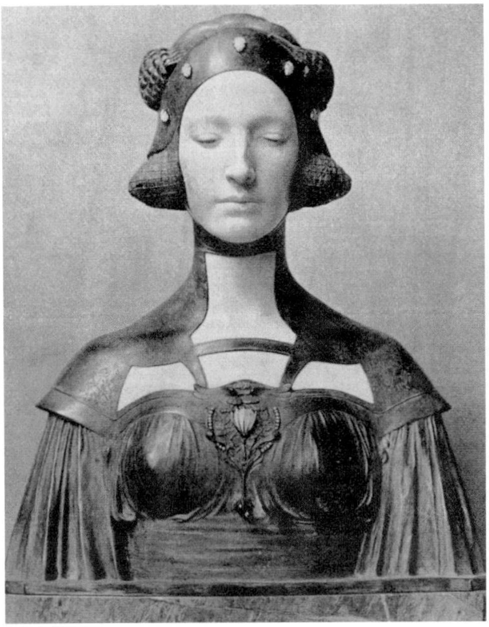

The *Exposition Universelle*, Paris of 1900 featured works by a cross-section of contemporary British sculptors, including Charles John Allen, Gilbert Bayes, Alfred Drury, Edward Onslow Ford, William Goscombe John, Andrea Lucchesi, Frank Lynn-Jenkins, James Pittendrigh MacGillivray, William Hamo Thornycroft and, most notably for this essay, George Frampton. Though not representative of all British sculpture, it could certainly be argued that the approaches this last artist adopted to the associated questions of sculptural form and meaning came to be regarded as archetypal. Indeed, as the new century progressed, growing numbers of sculptors saw Frampton's approach as something to be used as a benchmark.

The works Frampton exhibited at Paris – 'My Thoughts are My Children' (1894) and 'Mother and Child' (1894–5) – have long been noted as heralding the formal simplifications and contrasting allegorical convolutions of the sculptor's mature style. At the time, he was embracing Symbolist theories on the projection of meaning, such as the idea of the work of art as a cult object 'in which spirituality and exoticism are morbidly combined'.[1] In his relief work, this predilection for mystical subject matter was combined with a daringly decorative approach to form: patterns of flat planes demarcated by edges of the most linear precision. These features helped produce prophetically early versions of the decorative naturalism that came to dominate British sculpture in the years after World War I. With its emphasis on the notion of the artwork as a devotional focus and on the decorative impulse as displayed in the sculpture of Frampton and his contemporaries, this essay will suggest a slightly different context to that usually provided for early 20th-century modernism in Britain.

Frampton's enthusiastic use of coloured, precious and semi-precious materials – as seen, for instance, in his bust of 'Lamia' (1899–1900; Fig. 1) – confirms the fact that his aesthetic owed its development to a straightforward adoption, in France, of the concerns of the Art Nouveau. But the later ripening of his style into something approaching Art Deco arose out of his career in Britain. The sculptor's decorative instincts were first cultivated in the late 1880s, when he served in Paris as an

1 George Frampton, 'Lamia', 1899–1900

assistant to Antonin Mercié, whose influence on his apprentice is most apparent when we consider 'Amphitrite' (1889), made by Mercié using similar materials to those of 'Lamia', and with an awareness of the same Florentine Renaissance antecedents.

The decorative forms and mystical themes Frampton embraced during his time in France would later dovetail with the Beaux-Arts-inspired architecture and Symbolist design he saw while working in 'the Second City of the British Empire'. By the mid-to-late 1890s, when Frampton first worked there, Glasgow was already established as an industrial and cultural powerhouse, fully able to support a remarkable crop of local artists. The Glasgow-trained Charles Rennie Mackintosh receives most attention, but arguably more important from the point of view of sculptural decoration was the contribution made by those numerous indigenous designers profiting from a period of study in Paris, especially J. J. Burnet and J. A. Campbell. The Beaux-Arts aesthetic these architects imported was crossed with a historicist taste for the verticality of Scottish Renaissance facades, with sheer elevations accentuated by up-and-down channels of punched windows and sinuous, often incised sculptural detail. Burnet and Campbell's work formed an appealing and distinctive branch of the famous 'Glasgow Style'.

Burnet was particularly fond of sculpture, and his Glasgow buildings generated employment for numerous local artists. For his reconstruction of the Glasgow Savings Bank on Ingram Street (1894–9), however, the architect brought in Frampton, at the time an influential co-director of the Central School of Arts and Crafts in London. The collaboration was inspired, with Burnet laying the architectural foundations for an 'extravaganza [that] properly treats relief sculpture as an organic extension of the structure, not mere addition'.[2] Having begun his career as an architect's assistant, Frampton had an educated feel for the building's form, enabling him to integrate an allegorical programme the sheer variety of which had rarely been seen before in Glasgow. More familiar was the suppleness of the modelling, which has formal affinities with the schemes executed by sculptors working on Burnet's earlier buildings. Frampton's scheme is commonly assumed to have consolidated the New Sculpture in Scotland, the movement having arrived there with the appointment of Francis Derwent Wood as modelling master at the Glasgow School of Art, and yet we find William Birnie Rhind contributing French-style figures and Symbolist allegory to Burnet's Charing Cross Mansions (1889–91) several years before Frampton or Derwent Wood ever arrived in the city.

2 Francis Derwent Wood, Maquette for 'Music', *c.*1899

3 George Frampton, clay model, *c.*1899 for the bronze group 'St Mungo as Patron of the Arts' of the north entrance to Kelvingrove Art Gallery and Museum

Frampton's next Glasgow commission – the new art gallery then being built at Kelvingrove Park in the city's west end – was more prestigious, if more contentious. A diffident Glasgow Corporation had assigned the task of assessing the architectural competition to Alfred Waterhouse, a fashionable London designer with no experience of Glasgow. He selected an entry by fellow Londoners J. W. Simpson and E. J. Milner Allen, controversially ignoring submissions by Burnet and by Honeyman & Keppie, Mackintosh's employers. Citing good value for money and the need for 'a man of strong decorative feeling in his work, and in sympathy with our design', the architects hired Frampton to design the sculptural set-pieces and oversee the rest of the programme.[3] No other sculptor was considered. Frampton then chose incoming sculptors for the majority of the building's seven freestone figures, despite earlier assurances that 'as large a proportion of the work as they may be competent to undertake shall be allotted to Glasgow craftsmen'.[4] Derwent Wood contributed allegorical figures of Architecture, Painting, Sculpture and Music (*c.*1899; Fig. 2), the last of which might fairly be compared to Frampton's own design for one of the two figures supporting his bronze St Mungo at the building's north entrance (Fig. 3). It seems reasonable to suppose the two compatriots discussed their respective designs at length.

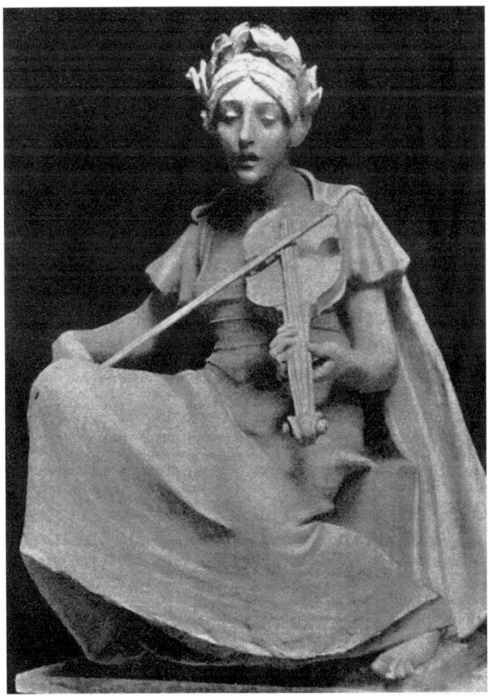

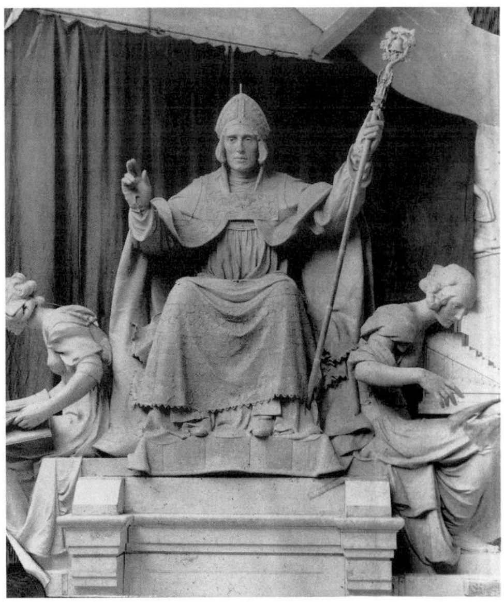

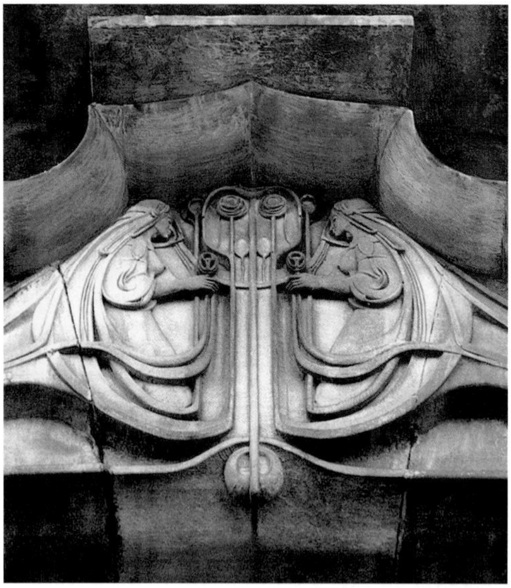

Frampton and Derwent Wood had plenty of points in common. They had both worked at the Slade in the early 1890s, and we know they shared a historicist interest in early Renaissance art, especially that of Donatello.[5] Frampton may have visited Derwent Wood at the Glasgow School of Art in Sauchiehall Street, and from there to Garnethill to see how work was progressing on the Mackintosh building.[6] Glasgow School of Art's new entrance block opened in December 1899, just as the final decisions on the supporting sculpture at Kelvingrove were being made. Mackintosh had actually wanted more sculpture for the Garnethill building than the school's governors were willing to pay for, but the one small piece of carved stonework he did see executed encapsulated his efforts to achieve a synthesis of meaning and function, form and context. The 'Tree of Knowledge' (*c.*1897–9; Fig. 4), designed by Mackintosh and carved by Holmes and Jackson for the lintel above the main entrance on Renfrew Street, was both enchanting and novel in terms of British sculpture, and its influence on Frampton deserves closer analysis.[7]

It is intriguing to speculate on the influence Mackintosh's art had on the spandrel reliefs at the north entrance of Kelvingrove Art Gallery and Museum. Frampton would already have absorbed Walter Crane's theories on the subject of spandrels, having joined the Art Workers' Guild a year before Crane left in 1888. He would also have known Crane's various commentaries on the architectural arrangement of figures, one of which appeared in the same edition as an illustrated report on Simpson & Allen's plans for Kelvingrove.[8] And yet where Crane's ideas were inspired by a largely baroque taste for dexterous, seemingly naturalistic contortions of form and perspective, Frampton's spandrels for the art gallery were low-relief processionals, clearly rooted in 'primitive' early Renaissance precedents. The deliberate rejection of modelled perspective in favour of a composition based more on pattern and linear form undoubtedly links Frampton's work to the primitivist designs of Mackintosh and the rest of 'The Four' (Margaret MacDonald, Frances Macdonald and Herbert McNair), as does the sculptor's tendency to use draperies and other representational forms as abstracted framing devices, as seen for instance in the angels' wings of his 'Love Teaching Harmony to the Arts' (*c.*1897–8;

4 Charles Rennie Mackintosh, 'Tree of Knowledge', *c.*1897–9)

5 George Frampton, 'Love Teaching Harmony to the Arts', *c.*1899

6 Frank Lynn-Jenkins, 'Spirit of Maritime Commerce', 1900–1

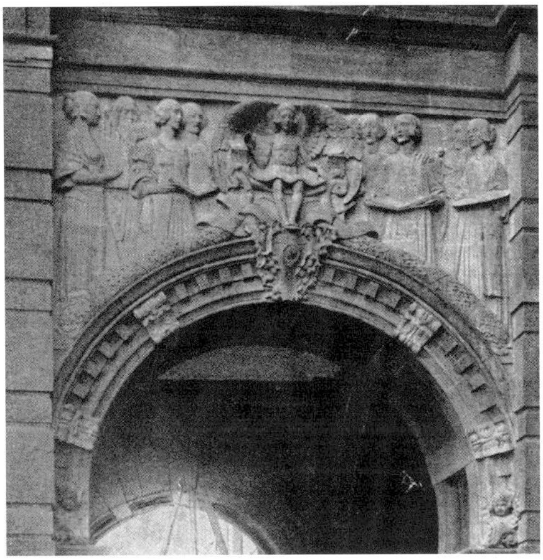

Fig. 5) on the spandrels at Kelvingrove, to the east of the main entrance. At the same time, Frampton's decision to use the semi-mythical character of St Mungo as a central allegorical figure for both the schemes he completed in Glasgow further indicates his strengthening dedication to Symbolism and his growing interest in primitivism.[9] Mackintosh drew similar inspiration from the cultural and artistic traditions of his homeland, regularly using these as fuel to drive his search for a new decorative style.

At T. E. Colcutt's Registry of Shipping for Lloyd's on Fenchurch Street, London, completed in 1901, the ornamental trends Frampton encountered in Glasgow were built upon not by the sculptor himself but by his colleague Lynn-Jenkins. Lynn-Jenkins, a fellow exhibitor at the *Exposition Universelle*, Paris of 1900, contributed lunettes and an 80-ft-long interior frieze, highlighted with ivory and mother-of-pearl and set in a technologically sophisticated background of electrotyped copper (1900–1; Fig. 6). The frieze picked up where Frampton left off with his spandrels at Kelvingrove, displaying a near-total rejection of naturalistic perspective. Instead, Lynn-Jenkins

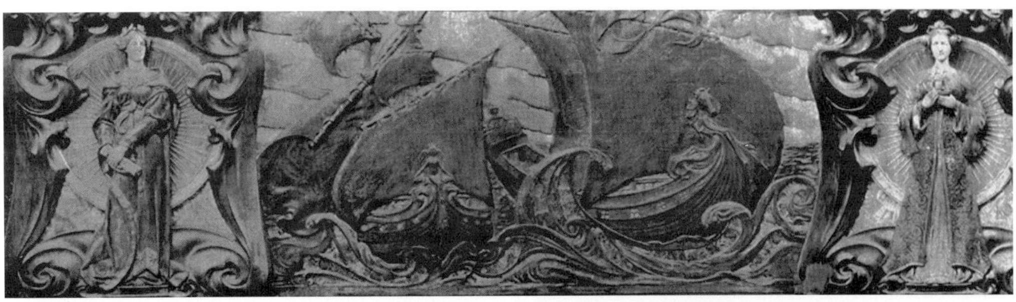

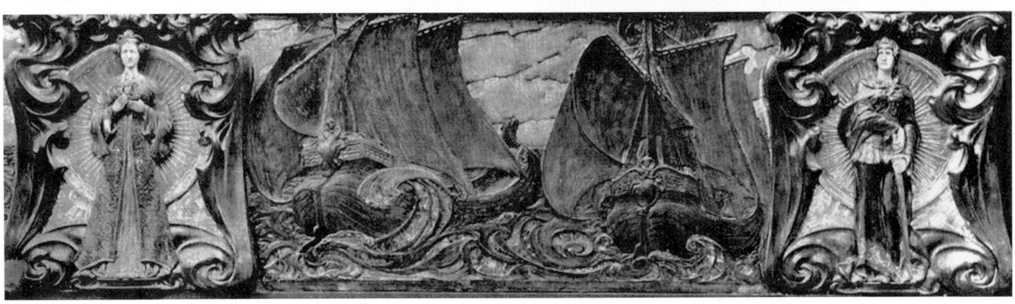

demarcated his low-relief planes using a decorative mixture of colour and line, so that a composition of allegorical figures representing Shipping, Commerce and the like, together with schooners and their billowing sails, came to resemble an abstracted design of pure form. Primitive, early Renaissance precedents were again being utilised as the inspiration for something that must have come across as startlingly modern, though contemporary crafts such as ceramic tiles and, more particularly, stained glass were also prominent in the sculptor's mind.[10]

It would appear, then, that the concerns that led in the 1910s and 1920s to key examples of early modernist sculpture were already germinating in the minds of Frampton and his contemporaries. The enthusiasm for novel materials, the promotion of decorative line over naturalistic structure, and the general interest in primitivism as a basis for exploring untapped varieties of form and meaning – all these issues came to the fore as the 20th century progressed.

The career of John Duncan Fergusson offers a particularly revealing example of how they would develop. Having shown paintings at the Paris International Exhibition of 1900, Fergusson would certainly have known Frampton's 'Lamia', and it seems telling that he would go on to produce artworks so illustrative of the progression between 1900 and 1925. Although he would never have endorsed the artistic forms Fergusson employed, Frampton would have been hard pressed to deny the relevance of his contemporary's discourse between primitivism and modernism, the local and the international. For both artists, heritage and tradition exerted unbreakable holds on the cultural identity of the individual, but Fergusson moved on from Frampton in the way he used this conviction as the basis for a dialogue between the ancient folklore of Britain and the contemporary modernism of continental Europe.[11] His 1924 sculpture, 'Eāstre, Hymn to the Sun' (Fig. 7), referred directly to the Saxon goddess of spring, but also to a modern ballet by Rimsky-Korsakov that the artist had seen performed by his partner, the dancer Margaret Morris.[12] The polished brass from which the head was cast aligned Fergusson with the fashion for exotic

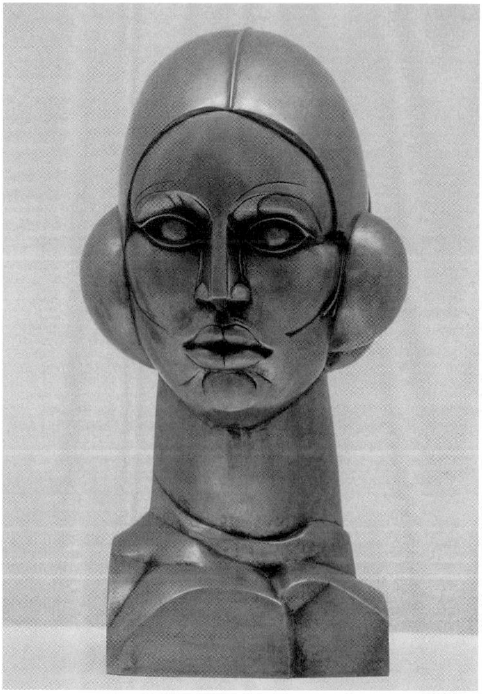

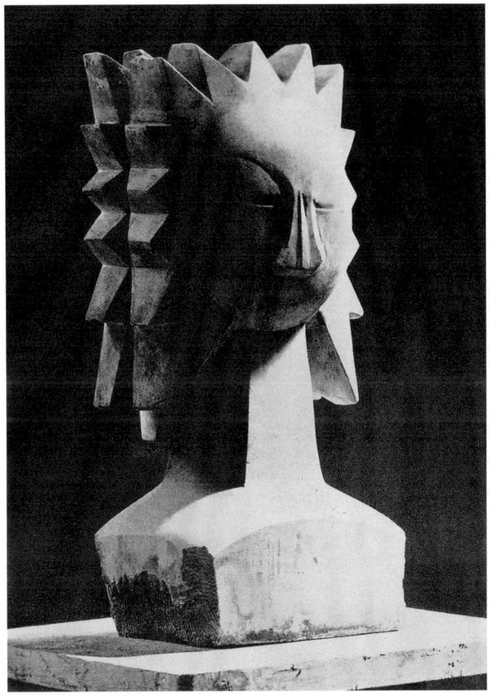

or eye-catching materials, used contemporaneously by Constantin Brancusi in Paris and Frank Dobson and Maurice Lambert in Britain, but anticipated by Frampton and Lynn-Jenkins at the century's outset. Morris acted as model for the sculpture, her features delineated by rigid, curving lines, her head constructed using a series of interlocking spheres and hemispheres. The helmet may have been included as a passing acknowledgement to Frampton's 'Lamia', but it also operated as a salute to the machine aesthetic. Formally and thematically, the head was a balanced blend of geometric primitivism and decorative modernity.

We can now use this framework to look at work by artists such as Henri Gaudier-Brzeska and especially Jacob Epstein. Epstein's 1912 sculpture 'Sunflower' (Fig. 8) made reference not only to the work of Brancusi, but also to the sculptor's developing interest in primitivism. An avid collector of African artefacts, Epstein was warned away from straightforward imitation by Brancusi, who feared such an approach would undermine the qualities both artists so admired in primitive African sculpture: its ability 'to impress, terrify and impart to the beholders a state of mind bordering on, or actually, hallucinatory'.[13] Epstein took the advice, and although his 'Sunflower' is readable in these idolatrous terms, the sculpture must also be seen, like Fergusson's 'Eāstre', through the lens of a modern western machine aesthetic. Its debt, similarly, to the western portrait tradition marks it out as an unmistakably European work, and yet there is no doubt Epstein was trying something new.

This 'moment' of a radical modernism predicated on the assimilation of classical European and primitive non-western traditions was extinguished abruptly by the outbreak of World War I. Epstein reached the end of the conflict exhausted, depressed and impoverished. With an unprecedented memorial-building programme being put in the hands of various Royal Academicians, the future of sculpture at the beginning of 1919 seemed to point towards an unabashed neo-classicism. But the modernist idiom did persist within London's fashionable salon society. Another exponent of what might be termed a Franco-primitive

7 J. D. Fergusson, 'Eāstre, Hymn to the Sun', 1924

8 Jacob Epstein, 'Sunflower', *c.*1912

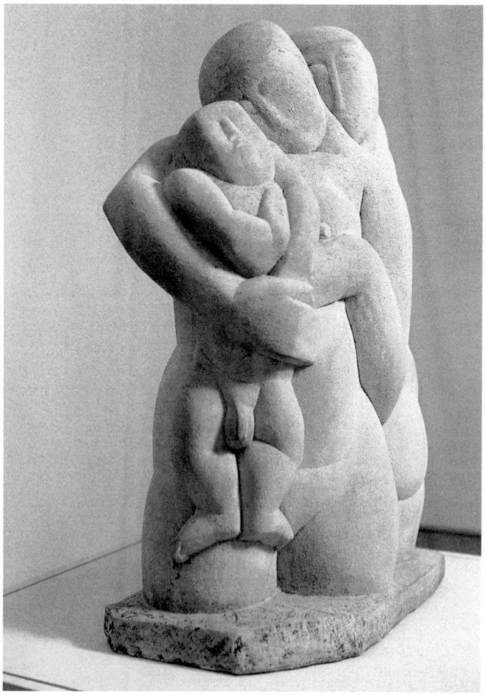

programme was Dobson, a sculptor patronised by the Bloomsbury circle.

Dobson's first one-man show was held at the Leicester Galleries in London in 1921. One of the sculptures he showed there was 'The Man Child', a figure carved in Portland stone (1921; Fig. 9). The work had a number of precedents, including 'Harlech', a tri-partite portrait by Fergusson, photographed by Alvin Langdon Coburn in 1920. Dobson's sculpture was similar in the way it analysed the relationship between tradition and progress. As carving a figure group from such a shallow piece of stone presented very particular problems, the sculptor may also have looked at 'Samson and Delilah', a work by Gaudier-Brzeska from 1913. There are strong formal and compositional similarities between Gaudier-Brzeska's whimsical lovers and the two female figures in 'The Man Child'. Dobson's figures interlock in a tight, solemn embrace, holding up the child to the viewer's inspection. Their downcast faces and the sphinx-like calm of the child suggest mourning and loss, but also stoical perseverance. It seems meaningful too that both the adult figures are female. With the adult male poignantly absent, lost in some nameless catastrophe, the implication seems to be that 'The Man Child' will eventually grow up and take his place. The sculpture is thus an optimistic, forward-looking commemoration, executed with primitivising intent: the memorial made ancient, but also modern.

In dealing with issues of design, beauty and the reproductive process, Dobson focused attention on the positive aspects of modernity and the primitive. These ideas were couched in the formal language of figurative memorial sculpture, an idiom the artist used to imply two important notions. First, he demonstrated, as Frampton had done before, that an interest in classicism and the primitive need not be mutually exclusive. Second, he provided a template for the coming artistic debates of the 1920s. 'The Man Child' linked the primitive with the modern by way of an image of suffering and future regeneration. And yet it was presented as a feat of technical ingenuity, with mere lip-service paid to tribal forms, and everything wrapped up in general ideas of pleasure and

9 Frank Dobson, 'The Man Child', 1921

beauty, as displayed in the poses of the women and the tenderness of their embrace. Dobson's sculpture represented 'primitive chic', an inoffensive fusion of Mediterranean classicism and tribal vernacular, offered up at the end of the Great War, and at the dawn of a decade famous for its ambiguous interests in 'savage' cultures.

Matthew Withey and Jonathan Blackwood

Notes

This essay has been edited by Penelope Curtis.

1 S. Beattie, *The New Sculpture*, New Haven, CT, and London, Yale University Press, 1983, p. 160.

2 R. McKenzie, *Sculpture in Glasgow: An Illustrated Handbook*, Glasgow, Foulis Archive Press, 1999, p. 45.

3 Glasgow City Archives (document C1/3/24), p. 643.

4 Ibid.

5 See, for example, S. Beattie, *The New Sculpture*, pp. 86–7, and S. Crellin, 'Hollow men: Francis Derwent Wood's masks and memorials, 1915–1925', *Sculpture Journal*, 2001, vol. VI, p. 82. In February 1921, many years after their collaboration in Glasgow, Frampton was one of the experts who endorsed sketch plans for the languid 'David' figure Derwent Wood designed for the Machine Gun Corps memorial at Hyde Park Corner, London. The design referred directly to Donatello's famous helmeted figure of the same biblical hero.

6 Glasgow School of Art has a relief bust by Frampton commemorating its one-time chairman of the governors, Sir James Fleming, the man chiefly responsible for raising the funds necessary to erect the building's entrance block. Set at the centre of a polished steel surround designed by Mackintosh, Frampton's panel was unveiled in 1903, though he must have started working on it much earlier. It seems fair, therefore, to assume the sculptor knew Mackintosh and the art school well.

7 Beattie, *The New Sculpture*, pp. 75–6. Beattie sets great store by Frampton's dissemination of the formal tree motif, citing it as a defining influence on the designs of W. J. Neatby for Doulton. The illustrations she chooses to support this proposal are unconvincing, however, and fail to explain the progression from the formal severity of Frampton's decoration for the fireplace of Linden Haus in Düsseldorf, executed in 1896, to the elegant complications of Neatby's terracotta panels for Orchard House in Westminster. Placing Mackintosh's 'Tree of Knowledge' – with its rhythmic undulations and radically decorative, compositional symmetry – at the middle-point in this development explains the jump more credibly.

8 *Magazine of Art*, 1892–3, pp. 92–4 and 131–6.

9 Again he seems to have been pre-empted in this interest by Birnie Rhind, who executed his own representation of St Mungo for the aforementioned scheme at Charing Cross Mansions, but it was probably due to Frampton's example that the 6th-century patron saint of Glasgow became a subject of such appeal for an emerging school of native sculptors. Having exhibited with Frampton at the Paris International Exhibition of 1900, MacGillivray, for one, was fired by his contemporary's primitivist fascination with local folklore, especially judging by the historically and dialectically accurate appellation of 'Thenew' he would later attach to his 1915 bust of St Enoch, the mother of St Mungo or, more correctly, 'Kentigern'.

10 Indeed, it is with this interest in stained glass that the links with the Glasgow Style become further apparent. According to the *Magazine of Art*, 1901, p. 18, Charles John Allen – Frampton and Lynn-Jenkins' collaborator at the Lloyd's building and a fellow exhibitor at the Paris International Exhibition of 1900 – was appointed in 1894 as instructor in sculpture and modelling at the Liverpool School of Architecture and Applied Arts. His colleague at the school, hired to provide tuition in decorative stained glass just a year or so before Allen went to work at Lloyd's, was none other than Herbert McNair, brother-in-law and long-time confederate of Mackintosh. See also *Magazine of Art*, 1901–2, pp. 294–301, for an informative article on Lynn-Jenkins.

11 J. D. Fergusson, *Modern Scottish Painting*, Glasgow, Collins, 1943, p. 210. Towards the end of his career, Fergusson wrote: 'Tradition, to me, is the spirit of the race or nation, which is always there and ready to help, as long as it is kept alive and nourished by creative contributions.'

12 Perth and Kinross Council Archives (Fergusson archive, document L1410). In a letter to John Ressich, dated 2 March 1927, Fergusson states that 'if you have "Hymn to the Sun", Rimsky Korsakov, sung by Galli Curce, you'd probably like her, it's a good record'.

13 E. Bassini and M. D. MacLeod, *Jacob Epstein Collector*, Milan, Ethnographic Arts Publications, 1989, p. 21.

In 1889, the English sculptor Edwin Roscoe Mullins (1848–1907) noted how 'With the Greeks, we know all their chief works were intimately allied to architecture, formed as part of it in fact', and wished 'that it were more so with us'. Sculpture, he felt, 'is "out in the cold", in harmony with nothing around it, and with no near background of buildings or even foliage to give it the sanctity of a home'.[1] Mullins' nostalgia reflected a pervasive view in late 19th-century thinking about sculpture. In the decades leading up to the new century, voices from across Europe, including John Ruskin, William Morris and Arts and Crafts figures like Walter Crane, Charles Baudelaire, Rainer Maria Rilke and Adolf von Hildebrand, were looking to the past in an effort to come to terms with looking at sculpture in the present.[2] The romanticising of older orders of art, including the Greek, medieval and Renaissance periods, seems to have been born out of a profound anxiety about sculpture's place and status in the modern world. Sculpture was felt to be increasingly isolated and detached, as the declining role of decorative schemes in modern architectural programmes divested it, as indeed painting and ornament, of what was once conceived as its primary function and purpose. Without the permanence, stability and dignity of architecture, sculpture seemed weak and vulnerable.

While these views were partly informed by a rejection of modern values, resisting sculpture's assimilation into the commercial world of commodities (its fetishisation, as Ruskin saw it), they can perhaps also be read more simply as a dissatisfaction with the contemporary experience of looking at sculpture. A building provided not only a physical and aesthetic framework through which sculpture was mediated; it also provided a readable context from which sculpture derived its meaning and function. Sculpture was so intrinsically and ideologically identified with architecture that its existence outside of this context necessarily altered the ways it was looked at and interpreted, and by the same token, redefined notions of what sculpture was and what it was for. As soon as it became free-standing, physically detached and isolated, its point of reference shifted inward, to its own intrinsic aesthetics; it acquired an autonomy and specificity that called for a new contextual evaluation.

The discomfort with sculpture's contemporary circumstances suggests there was a growing awareness that the visual and conceptual experience of sculpture had as much to do with its display and location as with the object itself. How a sculpture gave or withheld meaningfulness depended on how it was housed, shored up, enveloped or isolated by its surroundings. It was not until the turn of the century that the echoes of these ideas evolved from a nostalgic, retrospective sense of loss for sculpture's role in architectural schemes of the past into a forward-looking and creative rethinking about how sculpture could be encountered and experienced in the present. Only gradually did the sense of regret and disappointment transform into a positive desire for change – letting go of the notion of a sculpture defined through architecture, and embracing new approaches to sculpture-making and sculpture-seeing. From being thought of as a concrete, finite thing, defined by its physical limits, sculpture was reconstituted as an idea that extended, breathed and resonated in space. This was reflected not only in the way it was approached in practice, but also in how it was thought of, written about and, increasingly, displayed.

In art history, this shift has become most intimately linked with developments in Paris at the turn of the century, in particular with Auguste Rodin, who represents the moment when a passive, unwitting approach to sculptural display became activated into a conscious, creative act, resulting in a new type of practice that defined sculpture through a visualisation of ideas and processes.[3] Developments in the sculpture of Britain are more difficult to establish. No single figure like Rodin existed to represent modern concerns in a similarly overarching manner, and there was no comparably vast archive of visual and literary documents, such as the one that has allowed us to construct so comprehensive a history of Rodin's sculptural displays. Britain's exhibitions tended to place less emphasis on individual practices,

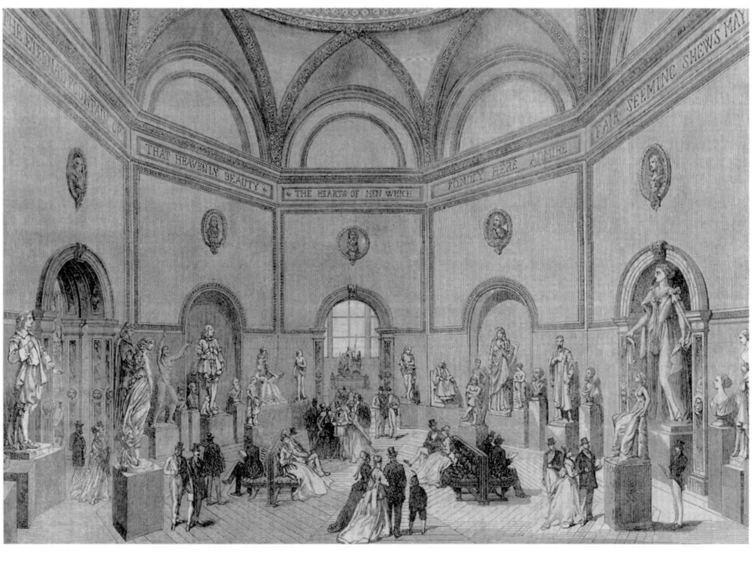

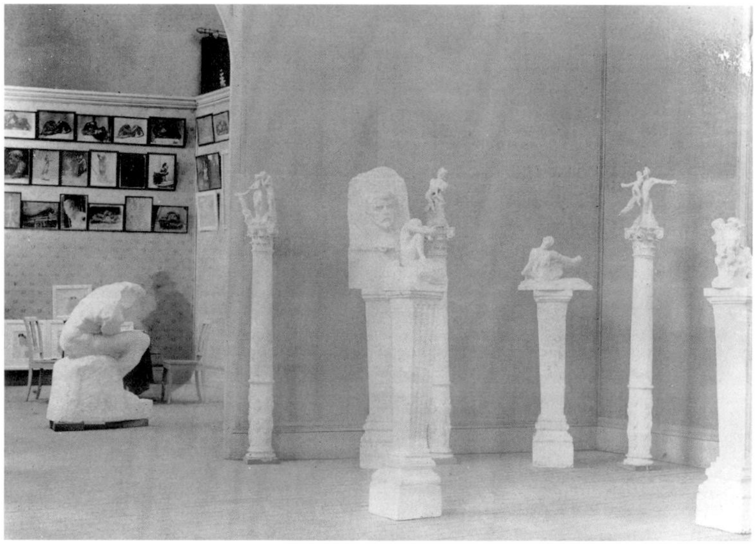

often treating British sculpture as a school that could be defined broadly by period and place; the appearance of the 'New Sculpture' of the 1880s, for example, was perceived as a collective British phenomenon, and did not result in the ascension of one sculptor. In today's art history, Britain continues to be identified with a more traditional ('Victorian') ideology, characterised by its resistance rather than its embrace of modernist concepts.[4] As a result, the role of British artists at the turn of the century in reconfiguring sculptural display has not been widely examined.

It is true that display culture in Britain did not alter as radically or as visibly as it did in France. But subtle shifts did occur. By looking closely at the reassimilation of contemporary sculpture around 1900, both in its physical environments and in its critical contexts, we can identify an artistic engagement with the sculptural encounter that had significant ramifications for the way sculpture in Britain was both made and perceived in the early 20th century.

In Britain, the powerful role institutions played in determining the fine art scene resulted in an exhibitions history quite different from that of France. Long after French artists had broken the grip of the salons' institutionalised selection of art,[5] the Royal Academy retained its position as the key showcase, and benchmark, for fine art, both through its exhibitions and through its affiliation system, which were important public markers of an artist's standing.[6] Displays at the Royal Academy were characterised by rooms crowded with the works of

1 'The Central Hall of the Royal Academy', *c.*1869, wood-engraving from an unidentified illustrated magazine

2 M. Bauche, 'Exposition de l'Alma', 1900

many artists,[7] with large sculptures grouped together in a dedicated 'sculpture hall' (Fig. 1). At a time when Rodin was exhibiting internationally in one-man pavilions – such as at the Pavillon de l'Alma at the Universal Exhibition, Paris, 1900,[8] (Fig. 2) or the 'Rodin Room' at the Düsseldorf exhibition, featured in *The Studio* in 1904[9] – solo exhibitions of contemporary sculpture were hardly seen in Britain.[10] This not only points to the limited opportunities sculptors had for raising their individual profiles; it also tells us something about how viewers were given to understand sculpture: as discrete, finite objects to be judged by their individual merits, and severed from the broader creative process out of which they emerged.

Mullins recognised this when he portrayed museums as inherently difficult spaces for viewing sculpture. Their 'great advantages', he warned, 'must not deaden us to their possible evil': in fostering 'the sight of isolated pieces of sculpture', the museum caused us to 'accustom ourselves to look at [sculptures], and enjoy them … purely as separate works'. The museum's 'evil' was to normalise the displacement of sculpture to the point where the viewer began to 'enjoy' it, and indeed expect it. Museum display, Mullins implied, was transforming artistic practice: 'One feels that the works of men like Bacon, Banks, Gibson, and others is misplaced, or, rather, as if it were not intended for any particular place at all, but were executed for a museum.'[11] Mullins' sentiments were reiterated by other critical voices in Britain, such as that of Edmund Gosse, a figure closely connected with contemporary British sculpture. Gosse complained more specifically of the 'pressure of space and ignominy of position' of sculpture at the Royal Academy, which 'do so much to ruin the effect of the best groups and statues'. He suggested 'distribut[ing] the principal figures through the rooms so as to give the sculptors a few more of those advantages which the painters enjoy in abundance; nor would it injure the effect of the pictures to confront them here and there with the cool and serene beauty of marble'.[12]

Gosse's suggestion was not simply based on an aesthetic preference; like Mullins, he was expressly criticising the practice of physically isolating sculptures in 'sculpture halls'. We can get a powerful sense of this isolation in prints and photographs recording sculpture displays in Britain and France during the late 19th and early 20th centuries. The similarities of the Royal Academy's sculpture hall of *c.*1869 (Fig. 1) and the set-up at the Musée du Luxembourg *c.*1900 (Fig. 3) suggest a generic, institutionalised type of display, in which sculptures were deposited together in a large room, away from the paintings, as if

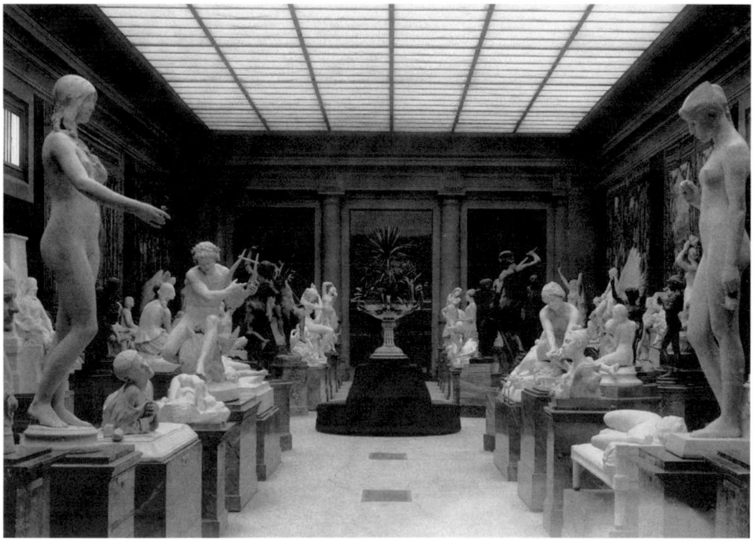

3 Sculpture hall in the old Musée du Luxembourg, *c.*1900

in a storehouse. On plinths resembling uniform wooden crates, life-size sculptures, mostly in plaster or marble, are loosely arranged around the architectural pattern of the space – in rows or around the rotunda. There is something almost tragic about the figures in these images. The statues become homogenised in their environment; they gesticulate into space from their platforms, but their gestures seem arbitrary and meaningless; the architect and writer Harry Bulkeley Creswell described the effect thus in 1900: '[an] air of insignificance ... settles like a blight upon a collection of sculptures that are set out only along the wall of a gallery, or grouped in a corner of a museum'.[13]

The call for a reconfiguration of exhibition spaces was echoed by writers on the continent. There are distinct parallels between Rainer Maria Rilke's thoughts on sculpture, published in his book *Rodin* in 1903, and the views expressed in Britain by the likes of Gosse and Mullins. In a passage that points to his acute sensitivity to the conditions of sculpture, Rilke ponders the near-impossibility of encountering sculpture in all its intended fullness:

> [Sculpture] had to be given its own certain place, in which no arbitrariness had placed it, and it must be intercalated in the silent continuance of space and its great laws. It had to be fitted into that space that surrounded it, as into a niche; its certainty, steadiness and loftiness did not spring from its significance but from its harmonious adjustment to its environment.[14]

Like his British counterparts, Rilke understood that it was precisely those spaces nominated for the purpose of looking at sculpture – spaces that, in a sense, turn around the notion of sculpture's relationship to architecture – that failed to convey a meaningful visual experience. The 'arbitrary' and artificial synthesis of sculptures and museums stifled the possibility of an imaginative sculptural encounter, seeming only to emphasise further their disconnection and alienation.

These different European voices indicate an emergent recognition of the special demands sculpture made on the viewer; an awareness that sculpture's strange oscillation between a physical existence as mere matter, and an almost magical ability to project a sense of livingness and animation, was intimately connected to how and where it was encountered. Creswell attempted to articulate this when he wrote: 'Though [sculpture] assumes to deal with concrete subjects … the precise channels of its appeal defy identification, as though, like music, it dealt in abstractions.'[15] The elusive, fragile balance between sculpture's figurative presence and its inert materiality was undone in conventional modes of display. A different kind of space was needed, one which would allow sculpture to be presented more sensitively and responsively, giving it room to expand and be mentally absorbed.

This new space was increasingly being sought outside traditional exhibition spheres. Rilke saw no future for sculpture in the public arena. He visualised a place that could somehow invoke sculpture's origin, where it could remain connected to the creative cycle from which it had materialised, and from there project itself into the imagination of the viewer. For Rilke, this environment was embodied in the relationship and proximity of the sculptor to his work: 'Rodin lived near his work and, like the custodian of a Museum, continuously evolved from it new meanings.'[16] Rilke thus transforms the 'museum' into a private space: the artist's home, the studio, an intimate, secreted domain where sculpture existed not as an isolated object, but as part of a continuously evolving process. Rilke's vision of a private 'museum' signalled an important adjustment in the relationship of sculpture and display.

This shift was recognised and articulated by other writers, including Gosse, who seems similarly receptive towards sculpture's complex nuances, sensing it had somehow to become integral and personalised within a space in order to resonate and shine. He envisaged a space that would counter the natural 'insensibility of the eye', a 'numb and irresponsive condition' where sculpture was present, visible, but

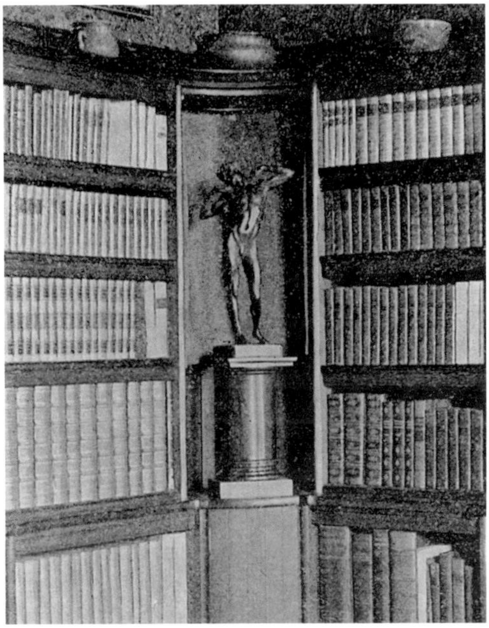

somehow not seen or perceived.[16] Only in the right surroundings could the eye be awoken and made privy to sculpture's effects:

> [T]he surroundings of a piece of sculpture are its atmosphere; it is not independent of them, they are part of the secret of its effect. A picture is self-contained. It carries its air and its distance and its foreground within the four walls of its frame … But a fine piece of sculpture becomes a portion of the room in which it stands.[18]

Like Rilke, Gosse imagined a new kind of space – uncontrived, personalised, and allowing a more natural encounter with sculpture. Where Rilke chose the studio, Gosse's private 'museum' was the intimate space of the home (Fig. 4).

The desire for an alternative sculptural encounter can be read as a direct response to the emergence of a new kind of sculptural practice, and this was not confined to developments in Paris. If Rodin represented a departure in French sculpture, the work of sculptors active at the same time in Britain was cast in a similar light. Critically recognised as the New Sculpture and taken into the fold of the Royal Academy, it was seen as a positive reaction to the disenchantment with modern sculpture that Ruskin had voiced half a century earlier. By the 1900s, writers and artists were able to link this disenchantment to the classicising ethos of the previous generation. Gosse, Mullins, Creswell and others understood that 'the early Victorian sculptors' had deliberately cultivated a sense of separateness and isolation around their work. John Gibson and his followers, Gosse felt, had 'kept up a sort of pompous mystery about their business',[19] while Mullins, similarly pointing to Gibson, lucidly hinted at the physical and metaphysical space that sculpture had previously occupied: 'the works represent a splendid gallery of an art that is dead, because created apart and away from the needs of the time and the sympathies of the nation'.[20]

4 Frederic Leighton, 'The Sluggard', bronze statuette, photograph from 1895

The new work, by Alfred Gilbert, Edward Onslow Ford, William Hamo Thornycroft, George Frampton, William Reynolds-Stephens, Gilbert Bayes and Frank Lynn-Jenkins, to name but a few, was seen as embodying qualities that fundamentally contradicted the neo-classicists'

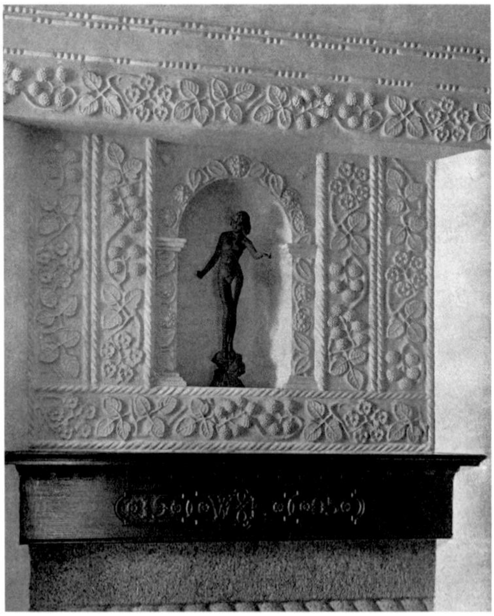

notions of 'sculpture proper'.[21] With an emphasis on modelling and detail, mostly translated into bronze rather than marble, sculptors were moving away from the broad, generalised planes of the classicising statue to a more particularised, intimate handling, often expressed in smaller sculptures and statuettes instead of 'heroic' statues. The use of a smaller scale brought the viewer closer, putting an accent on the finer minutiae of sculpture – the details in its surfaces, the richness of its textures and colours. The British statuettes of this period differed markedly from their earlier incarnations and from those produced in France, where a wider commercial market in statuettes had focused since the early 1800s on the reproduction, often in significant quantities, of well-known, popular statues.[22] British artists at the end of the 19th century treated small sculpture as a distinctive creative outlet, and tended to produce statuettes that were carefully crafted, finely finished, often unique and deliberately conceived on a small scale rather than as reductions.

Statuettes had previously been marginalised in critical discourse on account of their reductive and reproductive nature, but the new British statuette was seen as a serious sculptural genre, and began to assume an importance and status that had once been the preserve of life-size statuary. Its critical contextualisation was quite specific, however, taking into account the unique qualities evoked by its small scale and decorative appearance. A new syntax emerged that redefined these works as 'domestic', and reconstituted their role in terms of their relationship with intimate domestic spaces. This took place literally (inside the private home) and figuratively (in public exhibitions); indeed, there is a sense that the boundary between the two became blurred, as a ubiquitous notion of 'domesticity' began to inform the display and viewing of sculpture. So fluid was this exchange between home and gallery that it not only ran through art criticism but affected a broad literature on home interiors. While the home has perhaps always acted as a kind of private display chamber for personal collections of ornamental objects, memorabilia and souvenirs, the display of sculpture became much more specific and self-conscious in the 1900s. Journals like *The Studio* took the lead in demonstrating how sculptures should

5 Edward Onslow Ford, 'Folly', bronze statuette; George P. Bankart, chimney overmantel in raised plaster, photograph from 1908

6 View of the Franco-British Exhibition, 1908

be shown (Fig. 5),[23] while books on home interiors began to incorporate detailed instructions for arranging sculpture displays in the interior.[24]

The powerful influence that a domestic setting could exert on the perception of sculpture did not remain confined to domestic spaces; the 'atmosphere' of the home was deliberately recreated in the public arena. Although the fashioning of galleries as ideal imaginary homes was not a new concept (the Fine Art Society and the Grosvenor Gallery had already adopted such a strategy in the 1870s),[25] the specific implications for sculpture were only becoming apparent in the 1900s. The convergence of sculpture and domesticity was visible in international exhibitions, such as the Franco-British Exhibition in 1908 (Fig. 6),[26] as well as in museums and galleries. In Bulkeley Creswell's report of 1900, in which he called for British museums and galleries to adopt a 'new scheme of arrangement for sculpture galleries', the private interior was treated as a template for exhibition spaces specially designed to accommodate sculptures. The gallery would 'illustrate how a well-to-do citizen might avail of sculpture for beautifying his home'.[27]

A realisation of Creswell's concept can be found in the Fine Art Society's *First Exhibition of Statuettes by the Sculptors of Today, British and French* of 1902, which illustrates the evolving contiguity between public and private spaces. Featuring a large selection of statuettes by some of the best-known artists, the Society enveloped its exhibits in a homely feel. Marion Spielmann's essay 'Sculpture for the home', in the accompanying catalogue, tells us just how closely statuettes had become

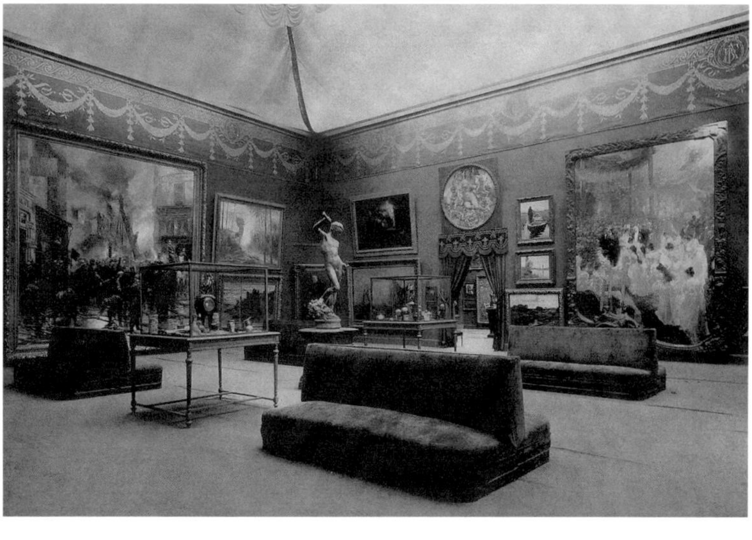

identified with the domestic. He described statuettes as intimate, private possessions that made possible a closer connection with the viewer. This new relationship suggested an evolution of the ideology around sculpture: 'Sculpture has hitherto had little attraction for us as a nation. We have usually regarded it with awe, sometimes with admiration, but rarely indeed has it inspired "the man in the street" with a desire for possession.'[28] In the homely spaces of the Fine Art Society's galleries, with their carpets, rugs, fireplace and statuettes set about the furniture and mantelshelves, the distancing 'awe' of the museum-bound statue was undone. Intimacy and closeness informed this new kind of sculptural encounter.

The efflorescence of a decorative, domestic kind of sculpture not only represented a new creative approach; it affected the way these objects were displayed, viewed and perceived. Its smallness and accessibility, and its suitability for display outside normal exhibition arenas, allowed sculpture to be absorbed and imagined in new ways. But perhaps its focus on decorative and domestic qualities has meant that British sculpture of this period tends to be construed as traditionalist in its approach and ideology. The concern with surfaces, finish, detail and outer appearance, at a time when formal conceptual issues were finding expression elsewhere, particularly in Paris, may be perceived as superficial and irrelevant. But this very quality can also be read as a modernising transformation, and one which was instrumental in reconfiguring the contexts in which sculpture could be seen. Its small, decorative nature stimulated an alternative vocabulary, opening up and modernising the very notion of what sculpture was and what it was for. In the transitional period of the early 1900s, it suggested that sculpture could be conceived, viewed and imagined in new ways.

Martina Droth

Notes

I thank Alex Potts for our conversations about sculpture displays, and Nicholas Mead for reading and commenting on earlier drafts of this essay. Thanks also to Diane Bilby, Alan Crookham, James Kay, Victoria Worsley and Laura Valentine for helping me in my search for images of British sculpture displays.

1 E. Roscoe Mullins, *A Primer of Sculpture*, London, Cassell & Co., 1889, p. 90.

2 See, for example, J. Ruskin, *The Two Paths, Being Lectures on Art and its Application to Decoration and Manufacture, Delivered in 1858–9*, London, Smith, Elder, 1859; W. Crane, *The Claims of Decorative Art*, London, Lawrence and Bullen, 1892); C. Baudelaire, 'The salon of 1856', in *Selected Writings on Art and Literature*, London, Penguin, 1992); R. Maria Rilke, *Rodin* (1902), trans. J. Lamont and H. Trausil, London, Grey Walls Press, 1946); A. von Hildebrand, *The Problem of Form in Painting and Sculpture* (1893), trans. M. Meyer and R. Morris Ogden, New York, Stechert, 1907.

3 Most recently in the exhibition and catalogue *Rodin en 1900: L'Exposition de l'Alma*, Paris, Musée du Luxembourg, Musée Rodin, Réunion des Musées Nationaux, Paris, 2001.

4 For an analysis of the persistent influence of traditional arts and crafts principles in the early 20th century, see M. T. Saler, *The Avant-garde in Interwar London: Medieval Modernism and the London Underground*, New York and Oxford, Oxford University Press, 1999. Thanks to Jon Wood for directing me to this book.

5 See P. Mainardi, *The End of the Salon: Art and the State in the Early Third Republic*, Cambridge and New York, Cambridge University Press, 1993).

6 See S. C. Hutchison, *The History of the Royal Academy*, London, Royce, 1986.

7 See D. Solkin, *Art on the Line: The Royal Academy Exhibitions at Somerset House, 1780–1836*, New Haven, CT, and London, Yale University Press, 2001.

8 Recently reconstructed in the exhibition *Rodin en 1900* at the Musée du Luxembourg (see n. 3).

9 'The Fine Arts and Horticultural Exhibition at Düsseldorf', *The Studio*, August 1904, p. 231.

10 To put this into a broader context of how exhibitions developed in Europe, see F. Haskell, *The Ephemeral Museum: Old Master Paintings and the Rise of Art Exhibitions*, New Haven, CT, and London, Yale University Press, 2000, p. 104.

11 E. Roscoe Mullins, 'The decorative uses of sculpture', *Journal of the Society of Arts*, 8 April 1892, p. 515.

12 E. Gosse, 'Sculpture in 1880', *Saturday Review*, 7 June 1880, p. 757.

13 H. B. Creswell, 'A new scheme of arrangement for sculpture galleries', *Architectural Review*, 1900, vol. 8, p. 204.

14 Rilke, *Auguste Rodin*, London, The Grey Walls Press, 1946, p. 9.

15 Creswell, 'A new scheme of arrangement for sculpture galleries', p. 202.

16 Rilke, *Auguste Rodin*, London, The Grey Walls Press, 1946, p. 36.

17 E. Gosse, 'The place of sculpture in daily life', *Magazine of Art*, 1895, p. 329.

18 Ibid., p. 372.

19 Ibid., p. 329.

20 Roscoe Mullins, 'The decorative uses of sculpture', p. 515.

21 Mullins makes the point that 'what is now called sculpture proper' was generally identified with 'free-standing' statuary. Roscoe Mullins, 'The decorative uses of sculpture', p. 512.

22 See, for example, J. Wasserman (ed.), *Metamorphosis in Nineteenth Century Sculpture*, Fogg Art Museum, Cambridge, MA, Harvard University Press, 1975; F. Rionnet, 'Goupil et Gérôme: regards croisés sur l'édition sculptée', in *Gérôme et Goupil: Art et Entreprise*, Bordeaux, Musée Goupil, Réunion des Musées Nationaux, 2001. Thanks to Pierre-Lin Renié for alerting me to this latter article.

23 'British wall and ceiling decoration', *Studio Yearbook of Decorative Art*, 1908.

24 See, for example, J. H. Elder-Duncan, *The House Beautiful and Useful*, London, Cassell, 1907, p. 22, which includes a meticulous description of how to accommodate statuettes correctly.

25 See S. P. Casteras and C. Denney (eds), *The Grosvenor Gallery: A Palace of Art in Victorian England*, New Haven, CT, and London, Yale University Press, 1996.

26 Statuettes, busts and decorative sculptures accounted for around half of the British sculpture on display. *Souvenir of the Fine Art Section, Franco-British Exhibition 1908, Compiled by Sir Isodore Spielmann Under the Auspices of the British Art Committee*, Derby, 1908.

27 Creswell, 'A new scheme of arrangement for sculpture galleries', p. 206.

28 *First Exhibition of Statuettes by the Sculptors of Today – British and French*, London, Fine Art Society, 1902. Thanks to the Fine Art Society for allowing me to consult their copy of this catalogue.

According to M. H. Spielmann, editor of the *Magazine of Art* and author in 1901 of *British Sculpture and Sculptors of To-day*, sculpture was not fully appreciated in Britain, or by the general public anywhere. People, he wrote, liked colour.[1] Nearly twenty years later, when there was an outcry over the exhibition of Jacob Epstein's 'Christ' at the Leicester Galleries in London, the critic Paul Konody reckoned 'the real sensation was not the untraditional and debatable gaunt figure of Christ in his winding sheet, but the fact that the public had awakened to an appreciation of sculpture'.[2]

Spielmann and Konody's agreement on the low level of interest in sculpture prevailing in Britain at the start of the century is borne out by a study of the range of images of contemporary sculpture available to the public in this period. Such a study also supports Konody's sense of a perceptible increase of interest in the years after World War I. Throughout this period, however, the individual wishing to find out what was happening in contemporary sculpture would require a considerable degree of determination. The amount of illustration in newspapers and magazines was relatively small, although it grew appreciably in the years after the war, whilst the number of books on contemporary sculpture published in Britain in this period was, by the standards of the later years of the century, extremely small.

Books

The publication of Spielmann's book in 1901 was prompted, he wrote, by 'the fact that there exists no book upon present or recent sculpture in Great Britain – nothing beyond occasional articles in the Magazines'. His book, however, would stand almost alone in the years to come amidst the myriad publications on classical and Renaissance sculpture, and the many books on contemporary painting. He intended his work to be comprehensive. With fifty-six artists represented, the book, he claimed, included examples of 'nearly every living sculptor of repute in Great Britain'. The largest numbers of illustrations were devoted to Alfred Gilbert, William Hamo Thornycroft and Thomas Brock, three artists who had, he suggested, established Britain in a very high place among the schools of the nations. Others well represented were Edward Onslow Ford, Alfred Drury and George Frampton. Ernest Short's well-illustrated *History of Sculpture* appeared six years later. Half of its length was devoted to Greek and Roman sculpture, but readers were also given a reasonably comprehensive account of 19th-century sculpture, with praise lavished on Auguste Rodin, Frederic Leighton and Alfred Stevens. Short concluded with a chapter on modern English sculpture, including Brock, Thornycroft, Gilbert, Onslow Ford, Harry Bates and Frampton.

The next such comprehensive work would be Kineton Parkes' two-volume *Sculpture of To-day*, published in 1921, the first two volumes in Chapman and Hall's 'Universal Art Series'. His selection of images was largely conservative, with four illustrations of works by Francis Derwent Wood, three by Thornycroft, and others by Frampton, Frederick Pomeroy and Henry Poole. However, he also included a stone 'Torso' by Eric Gill and a bronze 'Mask from Life' by Epstein. As an encouragement for viewers to engage with the subject, Parkes' work is also interesting for the author's provision of the names and addresses of the publishers of the photographs, allowing readers to obtain larger copies of the reproductions.

Academic artists could hope to have their works published in the various illustrated volumes accompanying the annual Royal Academy summer shows. Besides the Royal Academy's own *Royal Academy Illustrated*, there were rival publications issued by *Pall Mall Magazine*, the *Magazine of Art*, and the *Sphere & Tatler*. These all tended to follow the same pattern, starting with a major section of about 100–150 pages devoted to paintings, and then 10–15 pages of sculpture. This ratio of illustrations, ten paintings to one sculpture, hardly varied throughout the period, although in the exhibitions themselves the ratio was between 5:1 and 4:1, with the proportion of sculptures gradually increasing throughout the period.[3]

In the years before World War I, a plethora of books appeared on the nature of art, stimulated by the gradual impact of the Post-Impressionists and their successors. Clive Bell's *Art* is the best known, but like most of its contemporaries, it was unillustrated. Bell's later *Since Cézanne*, which appeared in March 1922, dealt almost exclusively with painting, with the exception of one chapter on 'Negro sculpture', and was also unillustrated. Roger Fry's *Vision and Design*, published in December 1920, although generously illustrated, had very few images of sculpture: two accompanying the essay on 'Negro art', and a comparison of three standing figures, including one from Rodin's 'Burghers of Calais' and Henri Matisse's 'The Back No. 1'.

There was even a general lack of monographs on the more popular contemporary sculptors. For instance, the first monograph on Gilbert appeared in 1929.[4] The one exception was Rodin, on whom numerous books were published, starting with a translation of Camille Mauclair in 1905, and rapidly followed by two books by Lawton in 1906 and 1907, and one by Kahn in 1909.

During and after the war, some short monographs on sculptors of the modern movement began to appear. In 1916 Ezra Pound wrote his memoir of Henri Gaudier-Brzeska;[5] in 1919 Westheim's book on Wilhelm Lehmbruck appeared, as did a volume in praise of Ivan Meštrović, with contributions from Sir John Lavery and others.[6] Maurice Raynal's book on Jacques Lipchitz was translated the next year, and in 1922 Horace Shipp published *The New Art* featuring the sculpture of Lawrence Atkinson.[7]

The first book on Epstein appeared in 1920, an expensive, large-format volume published by John Lane, with text by Bernard van Dieren. Its fifty plates illustrated a rather conservative choice from Epstein's oeuvre, mostly recent portrait busts, with only a few of his early works included, such as a detail of the tomb of Oscar Wilde, 'Cursed be the Day I was Born' and the upper torso of the 'Rock Drill'. There were no images from the British Medical Association building.

An interesting development in the 1920s was the appearance of various series of monographs on contemporary British artists. The first of these was Benn's *Contemporary British Artists*, edited by Albert Rutherston and launched in 1923. Each volume had a substantial text of twenty to thirty pages and approximately thirty-five good-quality, black-and-white illustrations. It was to run to sixteen volumes over five years, but only two of these dealt with sculptors: Epstein and Gill. The volume on Epstein, published in 1925, was written by the London Group painter Hubert Wellington, who was then Registrar of the Royal College of Art. Its images were rather more adventurous than those used by van Dieren, including one figure from the BMA building, the 'Rock Drill', 'Two Doves' and 'Venus'. This book was also innovative in the way it devoted pairs of pages to individual works, allowing them to be shown from different viewpoints.

In 1925 Fleuron began a similar series, 'British Artists of Today', each volume illustrated with seventeen black-and-white plates. Again the series featured painters primarily – Mark Gertler, John and Paul Nash, Gilbert Spencer and Duncan Grant – but included a 1926 volume on Frank Dobson, written by Raymond Mortimer. The series 'Masters of Modern Art' published by John Lane focused mostly on 19th-century artists, with volumes on Louis Barye and Rodin.

Given the dearth of British books on contemporary sculpture, it is small wonder that, when Anton Zwemmer took over Jäschke's foreign-language bookshop in Charing Cross Road in 1923 and developed a specialism in importing art books from Europe, his shop rapidly became, as Kenneth Clark wrote, 'an inevitable place of pilgrimage'[8] for the artworld. It was also a library for impoverished art students such as Henry Moore, who was able to browse undisturbed amongst books not only on contemporary European sculpture but also on the art of a variety of non-western cultures.[9] English-language books on contemporary art were available in other shops such as Foyle's, the largest of the Charing Cross Road's many bookshops. Elsewhere in London, the International Book Shop on the Strand and Tottenham Court Road advertised a range of books on European painters, mainly Post-Impressionists, and in 1925 P. H. Muir of 76A Oxford Street was advertising his second book catalogue, 'Art and the Moderns'.[10] Zwemmer's, however, was unusual in importing foreign-language art books, primarily in French and German. It was through these, and the various European art journals for which he became a distributor, that many people in Britain were able to see reproductions of contemporary European art in the 1920s.

Zwemmer's 1924 catalogue of art books[11] demonstrates again the preponderance of volumes on modern painting, such as Charles Marriott's *Modern Movements in Painting* and Jan Gordon's *Modern French Painters*. The number of titles on contemporary sculpture was small. However, there were foreign-language monographs on Alexander Archipenko and Ossip Zadkine in the series 'Les Artistes Nouveaux' and on Heinrich Campendonk in the series 'Junge Kunst'. There were also three books on Rodin, two in German and one in French,[12] as well as Carl Einstein's *Negerplastik* (Munich, 1920), featuring 116 full-page illustrations.

Zwemmer listed a few works that provided well-illustrated if limited surveys of contemporary European sculpture. In Alfred Kuhn's *Die neuere Plastik*, for instance, which contained seventy-seven full-page plates of work by German and Paris-based artists, readers could see two works each by Constantin Brancusi, Lipchitz, Ernst Barlach and Lehmbruck, three by Archipenko, and single works by Henri Laurens, Karl Schmitt-Rottluff and Max Pechstein, as well as Pierre-Auguste Renoir, Aristide Maillol and a number of lesser-known German artists.[13] Works by Zadkine were illustrated in a volume entitled *Le Néoclassicisme dans l'art contemporain*.[14]

Bookshops such as Zwemmer's also sold portfolios of reproductions of works of art. These had been available since the turn of the century,[15] but by the early 1920s the technology of colour printing had significantly progressed. In the later 1920s Zwemmer's developed a substantial business selling high-quality reproductions from various German publishers such as Piper, Hanfstaengl and the Marées Society. These reproductions appear only to have been of paintings, and mostly of works before 1900.[16] However, in 1924 Twenty-One Gallery in the Adelphi advertised for sale a portfolio of thirty reproductions published by the American *Dial* magazine under the title *Living Art*. The selection, according to the advertisement, excluded 'purely abstract work', though there was a 'definite denial of photographic naturalism'. These were colour reproductions, the product of two years' collaboration with the Ganymed Press in Berlin, and at the price of eight guineas per portfolio, they were not for the faint-hearted. However, those who invested were rewarded with ten illustrations of sculptures, including works by Brancusi, Archipenko, Lehmbruck and Frank Dobson.[17]

Newspapers and journals

In 1897 the *New York Tribune* became the first newspaper to reproduce photographs, using half-tone plates. Others were quick to adopt the process, giving better-quality images at only half the cost of the previous engraving process.[18] Newspapers benefited from photography's sense of immediacy and documentary accuracy, but at first they did not exploit the possibilities of the medium for reproducing works of art.

In the popular press, coverage of the arts was restricted to occasions when specific works became newsworthy, such as Epstein's figures for the BMA building. The broadsheets reported and reviewed art exhibitions regularly, but rarely incorporated photographs. Reviewers on *The Times*, for instance, were diligent in reviewing exhibitions in London, but the paper's photographs tended to be gathered on a single page of the newspaper, and mostly dealt with general news events. The Royal Academy summer show was an exception. By the mid-1920s many newspapers were devoting space to illustrations from this exhibition. In 1925, for instance, *The Times*, *Daily Sketch*, *Daily Mail*, *Sphere* and *Graphic* all ran photographs, but again these were devoted to paintings, not sculptures.

Among the plethora of literary and political periodicals published around this time, such as the *Nation*, *New Statesman* and *Fortnightly Revue*, many carried discussion on contemporary art, but usually without illustration. Even among those that specifically favoured the art of the modern movement, illustration was patchy, particularly for sculpture. Frank Rutter's *Art and Letters*, which ran from 1917, illustrated a number of contemporary painters, but made no reference at all to sculpture.

Although the subtitle of Wyndham Lewis' journal the *Tyro* includes the word 'sculpture' – 'A review of the arts of painting, sculpture and design' – Lewis' manifesto, 'The objects of this paper', refers several times to painters and painting, but never to sculpture.[19] All the illustrations in the paper refer to two-dimensional works, except one clay model by Dobson, 'Dancing Figures'. The second issue of the *Tyro* ran an article by Lewis entitled 'Plastic art', but this made no specific reference to sculpture other than a passing swipe at the Edith Cavell monument by Frampton. Of the seventeen illustrations in the large, glossy photograph section at the end of the issue, only three were of sculptures, two by Dobson and one by Lipchitz.[20] The rest were paintings and drawings, mostly by Lewis and Wadsworth.

Illustration in art journals depended on editorial inclination. The *Art Journal*, which launched a new series in 1900 and ran until 1912, focused primarily on painting and decorative art, although it touched on sculpture in relation to the Royal Academy and when Rodin was in the news. By contrast, the *Magazine of Art*, edited by Spielmann, gave considerable space to sculpture. In 1901, for instance, Spielmann ran articles on M. Nestor Antokolsky, Daniel Chester French, Edouard Lantéri, Stephan Sinding and F. J. Williamson ('Her late Majesty's Private Sculptor'). There were also numerous illustrations of work by sculptors such as Onslow Ford and Thornycroft. Volume 1 of the magazine's *New Series*, published in 1903, represented the work of thirty-seven sculptors, most of them still living.

Regular coverage of sculpture was also to be found in *The Studio* magazine, launched in 1893 for followers of the Arts and Crafts movement. It figured particularly heavily in the regular feature 'Studio-talk', a round-up of news and exhibition reviews from home and abroad. These reviews were usually illustrated.[21] Not many of the magazine's main articles dealt with sculpture in the early years of the century, although an article was run in 1913 on contemporary work from Japan. After World War I, the interest in sculpture seemed to grow. For instance, in 1920 there were articles on Epstein and Ernest Cole.[22] The *Burlington Magazine*, meanwhile, dealt primarily with art from before 1900, although its 'Monthly chronicle' provided a round-up of what was on at the London galleries, including contemporary sculpture, with the occasional illustration.[23]

Perhaps the most extensive and enthusiastic coverage of sculpture came in *Artwork*, a new periodical launched in 1924 'for artworkers and art lovers who do not confine their practice or love of art to painting', and boasting freedom from all groups and schools, with contributors including both 'reactionaries and rebels'.[24] The opening issue, besides running an illustrated article by Kineton Parkes on Meštrović, included several illustrations of sculptures, including some from the Royal Academy show of that year, and four plates from Gill's 'Stations of the Cross' for St Cuthbert's in Bradford. The Gill illustrations were interesting because they figured as a purely visual feature, without any accompanying text.[25] This level of interest was maintained in subsequent issues, with articles by Kineton Parkes and R. H. Wilenski, both well illustrated on glossy paper. The second issue also initiated 'A quarterly review of the art reviews'. This was a digest of a range of art magazines from Europe, America and Australia. In the first of these reviews, Parkes noted that 'with the renaissance of architecture, true sculpture is awakening to a new life also'. He noted that in all the thirteen magazines reviewed, 'sculpture in most of its forms finds an honourable place', and between them they covered twenty living sculptors, ranging from Joseph Csaky and Laurens in *L'Effort Moderne* to the Austrian Anton Hanak in *Deutsche Kunst*.[26]

Country Life, although more of a general interest magazine, came to develop an interest in sculpture. Launched in the 1880s with little arts coverage beyond the occasional piece on garden statuary and a gradual interest in architectural history, it frequently dealt with contemporary art after World War I, and ran a number of features on sculpture, always generously illustrated. The motivation for these articles was usually based on a contemporary event such as the beginning of the construction of the Edith Cavell monument, the opening of an exhibition by Eric Kennington, or the unveiling of Kennington's 'Memorial to the 24th Division'.[27]

Critical reaction

Spielmann's intention in his *British Sculpture and Sculptors of To-day* was to celebrate the 'radical change' which had come over British sculpture 'since the year 1875 or thereabouts'. Classicism, which he criticised for sameness, sickly-sweet, empty charm and lifeless skill, had been overtaken by a tendency towards realism and the picturesque, without detracting from the 'dignity of the conception'. The aim, he wrote, was 'to give life without actual realism – a suggestion of reality shrouded in poetry and grace'.[28]

Classicism, however, continued to have its adherents. Sir Charles Waldstein, one-time Slade professor of fine art and director of the Fitzwilliam Museum in Cambridge, delivered two lectures to the students of the Royal Academy in 1914, in which he upheld Greek classical sculpture as the pattern to which they should adhere. The Greeks, he said, aimed for ideal types, whereas modern art claimed it sufficient to copy an individual. He distinguished between Rodin's theory, which spoke of copying the individual, and Rodin's practice, which, in his best works, Waldstein felt, went beyond the individual appearance and expressed the character within.[29]

Among younger writers, there was a variety of opinions, though generally they shared a frustration with the Royal Academy. Under the influence of Post-Impressionism and Cubism, many were willing to entertain a degree of stylisation, while instinctively clinging to a traditional notion of sculpture as a means to express the inner character of a subject through representation. Thus, at the more conservative end, Amelia Defries wrote enthusiastically of the stylised animalia of Mateo Hernandez, praising this sculptor for the way he expressed the character of the animals. Then, with a nod towards the concept of primitivism, she commended his direct carving, saying that he carved 'with pre-historic frankness, and yet with the sensitive poetry of the civilised mind'.[30] These works, she felt, solved 'the aesthetic problem' and were more interesting than 'those few remaining Cubists who are satisfied with abstract form'. Hernandez's sculptures retained recognisable form and, in their simplification, communicated essential character.

Kineton Parkes made a similarly tamed use of the concept of primitivism when he commended Alan Durst as 'an authentic modern representative of the primitive artist, who is archaic by nature and training as well as by predilection and taste; one who takes what comes to his hand and subdues it to his spirit'.[31] From this perspective, Parkes' notion of primitivism meant simply responding to the nature of the materials, then imposing one's will upon them.

Towards the end of the period, Wilenski emerged as a leading critic writing in support of non-representational sculpture. In the tradition of Walter Pater, he argued that sculpture had its own unique and untranslatable beauty, and that the aim of the discipline was to make the block itself beautiful. Thus he praised what he called 'broadly Cubist sculpture', by which he meant work freed from the influence of painting and Greek or Renaissance modelling: 'sculpture confined relentlessly to the elements peculiar to itself'.[32]

Nigel Halliday

Notes

1 M. H. Spielmann, *British Sculpture and Sculptors of To-day*, London, Cassell, 1901, p. 4.

2 *Observer*, 27 January 1924, p. 8; quoted in Evelyn Silber, *The Sculpture of Epstein*, Oxford, Phaidon, 1986, p. 37.

3 In 1903, for instance, there were 788 oil paintings and 186 sculptures (4:1), out of a total exhibition of 1880 works. Thus sculpture represented 10 per cent of the exhibition. After the war the number of paintings decreased markedly, while the number of sculptures stayed constant: in 1925 there were 631 oils and 206 sculptures (3:1) in a total show of 1,419 works. Sculpture had increased its share to 14 per cent of the total.

4 Gilbert was featured in the series of 'Standard Monographs' issued by the *Art Journal* in *c.*1910, but these were probably reissues of the magazine's special Christmas editions devoted to individual artists. See advertisement in *Art Journal*, June 1911, inside back cover, listing thirty-five issues, almost all of which featured painters such as Frederic Leighton, Lawrence Alma-Tadema and William Quiller Orchardson.

5 E. Pound, *Gaudier-Brzeska: A Memoir*, London, John Lane, 1916, with a frontispiece and thirty plates. Works by Gaudier-Brzeska also featured in *New Paths: Verse, Prose, Pictures 1917–18*, a volume edited by Cyril Beaumont and M. T. H. Sadler, published in May 1918. It was dedicated to the memory of various poets and artists who had died in the war, including Gaudier-Brzeska. Dedicated to all the arts, its coverage of sculpture was limited, but the section of glossy plates included a drawing by Gaudier and his sculpture 'Weeping Figure', as well as Epstein's 'Head of W. H. Davies'.

6 P. Westheim, *Wilhelm Lehmbruck*, Berlin, G. Kiepenheuer, 1919, with eighty-four illustrations. Sir John Lavery et al., *Ivan Meštrović: A Monograph*, London, Williams and Norgate, 1919.

7 Horace Shipp, *The New Art: A Study of the Principles of Non-Representational Art and their Application in the Work of Lawrence Atkinson*, London, Cecil Palmer, 1922, with ten plates.

8 Kenneth Clark in *Anton Zwemmer: Tributes from Some of his Friends on the Occasion of his 70th Birthday*, privately printed, 1962, p. 57.

9 See Henry Moore's contribution to ibid.

10 Advertisement in *Artwork*, February–April 1925, vol. 1, no. 3, p. xvii.

11 'Catalogue No. 10 Fine Art'. There is also a section on art books in his general 'Catalogue No. 3' which is dated December 1924, but includes the Epstein volume in the series 'Contemporary British Artists', dated 1925. Copy in Zwemmer Archive, Hyman Kreitman Research Centre, Tate Britain.

[12] C. J. Burckhardt, *Rodin und das plastische Problem*, Basel, Basler Kunstverein, 1921, forty-six plates. R. M. Rilke, *Auguste Rodin*, Leipzig, Insel Verlag, 1920, ninety-six full-page illustrations. Coquiot's book is listed as '*Rodin* (1915)'. This is presumably *Auguste Rodin: Cinquante-sept Statues*, Paris, Bernheim-Jeune, 1915.

[13] Alfred Kuhn, *Die neuere Plastik von achtzehnhundert bis zur Gegenwart*, Munich, Delphin-Verlag, 2nd edn, 1922.

[14] Published in Rome, 1923, with sixty-six reproductions including work by Carlo Carrà, Ardengo Soffici and Georges Braque. The catalogue does not name the author. Judging by the price of seven shillings, the reproductions are unlikely to have been of high quality.

[15] For instance, in 1904 Chapman and Hall were offering 'Pictures for art education', carbon photographs made directly from the original, printed either 17 × 23 in or 20 × 32 in, mounted on board and suitable for framing. They also sold collections of ten reproductions, each about 5.5 × 8 in, under the title 'Masterpieces in art – Elson prints'. See advertisement in *Art Workers' Quarterly*, January 1904, vol. III, no. 9, p. xii.

[16] Hanfstaegl, however, extended into the 20th century with works by Franz Marc, Maurice Utrillo, Henri Matisse and Maurice de Vlaminck.

[17] Advertisement in *Artwork*, October 1924, vol. 1, no. 2, p. 118. The portfolio was issued in a limited edition of 500.

[18] See Lucia Moholy, *A Hundred Years of Photography*, Harmondsworth, Penguin, 1939, pp. 169–71.

[19] The object of the magazine, Lewis wrote, was 'To be a rallying spot for those painters, or persons interested in painting, in this country, for whom "painting" signifies not a lucrative or sentimental calling, but a constant and perpetually renewed effort ... There is actually at the moment no paper in this country wholly devoted to the interests of the great European movement in painting and design ... The number of painters experimenting in England in the European sense are very few.' The magazine, he adds later, is 'run entirely by painters and writers'. *Tyro*, no. 1, 1921, p. 2.

[20] The Lipchitz was an abstract form, entitled 'Sculpture'. Dobson's two works were entitled 'Family' and 'Woman Descending from a Bus'. The former is now known as 'The Man-Child' (Tate Britain, 1921; see N. Jason and L. Thompson-Pharoah: *The Sculpture of Frank Dobson*, London, Lund Humphries and Henry Moore Foundation, 1994, p. 124). The title of the latter is probably ironic, and the work is not listed by Jason and Thompson-Pharoah.

[21] See, for instance, the five photographs of the Rodin Pavilion, erected by the Technical Artists' Union in Prague, in *The Studio*, November 1902, vol. XXVII, no. 116, pp. 141–6.

[22] J. Harada, 'Modern tendencies in Japanese sculpture', *The Studio*, June 1913, vol. LIX, no. 243, pp. 13–20, with sixteen illustrations. M. Salaman, 'The sculpture of Ernest Cole', *The Studio*, January 1920, vol. LXXVIII, no. 322, pp. 140–8, with illustrations of five sculptures and four drawings. J. Cournos, 'Jacob Epstein: artist-philosopher', *The Studio*, July 1920, vol. LXXIX, no. 328, pp. 173–8, with illustrations of five portrait busts and 'The Christ'.

[23] See, for example, unillustrated review of Meštrović at Twenty-One Gallery, *Burlington Magazine*, June 1919, vol. XXXIV, no. 195, p. 253; unillustrated review of Epstein's exhibition at the Leicester Galleries, March 1920, vol. XXXVI, no. 204, p.146. Havard Thomas' 'Boadicea' was illustrated to accompany a note of the sculptor's death, June 1922, vol. XL, no. 231, pp. 248–53.

24 Editorial, *Artwork*, 1924, vol. 1, no. 1, p. iv.

25 An article by Gill appears later in the same issue, but the magazine does not draw attention to the connection.

26 K. Parkes, 'A quarterly review of the art reviews', *Artwork*, October 1924, vol. 1, no. 2, pp. 117–18.

27 H. Avray Tipping, 'The memorial to Nurse Cavell', *Country Life*, 6 December 1919, vol. XLVI, no. 1196, pp. 780–2, including five illustrations of plaster models and sections of the final work. C. Dodgson, 'The Kennington Exhibition', *Country Life*, 6 November 1920, vol. XLVIII, no. 1244, p. 616; illustrated with the low-relief 'P.B.I.' [Poor Bloody Infantry] (see J. Black, *The Sculpture of Eric Kennington*, Much Hadham, Henry Moore Foundation, 2002, pp. 22–3). C. Hussey, 'A new sculptor', *Country Life*, 4 October 1924, vol. LVI, no. 1448, pp. 526–8, with illustrations of four sculptures.

28 Spielmann, *British Sculpture and Sculptors of To-day*, pp. 1–3.

29 Sir Charles Waldstein (later Walston), *Greek Sculpture and Modern Art: Two Lectures Delivered to the Students of the Royal Academy in London*, Cambridge, Cambridge University Press, 1914. See also his *Art in the Nineteenth Century*, Cambridge, Cambridge University Press, 1903.

30 A. Defries, 'Mateo Hernandez, sculptor', *Artwork*, October 1924, vol. 1, no. 2, pp. 98–101, including six illustrations.

31 K. Parkes, 'The direct carvings of Alan Durst', *Artwork*, October 1924, vol. 1 no. 2, pp. 76–80. The article was accompanied by five photographs.

32 R. H. Wilenski, 'Form in sculpture', *Artwork*, February–April 1925, vol. 1, no. 3, pp. 138–44. The essay was accompanied by four pages of glossy plates, illustrating two Chinese figures; two images from Chartres Cathedral; two stone heads and a wood-carved nude by Dobson; a stone nude by Leon Underwood; and 'Sculpture from a Cottage Hearth' by Kennington.

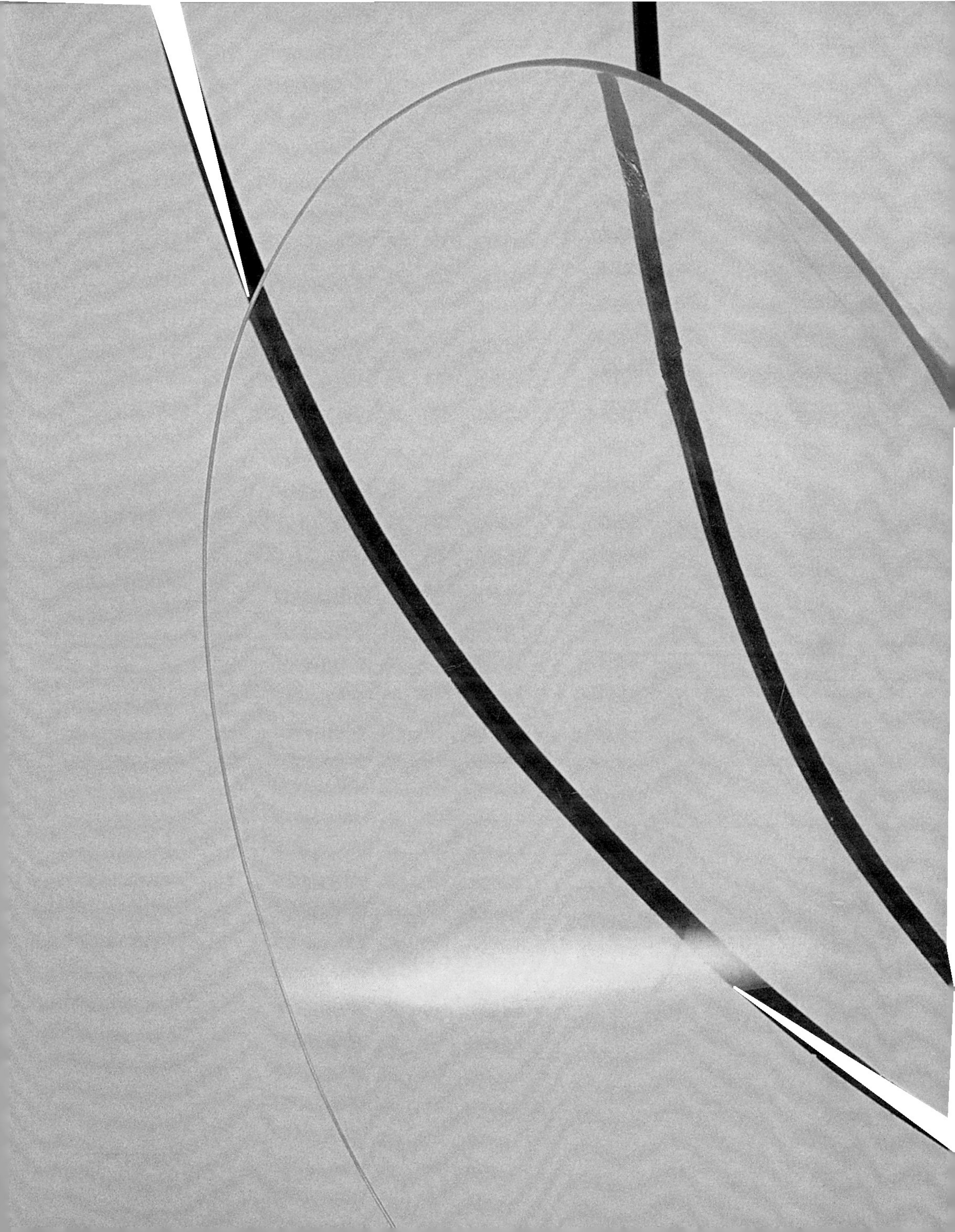

1925

■ William Hamo Thornycroft dies
■ Ian Hamilton Finlay born
■ John Skeaping and Barbara Hepworth marry
■ Gilbert Bayes becomes master of the Art Workers' Guild
■ Alan Durst (1925–40) and Henry Moore (1925–32) teaching at Royal College of Art (RCA) – Eric Gill turns down offer to teach there
■ London Artists' Association founded (Frank Dobson, Vanessa Bell, Duncan Grant, Raymond Coxon and others)
■ Charles Sargeant Jagger's Royal Artillery memorial and Francis Derwent Wood's Machine Gun Corps memorial unveiled at Hyde Park Corner, London
■ Jacob Epstein's memorial to W. H. Hudson ('Rima') unveiled, with great controversy, by the prime minister, Stanley Baldwin
■ Alfred Hardiman's sculptures for Westminster County Hall, London
■ The *Exposition des Arts Décoratifs et Industriels Modernes* in Paris (Gilbert Bayes wins gold medal and diploma of honour)
■ Constantin Brancusi exhibits at New Chenil Galleries, London
■ Hubert Wellington's book on Jacob Epstein published

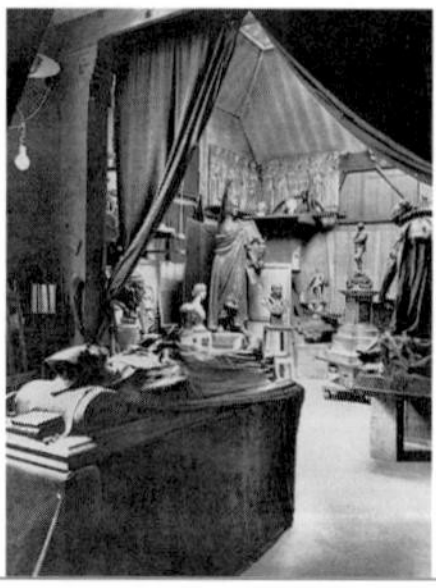

Sir William Hamo Thornycroft's studio at Melbury Road, London at the time of his death

1926

■ Ben Nicholson becomes chair of 7 & 5 Society
■ Alfred Gilbert's 'Clarence Tomb' in Windsor completed and his 'Eros' removed from Piccadilly
■ Gilbert Ledward professor of sculpture at the Royal College of Art (1926–9)
■ Francis Derwent Wood dies: memorial exhibition, Leicester Galleries, London
■ Jacob Epstein exhibits 'Visitation', Leicester Galleries, London
■ Adrian Stokes meets Ezra Pound at Rapallo
■ Raymond Mortimer's book on Frank Dobson published

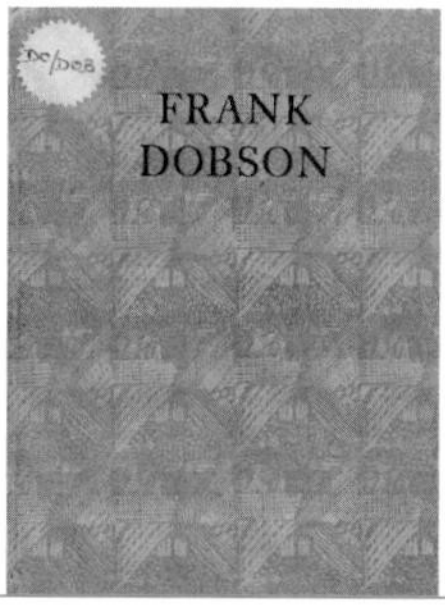

Raymond Mortimer 'Frank Dobson', London: Fleuron

1927

■ Constantin Brancusi 'Bird in Space' court case v. US Customs – Jacob Epstein one of Brancusi's defenders in court
■ St Ives Society of Artists founded
■ Merlyn Evans studies at Glasgow School of Art (1927–31)
■ Maurice Lambert's first solo exhibition at Claridge Gallery, London
■ Francis Derwent Wood and Edward Onslow Ford exhibition, Royal Academy, London
■ Kathleen Scott's first solo exhibition, Greatorex Galleries, London
■ J. K. M. Rothenstein's monograph on Eric Gill published
■ R. H. Wilenski's *The Modern Movement in Art* published by Faber and Faber

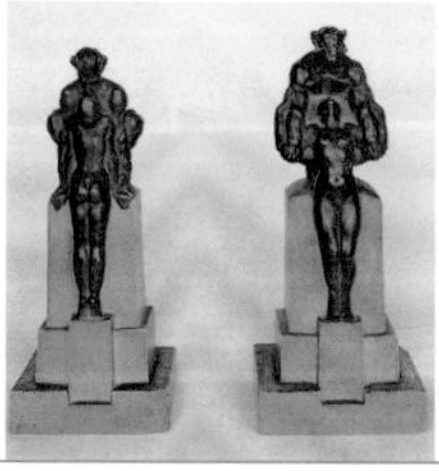

Charles Sargeant Jagger 'Two Maquettes for Fountain Garden Groups of Nymphs and Fawns'

1928

- George Frampton dies
- F. E. McWilliam studies at the Slade School of Fine Art (1928–31)
- Jacob Epstein, Eric Gill, Henry Moore, A. H. Gerrard, Eric Aumonier, Allan Wyon and F. Rabinovitch work on St James' Underground Headquarters, London
- Eric Kennington's Soissons memorial, started in 1925, unveiled in July
- *Modern and African Art* exhibition at Sydney Burney Gallery, London
- Eric Gill at Goupil Gallery, Moore at the Warren Gallery and Hepworth at Beaux-Arts Gallery, London
- Stanley Casson's *Some Modern Sculptors* and Isabel McAllister's *Alfred Gilbert* published
- Ralph Brown born

1929

- Louis Richard Garbe professor of sculpture at Royal College of Art (1929–46)
- Kenneth Martin and Mary Martin study at Royal College of Art (1929–32)
- Alfred Hardiman commissioned to do Earl Haig monument for Whitehall, London
- Eric Kennington commissioned to execute commemorative statue of Thomas Hardy in Dorchester
- Henry Moore moves from Hammersmith to Parkhill Road, Hampstead
- Eric Gill exhibits at Goupil Gallery and publishes *Art-Nonsense and Other Essays, and Engravings*
- Maurice Lambert and Antony Gibbons Grinling exhibit at Tooth's Gallery, London
- Kineton Parkes' essay 'Rights and wrongs of academy sculpture' published in *Apollo*
- *Epstein: Seventy-Five Drawings* published

1930

- Frank Dobson's facade for Hay's Wharf, Southwark
- Antony Gibbons Grinling relief for Cambridge Theatre, London
- Alan Durst exhibits at the Leicester Galleries and Tait McKenzie at the Fine Art Society, London
- Jacob Epstein carves 'Genesis'
- Austin Wright at Oxford University reading modern languages
- Important publications on sculpture include: Stanley Casson's *XXth Century Sculptors*, E. Aumonier's *Modern Architectural Sculpture*, G. Bayes' *Modelling for Sculpture* and H. S. Ede's *A Life of Gaudier-Brzeska*
- Anthony Hill, Elisabeth Frink and Bryan Kneale born

1931

- The *Island* magazine published
- Henry Moore resigns from the Royal College of Art
- F. E. McWilliam travels to France (with Robert Ross Scholarship from the Slade)
- The British Museum acquires Sumerian sculpture 'Gudea' from Sydney Burney
- Eric Kennington carves figures for the new Royal Shakespeare Theatre in Stratford-upon-Avon (unveiled in 1932)
- Charles Ricketts dies
- Barbara Hepworth joins 7 & 5 Society
- Barbara Hepworth and John Skeaping divorce
- Alan Durst executes figures for the Royal College of Dramatic Art, London
- Henri Gaudier-Brzeska exhibition at Bumpus Gallery, Oxford Street, London
- *Yugoslav Sculpture and Art Exhibition* travels Britain (visits Leeds, Birmingham,

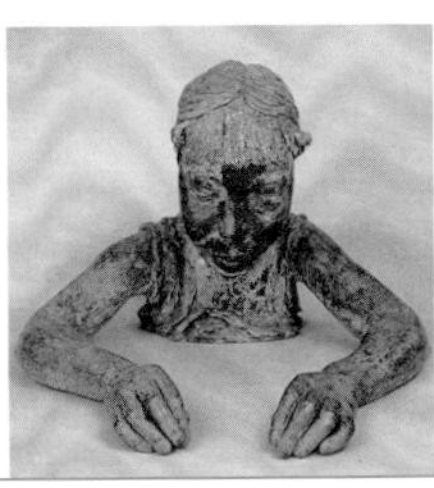

Jacob Epstein 'Peggy Jean (Sick Child)'

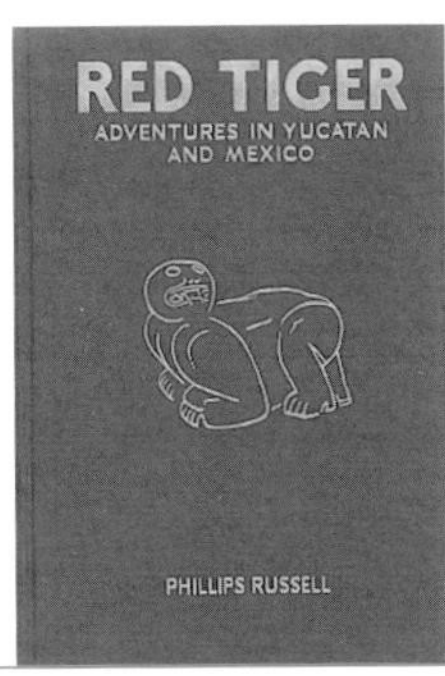

Leon Underwood 'Red Tiger: Adventures in Yucatan and Mexico', London: Phillips Russell

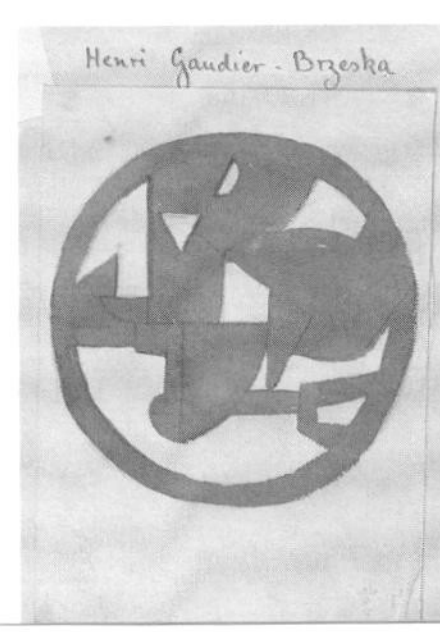

Watercolour by Henri Gaudier-Brzeska from Ede's *A Life of Gaudier-Brzeska*

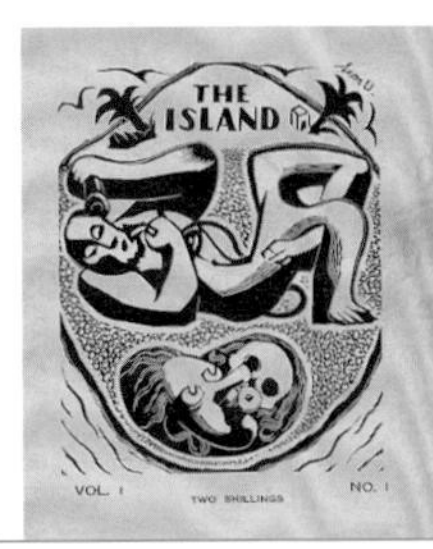

Front cover of 'The Island', London

Glasgow, Bradford, Belfast, Swansea and Manchester)

- Edward Bainbridge Copnall works on Royal Institute of British Architects figures (1931–4)
- Eric Gill establishes his own press, Hague and Gill
- Books include: H. S. Ede's *Savage Messiah*, A. L. Haskell's *The Sculptor Speaks* and Kineton Parkes' *The Art of Carved Sculpture*
- Edward Carter Preston's Liverpool cathedral sculptures (1931–37)

1932

- Alfred Drury's 'Sir Joshua Reynolds' unveiled at Burlington House, London
- Alfred Gilbert's Queen Alexandra memorial at St James', London
- Alfred Gilbert knighted and resumes Royal Academy membership
- Henry Moore becomes head of new sculpture department at Chelsea School of Art
- Gertrude Hermes' 'Fountain' and mosaics for Shakespeare Memorial Theatre, Stratford-upon-Avon
- Charles Wheeler's figures for the Bank of England, London
- Leon Underwood carves 'The Cathedral' and curates *Sculpture Considered Apart from Time and Place* at Sydney Burney's St James' gallery, London
- R. H. Wilenski's *The Meaning of Modern Sculpture* is published by Faber and Faber
- L. B. Powell's *Jacob Epstein* published
- Adrian Stokes' *The Quattro Cento* published

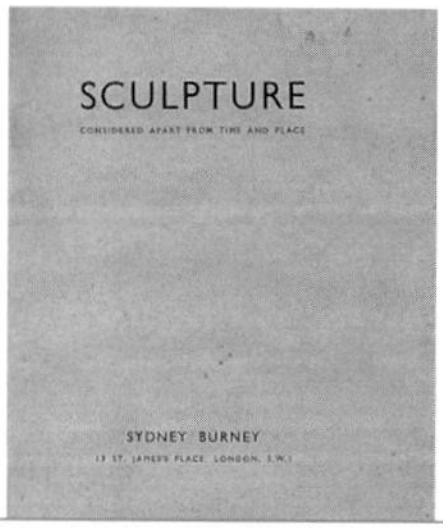

Front cover of 'Sculpture Considered Apart from Time and Place', Sydney Burney, London

1933

- *Art Now* by Herbert Read published
- Artists' International Association founded
- Louis Richard Garbe works with Royal Doulton producing ceramic figures (1933–9)
- Maurice Lambert unsuccessfully proposed as a member of Unit One by Paul Nash
- Books published on sculpture include: H. Maryon's *Modern Sculpture: Its Methods and Ideals*, L. Underwood's *A Short History of English Sculpture*, S. Jagger's *Modelling and Sculpture in the Making* and H. Brodzky's *Henri Gaudier-Brzeska 1891–1915*
- Adrian Stokes' articles on Moore and Hepworth for the *Spectator*
- Edward Carter Preston's 'Four Winds' sculptures for Cambridge University Library

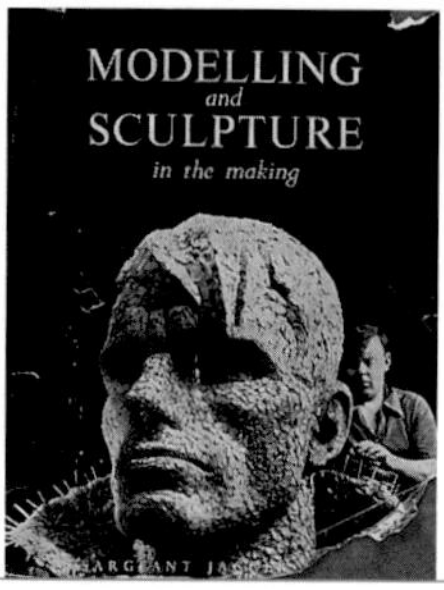

Front cover of Jagger 'Modelling and Sculpture in the Making'

1934

- British Council founded
- Alfred Gilbert and Charles Sargeant Jagger die
- Phillip King born
- Betty Rea secretary of Artists' International Association
- Kenneth Armitage studies at Leeds College of Art (1934–7)
- William Reid Dick trustee of Tate Gallery (1934–41)
- Gilbert Ledward founds Sculptured Memorials and Headstones firm
- Willi Soukop teaches at Dartington Hall (1934–40)
- Charles Wheeler executes decorative motif for South Africa House
- Hermon Cawthra's sculptures for Leeds Civic Hall
- Sydney Burney's *The Model Modern Art Gallery* exhibition at Chesterfield House, London
- Unit One at Mayor Gallery, London

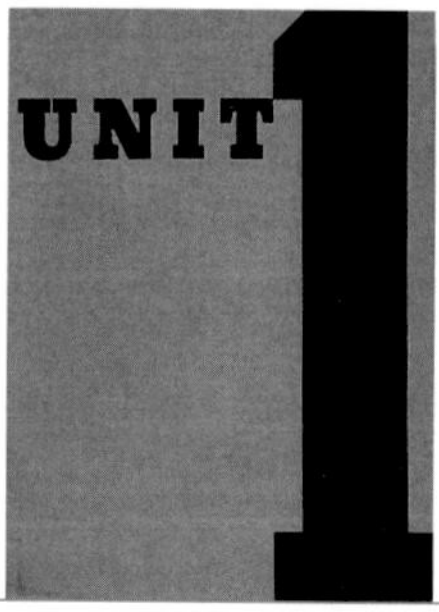

Front cover of 'Unit One', Cassel, London

1935

- Herbert Read edits *Unit One: The Modern Movement in English Architecture, Painting and Sculpture* and publishes book on Moore
- *Abstraction Création: Art Non Figurative 1934* exhibition
- Adrian Stokes' *Stones of Rimini* published by Faber and Faber
- Mark Boyle born
- Gaston Lachaise dies
- William Tucker born
- Proposal to remove Jacob Epstein's eighteen carved figures from the exterior of the British Medical Association building by the new owners, the government of Southern Rhodesia
- Naum Gabo moves to London
- William Reid Dick knighted and made president of Royal Society of British Sculptors (1935–8)
- Maurice Lambert makes decorative relief panels for Duchess Theatre, London and begins work on equestrian statue of George V
- Dora Gordine returns to England
- Siegfried Charoux moves to England
- Contents of Alfred Gilbert's studio bought by National Art Collections Fund
- T. E. Lawrence dies – Eric Kennington starts work on memorial to him privately
- Symposium on 'Revolutionary Art' held at the Artists' International Association in London and proceedings published
- R. H. Wilenski 'The place of sculpture today and tomorrow' published in *The Studio*
- Paul Nash's article 'Ben Nicholson's carved reliefs' published in *Architectural Review*
- Ivor Abrahams born

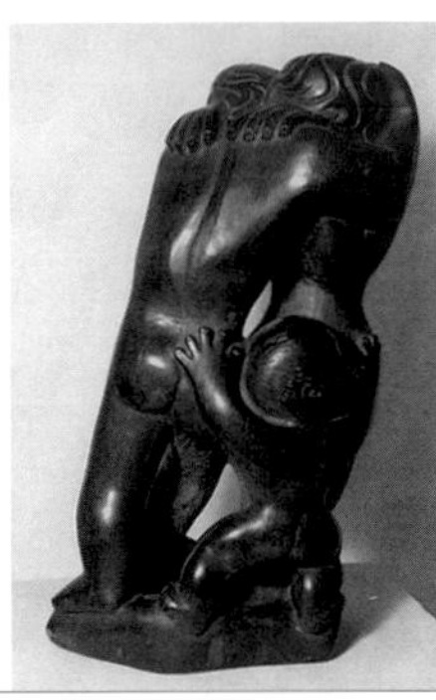

Leon Underwood
'The Family'

1936

- F. E. McWilliam moves to Steele's Road, Hampstead
- Bernard Meadows becomes studio assistant to Henry Moore
- *International Surrealist Exhibition* at New Burlington Galleries, London (including sculptors Henry Moore, Merlyn Evans, Eileen Agar and Paul Nash)
- *Abstract and Concrete* exhibition at Lefevre Gallery, London (then travelled to Liverpool, Oxford and Cambridge)
- Richard Bedford solo show at Lefevre Gallery, London
- Jacob Epstein begins his illustrations for Baudelaire's *Les Fleurs du Mal*
- Exhibition of Henri Gaudier-Brzeska's drawings at Zwemmer's Gallery, London
- Paule Vézelay exhibition at the Lefevre Galleries (with catalogue foreword by Paul Nash)

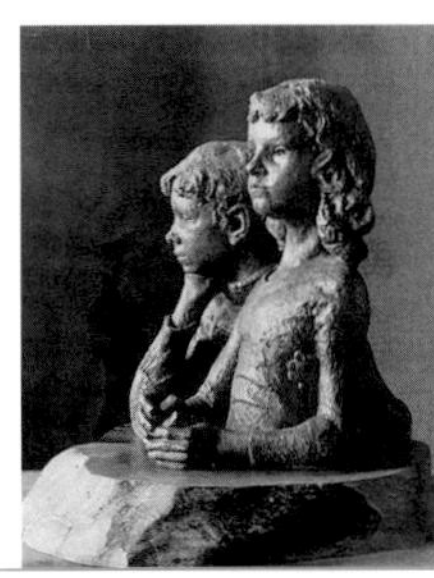

Gertrude Hermes
'Judith and Simon', portrait of her children

1937

- Michael Kidner reads anthropology at Cambridge University
- John Skeaping's *Animal Drawing* published
- Michael Sandle, David Annesley and Isaac Witkin born
- Alfred Hardiman's 'Earl Haig' monument unveiled, Whitehall, London
- Roland Penrose founds the London Gallery
- F. E. McWilliam moves into purpose-built studio-home in New Malden
- Gertrude Hermes designs 'Britannia' glass window for the British Pavilion at the *Exposition Internationale des Arts et Techniques* in Paris and Betty Rea executes murals for International Peace Campaign Room for the unofficial Peace Pavilion
- Raymond Mason studies at the College of Arts and Crafts, Birmingham
- Kenneth Armitage studies at the Slade (1937–9)
- Austin Wright visits Paris
- Selfridge's sculpture in celebration of coronation
- *Fantastic Art, Dada and Surrealism* exhibition, MoMA, New York
- *Surrealist Objects and Poems* exhibition, London Gallery
- *The First British Artists' Congress for Peace, for Democracy, for Cultural Progress* (Artists' International Association exhibition, Grosvenor Square, London)
- *Circle: International Survey of Constructive Art* published, edited by Ben Nicholson, Naum Gabo and Leslie Martin
- Giedion-Welcker's *Modern Plastic Art* published in English
- Henry Moore's article 'The sculptor speaks' published in the *Listener*
- Tim Scott born

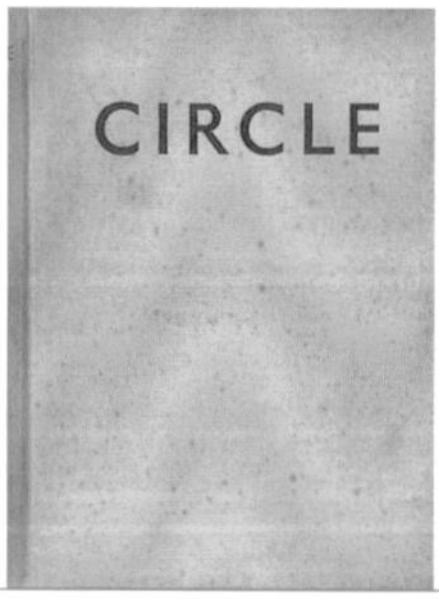

Front cover of 'Circle', Faber and Faber, London

1938

- William Reid Dick made Sculptor to King George VI (1938–52)
- Michael Ayrton in Paris (studio with John Minton)
- Piet Mondrian moves to London
- Leon Underwood's Brook Green School closes
- F. E. McWilliam makes masks of Chamberlain for May Day demonstration in London
- Jacob Epstein, Henry Moore and Stephen Spender receive honorary degrees from Aberdeen University
- Pablo Picasso's 'Guernica' shown at New Burlington and Whitechapel Galleries, London
- Britain's last participation in the Venice Biennale until 1948
- *London Life in Concrete* exhibition
- *Exhibition of Contemporary Sculpture* at Guggenheim Jeune Gallery, London

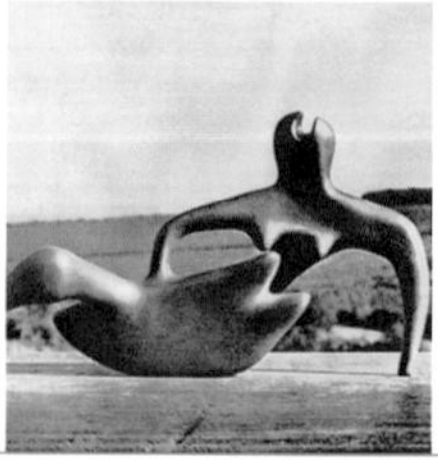

Henry Moore 'Maquette for Reclining Figure'

1939

■ Alan Durst's *Wood Carving* published
■ *Sculptured Memorials and Headstones* published by The Sculpture Centre, London
■ *AIA: The First Five Years*, 1933–8 published
■ Paul Neagu, Roland Piché and William Pye born
■ Edward Carter Preston's 'Nelson Figurehead' for S.S. Conway
■ Maurice Lambert serves as a captain in Royal Welsh Fusiliers (1939–41)
■ Peter Peri becomes naturalised British citizen
■ F. E. McWilliam has first solo exhibition London Gallery
■ Henry Moore resigns from Chelsea School of Art (which is relocated to Northampton for the war)
■ Jacob Epstein's 'Adam' exhibited at the Leicester Galleries, London
■ Eric Kennington's recumbent effigy of Lawrence is installed in St Martin's church, Wareham, Dorset
■ Eric Kennington begins work as portraitist for War Artists' Advisory Committee
■ Henry Moore's 'Recumbent Figure' enters Tate Gallery Collections, London
■ Artists' International Association's *Unity of Artists for Peace, Democracy and Cultural Development and Art for the People* exhibition at the Whitechapel Gallery, London
■ Jacob Epstein exhibition in Blackpool
■ Stanley Casson's *Sculpture of Today* published
■ Glynn Williams born

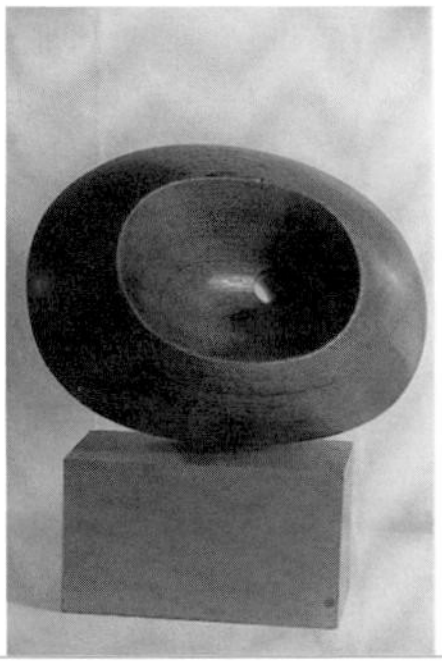

Barbara Hepworth 'Conicoid'

1940

■ Eric Gill dies
■ J. D. Fergusson founds the New Art Club in Glasgow
■ F. E. McWilliam joins the RAF
■ Hubert Dalwood apprenticed as an engineer to the British Aeroplane Company (1940–4)
■ Geoffrey Clarke studies at Preston School of Art (1940–1) and then at Manchester School of Art (1941–2)
■ Austin Wright moves to York (a conscientious objector during the war)
■ Eric Kennington's 'Tomb of T. E. Lawrence' at Wareham completed
■ Henry Moore and John Skeaping made official war artists – Moore starts 'Shelter Drawings' then leaves London for Perry Green
■ *Surrealism Today* exhibition at Zwemmer's
■ Eric Gill's *Autobiography* and Jacob Epstein's *Let There Be Sculpture* published
■ Clive Barker and Maurice Blik born

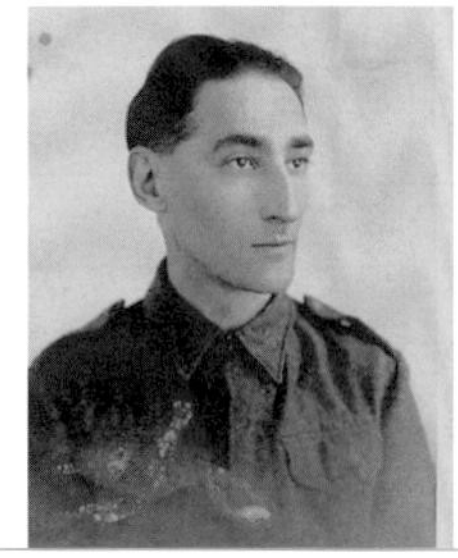

Laurence Josephs in the Army

1941

- Lynn Chadwick serves in Fleet Air Arm
- Donald Attwater's *Eric Gill: Workman* published
- Henry Moore begins 'Coalmining Drawings'
- Henry Moore becomes trustee of the Tate Gallery
- Graham Sutherland, John Piper and Henry Moore group exhibition at Temple Newsam, Leeds
- Barry Flanagan, Michael Kenny and Michael Craig-Martin born

1942

- Anthony Caro studies engineering at Christ's College, Cambridge
- George Fullard serves in army (1942–7)
- J. D. Fergusson founds the New Scottish Group
- Paule Vézelay moves to London
- Charles Wheeler made trustee of the Tate Gallery, London (1942–9)
- Gertrude Hermes in Canada, where she works as draughtsman for aircraft and ship-building factories
- Julio González dies
- Jacob Epstein and Matthew Smith exhibition at Temple Newsam, Leeds
- *New Movements in Art: Contemporary Work in England* exhibition at the London Museum
- *Imaginative Art Since the War* at Leicester Galleries, London
- Jacob Epstein exhibits 'Jacob and the Angel' at the Leicester Galleries, London
- Susan Hiller born

1943

- Henry Moore carves 'Madonna and Child' for St Matthew's church, Northampton
- Geoffrey Clarke serves in the RAF (1943–7)
- Raymond Mason studies at the Slade
- Paul Nash and Barbara Hepworth exhibition at Temple Newsam, Leeds, and Hepworth exhibition at Bankfield Museum, Halifax
- *Out of Chaos* film made about official war artists
- A.T. Broadbent's *Sculpture Today in Great Britain, 1940–1943* and G.E.H. Grigson's book Henry Moore published
- Carl Plackman and Stephen Willats born

1944

- Aristide Maillol dies
- Hubert Dalwood serves in Royal Navy (1944–6)
- F. E. McWilliam in India on military service (1944–6); teaches in art schools in New Delhi and Bengal
- Alfred Drury dies
- Eduardo Paolozzi studies at the Slade (1944–7)
- Selection of Henry Moore's 'Shelter Drawings' published
- Bruce McLean and Phyllida Barlow born

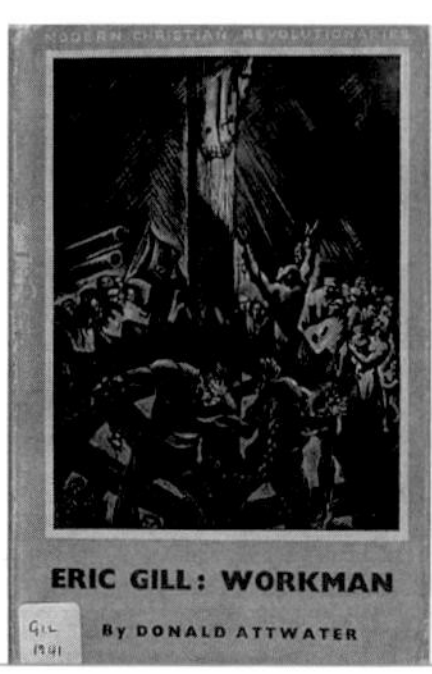

Front cover of 'Eric Gill: Workman', James Clarke & Co., London

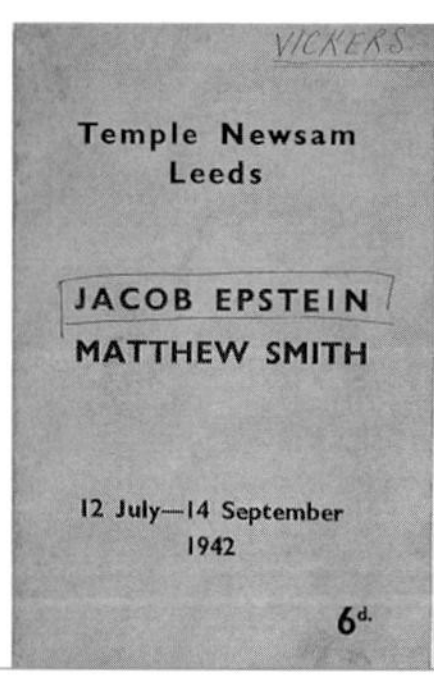

Jacob Epstein and Matthew Smith at Temple Newsam

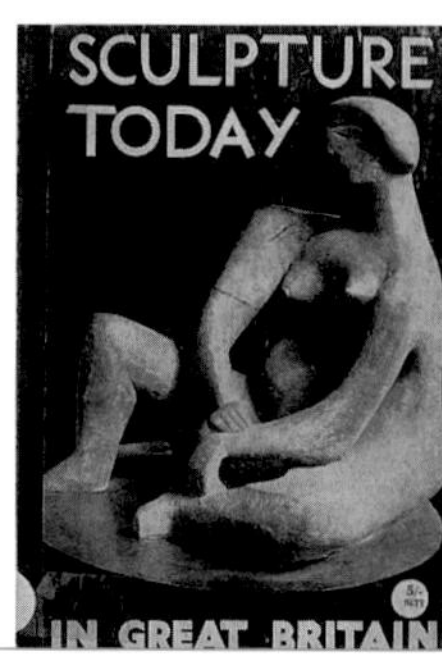

Front cover of Broadbent 'Sculpture Today'

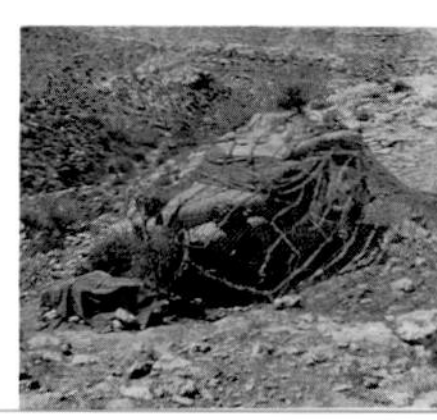

Edward Bainbridge Copnall 'Camouflage of Staff Car in Gazala'

1945

- Henry Moore appointed to the arts panel of the British Council
- T.W. Earp's *Frank Dobson: Sculptor* published
- Artists' International Association *Sculpture in the Home* exhibition, Heals', London
- Jacob Epstein's 'Lucifer' exhibited, Leicester Galleries, London
- Edward Bainbridge Copnall head of Sir John Cass College of Art (1945–53)
- Richard Long, John Hilliard, Martin Naylor, David Tremlett and David Nash born

1946

- Arts Council established and collection initiated
- Jacob Epstein executes portrait of Winston Churchill
- Paul Nash dies from pneumonia
- Naum Gabo moves to the United States
- Charles Despiau and Elie Nadelman die
- First solo show for Robert Adams at Gimpel Fils Gallery, London
- Paule Vézelay visits Paris
- Hubert Dalwood studies at Bath Academy of Art (to 1946–9)
- Kenneth Martin is visiting teacher at Goldsmiths' (1946–67)
- Henry Moore's first major retrospective is held at MoMA, New York
- Barbara Hepworth's first postwar solo show at Reid and Lefevre, London
- William Gibson's book *Barbara Hepworth: Sculptress* published
- Raymond Mason visits Paris and stays
- Jacob Epstein models portrait of Churchill
- Eric Kennington made portraitist to the Worshipful Company of Skinners, London; his first sculpture for an Anglican church interior
- First *Sculpture in the Home* Arts Council travelling exhibition (three to follow: 1950, 1953 and 1958)
- Barbara Hepworth exhibition at the Lefevre Gallery, London
- E. Newton's *British Sculpture 1944–46* published
- Stephen Cox, John Davies and Hamish Fulton born

1947

- Institute of Contemporary Arts founded in London
- Competition for sculpture on Waterloo Bridge, London
- First mobile by Lynn Chadwick, shown at the *Building Trades Exhibition*, London
- Lady Kathleen Scott-Kennet dies
- William Turnbull visits Paris (and lives there 1948–50)
- Anthony Hill studies at St Martin's School of Art, London (1947–9)
- Ghisha Koenig studies at Chelsea School of Art, London
- Franta Belsky's paratroop memorial in Prague
- F. E. McWilliam appointed by A. H. Gerrard to teach sculpture at the Slade (1947–68)
- Richard Wentworth born

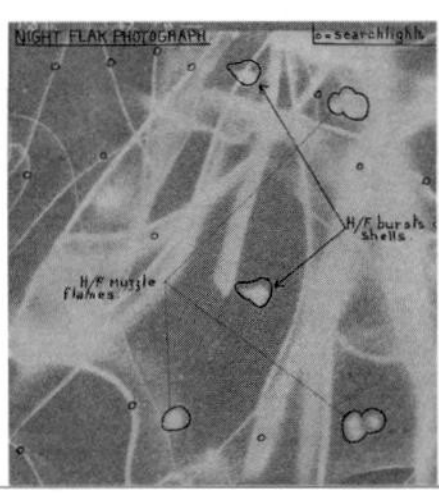

A.H. Gerrard
'Night Flak Photograph'

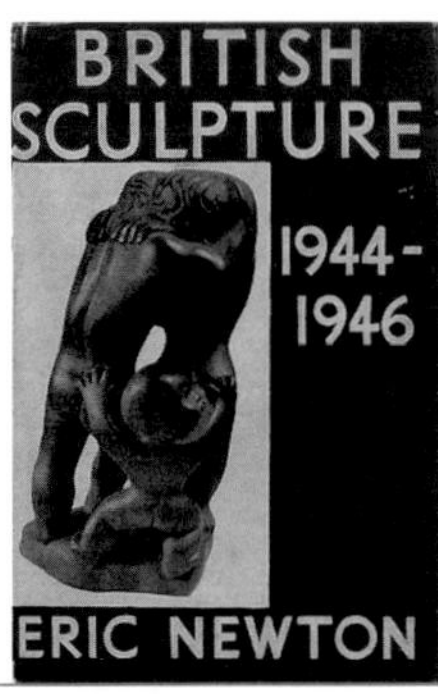

Eric Newton
'British Sculpture, 1944–46',
John Tiranti Ltd., London

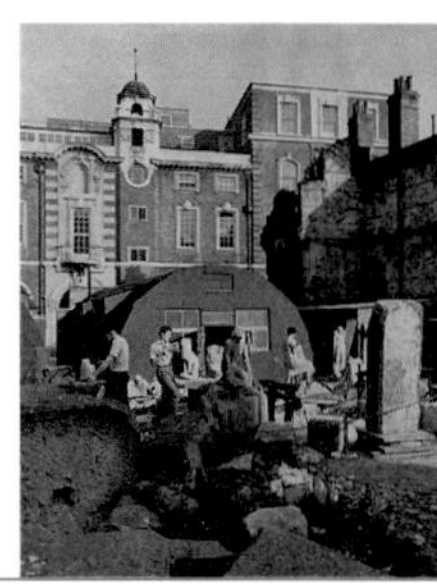
Edward Bainbridge Copnall
and students

1948

- Alfred Hardiman's Southwood memorial at St James' Church, Piccadilly, London
- Henry Moore awarded International Sculpture Prize at the 24th Venice Biennale
- *40 Years of Modern Art* exhibition at Institute of Contemporary Arts, London
- Bernard Meadows teaches at Chelsea School of Art, London (1948–60)
- Geoffrey Clarke studies at the Royal College of Art (1948–52)
- Arthur Fleischmann travels to England
- Bryan Kneale studies at Royal Academy Schools (1948–52)
- Siegfried Charoux carves stone figures for the School of Anatomy and Engineering, Cambridge
- First *Sculpture in the Open Air* exhibition, including Henry Moore's 'Three Standing Figures', held at Battersea Park and organised by the Arts Council
- Kathleen Scott memorial exhibition at Mansard Gallery, London
- Bill Woodrow, Chris Drury and Alison Wilding born

1949

- Henry Moore's 'Family Group' installed at Barclay School, Stevenage
- Jacob Epstein starts to make 'Youth Advancing' for the forthcoming *Festival of Britain* exhibition
- Anthony Hill studies at Central School of Art and Crafts (1949–51)
- British Council organises touring exhibition of Henry Moore's work
- *Sculpture in the Open Air* exhibitions, Kelvingrove Park, Glasgow
- Barbara Hepworth exhibition, Durlacher Bros Gallery, New York
- F.E. McWilliam exhibition, Hanover Gallery, London
- Nicholas Pope, Richard Deacon and Tony Cragg born
- Paul Nash's *Outline: An Autobiography and Other Writings* published by Faber and Faber
- Alfred Hardiman dies

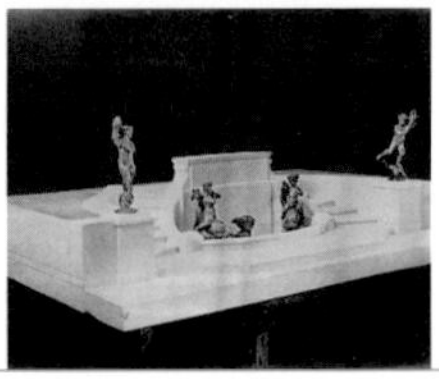

Alfred Hardiman's 'Southwood Memorial' maquette, for St James', Piccadilly

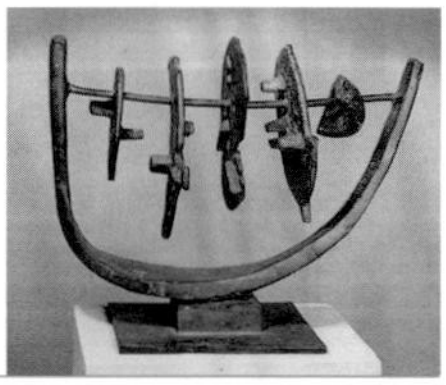

Eduardo Paolozzi 'Forms on a Bow'

In her *Sculpture: Themes and Variations – Towards a Contemporary Aesthetic* (1953), E. H. Ramsden characterised the late 19th-century sculptor as 'a virtuoso whose one consolation was to be found in an indiscriminate display of his technical powers – his skill in falsifying his material "to look like soft flesh", his dexterity in transforming his work into the negation of everything sculpture should be'.[1] The identity of the 20th-century sculptor was defined on the basis of a vilification of 19th-century naturalism and the gentleman-modeller. Modern sculptors were predominantly carvers working directly with the stone. The physical demands of the medium gave rise to ethical work of high seriousness. The sculpture itself was the expression of the character of the person who carved it. There was 'no place' in direct carving 'for any element of prevarication, levity or capriciousness ..., nor even a semblance of superficiality or self-consciousness in any phase of its execution. Throughout it must exhibit an integrity of purpose and a quality of inwardness that are beyond question'.[2]

In art schools, carving was usually taught as a craft for artisans rather than to artists. As direct carving was widely taken up in the 1920s and 1930s, the modern sculptor adopted the association with craft to project himself as a workman rather than a gentleman. Direct carving stood for the honest dignity of labour. It was a demonstration of heterosexual manliness and resistance to effeminacy.[3] Sculptors who carved were believers in the doctrine of 'truth to materials', meaning that the stoniness of the stone was undisguised and materials were not made to imitate non-sculptural forms such as flesh. The autonomous, self-referential sculptures that resulted were sometimes non-figurative but always rooted in a humanist feeling for the vitalist and organic. Truth to materials was equated with being true to the self. The autonomy and purity of the media meant the autonomy and probity of the individual. Because the stone was analogous to the self, inert matter was transformed into something that had what Henry Moore termed 'an intense life of its own'.[4] Rosalind Krauss wrote that in modernist sculpture '*behind* the surface of ... abstract forms an interior was always indicated, and it was from this interior that the life of the sculpture emanated', which Mignon Nixon has glossed as an 'expressive analogy between the imaginative space of art and the internal realm of the self'.[5]

Statements by modernist British sculptors in the 1930s and 1940s self-consciously paraded an identification with the object. In 1937, Henry Moore wrote that the sculptor 'gets the solid shape, as it were, inside his head ... he identifies himself with its centre of gravity, its mass, its weight'.[6] Barbara Hepworth described how 'one can either be the spectator of the object or the object itself. For a few years I became the object.'[7] The correspondence between the self and the object was a consequence of the doctrine of truth to materials. The form of the resulting sculpture was described as having evolved from an interaction between maker and material. In 1930 John Skeaping wrote that 'the material adapts itself to my ideas and unconsciously my ideas are created by my materials, and such is the harmony, I do not feel limited in my expression'.[8] The critic R. H. Wilenski wrote an extended polemic in defence of modernist sculpture in 1932. He explained that 'When the modern sculptors speak of carving they mean direct carving by the sculptor himself; and they regard direct carving as a kind of *collaboration between the sculptor and the substance*.'[9] Modelling, and by extension clay models enlarged and reproduced by mechanical means in marble, did not fit the criteria for truth to materials because clay had no fixed character. It could not generate a formal meaning inherent in the essential nature of the material. When modelling, the sculptor imposed a preconceived idea on the medium. In the pursuit of a compelling account of the inevitable progress of modernism, the work of those sculptors in the 1920s and 1930s who also modelled was downplayed or overlooked, as David Getsy has discussed in his contribution to this volume.[10] In direct carving, the encounter between the sculptor and the material meant the submersion of the self. Because it was about a dialogue between the material and the idea, the act of carving implied the completion of the self.

This essay covers the years of expansion and consolidation in modernist sculpture of the 1930s, following the innovations of the period before 1914, up to the establishment and incorporation of modernism in the welfare state of the 1950s. Although sculptors who had been identified with the New Sculpture in the 1890s were still active and were sometimes outspoken in their opposition to avant-garde sculpture of the 1920s, New Sculpture was no longer a reckonable force.[11] Unlike the period before World War I, this is not an era marked by conflict between competing camps holding incompatible views on the definition and practice of sculpture. Yet the process of establishing a distinctive sculptural identity after 1925 remained a matter of defining what it was not and imagining an opposite from which a new identity could emerge. Nineteenth-century sculptors were caricatured, for example in both Wilenski's and Ramsden's texts, as inauthentic falsifiers of true sculptural purpose. Similarly, modernist identity was most clearly articulated when it began to be identified as a paradigm to be overturned in the later 1960s and 1970s. For example, Kate Linker, writing about the feminine subject in minimalism, describes how

'Derrida has spoken of the *dis*semination of meaning, opposing it to the *in*semination of meaning performed by the author-function in our (masculine) Western metaphysical model', meaning modernism.[12] Mignon Nixon celebrated the fragmented work of Eva Hesse in the 1960s as an assertion of the part-object against the authority, and patriarchal authoritarianism, of the autonomous, self-referential and essentialising modernist object: In twentieth century art, the part-object punctures modernist aesthetics repeatedly, a prick of resistance to a full complement of totalizing systems: to utopianism, to abstraction, to Oedipus.'[13]

Wilenski's extended polemic debunking the 'Romantic prejudice' and the 'Greek prejudice' was a commonplace strategy in the 1930s for securing the credentials of modernist sculpture and consequently the integrity and authenticity of its maker. Ramsden's text from the 1950s continued to deploy the trope even though modernism was the dominant aesthetic. Henry Moore was so established in the 1950s that David Sylvester could describe his contribution to the Festival of Britain in 1951 as 'empty, if impressive, virtuosity'.[14] It would seem from Ramsden's text that it was essential to the realisation of a modern sculptor's identity that he was seen as a pioneering and oppositional, sometimes beleaguered and misunderstood figure.

For sculpture to be counted as progressive and successful in the 1930s, it had to be seen as an autonomous art. There were some simple socio-economic explanations for this. First, one social consequence of World War I was a general levelling out and simplification of the English class system accompanied by the terminal decline of the English aristocracy. The golden age of the artist as a fabulously wealthy public figure whose high social status sometimes led to elevation to the peerage had already been eclipsed before 1914. Artists in general began to emerge from a wider range of social backgrounds and to enter the profession through art school training, sometimes supported by bursaries and prizes. For an ambitious artist, such an education always had to be completed in London. Educational attainment became a recognised entrée for confirming middle-class status or enabling upward social mobility.[15] Artists were part of an expanded and more dominant but also levelled-out middle class. Sculptors participated in this general trend alongside painters.[16] Second, there was a sustained crisis in the role of the public monument and in architectural sculpture, both of which were crucial sources of income and public visibility for sculptors. Although the production of war memorials was considerable after 1918, the majority of the sculpturally significant were completed by

1925 and then mainly by sculptors of the New Sculpture generation of the 1890s, such as George Frampton, Albert Toft and Francis Derwent Wood. Most memorial production in most localities was undertaken by local stone masons and tradesmen, not artists.[17] As the protracted and very vehement controversy over Jacob Epstein's W. H. Hudson memorial in Hyde Park (1925) demonstrated, modernist sculpture did not square easily with monumental traditions. Because reputation and social standing were no longer to be secured by participation in public projects, modernist sculptors, working in isolation in studios rather than in collaboration with civic patrons and architecture, needed to mark a distinctive identity as pioneers and heroes.[18]

The absence of prestigious public commissions for monuments or architectural sculpture, of a public status, was much more crucial for the prospects of sculptors than for painters and had more radical implications for the economics of sculptural practice. It meant that mechanisms for distinction, or how to make one's mark in an increasingly democratised profession, became a matter of making innovative work independently and getting it recognised as such. Wilenski wrote in 1930 that the modern sculptor 'works in exactly the spirit of the research scientist'.[19] By the early 1930s, a sculptor announced his, and sometimes her, arrival as a modern by holding a significant solo exhibition in a private gallery that was regularly written up by major art critics. For example, Moore held his first important solo exhibition in 1931 at the Leicester Galleries, the leading London avant-garde gallery. Epstein wrote the preface to the catalogue, meaning an older modern sculptor endorsed the work of the younger. In December 1930, Wilenski had written an important article about Moore's work for *Apollo*, a month after an article by John Grierson about Hepworth and Skeaping appeared in the same journal. The ultimate endorsement was a purchase by a modern art museum, particularly the Tate. Works by Moore and Hepworth entered the collections of the relatively newly established Museum of Modern Art, New York, in 1936. The Tate acquired Moore's 'Recumbent Figure' (1938) in 1939; by 1941 he was a trustee of the gallery. Moore was also teaching two days a week, first at the Royal College of Art and then at Chelsea School of Art, which meant he was not dependent on sales for an income. After 1945 it became more common for modern artists who were recognised as significant to be teachers and independent practitioners, rather than commercially successful or associated with prestigious public commissions.

The failure of confidence in a recognised social purpose for sculpture as monument or architectural decoration was closely intertwined with the emergence of a more democratic social order, but such factors do not exhaust the meanings and investments in sculpture as an autonomous art. The identification of the self with the autonomous modernist object was never as totalising or as utopian as a later period would have it. The period when 'truth to materials' and direct carving were most actively pursued was also marked with anxieties and contradictions. Adrian Stokes, alongside Herbert Read, emerged as the major writer on modern sculpture in the 1930s. In his *Stones of Rimini* (1934), he described an apocalyptic vision of the death of art following the decline of architectural sculpture. Because modern buildings were made from modern materials such as steel, rooms could be any shape and the building was pure design with no use for ornament. Consequently:

> stone architecture dies, the mother of the European visual arts for more than two thousand years ... building will no longer serve as the mother art of stone, no longer as the source at which carving or spatial conception renews its strength ... should the growth of plasticity, of manufacture, in labour and in art, over-power carving activities altogether, there is then no future for visual art as hitherto conceived by the European races.[20]

In Stokes' account of sculpture, the viewer participates in the same fantasy about the material as the artist. In effect, if the artist is identified with the material, so is the viewer. Stokes writes, 'If we would understand a visual art, we ourselves must cherish some fantasy of the material that stimulated the artist, and ourselves feel some emotional reason why his imagination chose... to employ one material rather than another.'[21] Carving was a matter of bringing the stone itself to life. It was the antithesis of modelling, just as maleness was the opposite of femaleness, but the two processes, like male and female, were also interdependent. In a well-known passage, Stokes declared:

> Man, in his male aspect, is the cultivator or carver of woman who, in her female aspect, moulds her products as does the earth. We see both the ultimate distinction and the necessary interaction between carving and moulding in their widest sense. The stone block is female, the plastic figures that emerge from it ... are her children, the proof of the carver's love for the stone.[22]

Carving was 'an articulation of something that already exists in the block' and could 'never ... be entirely freed from its matrix'.[23] Directly carved sculpture facilitated fantasies about procreation and birth for both the artist and the viewer.

At a later date, Stokes would come to equate carving with Melanie Klein's depressive position, the point when the ego achieves a degree of integration, as though the sculpture was the site for projecting an integrated ego.[24] For example, in a few works around 1932 and 1933 Hepworth engraved a profile onto her carved sculptures as if literally inscribing the self.[25] Although critical writings and artists' statements sustained fantasies for both artist and viewer about bodily projection and introjection, the separateness of the block or its sculptural autonomy also marked out the impossibility of this fantasy.[26] The object could both be imagined as the self and also be experienced as radically other to the self, as male and female were interdependent and also opposed. Moreover, sculptures made in the 1920s and 1930s when 'truth to materials' was most actively pursued do not necessarily take the form of self-contained, ideal wholes implied by the fantasy. Anne Wagner, for example, has remarked on the signs of unease and incompleteness in Hepworth's work in the early 1930s, at odds with projecting fantasies about the object standing in for the integrated ego.[27]

A similar problem relates to the invention of parallels and a history for modern sculpture selected from cultures lying outside the classical and Renaissance canon that formed its immediate chronological precedent. An affinity with objects from other cultures or very early periods in European art, then sometimes termed primitive, and modern sculpture was made in the keynote exhibition *Sculpture Considered Apart from Time and Place* (1932), co-curated by Sydney Burney and the sculptor Leon Underwood, and including Moore, Hepworth, Gertrude Hermes and Richard Bedford alongside Amedeo Modigliani and Henri Gaudier-Brzeska. Their sculptures were juxtaposed with objects from faraway places such as the Orient, Africa and Polynesia and such distant periods as the prehistoric. As Underwood explained in the catalogue, 'earlier' works demonstrated more sculptural consciousness than later ones and were the appropriate precedents for modern art. Carved sculpture, in particular, was a metaphor for origins, especially the origin of the self. As Nixon puts it, modernism was 'a system of representation that claimed to encompass its own beginnings – and that invented its own mythic origins as a metaphor for all origins including the founding of subjectivity'.[28] According to Wilenski, writing in 1932, a marked disposition to study first principles and general laws was a feature of contemporary culture.[29]

The janus-faced character of modern sculpture, looking forwards to a progressive and humanist future and backwards to a cult of the primitive and a quest for origins as guarantees of its authenticity, found a voice in Alexander Korda's epic science-fiction film *Things to Come* (1935). The film tells the story of the destruction of the world through war and its ultimate reconstruction as a utopia where all social problems have been solved and surplus energies are used in creative art and science. Some scientists, however, desire to press on with scientific discovery and reach for the moon. The revolt of the people calling for a halt to progress is led by the sculptor Theotocopulos, whose persona is recognisably that of Epstein, the artist who represented the modern sculptor in popular imagination. The film closes with the mob led by Theotocopulos, storming the scientists' 'Space Gun' in order to put a stop to the interminable march of scientific progress or modernity. Sculptors, together with their directly carved objects, stood for archaic, eternal and universal values that, in Stokes' analogy with modern architecture, were at risk of imminent death from the onslaught of machine-age progress. In a telling phrase, Carola Giedion-Welcker, in her *Modern Plastic Art: Elements of Reality Volume and Disintegration* (1937), stated that 'Brancusi lives in a world of forms as simply and intimately as St Francis of Assisi dwelt amongst the birds' and compared him to Moore and Hepworth.[30]

Things to Come acted out collective fears of a coming war, especially that the advent of aerial bombardment would result in mass civilian deaths. It was one of a number of cultural productions in the 1930s predicting war, and imaging death and destruction as emanating from the sky.[31] Imagery in art, films and novels fuelled anxieties that England was no longer an impervious island nation protected by sea and cliffs. Analogies are sometimes drawn between the island and the body. An analogy between the self and the carved object could be extended to accommodate an image of a withdrawal into the self and/or the object for protection accompanied by melancholic fantasies of the death of the individual, the island or the nation. Such images were literally embodied in Epstein's 'Elemental' (1932), a figure curled up for self-protection or like an embryo or a corpse in an ancient burial site. The consolidation of directly carved sculpture as the most progressive modern form of sculpture in the 1930s coincided with the rise of fascism, which also put at stake the whole question of intellectual freedom. The doctrine of direct carving was not invented in the 1920s and 1930s but originated in the period before 1914, associated with the work of Epstein, Eric Gill and Gaudier-Brzeska. Gaudier-Brzeska called carving 'this virile art'.[32] The public image of the carver was very differently inflected, however, in the 1920s and 1930s. Gaudier posed as an avant-garde warrior, mercenary, libertarian and aggressive.[33] The sculptor with ambitions to be modern after World War I was likely to be a democratic socialist and an activist in anti-fascist campaigns, whose work found its rapport and its place in the new welfare state after 1945. Avant-garde artists before 1914 collaborated in volatile associations such as Vorticism and saw themselves as 'militants of a creativity to revive and liberate humanity', as Raymond Williams put it.[34] When artists regrouped in the 1930s it was against the background of severe economic recession and the threat of fascism. Their organisations, such as Unit One (1934) and Circle (1937) in which Moore and Hepworth were active, or the broad-based Artists' International Association, which also included Gill and Epstein, were politically progressive, committed to constructive social improvement and optimistic that modernist art was a democratic contribution to a better world.

Wilenski's *The Meaning of Modern Sculpture* argued that modern sculptors were against the individualism and nationalist isolation of 19th-century romanticism, and opposed to the image of the artist as a Bohemian:

> Modern culture, as I understand it, is an effort of the finer brains and spirits to relieve this desperate dissatisfaction [with the machine-ruled world] by repressing individualism, empiricism and local pretensions, and formulating concepts conducted not by individuals or individual nations but by civilised mankind pooling brains and imagination in the hope that collective thought may lead to concerted action and thereby avert the disaster which is feared.[35]

The development of artists' organisations in the 1930s was accompanied by the fostering of an international community for modernism, and British sculptors visited modern artists and studios in Paris. This community was enlarged when artist émigrés fleeing fascism began to arrive in England in the late 1930s, notably Naum Gabo, and when, with the fall of Paris, Britain became the only European nation with a superstructure capable of sustaining an avant-garde that was not occupied by Hitler. In 1953, Ramsden continued to argue that modernist sculpture's essential meaning concerned a widening of consciousness and that the 'impersonal supervenes over the personal and the identity of the individual becomes blurred'.[36] By 1945, international modernism had been adopted as the proper aesthetic for a free and anti-fascist West and the possession of a national modernist artist of international stature was an essential component for projecting national identity. In Britain, that role was fulfilled by Moore, Britain's representative at the newly revised Venice Biennale in 1948 where he was the winner of the prestigious international prize for sculpture. In 1950, Hepworth represented Britain. Throughout the postwar period, beginning with Moore, Britain's status as a significant contributor to modernist art has been consistently identified with its sculptors. In 1951, however, Moore observed that the 1920s and 1930s had 'tended "to make a fetish" of the "doctrine of truth to material"',[37] but by then the social pressures on sculpture, on modernism and on British national identity were much less urgent, and Moore and other carvers of the 1920s and 1930s were already being challenged by a new generation of sculptors with a different set of preoccupations.

Sue Malvern

Notes

1 E. H. Ramsden, *Sculpture: Theme and Variations – Towards a Contemporary Aesthetic*, London, Lund Humphries, 1953, p. 15.

2 Ibid., p. 12.

3 See 'Despite their classical origins and technical perfections, neither Thorwaldsen's Adonis nor Canova's Perseus can be said to recall the antique in any appreciable sense, but must by comparison be recognised to be altogether too exquisite and too effeminate to compete.' Ramsden, *Sculpture: Theme and Variations*, p. 7.

4 H. Moore, 'The Sculptor's Aims', 1934, reprinted in D. Sylvester (ed.), *Henry Moore: Sculpture and Drawings 1921–1948*, 5th edn, vol. 1, London, Lund Humphries and Zwemmer, 1957, p. xxxi.

5 R. E. Krauss, *Passages in Modern Sculpture*, London and Cambridge, MA, Thames and Hudson and MIT Press, 1977, p. 253, emphasis in the original; M. Nixon, 'Ringaround arosie: 2 in 1', in M. Nixon (ed.), *Eva Hesse*, Cambridge, MA, MIT Press, 2002, p. 211.

6 H. Moore, 'Notes on Sculpture', first published 1937, reprinted in Sylvester, *Henry Moore: Sculpture and Drawings 1921–1948*, pp. xxxiii–xxxiv.

7 B. Hepworth, 'The war, Cornwall, and artist in landscape 1939–1946', in *Barbara Hepworth: Carvings and Drawings*, London, Lund Humphries, 1952, n.p.

8 J. Skeaping, 'John Skeaping', *Architectural Association Journal*, February 1930, p. 302.

9 R. H. Wilenski, *The Meaning of Modern Sculpture*, London, Faber and Faber, 1932, p. 99, emphasis in the original.

10 Jacob Epstein, an important avant-garde pioneer of carving before 1914, returned to carving with a series of independent and challenging works in the 1930s, but his work was always difficult to accommodate and regarded with suspicion as hybrid. This identification could also be mapped onto his status as an outsider who was a Jew and not born in Britain.

11 The majority of its exponents were dead by the end of the decade. Frampton died in 1928, Brock in 1922, Thornycroft in 1925, Derwent Wood in 1926 and Gilbert in1934. Bayes, Goscombe John and Toft lived until just after World War II.

[12] K. Linker, 'A Feminine Subject for Minimalism?', in S. L Stoops (ed.), *More than Minimal: Feminism and Abstraction in the '70s*, Waltham, MA, Rose Art Museum, Brandeis University, 1996, p. 39.

[13] Nixon, *Eva Hesse*, p. 219.

[14] A. D. B. Sylvester, 'Festival sculpture', *The Studio*, September 1951, p. 75.

[15] Before 1914 artists born in London's East End such as Mark Gertler, David Bomberg and William Roberts had gained bursaries to the Slade. See the discussion in L. Tickner, *Modern Life and Modern Subjects: British Art in the Early Twentieth Century*, New Haven, CT, and London, Yale University Press for the Paul Mellon Centre for Studies in British Art, 2000. On social change, see D. Cannadine, *The Decline and Fall of the British Aristocracy*, New Haven, CT, and London, Yale University Press, 1990.

[16] It was not the case that, for Britain at least, sculptors who carved came from more humble backgrounds as argued by P. Curtis, *Sculpture 1900–1945: After Rodin*, Oxford, Oxford University Press, 1999, p. 94. It is arguable that sculptors in the 1920s and 1930s came from more varied backgrounds and this occurred at the point when a meritocracy began to emerge that was more securely established after 1945.

[17] See A. King, *Memorials of the Great War: The Symbolism and Politics of Remembrance*, Oxford, Berg, 1998.

[18] One of the ways they did this was through studio photographs. See J. Wood's essay, 'Close encounters: the sculptor's studio in the age of the camera', introducing the exhibition *Close Encounters*, Leeds, Henry Moore Institute, 2001, pp. 8–27.

[19] R. H. Wilenski, 'Ruminations on sculpture and the work of Henry Moore', *Apollo*, December 1930, vol. 12, pp. 409–13.

[20] A. Stokes, 'Stones of Rimini' (1934), in L. Gowing (ed.), *The Critical Writings of Adrian Stokes: 1930–1937*, vol. 1, London, Thames and Hudson, 1978, pp 258–9.

[21] Ibid., p. 186.

[22] Ibid., pp. 230–1.

[23] Ibid., p. 232.

[24] See the discussion in A. M. Wagner, 'Miss Hepworth's stone IS a mother', in D. Thistlewood (ed.) *Barbara Hepworth Reconsidered*, Liverpool, Tate Gallery Liverpool, Liverpool University Press, 1996, p. 57.

[25] See M. Gale and C. Stephens, *Barbara Hepworth: Works in the Tate Gallery Collection and the Barbara Hepworth Museum St Ives*, London, Tate Gallery Publishing, 1999, p. 35.

[26] See A. Potts, 'Carving and engendering of sculpture: Adrian Stokes and Barbara Hepworth', in Thistlewood (ed.), *Barbara Hepworth Reconsidered*, p. 49.

[27] A. M. Wagner, 'Miss Hepworth's Stone', p. 65.

[28] Nixon, *Eva Hesse*, p. 211.

[29] Wilenski, *The Meaning of Modern Sculpture*, p. 4.

[30] C. Giedion-Welcker, *Modern Plastic Art. Elements of Reality Volume and Disintegration*, English version by P. Morton Shand, Zurich, Dr H. Girsberger, 1937, p. 12.

[31] See my *Things to Come: Eric Kennington's 'War God'*, Leeds, Henry Moore Institute, 2001.

[32] Review of the Allied Artists' Association, in *The Egoist*, 1914, reprinted in E. Pound, *Gaudier-Brzeska: A Memoir*, New York, New Directions, 1970, p. 30.

[33] See P. Peppis, '"Surrounded by a multitude of other blasts": Vorticism and the Great War', *Modernism/Modernity*, vol. 4, no. 2, 1997.

[34] R. Williams, 'The politics of the avant-garde', in T. Pinkney (ed.), *The Politics of Modernism: Against the New Conformists*, London, Verso, 1989, pp. 50–1.

[35] Wilenski, *The Meaning of Modern Sculpture*, p. 4.

[36] Ramsden, *Sculpture: Theme and Variations*, p. 41.

[37] Quoted in D. Kosinski, 'Some reasons for a reputation', in D. Kosinski (ed.), *Henry Moore: Sculpting the 20th Century*, Dallas, Dallas Museum of Art, 2001, p. 22.

Architecture, Artisans and Applied Sculpture

When thinking about British sculpture in 1937, one might immediately recall the publication of *Circle* in July of that year. Like the formation of Unit One in 1934, this was a seminal moment for the British avant-garde. However, beyond the publicity and publications generated by *Circle*, there was another realm of sculptural endeavour populated with artists and artisans whose history this essay will attempt to recover.

The largest consumer of sculpture between 1925 and 1950 was, in its broadest sense, architecture. With few exceptions, however, architectural sculpture has been marginalised in historical discourse. Singling out the London Underground Headquarters project or Eric Gill's Broadcasting House ensemble, for example, has tended to separate the well-known names of British modernism, allowing them to transcend the history in which the majority are stuck.[1] However, new histories of sculptors whose work was closely, even primarily, engaged with architecture are emerging, and the study of the complex relationships between the sculptor and the wider world is being revealed.[2] The physical structure of a building, designed by an architect with the power to 'prescribe' sculpture, was commissioned as a consequence of macro-political, macro-economic and cultural infrastructures.[3] Sculpture was inextricably linked with a built environment reflecting the needs of government, finance, industry, commerce, transport, popular culture and Britain's status as an imperial power. The contingent relationships

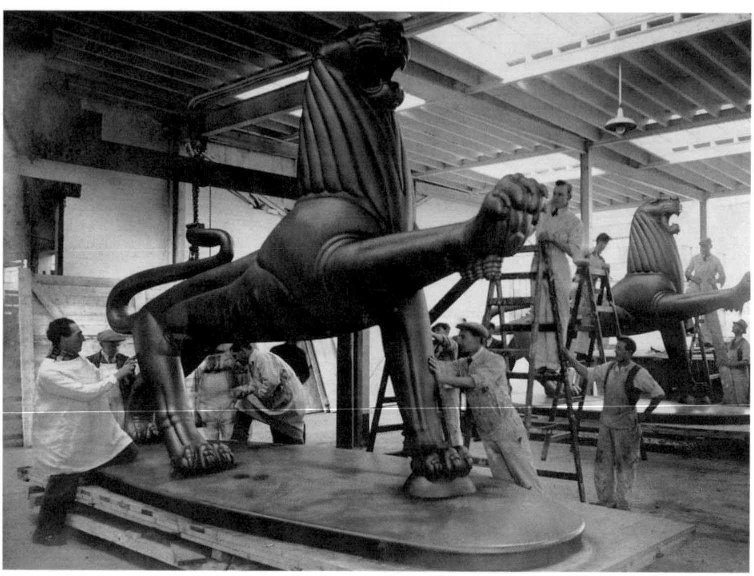

1 Alfred Hardiman with staff of Morris Singer Foundry finishing the bronze lions for Norwich City Hall, 1937

between these large-scale infrastructures and the micro-economy of a sculptor's studio practice necessitated a further network of essential connections: from the quarry and clay-pit, through merchants, delivery men, models, studio assistants and specialist artisans to larger craft businesses. The complexity of these stratified interconnections has implications for all sculpture.[4]

London as the 'Heart of the Empire' in the 1920s and 1930s has been closely examined in recent studies. Ian Black has described conditions and stylistic considerations specific to 'a series of imaginative geographies of empire' that led to the building of the City of London's bank headquarters, including the Bank of England.[5] The new colonial offices that were built and decorated in this period are obvious further evidence of Britain's imperial status. However, by the sterling crisis of 1931 it was clear that the natural as opposed to symbolic centre of the world economy was New York, and American influences on management structures and headquarters' grandeur were crucial to the development of buildings like Imperial Chemicals House and Unilever House.[6] Business rationalisation and the development of the empire as a free-trade area to rival the United States were taken seriously in the 1920s and 1930s for fear of a serious decline in Britain's status and economy.

The colossal building programmes which left much of central London iron-clad with scaffolding and covered in a layer of Portland stone dust from the early 1920s until the late 1930s offered many opportunities to architectural sculptors, from the traditional to the modernist. Competition was stiff; the value of a close relationship with an architect patron was incalculable. Even a short list of major projects reveals the names of some important figures in the field of architectural sculpture: Alfred Hardiman completed the sculpture of Westminster's County Hall in 1925–6;[7] Unilever House, Blackfriars (1932), supports work by Gilbert Ledward and William Reid Dick's Controlled Energy groups; Imperial Chemicals House, Millbank, has four allegorical figures by Charles Sargeant Jagger among other sculpture;[8] Bainbridge Copnall's works for Grey Wornum's RIBA appeared in 1934 and the sculpture by Charles Wheeler for Herbert Baker's rebuilding of the Bank of England (*c.*1928–*c.*1945) constitutes the largest single architectural sculpture commission of the era. In provincial cities some public buildings, like Leeds Civic Hall of 1934 with sculpture by Hermon Cawthra, were the products of job creation schemes. The deflationary effects of the slump of 1929–34, with consequent falling prices for raw materials and drastic reductions in labour costs, encouraged the *Architects' Journal* to claim in 1931 'Now is the time to build!'[9] Many

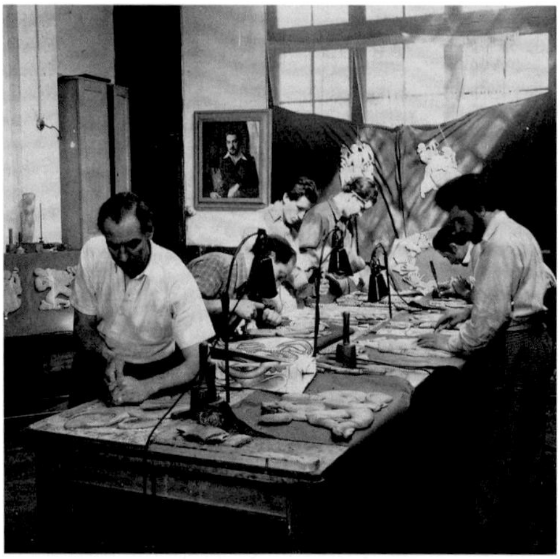

projects employed both individual studio sculptors and the skilled artisans of the best manufacturing businesses in the country.

Individual craft specialists have left few traces; some names survive, scattered among diverse histories, but beyond that records have been lost. But these tradesmen and colleagues in larger companies like Joseph Armitage, W. Aumonier and Sons, the Morris Singer Foundry, the Bromsgrove Guild and H. H. Martyn and Co. constitute a vital, neglected infrastructure of sculpture. They executed the designs of studio artists in bronze, reinforced plaster and stone, and often offered a complete design and manufacture service to the architect. The published histories of Joseph Armitage, the Morris Singer Foundry, the Bromsgrove Guild and H. H. Martyn and Co. are little known: there is no bibliography of art manufacturing businesses, nor even a list of known companies (Fig. 1). This is a serious lacuna, for the descriptions of working practices, names of craftsmen, contracts, photographs, records of wages and prices in these few publications all put vital flesh on the bones of sculptural production. The National Recording Project of the Public Monuments and Sculpture Association will greatly assist in expanding the histories of these companies and bring the names of other businesses and individual craftsmen to light.[10]

Patrick Eyres has recently drawn our attention to the work of Eric Aumonier, highlighting the ambiguity of his status as a marginal figure.[11] The nuances of definition between 'artist' and 'craftsman' seem not to have mattered to his client, Charles Holden. Aumonier's name was attached to two well-known works: the 'South Wind' relief for the London Underground Headquarters and 'The Archer' for East Finchley tube station, but he is otherwise anonymous as a practitioner within the family business, W. Aumonier and Sons. *Modern Architectural Sculpture*, published in 1930 and edited by Eric's father, William Aumonier, surveys contemporary work from Europe and the USA, though the definition of 'architectural' is sometimes quirky; not all the works are necessarily site or context specific. Crucially, as a craftsman, the editor differentiates between works that he generically attributes to a company, and those to which he ascribes the name of an individual maker, even though he may have been in a company's employ. Isolating

2 Bainbridge Copnall (foreground, left) with assistants carving relief decorations for the liner Queen Elizabeh, 1939.

3 Selfridges by night, part of London's flood-lighting scheme to celebrate the Coronation in 1937.

these individuals' names from the companies they worked for clearly indicates seniority and skill, but may also suggest that, like Eric Aumonier, they took personal commissions. By cross-referencing this and other texts with the histories of craft businesses, we gain a fuller understanding of employment practices and professional status and can more accurately attribute monumental and architectural sculpture in the middle of the 20th century.[12]

Walter Gilbert, whose work in stone and glass is illustrated in Aumonier's book, was a key figure in the rise of the Bromsgrove Guild before World War I. He joined H. H. Martyn and Co. in 1919 as a director on the considerable salary of over £600 a year. Some key craftsmen moved with him to Cheltenham and his decision to share with Martyn's the contract for work on G. G. Scott's Liverpool Anglican Cathedral, originally granted to the Bromsgrove Guild, caused a rift that severed any future sub-contracting relationship.[13] Like many businesses, the Cheltenham firm worked across the empire, providing monuments, memorials and decorative sculpture. The panelling, bronze work, decorative plaster, stonework and furniture in wood and nickel silver for the new Lal Bagh Palace, built for the Holkar of Indore in 1921, was one of their largest contracts.[14] The market for luxury decorative objects crashed in the slump, and although an employee estimated that Martyn's had 75 per cent of the architectural work in the country at the time, wood and stone carving declined and only the foundry kept the firm going.[15] Canny diversification had led the board of Martyn's to establish the Gloster Aircraft Company in World War I and enabled them to focus on specialist casting and aircraft production again in 1939 when times were fallow for sculpture. Although stone carving was drastically reduced by 1950, restoration projects to repair bomb damage still employed older craftsmen and foundry skills benefited postwar sculptors. In the 1950s and 1960s, Henry Moore, Lynn Chadwick, John Skeaping, Oscar Nemon, Edward Bainbridge Copnall and William MacMillan all had works cast by H. H. Martyn and Co. During the slump, Morris Singer's workforce was slashed from thirty to forty down to five plus one apprentice, but gradually rose again to forty-six by the mid-1930s. In 1948 the workforce of forty-five was regarded as low for the large volume of work the company had taken on.[16]

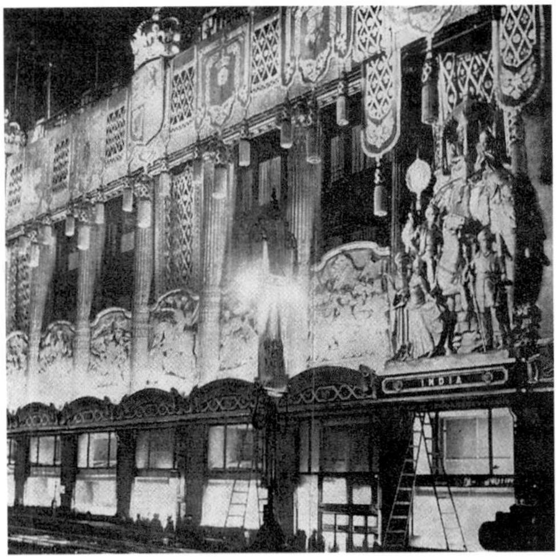

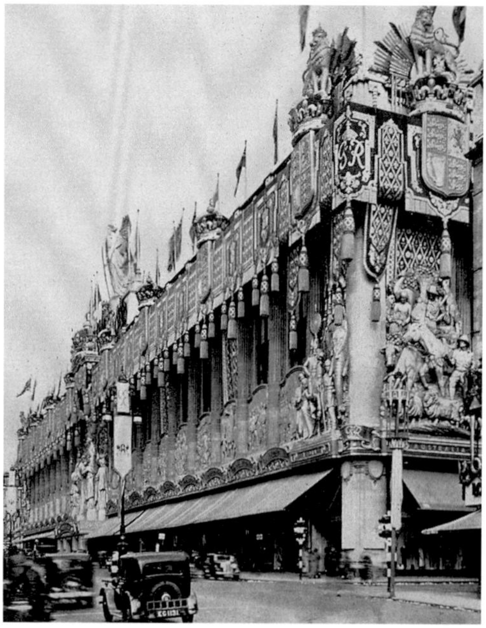

As the major fitter and decorator of British liners from the late 1920s until the *QE2* in 1969, Martyn's enabled naval architecture to carry British sculpture overseas to the outposts of the empire and New York.[17] These ships constituted significant floating spaces for display. The *Queen Mary*, first planned in 1926 but whose maiden voyage was suspended by the slump until 1938, had sculpture by Skeaping, Maurice Lambert and Bainbridge Copnall. The *Mauretania* (maiden voyage 1939) displayed 'The Creation of Speed' by A. H. Gerrard, who had contributed to the London Underground Headquarters, and 'North Atlantic' by Barney Seale. The interior of the *Queen Elizabeth*, completed in 1940 but used as a troop ship until her maiden voyage in 1946, was subtly designed by Wornum with sculpture by Bainbridge Copnall (Fig. 2), with whom he had worked on the RIBA building, and Lambert.[18] It was this type of modish chic modernity, acceptable to the wealthy middle-class passengers on these floating palaces, which Oliver Hill and Frank Pick promoted at the *Exposition Universelle* in Paris in June 1937.

Hill's British pavilion exuded a simple 'lightweight modernism' in its structure and contents.[19] Pick was chairman of the Council for Art and Industry, which organised the British exhibition. Well known as an enlightened patron of art for London Underground, in Paris Pick chose to show a type of modernism that was tamed and purged of excessive politics, in sharp contrast to the authoritarian excesses of the German, Italian and USSR pavilions.[20] As Paul Greenhalgh has pointed out, contrary to the naïve wishes of the organising committee that the *Exposition* should symbolise 'a universal will to peace', the result was 'the cultural equivalent of the military engagement shortly to follow'.[21] In Paris there was no emphasis on Britain's imperial power but on a kind of Bond-Street-and-Sussex life, represented in themes of 'le weekend', 'le sport', 'le tennis' and 'le five-o-clock'. Sporting goods, pottery, books and textiles represented Britain's contribution to the civilisation of Western Europe.

4 In the completed Selfridge's display Hermon Cawthra's *India* and Harold Youngman's *Canada* can be seen on the right hand side.

Pick's foreword to the catalogue crackles with political charge in the context of the terrible events in Spain, the rise of fascism and the rupture in the German artworld evinced by the exhibition *Entartete Kunst* of the same summer: 'Democracy to us means more than a mode of government: it means a fashion of living which leaves men and women free to express themselves as they will in what they have, or wear or do or use, as long as each respects the like freedom of his neighbour.'[22] However, Pick restrained Hill's desire for more radical modernism: though Pick employed László Moholy-Nagy to design posters for the London Underground in the 1930s, Hill's wish for him to design a photo-mural display for the pavilion was refused: 'The pavilion is a British pavilion and Mr Moholy-Nagy has not got the British tradition, I fear. We must not be tempted to copy the latest continental tricks.' Clearly radicalism was safe on home ground, but open to misinterpretation when promoting Britain abroad.[23]

Among many artists who participated, three sculptors contributed to the scheme. All had worked with Hill at the Dorland Hall exhibitions of *British Industrial Art in the Home* of 1933 and1934. Charles Wheeler's twice-life-size figures representing 'Art' and 'Industry' were captioned by Pick: 'Life without Industry is Guilt' and 'Industry without Art is Brutality'. Skeaping's mural for the exterior of the pavilion was again on the theme of art and industry, and Gertrude Hermes made a sculptured glass window of Britannia in conjunction with the manufacturers, Pilkington.[24] These sculptors represented a specific form of modernity within a British tradition that Pick and Hill required for the promotion of Britain abroad. Gill, who had also exhibited at the Dorland Hall exhibition in 1933, refused Hill's request to make a coat of arms for the entrance to the pavilion, protesting his hatred of international exhibitions as merely 'foreign trade shows', and his detestation of 'faux medievalism … in association with modernity'.[25] Hill's archive shows that at least two members of the Royal Society of British Sculptors (RBS), Barney Seale and C. L. J. Doman, sought employment on the Paris pavilion and he also received a letter on behalf of an artisan seeking work. The chairman of the Industrial Art Committee of the Federation of British Industries (now the CBI) recommended George Holman, 'a sculptor experienced in modelling, casting, moulding and carving in stone and wood'. He had been working as a modeller and technical adviser in an anatomical models firm, and was anxious to explore possibilities in connection with the British pavilion.[26] It is important to note the willing engagement, for whatever reasons, of many artists with industry, trade and commerce; beyond these particular shows, in a direct collaboration with manufacturing industry and retailing, Frank Dobson designed a mannequin for the display of lingerie, 'The Charnaux Venus', that was unveiled in Selfridge's in 1934.[27]

The subtle modernism of the British pavilion's design was admired in the architectural press, but the unity of the concept was misunderstood by some members of the Design in Industry Association. Pick had not wanted the well-mannered ensemble to be spoilt with brash crowd-pulling displays, but conceded that future shows would need 'some stunt to please the groundlings'.[28] The British pavilion promoted a modern look in its architecture and sculpture, both of which signified restraint in the rejection of extremes.

In stark contrast, a 'stunt for the groundlings', *con brio*, was the decoration of Selfridge's store to celebrate the coronation of George VI on 12 May 1937 (Fig. 3).[29] The scheme was a perfect example of the 'splendid anachronism of the [British Empire's] pageantry at the time of George V's silver jubilee and George VI's coronation' that David Cannadine has explained was 'deliberately projected as a powerful and reassuring antidote to the high-tech parades and search light rallies in Mussolini's Italy, Stalin's Red Square and Hitler's Nuremberg'.[30] Temporary sculptural decorations whose grand motif was 'The Empire's Homage to the Throne' encrusted the facades of the store for a month and cost a staggering £50,000. Gordon Selfridge, an anglophile American with a personal tendency to wild extravagance and showmanship, wished to show loyalty and to benefit commercially from the cult of personality that identification with a royal event offered.[31] Decorative schemes for the *World's Columbian Exhibition* in Chicago

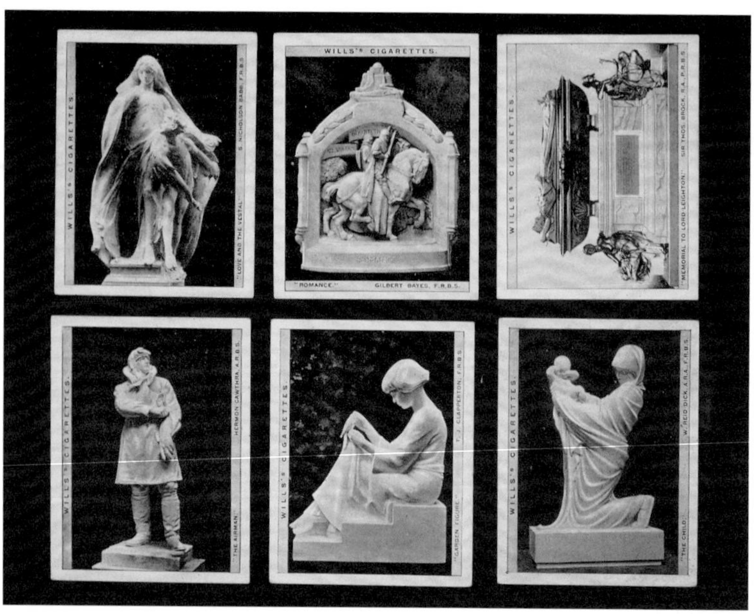

5 The First six cigarette cards from W. D and H. O Wills' set *Modern British Sculpture* of 1928. S. Nicholson Babb, Gilbert Bayes, Hermon Cawthra, Thomas Clapperton and William Reid Dick also contributed to the Selfridge's scheme; Thomas Brock died in 1922.

(1893), or even the temporary monuments in New York like the Dewey Arch of 1909, may have informed his display policy in London.[32]

Across the Oxford Street front, eighteen panels, each 20 ft high, illustrated British history from the Druids to the Armistice; at the four corners of the building were 35 ft high groups in gilded three-quarter relief depicting the great dominions of Australia, Canada, India and South Africa. Sir William Reid Dick's eponymous group, 58 ft across and 38 ft high, occupied the centre of the building, while 150 ft above the pavement Gilbert Bayes' figure 'Let Peace Prevail' symbolised the mood of the country. On Orchard Street, the sun shone on Tower Bridge in Clara Fargo Thomas' vast painting 'The Great Ports of the British Empire' and radiated its beams to the corners of the empire on which it never set. Australia, Canada and South Africa were depicted as masculine territories, brimming with agricultural bounty and mineral wealth, while India was decorative and exotic.[33] Cawthra's 'India' and Harold Youngman's 'Canada' (Fig. 4) were cast by H. H. Martyn and Co., but archives do not confirm the manufacture of the entire scheme.[34] Opinions about the decorations varied. One member of the Arts Club thought them 'the best seen in London for years', whereas E. M. Forster predictably 'thought them awful'.[35] However, it is clear from the mass-observation record of the day that, whatever the critical opinion, Selfridge's was one of the major sights of London, dazzling to provincial visitors.[36]

The iconographic fantasies of empire and British history illustrated by the sculpture would have been readily assimilated by the crowds that blocked the street to gape at the spectacle. The Empire Marketing Board's promotion from 1926 to 1933 of empire links and resources kept the idea of a real and imagined empire to the fore.[37] Political and commercial imperatives led the Empire Day Movement to exhort schools and other members to make it widely known that 'Empire Trade is of immense value to the entire population, above all to the working classes … it is the world's greatest influence for freedom, peace and prosperity'.[38] Popular imperialism was everywhere: posters, newspapers, biscuit tins, cigarette cards and school texts were emblazoned with imperial imagery and suffused with history, myth and adventure. Sculpture also engaged with these popular ephemera: in 1928 William Reynolds-Stephens, president of the RBS, launched a set of thirty cigarette cards of 'Modern British Sculpture' for W. D. and H. O. Wills (Fig. 5).[39] The selection of work by twenty-seven sculptors was eclectic: Sir William Hamo Thornycroft, Sir Thomas Brock, Sir George Frampton and Frederick William Pomeroy had recently died, but their inclusion indicated both Reynolds-Stephens' taste and the endurance of the New Sculpture. Jagger's Royal Artillery memorial, Ledward's Guards' memorial, Alfred Oakley's carving 'Malua', and the striking bronze head 'The Boxer' by Hardiman represented the work of younger sculptors. The widespread distribution of these cards was designed to educate popular taste and to assert that monuments and traditional figuration constituted the mainstream of modern sculpture (Fig. 6).

Of the seventeen sculptors who contributed to the Selfridge's decorations, all but one of whom were members of the RBS, eight had their work represented in the cigarette cards, ten had made sculpture for the *British Empire Exhibition* at Wembley in 1924, and six had done all three. Although many visitors to the Wembley exhibition preferred the dodgems to the wonders of the empire, one of the most popular didactic attractions had been the pageant.[40] It is clear from Jeffrey Richards' descriptions of the numerous tableaux representing the dominions and British history that the Selfridge's imagery derived from it, at least in part.[41] The illustrative style also evoked history painting and contemporary feature films such as *Clive of India* (1935), *Drake of England, Rhodes of Africa* (1936) and *The Iron Duke.*[42] British sculptors' involvement with the entertainment industry was varied, from Kathleen Scott's portrait of the child star Sabu, made when he was in London filming Korda's *Elephant Boy* in 1938, to decorating the palaces of pleasure.[43] Among others, Bayes made reliefs for the Saville Theatre and Cawthra produced the proscenium relief for Sadler's Wells as well as many pieces for Odeons and other cinemas, much of it cast by H. H. Martyn and Co. Newbury Abbot Trent, who contributed to the Selfridge's decorations, spent most of the 1930s producing sculpture for the interiors and exteriors of Gaumont British Cinemas. Eric Aumonier's cinema sculpture was made by the family firm.[44] Demand for scenery and props also provided employment opportunities for craftsmen.[45]

In 2000, Sam Taylor-Wood wrapped the 'temple of shopping', Selfridge's, in a 900 ft printed artwork. 'XV Seconds' portrayed images of iconic 'gods' of popular culture in a photographic allusion to a classical frieze.[46] High-tech industrial materials and production processes may seem far removed from traditional craft skills but the proto-wrapping of 1937 resonates here: the boundaries of high art, popular culture and mass consumerism seem equally unstable. In both cases the commissioner and the artists are known, but we must delve deep to find the identities of those who translated the concepts and models into fully realised, functional artworks.[47] Unlike in the film industry, the list of credits for sculpture does not extend to artisans and technicians.

The status in contemporary discourses of Taylor-Wood's engagement with architecture and popular culture is in stark contrast to the debased position of architectural sculptors in critical histories of the 20th century. Three sculptural episodes of May, June and July 1937 – Selfridge's, the British pavilion in Paris and the publication and exhibition *Circle* – may crudely exemplify a qualitative and temporal progression from 'low' to 'high' art. Critical and historical attention has been in inverse proportion to the size of the projects and the numbers of individuals involved. The groupings of sculptors engaged in these disparate events occupied their own places in the spectrum of production, but required contingent infrastructures in the same changing world. Quarries and foundries supplied modernist and traditionalist alike; businesses that developed in the heyday of architectural sculpture invested in technology and skills that later facilitated the production of important postwar works. Many studio sculptors would have sympathised with Hilaire Belloc's aphorism 'It is the duty of the wealthy man to give employment to the artisan'. This essay has endeavoured to illustrate the crucial role of the artisan in the infrastructures of British sculpture.

Sarah Crellin

Notes

I would like to offer my grateful thanks to Ann Compton, Ian Leith, Catherine Moriarty, Jeffrey Richards, Dennis Wardleworth and Gillian Whiteley for their valuable conversations and correspondence during the preparation of this essay.

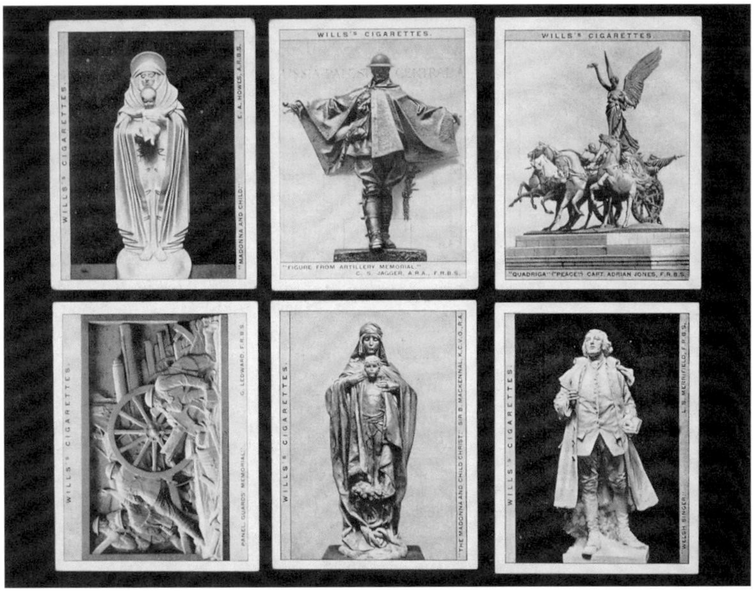

6 *Modern British Sculpture* cigarette cards illustrating works by Allan Howes, C.S. Jagger, Adrian Jones, Gilbert Ledward, Bertram Mackennal and F.W. Pomeroy.

1 R. Cork, 'Overhead Sculpture for the Underground Railway', *Art Beyond the Gallery*, New Haven and London: Yale University Press, 1985, for example, quotes architect Charles Holden's desire to reflect 'as far as possible the whole gamut of contemporary thought in sculpture', but includes no discussion of other architectural work in London.

2 See for example forthcoming monographs on Gilbert Ledward, Charles Sargeant Jagger and Charles Wheeler, to be published by Lund Humphries and funded by the Henry Moore Foundation. Dennis Wardleworth's unpublished Ph.D. thesis, 'Building the Modern Corporation: Corporate Art Patronage in Inter-war Britain', Southampton Institute, 2002, examines the economic, management and artistic influences on the design and decoration of industrial headquarters.

3 For the 1930s, see D. Mellor, 'British Art in the 1930s: Some Economic, Political and Cultural Structures', in F. Gloversmith (ed.), *Class, Culture and Social Change: A New View of the 1930s*, Sussex, Harvester Press,1980, pp. 185–207. For the effect of the slump on modernism, see A. Stephenson, 'Strategies of Situation: British Modernism and the Slump *c.*1929–1934', *Oxford Art Journal*, 1991, vol. 14, no. 2, pp. 30–51.

4 The exhibition *Close Encounters: The Sculptor's Studio in the Age of the Camera*, Henry Moore Institute, Leeds, 2001, by contrast, showed how the studio as a site of individual sculptural endeavour was deliberately constructed in photographs. For more on this, see Jon Wood's introduction to this exhibition, pp. 8–27.

5 I. S. Black, 'Imperial Visions: Rebuilding the Bank of England, 1919–39', in F. Driver and D. Gilbert (eds), *Imperial Cities. Landscape, Display and Identity*, Manchester, Manchester University Press, 1999, pp. 96–113, p. 110. See also his 'Rebuilding "The Heart of the Empire": Bank Headquarters in the City of London', *Art History*, November 1999, vol. 22, no. 4, pp. 593–618.

6 See Wardleworth, 'Building the Modern Corporation: Corporate Art Patronage in Inter-war Britain'. For a short article on the architecture of Unilever House, see C. Aslet, 'Unilever House Blackfriars', *Journal of the Thirties Society*, 1981, no. 1, pp. 18–21.

7 The sculpture for the western half of the building was made by Ernest Cole.

8 W. B. Fagan's panelled doors were cast in silver-bronze by the Bromsgrove Guild, who produced all the metalwork for the building and for Thames House nearby (1931).

9 'The Day of Cheap Building' and 'Now is the Time to Build', *Architects' Journal*, 21 January 1931, pp. 1 and 132–3. This includes a list of raw materials prices and illustrations of Thames House, Millbank, the Dorchester Hotel, Broadcasting House and the Masonic Peace Memorial building, Great Queen Street.

10 E. Armitage, 'Joseph Armitage, Craftsman, 1880–1945', *Journal of the Thirties Society*, 1982, no. 3, pp. 25–30. For H. H. Martyn and Co., see J. Whitaker, *The Best*, Cheltenham, published by the author, 1985, a substantial book chronicling the remains of archives that the author rescued from destruction. For the Bromsgrove Guild, see Q. Watt (ed.), *The Bromsgrove Guild*, Bromsgrove, 1999. For the Morris Singer Foundry, see D. S. James, *A Century of Statues: A History of the Morris Singer Foundry*, Basingstoke, 1984. These vital histories were compiled by family members and local historians. The latest volume in the series 'Public Sculpture of Britain' is P. Ward-Jackson *Public Sculpture of the City of London*, Liverpool, 2003.

11 P. Eyres, 'The Archer: Eric Aumonier's Icon of Urban Travel and of the Pre- and Post-war London Underground', *Sculpture Journal*, 2002, vol. VIII, pp. 36–53, especially pp. 42–44. See also W. Aumonier (ed.), *Modern Architectural Sculpture*, London, The Architectural Press, 1930, pp. 128, 130, 131 and 159.

12 For craft wages, see the article on Joseph Armitage and the books on the Bromsgrove Guild and H. H. Martyn and Co. cited at note 10. For comparison with miners' wages in 1937, see G. Orwell, '*The Road to Wigan Pier*', London, Penguin, 2001, pp. 69–72.

13 Reading across the histories of H. H. Martyn and Co., the Bromsgrove Guild, Aumonier's *Modern Architectural Sculpture* and P. Curtis, 'The Sculptural Scheme in the Anglican Cathedral: Sculpting to Order?', in P. Curtis (ed.), *Patronage and Practice: Sculpture on Merseyside*, Liverpool, Tate Gallery Liverpool, 1989, pp. 94–101, provides a fuller picture of the sculptural enterprise than can be obtained from any individual text.

14 The Italian renaissance style of the palace contrasted strongly with the modernism of the Maharaja of Indore's palace, designed by E. Muthesius and displaying his collection of Brancusi sculpture.

15 Whitaker, *The Best*, p. 105.

16 James, *A Century of Statues*

17 See A. Forsyth, 'Floating Palaces: British Liners of the 1930s', *Journal of the Thirties Society*, 1984, no. 4, pp. 10–15.

18 For Lambert's contributions to the *Queen Mary* and *Queen Elizabeth*, see V. Nicholson, *The Sculpture of Maurice Lambert*, Lund Humphries, London, 2002, pp. 69–70.

19 A. Powers, 'Oliver Hill as Exhibition Designer', *Journal of the Thirties Society*, 1991, no. 7, pp. 28–39.

20 For Pick's London Transport role and discussion of various commissions, see Cork, 'Overhead Sculpture for the Underground Railway', pp. 249–317, and Eyres, 'The Archer: Eric Aumonier's Icon of Urban Travel and of the Pre- and Post-war London Underground'.

21 P. Greenhalgh, *Ephemeral Vistas. The Expositions Universelles, Great Exhibitions and World's Fairs, 1851–1939*, Manchester, Manchester University Press, 1988, p. 130.

22 F. Pick, foreword to catalogue of British pavilion, p. 307, cited in Powers, 'Oliver Hill as Exhibition Designer', p. 35.

23 Letter from Pick to O. Hill, 14 October 1936, cited Powers, 'Oliver Hill as Exhibition Designer', p. 35.

24 See Powers, 'Oliver Hill as Exhibition Designer' and Powers, 'The Paris Exhibition of 1937', *Matrix*, 1996, no. 16, pp. 88–94. Patrick Eyres has shown that Hermes' window was to be recycled for use on a London Underground station: Eyres, 'The Archer: Eric Aumonier's Icon of Urban Travel and of the Pre- and Post-war London Underground', p. 41.

25 Letter to Hill, Oliver Hill papers, RIBA archive, HiO/66.

26 Letters from Doman and Seale and letter from C. Tennyson to O. Hill, 23.9.36, RIBA archive HiO/66.

27 In 'Art and Commerce: A New Departure', *Architectural Review*, May 1933, vol. LXXIII, pp. 210–11, Charnaux received lavish praise for commissioning a sculptor to design their mannequin. For discussion, excluding sculpture, of modernist artists' engagement with industry, see Stephenson, 'Strategies of Situation: British Modernism and the Slump *c.*1929–1934', *Oxford Art Journal*, vol. 14, no. 2, pp. 30–51.

28 Hill to Pick, 1 September 1937, HiO/63/1, cited Powers, 'Oliver Hill as Exhibition Designer', p. 36.

29 For full descriptions and images of the scheme, see *Selfridge's Decorations for the Coronation Souvenir Brochure*, London, 1937.

30 D. Cannadine, *Ornamentalism. How the British Saw Their Empire*, London, Allen Lane, 2001, p. 130.

[31] See R. Pound, *Selfridge*, William Heinemann, London, 1960, for the full rags-to-riches-to-rags story. Selfridge became a British subject in July 1937 after almost thirty years in England.

[32] For Selfridge's previous decorative 'stunts', see Pound, *Selfridge*. For the American connections, see M. H. Bogart, *Public Sculpture and the Civic Ideal in New York, 1890-1930*, Chicago, Chicago University Press, 1989.

[33] Posters with striking iconographic similarities include one of India for the P&O shipping company reproduced in D. Judd, *Empire*, London, 2001, opposite p. 298, and E. Dinkel, 'The Empire by Underground', 1932, reproduced in Driver and Gilbert, *Imperial Cities. Landscape, Display and Identity*, fig. 1.

[34] Whitaker, *The Best*, p. 74–5. I have not yet been able to prove the tantalising oral testimony that the entire scheme eventually decorated a maharaja's palace in India.

[35] Letters to *New Statesman* from M. Buckmaster and E. M. Forster, who in a purple passage derided the decorations as 'tassels and tomfoolery'. No dates, cited in Pound, *Selfridge*, p. 239.

[36] H. Jennings and C. Madge (eds), *May the Twelfth. Mass-Observation Day-Surveys 1937*, London, 1937 and 1987, passim. I am grateful to Jeffrey Richards for drawing my attention to these records.

[37] S. Constantine, '"Bringing the Empire Alive": the Empire Marketing Board and Imperial Propaganda, 1926–33', in J. MacKenzie (ed.), *Imperialism and Popular Culture*, Manchester, Manchester University Press, 1986, pp. 192–231.

[38] EDM annual reports 1930s cited MacKenzie, *Propaganda and Empire*, p. 235.

[39] No archive records for this set survive. William Reynolds-Stephens was the likely instigator of the set: he was PRBS, the set includes three of his own works and there are well-informed texts on all the cards. For the use of cards as vehicles of education and imperial propaganda, see MacKenzie, *Propaganda and Empire*, pp. 94–5. I am grateful to Murray Cards International for their assistance.

[40] For discussion of the exhibition, see Judd, *Empire*, pp. 273–96. For intellectual derision about the exhibition, see MacKenzie's introduction to *Imperialism and Popular Culture*, p. 7. See also *Catalogue of the Palace of Arts. British Empire Exhibition*, London, 1924.

[41] J. Richards, *Imperialism and Music*, Manchester, 2001, especially pp. 201–5.

[42] J. Richards, 'Boy's Own Empire: Feature Films and Imperialism in the 1930s', in MacKenzie, *Imperialism and Popular Culture*, pp. 140–64.

[43] Lady Kennet, *Self-Portrait of an Artist*, London, 1949, p. 309, and illustrated in Louisa Young, *A Task of Great Happiness*, London, 1995.

[44] For these, cross-reference L. Irvine and P. Atterbury, *Gilbert Bayes: Sculptor, 1872–1953*, Shepton Beauchamp, 1998; S. Crellin, unpublished MA thesis on Hermon Cawthra, University of Leeds, 1995; W. Aumonier, *Modern Architectural Sculpture*, and D. Atwell, *Cathedrals of the Movies*, London, The Architectural Press, 1980. Atwell discusses the work of M. Alexander and Sons of Newcastle, for whom John Alexander carried out interior design and sculpture manufacture for numerous cinemas in Britain, pp. 112, 122.

[45] When war broke out, Wheeler's assistant, Willie Wilkinson, joined the film industry. C. Wheeler, *High Relief*, London, Country Life Books (Hamlyn) 1968, p. 126. The Bromsgrove Guild also lost craftsmen to the scenery department of a film company.

[46] See illustrations and descriptions of the work at www.whitecube.com.

[47] The complex manufacture and installation of 'XV Seconds' was coordinated through creative marketing consultants General Assembly.

In 1930, the critic John Grierson judged that the time was ripe to offer a verdict on 'the new generation in sculpture'.[1] By this large phrase he meant a small set of artists: John Skeaping, Barbara Hepworth and Henry Moore. What they did new was relatively simple, he suggested: their art had begun to develop 'a certain looseness of limb'.[2] The mobile metaphor is bodily and youthful: it wants to speak to what is innovative in their confident ease. Like their works, the new carvers are fresh and footloose: not only have they left behind Epstein's 'hacking and harrowing', but even the simple-minded obviousness of a Dobson has ceded to their more mobile hands and brains.[3]

Grierson, it should be noted, was not entirely certain of the reasons for this development, nor why it led in the direction it had. At issue was what to make of their chosen subjects: 'snakes and toads and birds and antelopes and horses and babies and negro women'. The selection could not be merely accidental or formal: such topics suggested that beneath or within the standard sculptural issues (form, surface, materials) lay a 'deeper quest altogether'. The new generation, Grierson concluded, was possessed of a 'quickened consciousness of organic life'.[4] In retrospect, this may not seem an entirely surprising conclusion, not least given the main lines of these artists' future reputations, public statements and careers. More fraught, despite its familiarity, is the limited list of relevant subjects, those animals and ('primitive') humans in which 'the organic' can most easily be found. But neither the organic as such nor its putative locus is Grierson's main point. The combination seemed novel enough to need explaining, and he gave it a try. 'It may be,' he wrote, 'that the cinema has done something to open our eyes in this respect, with its power of revealing the constructions of plant life, animal life, and all life together in motion. It would be still more accurate to say that biology is getting into our blood. Certainly we become more conscious of the sculptural relations between these different worlds.'[5]

Nowadays, we would be quick to say that Grierson was rather awkwardly invoking such changes in the human sensorium as were brought on by technological innovation, as did other cultural commentators in the 1930s. What is remarkable in Grierson's case is his sense that the new vehicles of vision allow 'all life' to be seen as *sculptural* in its basic forms. The shapes the camera tracks, moreover, are as infectious as they are vividly plastic and material: not only do they course through our bloodstream, changing our make-up, but they find their expression in the special vitality of the new sculpture, in what was so oddly termed its looseness of limb.

Grierson's is a too-simple theory of a complex moment, yet to his credit he realised that some explanation was in order and tried his best. British sculpture had changed in ways that demanded a reckoning couched in some larger cultural terms. The critical issues behind those transformations lie, I think, in whether or not the new forms could be seen as actively giving access to organic or natural experience, rather than more passively construing it, and how such an imaginative experience could be tenable, let alone relevant, in the modern world. Hence the odd leap from babies to cinema, and thence on to biology and blood.

No recent account of those transformations seems to me more suggestive than that offered by Charles Harrison, particularly as it concerns sculpture's modernity: around what issues, asks Harrison, was the new practice said to cohere?[6] By 1930, the term 'sculpture' no longer summoned a finite and time-honoured category, one composed of distinct objects produced from cast and mould. Literary reference and the decorum of the classical tradition yielded to new certainties: sculpture now designated, and opened onto, certain innate categories of experience that might be classed as simultaneously distant and immediate: landscape and memory figured here largely, as did the childish and anti-classical. The very notion of tradition (its sites and materials) was being invented anew. By these lights sculptural experience was now to be found in key modern antinomies: its effects revolved around experiences grasped as simultaneously present and distant, vividly material, yet giving access to various figural reservoirs that condensed both personal and cultural pasts. What was modern was the expectation that the work of art could find its relevance in an urgent physicality somehow capable of summoning – the ambition is staggering – both the experiential and the psychic world.

Harrison's point is clear and, I think, largely right: as he recognises, the regressive inclusions of the new sculpture (its opening up of itself , not only to babies, horses and Negro women, but also to the use of evocative, often apparently 'native', woods and stones) did not prevent Moore and Hepworth from simultaneously insisting on the radical autonomy of their sculptural objects, not least as regards their chosen forms. Moore, for example, wrote enthusiastically of sculpture having within it 'a pent-up energy, an intense life *of its own*, independent of the object it might represent' (my italics).[7] Hepworth, for her part, claimed that in sculpture, 'the conception itself, the quality of thought that is embodied, must be abstract – an impersonal vision, individualised in the particular medium'.[8] These statements have more in common than their date of 1934: each wills into being the dream of an artistic autonomy that is not mere abstraction – though for Hepworth, certainly, it 'must be abstract'. Autonomy here lays claim to a special self-sufficiency for the artwork: not only does it contain its own reined-in energies but it can make the artist's own mental activity into something impersonal, in which individuality has been ceded to wood or stone. Sculpture must be highly individual, as well as actively impersonal – this seems to be Hepworth's not-quite-contradictory point. Despite their differences, both artists imagine a special role for a sculptural object: with the life of the one, and the individuality of the other, sculpture needs little from anyone or anybody – this is what autonomy means.

It is striking in retrospect, however, just how difficult it is to fit these various accounts together to approach something like a whole. The problems inevitably collect around the issue of just how actively British sculpture might be connected – or not – to the contemporary world. The loose relation Grierson imagined between cinematic vision and carving *c.*1930 is countered by the various insistences on autonomy offered by the artists, claims that have about them the sense that sculptural meaning *should be self-evident* – which is to say, lodged in the form itself. Harrison straddles the divide, not quite ceding to Moore and Hepworth their claims for autonomy, yet still not quite suggesting, as does Grierson, however dimly, that these issues of form and meaning concern the uncertain terms in which sculpture should or might enter a distinctly modernising world.

Not, of course, that anyone then securely knew the answer to that quandary; not Grierson, not Hepworth, not Moore. And surely sculpture in the interwar period demonstrates, in its inevitable intersections with traditional sites and vehicles of meaning, just how deep the uncertainty lay. Consider the agonies undergone by both sculpture and its viewers, when carvers were called upon to do a traditional allegorical job. The team of seven sculptors (or eight, if we count Jacob Epstein) asked to decorate the head office of the London Underground used allegory, all too irrelevantly: their personifications of wind power, however muscular or simplified the archaising bodies that attempt the conjuring (the requisite puffing and floating was hard to pull off), were themselves already conceptual archaisms, even before they were ever unveiled.[9] When the bodily and natural is used to clothe the technologies of a mass society, the everyday literalness of the latter means that the inevitable cognitive tensions cannot be annealed. The inevitable strain between fact and fiction – it rests on the conflation of the energies of wind and train – here reaches breaking point. If it is true, as Roger Fry remarked in his *Last Lectures*, it is only 'in fixed and well-ordered civilisations that large scale architectural works can be carried out', it does not follow that the mere existence of enormous structures (Holden's building is especially gigantic) in and of itself says anything particular about the vitality of coherent meaning within the relevant social world.[10]

We might say that British interwar culture relied on sculpture to figure for it, as both threat and promise, the failing coherence – the growing incoherence – of the contemporary experience. Epstein seems to have shouldered that burden with uncommon zeal. It is instructive in this context both that his chosen procedure was so insistently allegorical, and that allegory for him meant carving in stone. Witness the great series of carvings that he executed from 1930 onwards: the sequence began with 'Genesis', continued with 'Behold the Man', 'Consummatum Est' and 'Adam', and ended with 'Jacob Wrestling with the Angel', his last carved work.

Carving for Epstein can operate allegorically – this is, quite separate from the issue of his chosen subject – because for him (as opposed to Hepworth, Moore and Skeaping) a single carved figure can combine multiple figural histories and formats, while also guaranteeing variety of surface and style. Carving is allegorical, that is to say, because as Epstein does it, the stone figure is simultaneously monolithic and, yet not a single thing.

This is not merely a question of smooth versus rough, though of course in any carved figure such contrasts carry real declarative force. Take 'Genesis' as the key case in point: the figure is visibly a fragment, but also declaredly a study in fullness (1931; Fig. 1). And it likewise combines within a single marble a series of further contrasts able to cohabit, despite their insistent production of sensations of difference, without quite forcing the figure to fall apart. Tick off the oppositions one by one: there is first of all the fundamental contrast of black versus white. There is the measure of difference between the conventionalised mask of the face (with its evocations of Pablo Picasso, as well as the primitive) and the implicit naturalism of the body, which is alive enough to be pregnant (programmatically, it is by definition 'quick with life'). The mask/body opposition, moreover, plays itself out as a matter of form and volume: the face is the site of planarity and concavity, whereas the body – breasts, belly, buttocks – is all convexity, rounded out into globe after weighty globe. But speaking of the

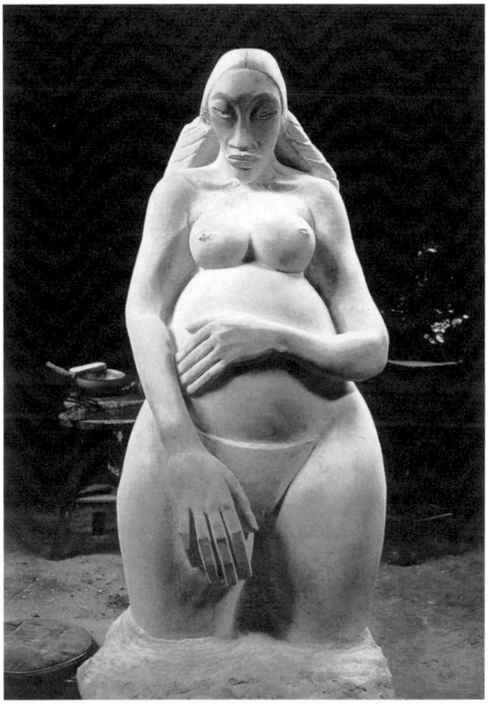

breasts: these organs too demonstrate again that the logic of difference that motivates the figure is closely linked to the way that Epstein uses carving allegorically, as his chosen mode. The proof lies first in the realisation that the breasts, with all their careful glowing polish, have been given different sizes, as if at this bodily site, with its evident narrative and erotic importance, a mimetic naturalism demands its say. But look at the nipples: in the centre of each breast, Epstein has gestured towards their crucial presence via a rough-worked tumescence or outcropping – that is all. Its presence catalyses a reversion, even a regression: mimesis returns to stone.[11]

This pattern of rupture and opposition matters to 'Genesis', I think, because it places the work in something like an adequate relation to complex circumstances of signification which themselves are the disjunctive aspects of some larger social whole. The sculpture bears reference to more than biblical narratives of origin: it speaks of art and colonialism, of the politics of birth and reproduction, of racism and anthropology: the endless responses of contemporary viewers make it clear that the net of reference was cast wide. That this is the result of the sculpture's allegorical operations there can be little doubt. Allegory here, to invoke the verdict of R. H. Wilenski on the sculpture, is lodged in the body: the work, he wrote awkwardly, is the 'embodiment of a genesis idea'. Unlike Frank Dobson, say, whose allegorical titles ('Truth', for example) were irrelevant ('it was only called *Truth* because it had to be called something'), 'the word "Genesis" here helps us to comprehension and sanctions the retention of the first incoming associated ideas'.[12]

To invoke Epstein in this context is to make him stand in for a more generalised uncertainty about how a modern sculpture should operate: the question, to repeat, concerned how it should make its forward-looking points. Hence the vogue for modernising materials: if Epstein did not much go in for such gimmicks, others did. Maurice Lambert was known not just for using high-gloss metals, but for even greater venturesomeness with media: in a single 1932 exhibition, he displayed works using not just a wide array of the English stones then

1 Jacob Epstein, 'Genesis', 1931, Serravezza marble

voguish (Derbyshire alabaster, Ham Hill stone, Course Hill sandstone), but also various combinations of lead, antimony, iron, plastic wood, cellulose, bronze, copper, aluminium and plate-glass. He also knew the ways of plywood, cellonite and concrete.[13] It was enthusiastically claimed of this array and its high-wire deployment (Lambert specialised in open and aerial formats, Fig. 2) that 'only the medium chosen could have expressed the subject'.[14] Yet the assertion loses its force entirely when we learn that Lambert's chosen subjects – 'Germinating Seed', 'Herring-Gulls', 'Helen of Troy' – are not all that far distant from the topics that Grierson's 'new generation' lent their 'quickened consciousness' of organic life. This is so even once we acknowledge the polemical difference between the corrective ambitions of 'Helen of Troy' as a sculptural subject and the more current allegiances to the 'primitive mother' theme.[15]

It is hard, in retrospect, not to think of Lambert, despite his contemporary celebrity and fashionable modernity, as only barking vainly at Moore's and Hepworth's heels. The problem for the latter two artists in particular was how, even under these confused conditions, to maintain some semblance of the formal autonomy to which, with their determinedly material and non-allegorical procedures, they aimed to stake a claim. For both these artists, autonomy could only be paradoxical at best. It was sought at a time when neither was above exhibiting on the rooftop at Selfridge's, or shy about envisioning their sculpture as table-top or garden items made to play a private, even avowedly domestic role.[16] Not only did their carving usually involve establishing some underlying

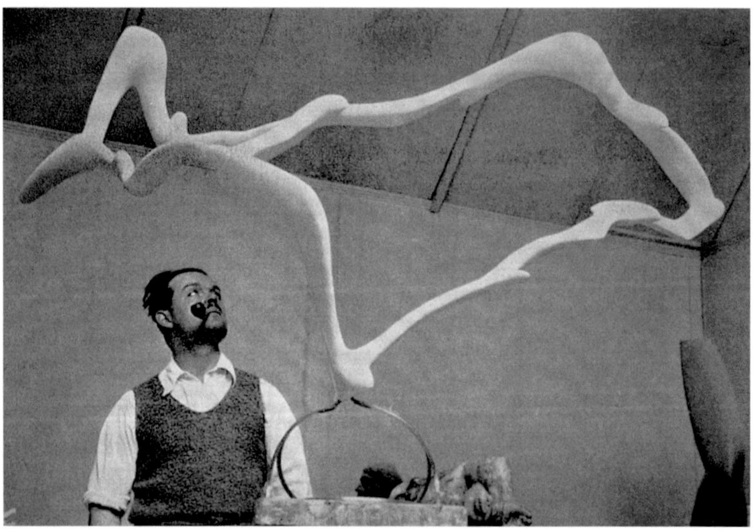

2 Maurice Lambert in his studio with 'Herring-Gulls', early 1930s

3 Henry Moore, 'Reclining Figure' 1939, elmwood, in foreground at the *Surrealism Today* exhibition at the Zwemmer Galleries, June 1940

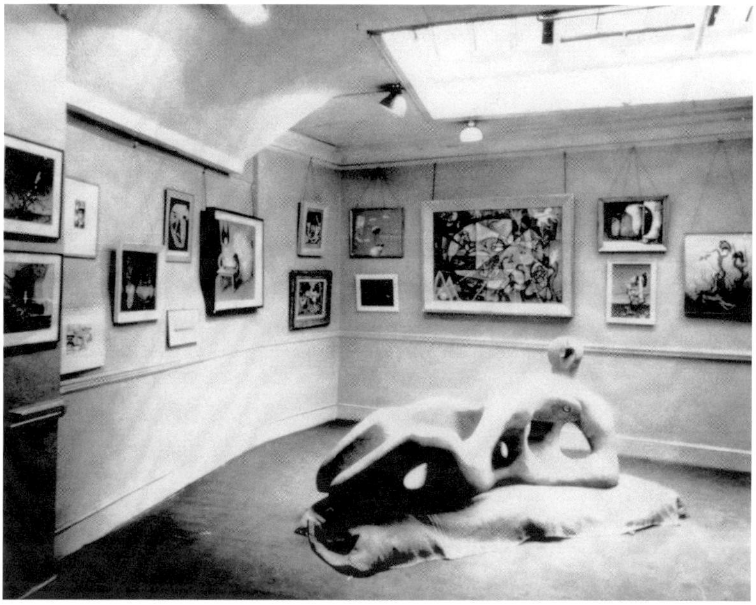

experience of unity – this even for objects that have internal contrasts, or the works that have been opened to vision, or conjured out of several separable parts. They also seem to have understood autonomy as the only possible condition of relationship between objects and viewers: I think, moreover, both artists made this paradox their own. Or, perhaps better stated, they suspected that the kinds of autonomy they sought for their sculpture were fragile, relied on viewers, and had to be argued for. Though Moore, for example, could write of the work of sculpture having a 'pent up energy, an intense life of its own', he was also well aware that such energies gained their force (or lost it) in relations of consumption and display. The stories of the artist siting and resiting his sculptures are legion: even more eloquent is the emphasis he put on photography as the vehicle of the ideal space of relation, one that could not only posit a position for object, site and viewer, but also keep its key elisions and connections safely insulated, free from time and change.[17] In such images, which Moore often took himself, a sculpture gains autonomy the more actively it connects (a viewer) with a view. And Moore's indoor installations raise similar issues: whether his objects appear in cases or on bases, or lack such mediations, the chosen tactic puts objects and viewers (as well as other sculptures) into contact on more than passing terms. When in 1941 his elmwood 'Reclining Figure' (1939; Detroit; Fig. 3), was exhibited atop a blanket which in turn seems to cover a low cushion or mattress, it seems clear that an utterly intimate and animate relationship is imagined by the installation, and perhaps even that the energy within the figure – it is visual as well as spatial – is seeking some sort of engagement or release.[18] Certainly the blanket tries to make the sculpture present *as a body*, as well as a thing or a dream.[19]

It is considerably more difficult to be certain how Hepworth imagined her sculptures and their possible relationships, whether to viewers or to the artist's self. Yet there is one declarative instance of her summoning a context able to define the forms and meanings of her art. Its site is textual: it occurs in *Circle*, the manifesto-cum-anthology of a group of artists who in 1937 aimed at a 'new cultural unity': Hepworth had a hand in the volume's layout, and certainly would have determined the images that conclude her own visionary and diagnostic contribution to the whole.[20] Sweepingly titled 'Sculpture', though in fact a defence (and redefinition) of abstract and Constructivist sculpture, her essay concludes with uncommon force: 'A constructive work is an embodiment of freedom itself and is unconsciously perceived even by those who are against it. The desire to live is the strongest universal emotion, it springs from the depths of our unconscious sensibility – and the desire to give life is our most potent, constructive, conscious expression of this intuition.'[21] Hepworth meant these words to be stirring, as well as deeply polemical: by these lights Constructivism is *constructive*: a positive act of making, it builds life. But this is not all the sculptor aims to say. What follows, directly enough to make it part of the essay, is a page with three photographs (Fig. 4). Each shows a partial view of Stonehenge: they are doubtless Hepworth's own work.

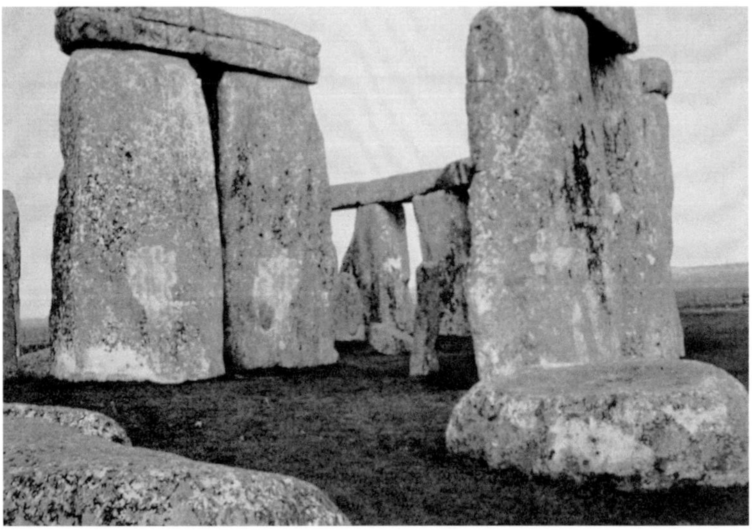

4 Photograph of Stonehenge from *Circle*, 1937

5 Barbara Hepworth, 'Single Form', 1937–8, holly

Not only are the standing stones shot to echo the monoliths the artist was then herself carving in miniature; they are also aligned, as befits a manifesto, with a view of constructive sculpture as a vehicle capable of representing an elemental desire – nothing less that the 'desire to live'.

What needs emphasising in this context are the historical circumstances and visual contingencies of Hepworth's resonant declaration. Note that this version of Constructivism is a theoretical and sculptural anomaly, a mutant or sport, or so we should conclude on the basis of what we should now term, following Hepworth, one of her contemporary 'constructive' works, 'Single Form' (1937–8; Leeds, Fig. 5). The work both figures and is a monolith, and as such it has none of the qualities customarily attributed to Constructivism in its various iterations: neither the transparency of a Gabo nor the fragmentary surfacelessness of Picasso's constructed work. (When in the years during and after World War II Constructivism (re)enters British sculptural practice, it often does so by supplying, mostly incongruously, fraught effects of surface to essentially linear form.) The key to the piece is simply its standing presence, a standing that suggests that the artist was actively and polemically reading out – and speaking back to – the fallen stones and shadows that, in her chosen photographs, collect in the visual field. It seems right to suggest that, given their context and imagery, these images speak of history and time. And Hepworth's sculptural conversation with them establishes a relation that complicates any easy assertion of sculptural autonomy. Has there ever been such a thing as an autonomous artwork? It is time to let that shibboleth fall by the wayside, not least in the case of sculpture. Relation, we might say, is the sculptural principle, or so I have argued here.

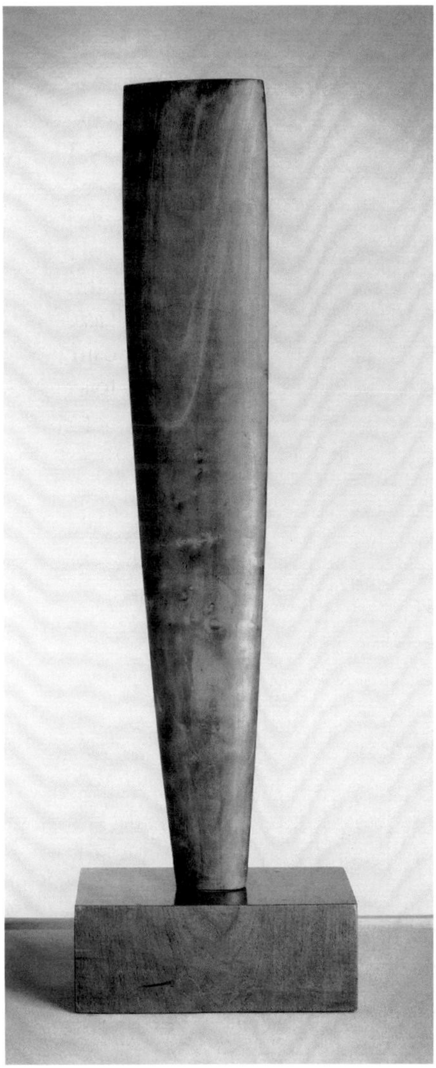

Anne Wagner

Notes

1 J. Grierson, 'The new generation in sculpture', *Apollo*, November 1930, vol. 12, pp. 347–51.

2 Ibid., p. 348.

3 Ibid.

4 Ibid., p. 350.

5 Ibid.

6 C. Harrison, 'Sculpture and the new "New Movement"', in S. Nairne and N. Serota (eds), *British Sculpture in the Twentieth Century*, London, Whitechapel Art Gallery, 1981, p. 104.

7 H. Moore, 'Statement for Unit I', 1934, reprinted in P. James (ed.), *Henry Moore on Sculpture*, New York, Viking Press, 1966, pp. 69–72; this citation, p. 72.

8 B. Hepworth, 'Statement for Unit I', 1934, as cited in Harrison, 'Sculpture and the new "New Movement"', p. 106.

9 On the London Underground sculptures, see R. Cork, *Art Beyond the Gallery*, London, Yale University Press, 1985, pp. 249–96.

10 R. Fry, *Last Lectures*, Boston, Beacon Press, 1962 (first published Cambridge, 1939), p. 37.

11 This paragraph condenses ideas explored at length in my forthcoming book *Brave New Womb: Modernist Maternity and British Sculpture*, chapter 5.

12 First published in the *Observer*, 8 February 1931, Wilenski's observations on 'Genesis' and allegory were later incorporated into his *The Meaning of Modern Sculpture*, London, Faber and Faber, 1932, p. 146.

13 See T. Friedman, 'A modernist masterpiece by Maurice Lambert', *Leeds Art Calendar*, 1988, no. 102, p. 106.

14 *Birmingham Post*, 14 June 1927, as cited in Friedman, 'A modernist masterpiece by Maurice Lambert'.

15 Lambert, that most conservative and fashionable of artists, was to rewrite the 'primitive mother'.

16 The Selfridge's show was held in summer 1930.

17 For attention to Moore's use of photography at the beginning of his career, see my 'Henry Moore's mother', *Representations*, Spring 1999, no. 65, pp. 93–120.

18 The photograph is illustrated in Nairne and Serota (eds), *British Sculpture in the Twentieth Century*, p. 122, as well as briefly discussed – in rather different terms than those used here – in A. Gruetzner, 'The surrealist object and surrealist sculpture', loc. cit, pp. 113–23.

19 The question of the operations of the sculptural base is broached by Y.-A. Bois, 'The sculptural opaque', *Sub-Stance*, 1981, no. 31, p. 30. Bois helpfully rehearses the main arguments concerning space, base and illusionism in 20th-century sculpture.

20 For a discussion of Hepworth's contribution to *Circle*, see M. Gale and C. Stephens, *Barbara Hepworth: Works in the Tate Collection and the Barbara Hepworth Museum, St Ives*, London, Tate Publishing, 1999, pp. 66–70. The authors establish Hepworth's role in *Circle*'s design.

21 B. Hepworth, 'Sculpture', *Circle: International Survey of Constructive Art*, New York, Praeger, 1971 (first published 1937), p. 115.

From the evidence of cartoons published in the British satirical weekly *Punch* in 1933, encountering modern sculpture in the art gallery and in the home demanded careful management if the artistic seriousness and aesthetic autonomy of the art object was not to be undermined. One problem, highlighted in the 22 February cartoon (Fig. 1) was that in so far as the gallery space staged a dramatic encounter between the sculptural object and the modern spectator, the precarious nature of this charged exchange could not guarantee clarity of interpretation. Since any informed understanding of the artwork's meaning was contingent upon the viewer's wider knowledge, artistic expertise and personal investments, and invoked assumptions about the correspondence of art to the social world, interpretation could easily falter, thereby inducing incomprehension or perhaps hilarity.[1] In such an event, any absorbed and serious interrogation could readily collapse into self-conscious theatre or ludicrous spectacle (as the *Punch* cartoon emphasises). At a private view, the modernist artist dressed in clichéd bohemian garb stands conspicuously with his hand on hip in a camp pose and stares intensely at the snake-like abstract form. To the assembled crowd of art lovers, including a female art student and a bemused mother with frightened daughter, he demonstrates his 'professional' knowledge and superior aesthetic taste by dismissively condemning the artwork: 'H'm – a bit *obvious*, isn't it?' Set up on a pedestal for the trained eye of the artist, the potential of the abstract

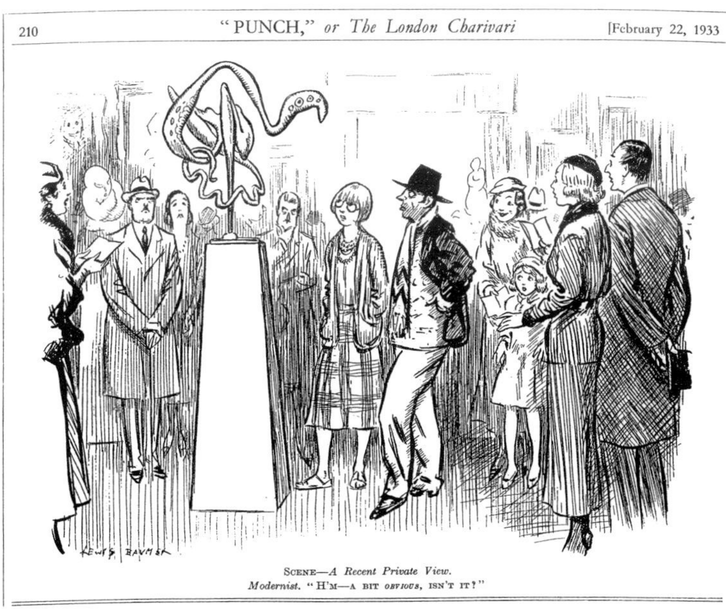
210 "PUNCH," *or The London Charivari* [February 22, 1933

SCENE—*A Recent Private View.*
Modernist. "H'M—A BIT *OBVIOUS*, ISN'T IT?"

1 'A Recent Private View', *Punch*, 22 February 1933

2 'The Modern Home', *Punch*, 2 August 1933

sculpture with its unnatural distortion and dynamic spatial form to compel attention and its ability to demonstrate aesthetic credibility have been decisively deflated. The perceived 'obviousness' of its pythonic referent undermines the sculpture's artistic sophistication and its hackneyed descriptiveness impairs any claims to its aesthetic autonomy. If only temporarily, the abstract form is reduced in the audience's eyes (and in the minds of *Punch*'s readership) to a discredited reptilian sham and the seemingly weird and unnatural languages of modern sculpture (like the eccentric dress and outré manners of the bohemian–artist) become an easy target for popular ridicule.

Issues relating to the display and staging of modern sculpture in the home emerge in another *Punch* cartoon of 2 August 1933 (Fig. 2). Within the contemporary home, the very absence of sculpture or indeed any sort of decoration is what is remarkable. In the sparsely furnished, Le Corbusier-inspired minimal flat, the fashionably dressed, single woman is criticised by her stylish taller friend with the words 'But, my dear, why the table?' As *Punch* amusingly indicated, if to the zealous, puritanical eye of the new woman the inclusion of the solitary Isokon dining table risked compromising the severe minimalist aesthetic of the solo flat, what restrictions did such conditions place upon the display of modern art in the home? Amongst this new constituency of modern, single householders whose tastes in interior decoration, fashion and furnishing style embraced all-white minimalist decors with large glass or metal panels, the appeal of modern sculpture rested upon its compatibility with these stark aesthetic criteria.[2]

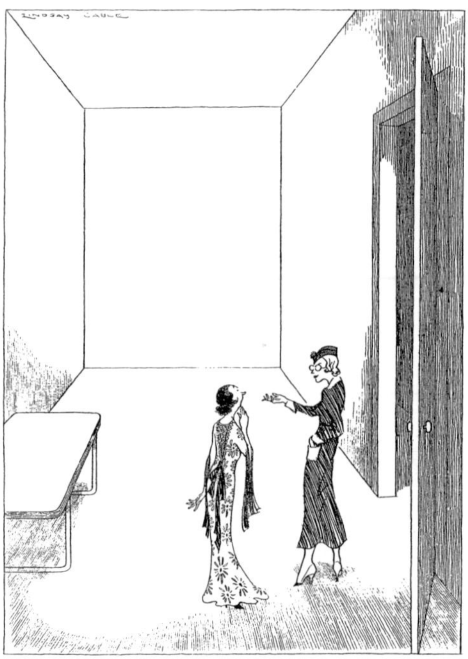

THE MODERN HOME.
"BUT, MY DEAR, WHY THE TABLE?"

In the following year, Herbert Read argued against this populist trend, proposing that 'sculpture is not a cabinet art suitable for drawing rooms or boudoirs, it is a monumental art demanding much elbow room'.[3] Nevertheless, for many sculptors during the bleak Depression years, given the lack of communal and state support and the high material costs associated with monumental sculpture, what was urgently needed were new commercial outlets as well as relatively affluent, art-purchasing individuals. Emerging in the early 1930s, amongst these younger audiences modern sculpture was divorced from previous classicising and monumental conventions, and earlier Cubist languages had become divested of their radical 'avant-gardist' credentials. More informal subjects and more intimate modes of viewing meant that domestic sculpture had become increasingly identified with an 'International Modern' furnishing style popularised in the growing number of large- circulation fashion, design and ideal home magazines.[4] This response was, at least in part, a sign of the commercial success of Cubist motifs and languages within the luxury goods markets (particularly in *haute couture* fashion, textiles and de luxe interior decoration following the impact of the 1925 *Exposition des Arts Decoratifs et Industriels Modernes* in Paris). Monitoring this trend in their 1929 study of *The New Interior Decoration*, Dorothy Todd and Raymond Mortimer noted with some degree of irony that the marketplace and the demand for 'boudoir modern' styles had tamed cubism. 'Painting like Picasso's [they claimed] made a renaissance of interior decoration possible' and 'Marie Laurencin and Braque have insinuated themselves into public favour'. You cannot go into a milliner's or even a hosier's today without seeing cubist design ... and you are exhorted to buy meat extracts and laxatives in a language derived from Picasso.'[5]

Increasingly familiar as decorative additions within a modern architectural scheme, modern sculpture or monochrome reliefs complemented many of the styling features of the contemporary 'House Beautiful'. Strategically placed besides the chic Art Deco cocktail cabinet or on the latest Bauhaus-inspired tubular stainless steel side table, such carefully proportioned sculptures were often carved from expensive exotic woods, incorporated hand-polished metal surfaces or delicate glass, ebony, silver or gilt inlay, or employed the latest hi-tech materials. 'Do not think of them', urged *Vogue*, 'over mantelpieces, but above a chromium radiator ... in a delightful modern interior.'[6] In the case of Henry Moore's 'Maquette for Reclining Figure' (1938; Fig. 3), the intended location was on a shelf in an alcove in Berthold Lubetkin's ultra-modern penthouse flat built by Lubetkin and Tecton at High Point II in Highgate between 1936 and 1938. Illuminated by a wall of plate glass and set amidst Bauhaus-designed furniture by Walter Gropius and Marcel Breuer, the simplified and organic language of the small bronze figure complemented the strict economy of design and form that were the hallmarks of Lubetkin and Tecton's austere modernist aesthetic.[7]

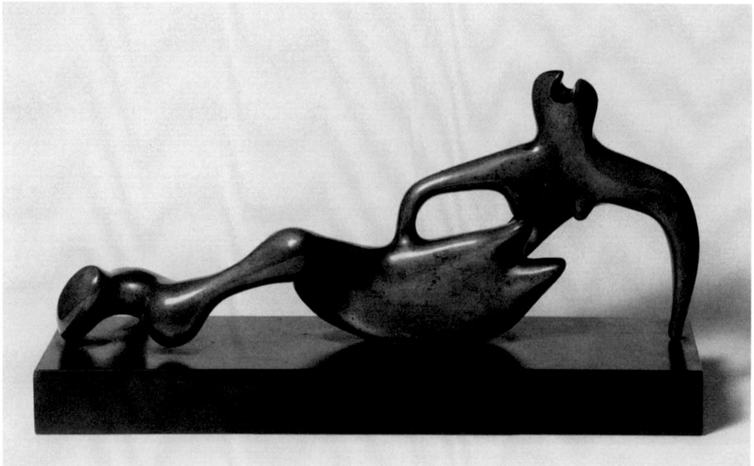

These more informal modes of staging and viewing in the domestic environment went hand in hand with similar developments in the commercial art gallery. To offer one example, the Mayor Gallery in London was completely refurbished in 1933 by leading architect and interior designer Brian O'Rourke, in a streamlined style similar to that used in Cunard's liners *Orion* (1935) and the *Queen Mary* (1936). The Mayor premises had a startling white and orange-vermilion exterior and a split-level layout with white roughcast walls, hidden lighting and stainless steel tubular furniture. The gallery was, as many commentators pointed out, 'the last word in modernity', heralding 'the Bauhaus [coming] to Cork Street'.[8] Critics saw abstract art and the gallery design as complementary. P. G. Konody in *The Daily Mail* praised 'the very interior on different levels, the rustless steel furniture, hidden lighting and severe simplicity [for] having the effect of a cubist picture'.[9] Both *Vogue* and *Harper's Bazaar* applauded the Mayor Gallery design for its 'modern taste', with the *Harper's Bazaar* critic going so far as to claim that 'the essential lack of ostentation central to the Mayor Gallery exhibition ... makes its effect a cumulative one. [For] in these circumstances [modern art] becomes intelligible.'[10]

Such fashionable framings, as Anthony Bertram recorded in *Design for Today* (May 1934), had a significant impact upon how contemporary sculpture was evaluated since 'the gallery feeling is replaced by a room feeling; the [artworks] are part of a decorative scheme rather than goods displayed for sale'.[11] Recognising the significance of showing sculpture in commercial premises that promoted such a broad

3 Henry Moore, 'Maquette for Reclining Figure', 1938

4 Naum Gabo, 'Construction in Space: Soaring', 1930

allegiance of modern art with continental architecture and design to wider audiences, exhibition societies such as the London Group in its 1930 annual show turned to the London department store, Selfridge's, to display its members' work and were praised by the press for their enterprise. In its landscaped West End Roof Garden above Oxford Street, sculptures by Barbara Hepworth, Maurice Lambert, Moore and John Skeaping were displayed as contemporary fittings for the modern home and as pleasing garden and grotto ornaments. As one reviewer noted:

> As houses and flats are now so small that there is little room for sculpture … Statuary is to be given a place in the rich man's garden if space cannot be found for it indoors … The result is that the sculptor has had to change his medium. Concrete is coming into its own sharing with pottery the power of weather resistance.[12]

Urged by *The Times* in October 1932 'to extract aesthetic virtues out of economic necessities' during the Depression years, sculptors were actively encouraged to 'evolve a style which is likely to harmonise with the kinds of domestic interior now in favour … For that reason [they] must work small, avoid intricacy, violent contrasts and distorting details.'[13] The correctness of this 'new marriage' of modern sculpture with industrial design and domestic architecture, 'combining elegance with economy', was further reinforced by furnishing displays such as *Modern Living* at Whiteleys department store in Bayswater in 1934 and the 1936 exhibition *Modern Pictures in Modern Rooms* held at the Duncan Miller design studio in London. Abstract sculpture by Moore, Hepworth and Eileen Holding alongside works by Constantin Brancusi, Naum Gabo and a mobile by Alexander Calder were enticingly displayed in an 'authentic' contemporary setting seemingly at home with the informal and intimate conditions of viewing that such a domestic milieu demanded.[14] As Gabo's 'Construction in Space: Soaring' (1930; Fig. 4) attested, modern materials such as the celluloid cones and the delicate skeletal supports suggested the sensation of rotation and flight and implied a dynamic, mechanical aesthetic that was clearly identified with progressive Constructivist principles by the mid-1930s. Recognising the advantages that such

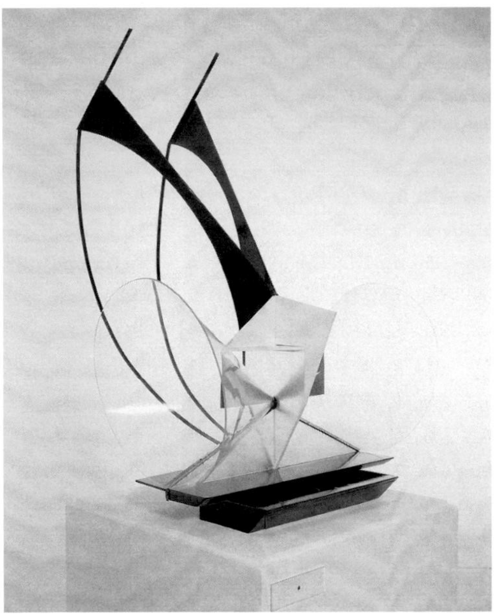

commercial enterprise and private patronage held, the Arts Council of Great Britain eagerly promoted the opportunities for sculptors available within the domestic market through its *Sculpture in the Home* exhibitions of 1946, 1950–1, 1953 and 1958. In these exhibitions, reasonably priced works were offered for sale against a background of contemporary furnishings and designs.

If the impact of staging and focused lighting to highlight the formal purification and surface qualities of abstract sculpture in both the modern gallery and the contemporary home was recognised, the importance of colour as 'a decorative factor and viewed in its psychological aspect' was also keenly exploited. *Decoration* in January 1936 advised its readers that 'To-day colours must perform a dual function: they must be varied and interesting as decorations, but they must at the same time be so handled as not to intrude themselves on nerves worried by the speed of modern living conditions.'[15] Emerging concurrently with new ideas about the psychological impact of the gallery design and display upon aesthetic contemplation and the need to produce a sympathetic environment within which the modernist sculpture could 'speak' without interference from other works, the interior space for sculpture became increasingly all-white, bleached of bright colour and divested of conflicting ornamental patterns. The 1936 *Abstract and Concrete* show at the Lefevre Gallery and the *Constructive Art* show at the London Gallery in 1937 convincingly demonstrated how carefully choreographed display using modern lighting could dramatise aesthetic effects. It could also reinforce the sense of a coherent movement developing in Britain as part of a common international commitment to the unification of art, design and architecture.

In his contribution to *Circle: An International Survey of Constructive Art* (1937), in which works by Hepworth, Gabo, Moore and Holding were illustrated, Lewis Mumford addressed what he saw as the responsibility of the museum to protect the art object from 'the purposeless congestion and complete intellectual bewilderment' of the modern metropolis.[16] According to the American sociologist, contemporary steel-framed architecture, glass and synthetic building materials were highly appropriate to the frequently changing interior arrangements that the modern museum, like the modern home, demanded. Citing Mies van der Rohe and Clarence Stein as exemplars of this updated approach, he argued that the art museum required 'a flexible interior … encased in glass … in which the internal arrangements can be completely recast by a flexible system of partitions'. For Mumford, abstract art, like modern architectural styles and design materials, constituted 'ideal symbols of this new attitude towards life'. What was required from the art professional was the creation of an ideal environment that would be responsive to art's aesthetic needs and within which 'the art object [could be detached] from both its long-dead past and from its disruptive turbulent present'.[17] Reiterating modernist curatorial beliefs, Mumford believed that 'pure' art demanded such conditions of display since what it connoted was not 'what it carries over from the past' but 'what it signifies against the background of our own experience'. Thinking about the need to distance abstract art from its social context, he concluded that:

> Indeed the more complete the detachment, the more effectively we can screen a symbol from what it meant to another generation, the more specific and final is our own response. For a work of art is not a monument: if it has life at all, it exists as a contemporary fact: a museum properly designed, with ample facilities for storage and preservation as well as for show, serves to enlarge the contemporary experience.[18]

By interrogating naturalistic sculpture's spatial conventions and its modes of display, abstraction had enlarged sculpture's traditional formal vocabularies (and responsibilities) beyond figuration, monumentality and commemoration. Abstract art's supporters also zealously promoted a radical self-consciousness about how visual signification

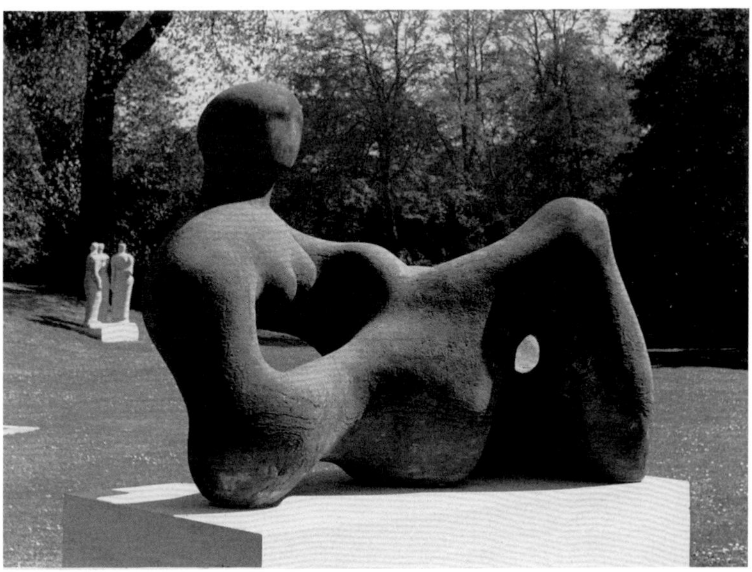

5 Henry Moore, 'Recumbent Figure', 1938

6 Photograph of Jacob Epstein's 'Lazarus' in Battersea Park, 1951

7 Barbara Hepworth, 'Maquette for Waterloo Bridge', 1947

operated and the terms within which it might be theorised. More alert to the expressive powers of pure form as exemplified by Hepworth's 'Single Form' (1937), the sculptural object assumed (and was accredited with) a self-sufficiency that endowed it with a compelling primeval and mythic immediacy.[19] Claims for the universality of abstraction across cultures focused debates about the integrity of abstract sculpture on geometricisation with its perceived indebtedness to totemic form and to 'primitive' precedents. Jacques Lipchitz's bronze 'Figure' (1926–30), when shown at the Institute of Contemporary Arts' *40,000 Years of Modern Art* (1948–9) held in the Academy Cinema basement, clearly invoked this correspondence between the 'primitive' and the 'modern'. Lipchitz's work also demonstrated in perhaps an unexpected way the ability of abstract art to generate controversy. When it was unveiled to unsuspecting London shoppers in Oxford Street to publicise the exhibition and to garner popular opinion on abstract art, 'Figure' provoked strong, mostly derisory, reactions.[20]

Outside the gallery, conditions favoured more flexible and informal interactive protocols. Artists keenly exploited sculpture's distinctive spatial and kinaesthetic potentialities, especially when the sculptured object was relocated within an open air or parkland setting. Jacob Epstein's William Henry Hudson memorial (1925), when encountered in the bird sanctuary on a stroll through Hyde Park, offered a charged moment of viewing that was less securely mediated by those aesthetic conventions deployed within the museum space. Rima, the dryad-heroine of Hudson's best-selling adventure story *Green Mansions: A Romance of the Tropical Forest* (1904), was depicted in a daring mixture of 'primitive' and classical styles; the model for Rima was a well-known cabaret performer and notorious *femme-fatale* Dolores whom the sculptor had met in 1912.[21] Unveiled on 19 May 1925 to public outrage, the female figure's misshapen features were seen by its detractors to intimate Epstein's political anarchism and to reflect his 'alien' Jewish identity. By extension, the crude stylisation of the

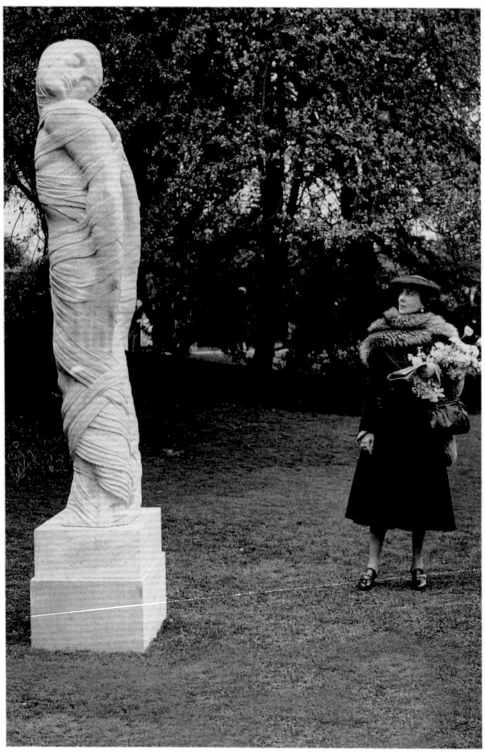

woman's face and arms and the geometric deformity of the bird's wings recast European femininity and British wildlife in a distinctly unfamiliar, unnatural way, one that for many contemporaries carried dubious moral and sexual innuendos.[22]

Recognising that sculpture was ideally suited to being encountered communally within a landscape setting that informed and inflected its interpretation, Moore was commissioned by the émigré Russian architect Serge Chermayeff to provide a reclining figure for his modernist Bentley Wood villa in Halland (1935–8). Moore produced his 'Recumbent Figure' (1938; Fig. 5), aware that it acted as 'a mediator between the modern house and the ageless land', with the horizontal figure echoing both the low-lying design of the timber-framed, cedar-clad house and the gentle rolling forms of the South Downs seen through and around the durable, Green Hornton stone figure.[23] Later Moore recalled how the reclining female form established and marked out a 'far seeing gaze': one that the spectator on the garden terrace could adopt and replicate by looking 'out across a great sweep of the Downs' with their 'gaze gathering in the horizon'.[24]

By the time of the London County Council series of outdoor sculpture exhibitions (in Battersea Park in 1948 and 1951, and in Holland Park in 1954) and the Kelvingrove Park, Glasgow *Sculpture in the Open Air* show (June–September 1949), the casual encounter has become carefully choreographed to such an extent that some critics lamented modern sculpture being 'dotted about' in 'highly artificial conditions'. As the photograph of Epstein's 'Lazarus' (1947–8; Fig. 6) demonstrates,

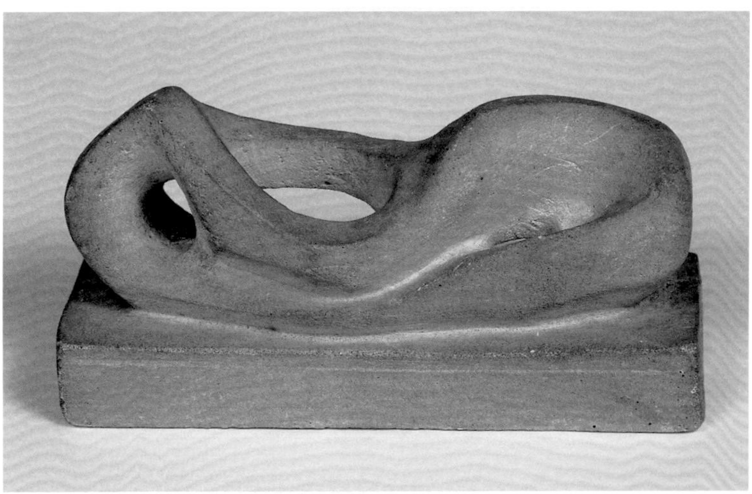

the spectator with guide in hand respectfully confronts the spectre of Lazarus emerging from his swathing bands in Battersea Park in 1951. Whilst some critics argued that open-air exhibitions reduced sculpture to a form of ornamental landscape gardening and made it look absurd, guide-lecturers freely available on site attempted to offer informative commentaries and to explain modern art in terms that were accessible to 'the ordinary citizen and the ratepayer'.[25]

As modern sculpture forced a rethinking of the material restrictions that such a public function demanded, it also interrogated the formalised interrelationship of decorative sculpture to its support and to its architectural surroundings. Ambitious schemes such as Frank Pick's new stations for the London Underground system, like Charles Holden's Underground Railways Head Offices in St James' (1928–9), saw sculpture in an unprecedented way as a visible and integral part of innovative urban redevelopment.[26] As Holden maintained, a respect for the sculptor's conception and towards his or her chosen material signalled an intellectual integrity and honesty to material ethos that was remarkably modern in attitude: 'I like sculpture to look like stone and, having a great respect for stone, I hate to see it decimated into the semblance of a plaster cast.'[27] Commissioning an impressive mix of senior (Eric Gill and Epstein) and younger artists (Eric Aumonier, A. H. Gerrard, Moore, F. Rabinovitch and Allan Wyon) to complete the sculptural programme on the head offices, the works were carved in relief directly into the Portland stone. With the exception of Epstein, who produced monumental figures of 'Day' and 'Night' for the ground floor entrances, the others were commissioned to carve flying figures symbolising the four winds that would be located on the seventh storey in the final building. Although generating lengthy press criticism (especially of Epstein's carvings), the Underground headquarters achieved the rare distinction of integrating modernist aspirations within a prominent monumental scheme. As James Bone applauded in the *Manchester Guardian*, the project 'succeeded in making people look at and even think about architectural sculpture … [since] it commands our attention and makes us think about the nature of sculpture'.[28]

Similar aspirations for the integration of public sculpture within urban redevelopment occurred in the post-World War II period. The construction of the new Waterloo Bridge in London by Giles Gilbert Scott from 1937 to 1942 envisaged that 'sculptors of high repute' – Frank Dobson, Epstein, Hepworth, Eric Kennington, Moore and Sir Charles Wheeler – would submit figure-group models for the Portland-stone-faced bridge. Although the works were never completed, the brief

8 Gjon Mili, photograph of Henry Moore in studio making a light drawing with 'Family Group', *c.*1949

from the London County Council was that they should have 'a simple and compact outline with a low horizontal sculptural treatment. The silhouette, as seen from a distance, should form part of the lines of the bridge's design.'[29] Hepworth submitted three drawings and a maquette (Fig. 7). As part of her vigorous commitment to the key role that sculpture would have in relation to postwar social and cultural regeneration, Hepworth's hollowed and undulating horizontal form offers the spectator (the passing pedestrian when located on the bridge, or the river-borne traveller when viewed from the Thames below) an unexpected and intriguing 'animated instability'. As Alex Potts has observed about a similar wood-carving, 'Pendour' (1947–8): 'the animation is much more kinaesthetic, and located in the continually shifting apprehensions of the work to be had as one circulates around it and as hollows and cuts come in and out of view'.[30] This kinaesthesia, like the correspondence of sculptural form to river setting and of sculpture to modern architecture, underlined the urgent social responsibility that Hepworth, like many of her contemporaries, felt about the place that modern sculpture had in the reconstruction of Britain's bomb-damaged cities.

The desire to stage sculpture in ways that would dramatise, even defamiliarise, earlier conventions of sculptural display shaped new and spectacular group exhibitionary practices. Incorporating strange objects and 'primitive' forms in striking juxtapositions with contemporary sculpture that often evoked explicit sexualised associations, the 1936 London *International Surrealist Exhibition* and the *Surrealist Objects and Poems* show at the London Gallery in 1937 achieved highly elaborate modes of interplay between artwork and viewer.[31] Whether it was a sudden encounter with 'primitive' object, 'where human attributes are implied, rather than openly confessed'[32] (exemplified by F. E. McWilliam's 'Bending Figure', 1935), or contemplating evocative found objects set against a photo-collage eliciting a Freudian scenario by association (such as Paul Nash's 'Only Egg', 1937), this psychoanalytically charged meeting was one in

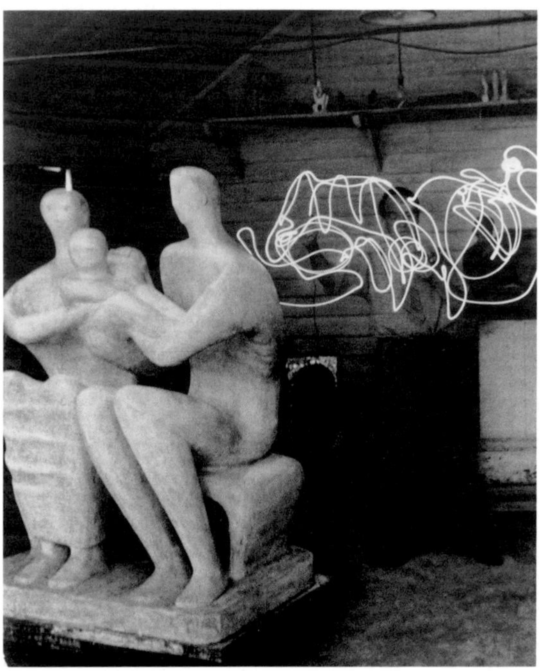

which the subversive possibilities and erotic potentialities of the sculptural imagination freed from late 19th-century contextual constraints were celebrated.

In January 1953, for the first time, television cameras went into the Tate Gallery and amongst the artworks broadcast to avid British audiences was Moore's 1938 'Recumbent Figure'. From Chermayeff's terrace overlooking the South Downs, it had been bought by the Contemporary Art Society in 1939 and presented to the gallery. Subsequently lent to a trade fair in New York, the sculpture had spent the years between 1939 and 1945 in the courtyard of the recently redesigned Museum of Modern Art in New York. Repatriated after the end of the war and then displayed at the first Battersea open-air sculpture exhibition in 1948, Moore's work had undertaken a European tour in 1949–50 that included being exhibited to acclaim in Hamburg and Düsseldorf, which were then British-occupied territories. In the television programme, the reclining female form was shown installed in the recently reopened national collection of British art. Through the technological advances of the mass media, more viewers than ever before would see Moore's work in a way that could not have been anticipated when it was created only fifteen years earlier. Television would also encourage sculptors like Moore, captured in Gjon Mili's 1949 photograph of him making a light drawing with his 'Family Group' (Fig. 8), to be alert to and to exploit the potentialities that the medium held for self-promotion and for forging artistic celebrity. Mirroring the dramatic impact that photography had had in the popular imagination, television similarly had the capacity to go behind the scenes and to anchor the aesthetic integrity of the artwork to the presence of the maker in that unique site of creation: the sculptor's studio.[33] Such startling and dynamic televisual modes of seeing would generate new and spectacular ways of displaying modern sculpture.[34] Television would also carry far-reaching implications for how the encounter with freestanding, three-dimensional form might be choreographed afresh and how the phenomenology of viewing modern sculpture might be understood and accounted for.

Andrew Stephenson

Notes

1 A. Jones and A. Stephenson, *Performing the Body/Performing the Text*, London, Routledge, 1999, pp. 2–3.

2 For the minimum flat, see Hayward Gallery, *Thirties: British Art and Design before the War*, London, Arts Council of Great Britain, 1979–80, pp. 267–8.

3 H. Read, *Henry Moore: Sculptor*, London, Zwemmer, 1934, p. 7.

4 For the popularisation of minimalist decoration, see D. S. Ryan, *The Ideal Home Through the 20th Century*, London, Hazar Publishing, 1997, pp. 70–2.

5 D. Todd and R. Mortimer, *The New Interior Decoration: An Introduction to its Principles and International Survey of its Methods*, London, B. T. Batsford, 1929, pp. 12–13.

6 Unidentified review in *Vogue*, 7 March 1934, contained in the Mayor Gallery Press Cutting Albums, Tate Archive, London (TAM9C).

7 See J. Peto and D. Loveday (eds), *Modern Britain 1929–39*, London, Design Museum, 1999, pp. 37–9, 45–6, 89–94.

8 'The Mayor Gallery', *The Daily Mail*, 13 April 1933, Mayor Gallery Press Cutting Albums, Tate Archive, London (TAM7B).

9 P. G. Konody, 'Gayest Art Show: Last Word in Modernism', *The Daily Mail*, 20 April 1933, Mayor Gallery Press Cutting Albums, Tate Archive, London (TAM7B).

10 'London Scene', *Vogue*, June 1933 and 'The Mayor Gallery', *Harper's Bazaar*, June 1933, Mayor Gallery Press Cutting Albums, Tate Archive, London (TAM7B).

11 A. Bertram, 'Selling Pictures: An Organisation and a Gallery', *Design for Today*, May 1934, p. 160, Mayor Gallery Press Cutting Albums, Tate Archive, London (TAM7B).

12 'Selfridge's West End Roof Garden exhibition', *Nottingham Journal and Express*, 31 May 1930, press cutting contained in London Group Papers, Mansard Gallery, Tate Archive, London.

13 R. Hinks, 'Sensible Preface', *The Times*, 10 October 1932, press cutting contained in London Group Papers, Mansard Gallery, Tate Archive, London.

14 See J. Beckett, 'Circle: The theory and patronage of constructive art in the thirties', in J. Lewison (ed.), *Circle: Constructive Art in Britain 1934–40*, Cambridge, Kettle's Yard Gallery, 1982, pp. 11–19.

15 'Book Reviews: "Colour in Modern Interiors"', *Decoration*, January 1936, p. 52.

16 L. Mumford, 'The death of the monument', in J. L. Martin, B. Nicholson and N. Gabo (eds), *Circle: International Survey of Constructive Art*, London, Faber and Faber, 1937, p. 268.

17 Ibid., pp. 266–7.

18 Ibid., p. 267.

19 See M. Gale and C. Stephens, *Barbara Hepworth: Works in the Tate Collection and the Barbara Hepworth Museum St Ives*, London, Tate Publishing, 2001, p. 69.

20 Press responses are discussed in B. Taylor, *Art for the Nation: Exhibitions and the London Public 1747–2001*, Manchester, Manchester University Press, 1999, pp. 195, 198.

21 T. Friedman, *The Hyde Park Atrocity: Epstein's Rima – Creation and Controversy*, Leeds, Henry Moore Centre for the Study of Sculpture and Leeds City Art Galleries, 1988, pp. 15, 21–3.

22 Ibid., pp. 33–7.

23 Moore quoted in P. Curtis, *Sculpture 1900–1945: After Rodin*, Oxford, Oxford University Press, 1999, p. 233.

24 Moore quoted in P. James, *Henry Moore on Sculpture*, London, McDonald, 1966, p. 99.

25 Letter from Assistant Clerk to London County Council to Eric Newton, 14 January 1948 quoted in Taylor, *Art for the Nation: Exhibitions and the London Public 1747–2001*, p. 192.

26 See R. Cork's discussion of 'Overhead sculpture for the Underground railway', in R. Cork, *Art Beyond the Gallery in Early 20th Century England*, New Haven, CT, and London, Yale University Press, 1985, pp. 249–96.

27 Holden, unpublished notes, n.d., preserved in the archives of Adams, Holden and Pearson, London, quoted in Cork, *Art Beyond the Gallery in Early 20th Century England*, p. 256.

28 *Manchester Guardian*, 20 July 1929 quoted in Cork, *Art Beyond the Gallery in Early 20th Century England*, p. 293.

29 London Metropolitan Archive LCC/MIN/214, p. 84, quoted in Gale and Stephens, *Barbara Hepworth: Works in the Tate Collection and the Barbara Hepworth Museum St Ives*, p. 104.

30 A. Potts, *The Sculptural Imagination: Figurative, Modernist, Minimalist*, New Haven, CT, and London, Yale University Press, 2000, p. 152.

31 For installation photographs of the *International Surrealist* exhibition, see A. Robertson, M. Remy, M. Gooding and T. Friedman, *Angels of Anarchy and Machines for Making Clouds: Surrealism in Britain in the Thirties*, Leeds, Leeds City Art Galleries, 1986, pp. 208–12. For discussion of the *Surrealist Objects and Poems* exhibition, see M. Remy, *Surrealism in Britain*, Aldershot, Lund Humphries, 1999, pp. 112–20.

32 P. Nash, 'F. E. McWilliam', *London Bulletin*, 1 March 1939, no. 11.

33 See J. Wood, *Close Encounters: The Sculptor's Studio in the Age of the Camera*, Leeds, Henry Moore Institute, 2001, pp. 8–27.

34 For an analysis of the impact of television upon attention, see J. Crary, 'Spectacle, attention, counter-memory', *October*, Fall 1989, no. 50, pp. 97–107.

'Modern sculpture ... is an aspect and a symbol of the living creative culture of our day.' R. H. Wilenski, 1932[1]

'Culture was everywhere but you could barely afford it.' John Baker, referring to 1937, the year he founded the Readers' Union.[2]

Between 1925 and 1950 the relationship between contemporary sculpture and its British viewers was transformed at every level by the published material through which critical exegesis and photographic reproduction were mediated. While undoubtedly true, for example, that 'more than any other work of the interwar years, "Rima" dictated public perceptions about the avant-garde', it was however largely cartoons and articles about the sculpture that provoked and constructed a hostile reaction to Jacob Epstein's memorial to W. H. Hudson from the moment it was unveiled in 1925.[3] The same year a photographically illustrated volume on Epstein's work appeared in the series on contemporary British artists published by Ernest Benn in which the author of the introductory essay remarked: 'We do not habitually oppose sculpture – we ignore it. ... The difference between the sculpture room at the Royal Academy – almost the only exhibition in London, be it said, where sculpture can now be seen, and an exhibition of Epstein's work is enormous.'[4] This is to ignore two of the most publicly visible forms of new work – war memorials and architectural decoration – but 'H. W.' does justifiably highlight the reason why public response veered between apathy and outrage: contemporary sculpture of all other kinds was simply not that easy to see.

In 1921, ten years after acquiring its royal title, the Royal Society of British Sculptors (RBS) had produced an official record of members' work, and in his foreword A. L. Baldry lamented that the aim of becoming an exhibiting society had not yet been realised: 'It is more or less [as] a substitute for an exhibition that this book has been planned.'[5] Priced at 7/6d, for years the standard cost of a well-illustrated art book, no follow-up appeared until 1939, when an edition limited to 550 copies and published by *Country Life* referred to its predecessor as 'a book of reproductions'.[6] While the RBS books were produced at the instigation of sculptors to raise their status, and to give sculpture much-needed public exposure in lieu of exhibitions, the photographs themselves suggested a particular reading that stemmed from a much earlier tradition.

Viewing sculpture as a succession of silhouettes had been reinforced by styles of photographic reproduction since the mid-19th century when the Florentine firm of Alinari first cornered the market for images of art and architecture. Buildings and relief sculptures were usually photographed from close up and directly in front, and sculpture in the round tended to be strongly lit and placed against a blank background of contrasting tone which emphasised overall shape and edge.[7] Alinari's images were popular with museums and book publishers not only because of their dramatic quality, but also because they were easily ordered from catalogues and cheap. In the period 1925 to 1939, changes in the way sculpture was reproduced in illustrated books played a particularly important part in the restructuring of ideas about how to approach sculpture itself.

Modern Architectural Sculpture, published in 1930 by the Architectural Press in a limited edition, was lavishly illustrated and widely distributed. Subscribers included public libraries; bookshops such as Foyles, Bumpus and Zwemmer's; art colleges; the Boots Booklovers' Library; and institutions as far afield as Sydney, Toronto, Tokyo, Lahore and Cairo. The aesthetic of the photograph, however, sometimes works against the sculptor's intention, as in the case of Epstein's 'Night' and 'Day' on the facade of the London Underground building at St James'. Epstein later remarked that the negative critical reception really began when, without his authorisation, these works were photographed separately, divorced from their context, and at eye level, whereas they were meant to be seen from below, at the exact height at which they were placed.[8]

As sculptors increasingly took photographs of their own work or exerted control over how their sculpture should be reproduced, so three-dimensionality, site and haptic rather than optic qualities came to the fore. So too did alternative subjects of sculptural photographs: the artist was increasingly shown in his or her studio engaged in the process of making, in a relationship with the object and the viewer.[9]

Forty London Statues and Public Monuments by Tancred Borenius, published by Methuen in 1926, provides an illuminating contrast to 'the book as exhibition'. Photographs of sculpture in situ were specially commissioned from E. O. Hoppé, whose atmospheric images, though selective in viewpoint, are unusual in that context prevails over content: London is a wintry city of white skies and bare trees, wet streets and tall buildings almost blotted out by fine rain. None the less Borenius criticises the Royal Artillery Memorial memorial at Hyde Park Corner by Charles Sargeant Jagger according to traditional criteria: 'The general silhouette, from whatever angle it is viewed, has no real beauty of rhythm.'[10] Borenius concludes with what, for the time, was a controversial assessment of 'Rima' which would, he believed, eventually be recognised as a performance not of power but of taste and skill.

While the press might engineer a *succès de scandale*, it was for book publishers to generate interest that was more informed and sustained. Apart from biographies, an average of thirty new titles on sculpture were published in each five-year period between 1926 and 1941, of which just under a third were devoted to the modern period.[11] Wartime shortages of manpower, machinery and, above all, paper meant that far fewer were published in the early 1940s, but more surprisingly, not a single title on modern sculpture appeared in the early 1950s. By then more significant than the quantity of books on sculpture was the unprecedented number of new readers.

To Geoffrey Faber who, in the late 1920s, wished to associate his new firm with the artistic as well as the literary avant-garde, a book on Epstein, preferably written by the artist himself, seemed an obvious choice. Although his approach did not succeed and Epstein's conversations with Arnold L. Haskell were published by Heinemann in 1931, one of 'Rima''s few supporters, the *Evening Standard* critic R. H. Wilenski, did at this period become a Faber author.[12] *The Modern Movement in Art* was first published in 1927 and appeared in a cheaper edition in 1935, specifying on the dust jacket that four large impressions had been sold since its first publication, and in those seven years it had become a standard work.[13] The flyleaf bears a generous and revealing tribute from the author: 'This book is dedicated to Geoffrey Faber who invited me to write it and has helped me enormously by criticizing the first drafts.'

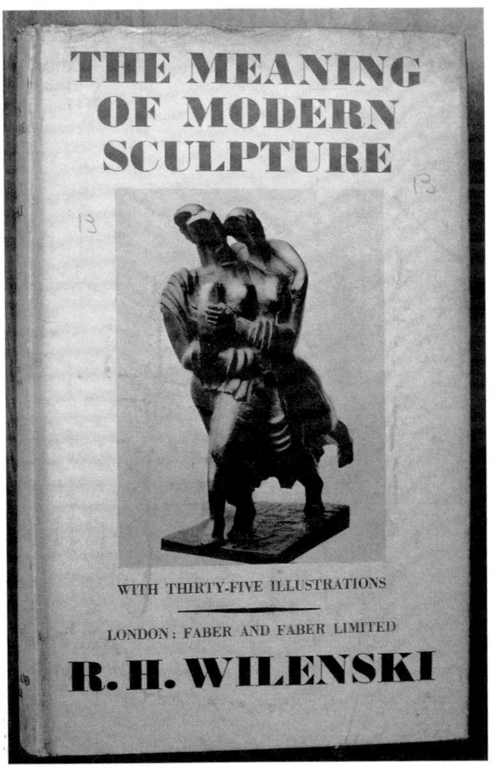

1 Wilenski, *The Meaning of Modern Sculpture* (1932), front cover

In 1932 Faber published another book by Wilenski, *The Meaning of Modern Sculpture*, which had begun as a lecture at the Victoria & Albert Museum (Fig. 1). As the author explained to his publisher: 'It is really two books in one – an attack on the Greek sculpture camp and a book on the modern experiments. It is also really a book on Epstein!'[14] The Faber catalogue for autumn 1932 plays up the polarisiation of critical views: 'This challenging book ... not only defines the artistic creed of the modern sculptors and the influences which have formed it, but also attacks the methods of archaeologists and historians of Greek sculpture, whom Mr Wilenski describes as "professional propagandists for the reputations of certain sculptors in ancient Greece, whose works no longer exist."'[15]

In the early 1930s a number of popular surveys and critical introductions were published to take account of the widely observed increase both in sculptural activity and in public interest. Among them were Eric Underwood's *A Short History of English Sculpture*, published by Faber in 1933, and Stanley Casson's *Some Modern Sculptors* and *Twentieth-Century Sculptors*, both published by Oxford University Press. Casson, like Borenius, deplored 'the horrible war memorials that deface so many of the towns and villages of Europe'.[16] Their proliferation had two contrasting results: while to many critics they represented all that was wrong with contemporary sculpture, they did alert even people living far from cities to the activity of modern sculptors. An archaeologist specialising in Ancient Greece, Casson was antipathetic to sculpture as personal expression, particularly the work of Auguste Rodin, and he criticised Epstein for a lack of truth to materials in that he made bronze look like metallic clay. Rather, he favoured work that reflected the spirit of a race or an age and found these qualities in carvings by Ivan Meštrović, whose 'Angel' at Cavtat was chosen for the frontispiece.[17] Internal correspondence between colleagues at OUP revealed that they had doubled the projected number of plates to thiry-two, arguing: 'I think the public very much like pictures in a book of this sort, and I don't see why we shouldn't sell a great many copies of such a book at 7/6.'[18]

Twentieth-Century Sculptors of 1930 was published in reponse to demand for the first book and to introduce more recent developments.[19] Some years later in an internal memo, the publisher was moved to exclaim:

> I cannot look at the accounts of these two books without shame. Nevertheless, though the printing was bad, or rather the price was right but the production was too lavish, the books have actually *sold* well for such a subject, it seems to me, and I think that it might well be worth while to use the magnificent series of blocks to make a new picture book, with a very short new text'.[20]

Such 'picture books' were steady but not large sellers, and in 1941 Casson's two volumes were still selling at the rate of about 25 a year.[21]

The Studio also published a number of important books about sculpture in the 1930s and 1940s, notably Jagger's *Modelling and Sculpture in the Making* of 1933. Photographs such as 'Pointing Machine in Position' (showing the development of his sculpted portrait 'Shackleton') are as much about the potential of photography as they are revelatory of the sculptural process. The shadow of the sculptor is used to create an image that seems to show a larger and more ghostly figure sculpting Jagger himself. Other images, however, are reused from previous publications, such as Bourdelle's 'Vierge d'Alsace' which had already appeared in *Some Modern Sculptors.* Casson was a regular contributor to *The Studio* magazine for which, in 1939, he supplied the commentary in a special spring number devoted to *Sculpture of Today.*[22] While discussing sculpture primarily as architectural decoration or as a design for open public space, Casson also noted the opportunities offered sculptors by interior designers and manufacturers.[23] To further illustrate his belief in the importance of truth to materials, he selected four images of bronze heads, three of which still looked as if made of clay, and one of which was a portrait of Hitler entitled 'The Leader', by Arno Bleker (Breker, *sic*).

Two books were published in the mid-1930s which, though compiled or written by one individual, allowed artists to speak for themselves, verbally and visually. Herbert Maryon's international survey *Modern Sculpture: Its Methods and Ideals*, published by Pitman in 1933 with 354 photographs, was presented as innovative in that modern sculpture was discussed from the sculptor's viewpoint, while *Unit One: The Modern Movement in English Architecture, Painting and Sculpture*, edited by Herbert Read and published in 1934, included what became one of Moore's best-known statements: 'Complete sculptural expression is form in its full spatial reality.'[24] To show that sculpture in the round had no two points of view the same, that it was essentially asymmetrical and organic, a single two-dimensional image could not suffice, and Moore later insisted on the reproduction of at least three or four views of each sculpture.[25]

Just as artists and critics sought to uphold a particular tradition, attitude to modernism, or set of aesthetic values, so publishers tried to hold on to their most successful writers, and at the same time to establish in the mind of the public a specific look to their books whose target audience was designated by price, design and advertising. The de luxe Architectural Press book *Modern Architectural Sculpture* sold by subscription, while OUP and *The Studio* in the late 1920s and 1930s published moderately priced books for the intelligentsia, and Geoffrey Faber identified his firm with the avant-garde. In this context it is important not to forget the role of literary advisers, whose influence was exerted long before that of the reviewer: a 'hardened professional reader' such as Herbert Read had the power to recommend acceptance or rejection of a manuscript, and might perform the same service for several different firms.[26]

Analysis of empirical data such as when a book was published, the size of its print run, sales and distribution, number and frequency of new editions, and length of time it stays in print all help build a picture of the book-buying public, but the impact of a book is not necessarily in direct proportion to the number of readers who own a copy. Impecunious artists and students borrowed or browsed: they could not always afford to buy. Moore, for example, acknowledged his formative influences to have been not only his visits to the British Museum, but also well-illustrated books – on sculpture from Peru, China and Ancient Egypt – and the continental publications such as *Minotaure* that he saw on his frequent and regular visits to Zwemmer's bookshop in the Charing Cross Road.[27]

When no one else was willing, it was Anton Zwemmer who undertook to publish Read's first book on Moore.[28] Design and printing of this slim volume was undertaken by Percy Lund, Humphries and Co. Ltd, thus beginning a long association with the sculptor and his work which continues to this day. Accompanying thirty-six plates showing Moore's sculpture and drawings, Read's 'appreciation' earned him £20, Moore himself contributing £30 from the sale of a sculpture to the cost of publication. At 1,500 copies, the print run was relatively small, but sales were even smaller: only twenty were sold in the first few years, and the bulk of the edition later went to Japan.[29] The *Yorkshire Post* pointed out that 'Since Henry Moore does not exhibit often, a book like this is doubly valuable, for the exceptionally fine photographs give a clear idea of the power and scope of his art.'[30] This first monograph on Moore was mainly admired for its production values and appearance, reflecting the widely held view that art books were primarily to admire and consult; they were exhibition substitutes not yet aimed at a mass market.

Although the significance of pre-war publishing cannot be measured exclusively in quantitative terms, new developments in targeting a mass readership brought about increases in scale that led to a wholly new phenomenon: mass purchase of books on art. In 1935 Allen Lane created Penguin to sell cheap reprints of contemporary fiction which were initially priced at 6d, and distributed in Woolworths. Two years later, the Readers' Union began to issue re-editions of texts selected from the lists of sixty-four publishers, including Heinemann, Faber and OUP. Offering a wide range of contemporary fact and fiction for 2/6d a month, the book club acquired a membership of nearly 50,000 and sold over seven million books.[31] In total it published 417 volumes, many of them illustrated and all of them well and distinctively designed, including, for example, texts by Read and Casson, and in 1942 Epstein's *Let There Be Sculpture*, first published by Michael Joseph in 1940.

The first three Phaidon Press books to be published in England appeared in 1938 and were praised both for the quality of their photographic reproductions and their modest price.[32] Although not devoted to modern sculpture, Phaidon books were influential in drawing attention to qualities of texture and handling of material through the way in which sculpture was photographed, notably by Ilse Schneider-Lengyel for the volumes on *Rodin* and *The Sculptures of Michelangelo* (both published in 1939), and *Donatello* (1941). The layout, equally influential, was designed by Ludwig Goldscheider, who often cropped images to focus on a particular detail.

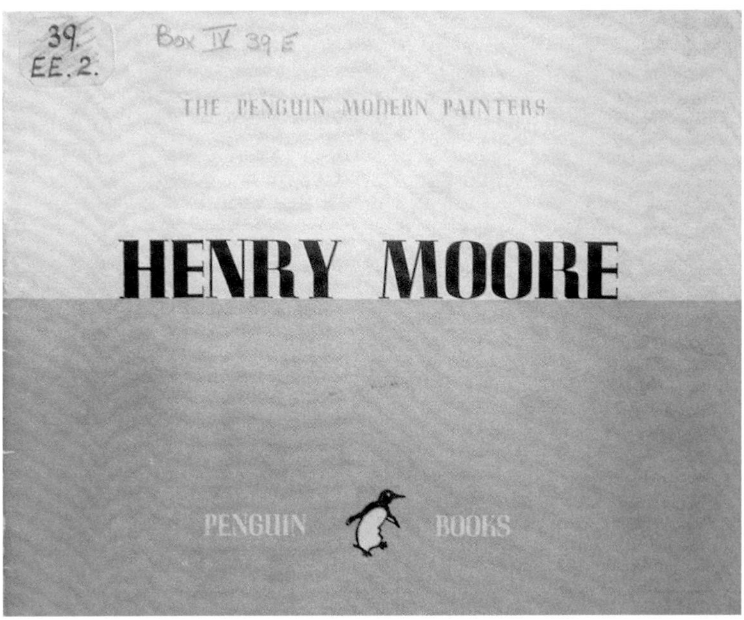

2 Grigson, *Henry Moore* (1943), front cover

3 Grigson, *Henry Moore* (1943), inside pages (double page spread)

Throughout World War II, paper was in extremely short supply and had to be rationed, but as the quotas represented a proportion of what each firm had used in 1938, and this had been a very successful year for Penguin, Allen Lane used his generous allocation to launch a number of different series that looked to a postwar future, among them 'Penguin Modern Painters' (Fig. 2). In July 1942 Kenneth Clark, as series editor, issued the names of eight authors and nine 'painters' (including Henry Moore, first on the list) to whom contracts should immediately be sent. Although dated 1943, the volume devoted to Moore was published with three others in the series in April 1944, and sold for 2/6d. A slim paperback, it contained no reproductions of sculpture, only thirty-two drawings, sixteen of which were in colour (Fig. 3). Each of the first four titles was subsequently reprinted, with an additional 15,000 for *Henry Moore*, so that of all the volumes published up to the end of 1948 it had the largest print run: over 56,000, sales by then having reached 48,000.[33]

Also in 1944, the first major monograph on Henry Moore, introduced by Herbert Read with copious illustrations of both drawings and sculpture, was co-published by Percy Lund, Humphries and Anton Zwemmer. This book was significant for Moore in establishing him as a serious artist, just as the publication of his drawings in Penguin had endeared him to the general public far more effectively than earlier reproductions of his sculpture alone.

Between 1925 and 1950 public awareness of, and pride in, British sculpture grew markedly, a development which has been only partially accounted for in the major surveys that have identified key promotional institutions and advocates, explored the language and form of sculpture

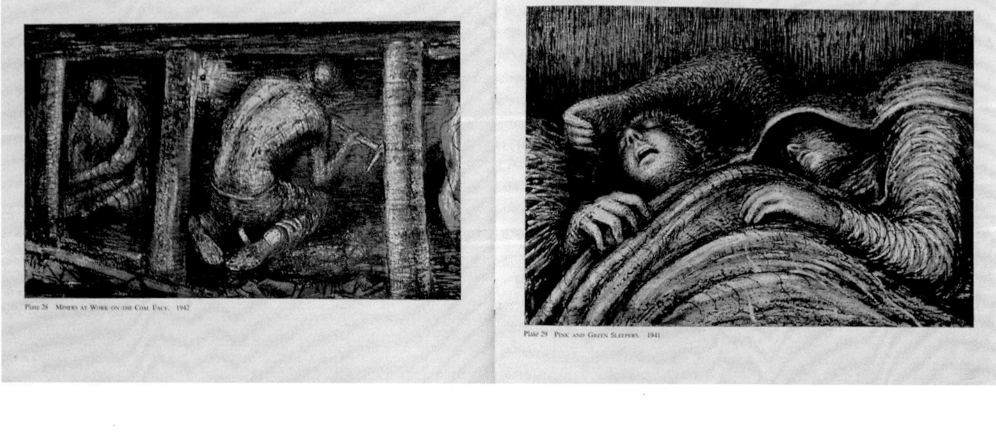

itself, or showed sculpture occupying an extended spatial environment.[34] It was a change that had as much to do with a revolution in communication as with the dominance of a few individual artists such as Epstein or Moore, and prolific critics such as Casson, Wilenski and Read. Books originated from a variety of sources: BBC radio broadcasts written up in the *Listener*; public lectures at the Victoria & Albert Museum; ideas that emanated from proselytising publishers for the modern movement such as Geoffrey Faber, or for a mass market as imagined by Allen Lane or the founders of the Phaidon Press and the Readers' Union.

From intuitions that there might exist a culture-hungry mass public to the business and design decisions that succeeded in identifying a market and attracting purchasers in unprecedented numbers, relationships between publisher and reader, between sculpture and its reproduction, and ultimately between object and viewer, altered in ways that profoundly affected the individual reception and public place of sculpture in contemporary national life. Cumulatively, publications on sculpture played a major role in repositioning sculpture as a significant form of contemporary culture and establishing a new relationship between the public and sculpture independent of function or architectural support. It was not just critical commentaries and theoretical texts that helped bring about this change, but the way in which photographs of sculpture were taken, selected and circulated, and above all, those structural innovations in publishing that affected the sales and distribution of the books in which they played a vital part. With proof that a mass market for culture did indeed exist, for the first time books about sculpture and sculptors sold in their tens of thousands, and helped create a wholly different context for public attitudes in the 1950s.

Valerie Holman

Notes

Material cited in the text and referred to in footnotes 18, 20 and 21 is reprinted by permission of the Secretary to the Delegates of Oxford University Press. The author would also like to thank Faber and Faber and Penguin for permission to cite material in this essay which is drawn from their archives.

1 R. H. Wilenski, *The Meaning of Modern Sculpture*, London, Faber and Faber, 1932, p. xvii.

2 J. Baker, *Low Cost of Bookloving: An Account of the First Twenty-One Years of the Readers' Union*, London, Readers' Union, 1958, p. 7.

3 T. Friedman, 'The Hyde Park atrocity: Epstein's "Rima" – creation and controversy', Leeds, Henry Moore Centre for the Study of Sculpture and Leeds City Art Galleries, 1988, p. 43.

4 'H. W.' (Hubert Wellington), *Jacob Epstein*, series on Contemporary British Artists edited by Albert Rutherston, London, Ernest Benn, 1925, p. 7.

5 A. L. Baldry, *Modern British Sculpture: An Official Record of Some of the Works by Members of the Royal Society of British Sculptors*, London, Academy Architecture, 1922, n.p.

6 7/6d remained something of a benchmark and an indication to the prospective purchaser of what he could expect: it was, for example, the price at which Phaidon launched their books in England a decade later.

7 See V. Holman, '"Still a makeshift"? Changing representations of the Renaissance in twentieth-century art books', in R. Palmer and T. Frangenberg (eds), *The Rise of the Image: Essays on the History of the Illustrated Art Book*, London and Vermont, Ashgate, 2003.

8 *The Sculptor Speaks: Jacob Epstein to Arnold L. Haskell – A Series of Conversations on Art*, London, William Heinemann, 1931.

9 See J. Wood, *Close Encounters: The Sculptor's Studio in the Age of the Camera*, Leeds, Henry Moore Institute, 2001.

10 T. Borenius, *Forty London Statues and Public Monuments*, London, Methuen, 1926, p. 30.

11 Information from J. D. Stewart (ed.), *The English Catalogue of Books (Books issued in the UK)*, reprinted with the permission of The Publisher's Circular Ltd, London, by Kraus Reprint Corporation, Millwood, New York, 1979. Volume XII, for example, covers the five-year period January 1926 to December 1930.

12 In total Faber and Faber published nearly forty books by R. H. Wilenski.

13 In the next thirty years *The Modern Movement in Art* went through four editions.

14 Faber and Faber Archives, R. H. Wilenski to Richard de la Mare, 1.6.1932.

15 Faber and Faber catalogue for autumn 1932.

16 S. Casson, *Some Modern Sculptors*, Oxford, Oxford University Press, 1928, p. 6. Photographs of pre-20th-century sculpture are largely from the firm of Alinari.

17 Casson wanted to reproduce half a dozen photographs from an untranslated article by Strzygowski and in addition wrote to OUP a month later to express his delight at finding the very man who had ordered and paid for the Ragusa Mausoleum! (Casson obtained from the Racic family not only a complete series of photos of the monument and permission to use them, but also what he considered to be fine photos of unknown Meštrović sculptures, which were in his house. OUP Archives, LB 6130.)

18 Oxford University Press Archives, LB 6130, A. Norrington to H. Milford, 13 February 1928. Interestingly, Norrington believed he could sell more copies at 7/6 with thirty-two plates than at 6/- with sixteen plates. In the event, the print run seems to have been just over 2,000, average for an art book of this type.

19 In this volume Casson shows a transfer of allegiance: 'There is no more influential sculptor today than Carl Milles. He can be considered more than any other as the sculptor par excellence of the twentieth century.' Casson, *Twentieth Century Sculptors*, Oxford, Oxford University Press, 1930, p. 25.

20 OUP archives, LB 6130, A. Norrington to the Secretary, 23 September 1935.

21 In 1946 the New York office of OUP wrote to Oxford on behalf of Jack C. Rich, then preparing his book on *The Materials and Methods of Sculpture*, asking if he could have 'the glossy prints of some of the plates appearing in two of Stanley Casson's books'.

22 *The Studio: An Illustrated Magazine of Fine and Applied Art: Sculpture of Today*, commentary by Stanley Casson (1939 special spring number of *Studio* edited by C. G. Holme), London/New York, 1939, 144 pp. See also S. Casson, 'The role of sculpture in contemporary life', *The Studio*, January (on Europe), and July (on America) 1939.

23 'Frank Dobson has been employed by a corset manufacturer to make a model for the thousands of plaster torsos which exhibited the corsets in a thousand shop-windows.' Casson in *The Studio: An Illustrated Magazine of Fine and Applied Art: Sculpture of Today*, p. 17. In 1949, when Alec Miller wrote *Tradition in Sculpture*, also published by *The Studio*, his chapter on the 20th century included the remark that the costumier's dummy could be likened to the Praxitelean ideal – a veiled reference to Dobson? In a tribute to the late Stanley Casson he called him 'The most acute and perhaps best equipped writer on modern sculpture.'

24 Henry Moore in H. Read (ed.), *Unit One: The Modern Movement in English Architecture, Painting and Sculpture*, London, Cassell, 1934, p. 29.

25 In *The Complete Sculpture*, at least from volume 3 onwards, virtually all the black-and-white photographs were taken by Moore himself. Information from John Taylor, Editorial Consultant, Lund Humphries Publishers.

26 To supplement his income, Read acted as literary adviser to Heinemann in 1933, then in 1937 took up the same position at Routledge, where he was a director for twenty-five years. He simultaneously read for Faber – manuscripts by authors as diverse as E. H. Gombrich and Salvador Dali.

27 See Henry Moore's contribution to *Anton Zwemmer. Tributes from Some of his Friends on the Occasion of his 70th Birthday*, privately printed, 1962, p. 19.

28 H. Read, *Henry Moore, Sculptor: An Appreciation*, London, A. Zwemmer, 1934.

29 See N. V. Halliday, *More Than a Bookshop. Zwemmer's and Art in the 20th Century*, London, Philip Wilson Publishers, 1991, p. 211.

30 Henry Moore Foundation Archive. Press cuttings: *Yorkshire Daily Post*, 28 May 1934.

31 Baker, *Low Cost of Bookloving: An Account of the First Twenty-One Years of Readers' Union*, p. 7.

32 See H. Miller, 'The business of art book publishing' in V. Holman (ed.), *The Early History of the Phaidon Press, 1923–1967*, a special issue of *Visual Resources*, vol. XV, no. 3, a Harwood Academic Publishers International Journal, 1999.

33 Information from Penguin Archives.

34 See J. Glaves-Smith, 'Sculpture in the 1940s and 1950s: the form and the language', and R. Calvocoressi, 'Public sculpture in the 1950s', in S. Nairne and N. Serota (eds), *British Sculpture in the Twentieth Century*, London, Whitechapel Art Gallery, 1981, and P. Curtis, *Sculpture 1900–1945: After Rodin*, New York, Oxford University Press, 1999.

Sculpture in 20th-century Britain **1950–75**

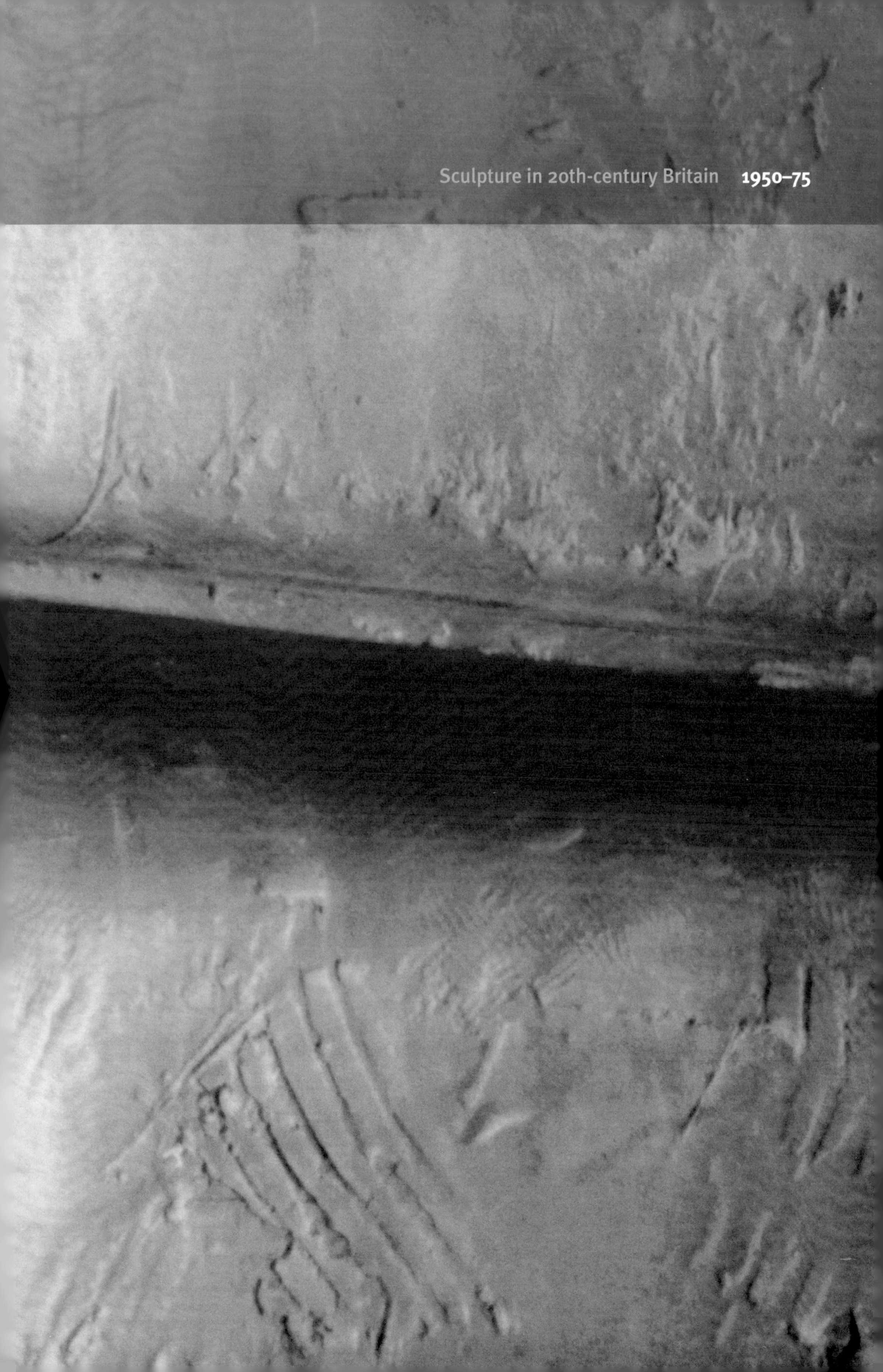

1950

■ E. C. Gregory sets up the Gregory Fellowships at Leeds University; Reg Butler becomes the first fellow in sculpture (1950–2)
■ The Contemporary Arts Society presents the London County Council with Henry Moore's 'Three Standing Figures' (1948)
■ Sigfried Giedion lectures on 'Palaeolithic Art and Modernism' at the Institute of Contemporary Arts, which influences William Turnbull who has his first solo show at the Hanover Gallery
■ Barbara Hepworth exhibits at the Venice Biennale
■ Antony Gormley born
■ Alan Durst's article 'Sculpture can survive' appears in *The Studio,* December 1950

1951

■ Festival of Britain (May–September); large number of new sculptures commissioned for the event
■ November issue of *Harper's Bazaar* uses sculpture as a backdrop for its fashion advertisements
■ John Read (son of Herbert) makes a TV film on Henry Moore
■ The Sculpture Biennales at Middleheim Sculpture Park, Antwerp begin
■ Reg Butler starts teaching at the Slade School of Fine Art (1951–80)
■ *Artists for Peace* exhibition at the Artists' International Association, London
■ *Growth and Form* exhibition at the Institute of Contemporary Arts, London
■ Anthony Caro becomes an assistant to Henry Moore

1952

■ The British Pavilion at the Venice Biennale includes Lynn Chadwick, Robert Adams, Reg Butler, Bernard Meadows, William Turnbull, Geoffrey Clarke, Kenneth Armitage, Eduardo Paolozzi and Henry Moore
■ Henry Moore gives his lecture 'The sculptor in modern society' to the International Conference of Artists at the Venice Biennale organised by UNESCO (22–8 September)
■ The Arts Council distributes sculptures from the Festival of Britain: Barbara Hepworth's 'Contrapuntal Forms' to Harlow Town, Frank Dobson's 'Woman and Fish' to Northampton and Jacob Epstein's 'Youth Advancing' to Manchester
■ First Constructivist exhibition takes place at Adrian Heath's studio, 22 Fitzroy Street, London
■ Kenneth Armitage has first solo show at the Gimpel Fils Gallery, London
■ Independent Group formed and Eduardo Paolozzi gives an illustrated lecture, 'Bunk'
■ Victor Musgrave opens Gallery One
■ Anthony Caro leaves Royal College of Art and begins teaching at St Martin's School of Art
■ *Barbara Hepworth: Carvings and Drawings,* the first major monograph on Hepworth is published, with introduction by Herbert Read and notes by the artist

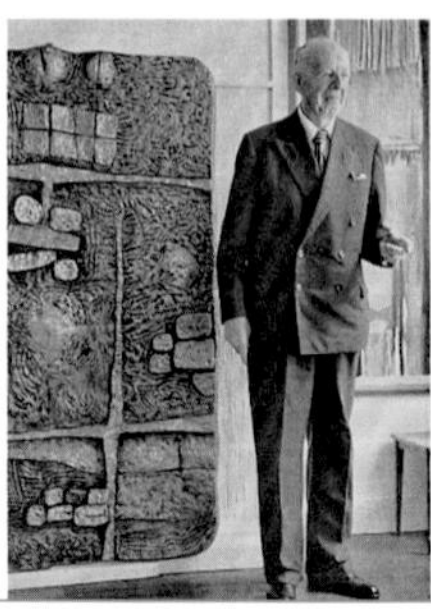

Photograph of E. C. Gregory

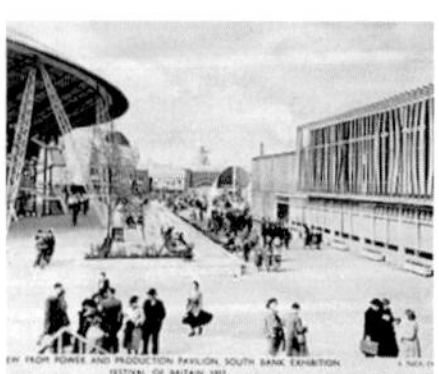

Souvenir postcard of the Festival of Britain

Images from Geoffrey Clarke's dissertation 'Exposition of a belief' for the Royal College of Art

1953

■ Lawrence Alloway identifies a generation of British sculptors using new material and techniques in his *Artnews* article 'Britain's new iron age'
■ Reg Butler wins the *Unknown Political Prisoner International Sculpture Competition* organised by the Institute of Contemporary Arts. At the exhibition of the entries at the Tate Gallery his maquette is vandalised; Herbert Read gives four lectures at the Institute on 'The aesthetics of sculpture' as accompanying events
■ Henry Moore's 'Reclining Figure' at Temple Newsam, Leeds is daubed with blue paint
■ Removal of the Artists' International Association's political clause
■ *Parallel of Life and Art* exhibition at the Institute of Contemporary Arts, London
■ The London County Council Sculpture School at Camberwell opens
■ Jacob Epstein is awarded an honorary doctorate from Oxford University and refuses an invitation to join the Royal Society of British Sculptors
■ Gilbert Bayes dies and Richard Wilson born
■ *An Exhibition of the Sculpture of Matisse* at the Tate Gallery, London

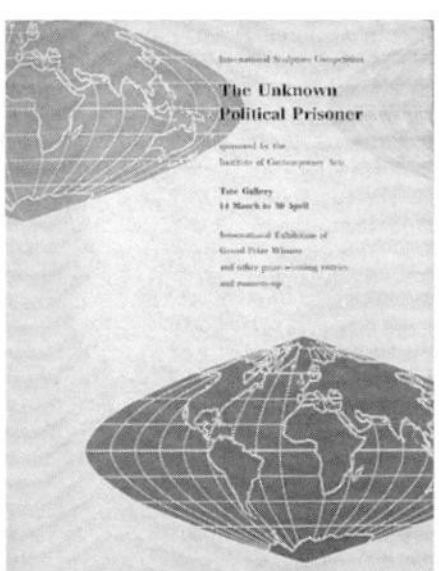

The *Unknown Political Prisoner International Sculpture Competition* exhibition catalogue

1954

■ Jacob Epstein is knighted; speaks on BBC Radio 'Sir Jacob Epstein on modern art'
■ Gilbert Ledward is made president of the Royal Society of British Sculptors, a post held until 1956
■ *Figures in Landscape* film on Barbara Hepworth directed by Dudley Shaw Ashton and major retrospective of her work at the Whitechapel Art Gallery
■ Lawrence Alloway's *Nine Abstract Artists: Their Work and Theory* published
■ John Latham co-founds the Institute for the Study of Mental Images
■ Kenneth Armitage's first New York solo show at the Bertha Schaefer Gallery
■ TUC competition for two monuments in their headquarters in London judged by J. M. Richards and Herbert Read but no prizes awarded
■ Dodo Society formed at the Royal College of Art by Bruce Lacey, Len Deighton, Ted Dicks and John Sewell
■ *Paule Vézelay: Lines in Space and Their Shadows* at the Leicester Galleries, London

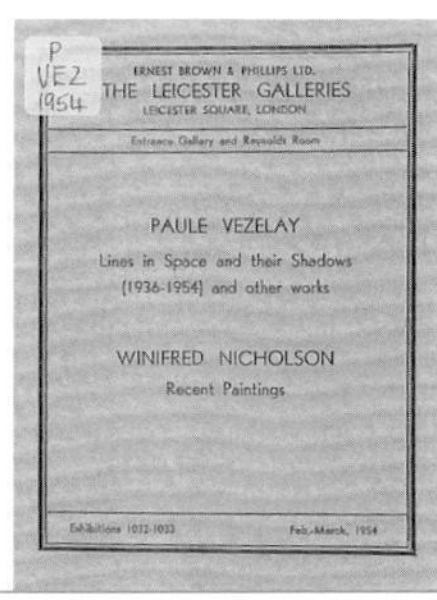

Paule Vézelay exhibition catalogue

1955

■ First *Documenta* international exhibition, Kassel, Germany
■ *Looking at People* exhibition at the Whitworth Art Gallery, Manchester, curated by John Berger and including Betty Rea; travels to Moscow in 1957
■ Retrospective of Michael Ayrton's work at the Whitechapel Art Gallery, London
■ Stephen Gilbert produces his 'House Neovision' with Peter Stead
■ *International Open Air Sculpture Exhibition*, Sonsbeek, Holland
■ Hubert Dalwood becomes Gregory Fellow (1955–9)
■ The British exhibits from the 1952 Venice Biennale travel to Germany
■ Patrick Heron's *The Changing Forms of Art* published

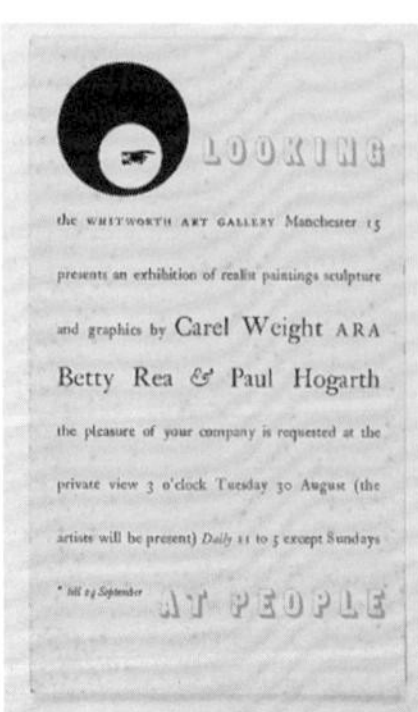

Private view card for the *Looking at People* exhibition

1956

■ Lynn Chadwick wins International Sculpture Prize at the Venice Biennale
■ Herbert Read's *The Art of Sculpture* published
■ London County Council starts its 'Patronage for arts' scheme investing £20,000 per annum in sculpture for schools and estates
■ Arts Council begins its survey exhibitions, *Some Contemporary British Sculpture*, held almost annually until 1966
■ *This is Tomorrow* exhibition at the Whitechapel, London, a collaboration/integration of sculpture, painting and architecture
■ Andy Goldsworthy and Cornelia Parker born
■ *Henri Gaudier-Brzeska 1891–1915: An Exhibition of Sculpture, Pastels and Drawings* organised by the Arts Council
■ *Young British Sculptors*, an exhibition touring Sweden 1956–7 organised by the British Council

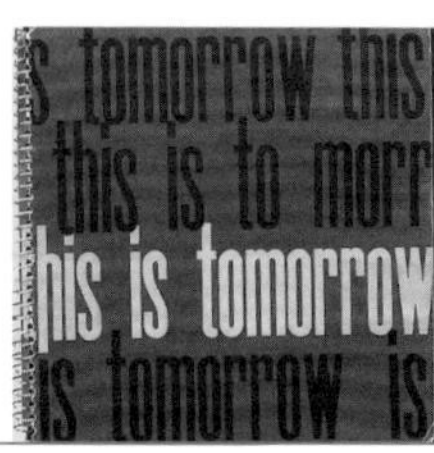

This is Tomorrow exhibition catalogue

1957

■ Yves Klein exhibits at Gallery One, London
■ Austin Wright wins the Purchase Prize at the São Paulo Bienale
■ Leon Underwood's experiments in bronze casting disprove the British Museum's theory about the casting of the Mesopotamian axe heads. Underwood shows sculpture at Zwemmer Gallery, London, with Jacob Epstein, Henry Moore, Barbara Hepworth and Marino Marini in June
■ Lynn Chadwick's first exhibition in America at the Saidenberg Gallery, New York

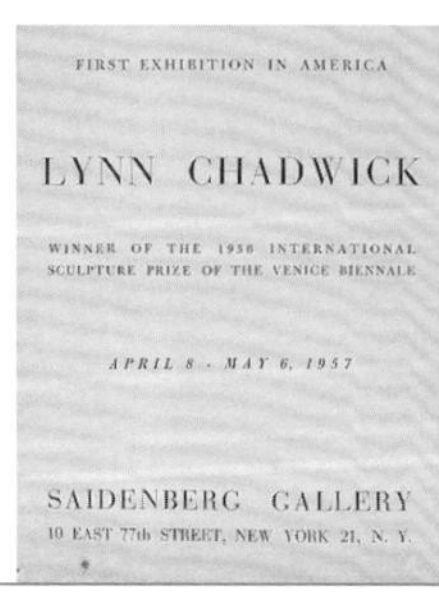

Lynn Chadwick exhibition catalogue

1958

■ Kenneth Armitage receives the David E. Bright Foundation Award at the Venice Biennale
■ John Berger publishes *A Painter of Our Time* whose protagonist is partly based on Peter Peri; it is withdrawn from sale after a month because of its Communist sympathies
■ Despite protests, Huddersfield buys Henry Moore's 'Falling Soldier' for £1,500 and UNESCO commission a 'Reclining Figure' for Paris head-quarters
■ Artists' International Association's 25th anniversary exhibition
■ Clement Greenberg publishes his article, 'Sculpture in our time' in *Arts Magazine*, June, in which he claims 'eyesight has more freedom of movement and invention within three dimensions than within two'

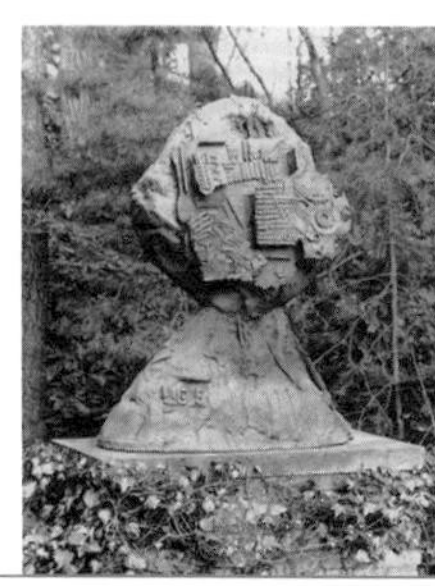

Eduardo Paolozzi's 'AG5'

1959

- Anthony Caro first visits USA on a Ford Foundation Grant. He is encouraged by Clement Greenberg and sees David Smith's work
- Kenneth Armitage retrospective at the Whitechapel based upon the XXIX Venice Biennale of 1958
- Jacob Epstein dies
- Barbara Hepworth visits New York for her first exhibition, at the Galerie Chalette
- Eric Kennington elected Royal Academician
- Michel Seuphor's *The Sculpture of This Century: Dictionary of Modern Sculpture* published
- John Read directs a TV film on Reg Butler
- First prize for British sculpture to Hubert Dalwood and second prize to Ralph Brown at *The John Moores Liverpool Exhibition 2: 1959*

1960

- Geoffrey Clarke and Eduardo Paolozzi represent Britain at the Venice Biennale; Paolozzi wins the David E. Bright Foundation Award
- Allen Jones expelled from the Royal College of Art for rebellious behaviour
- Bernard Meadows appointed professor of sculpture at the Royal College of Art
- Austin Wright has first retrospective exhibition, held at Wakefield City Art Gallery and then at Cartwright Hall, Bradford
- *Five Sculptors* exhibition at Hatton Gallery, Newcastle upon Tyne (also showed at Manchester, Leicester, Nottingham and Birmingham) exhibiting work by Elisabeth Frink, F. E. McWilliam, Uli Nimptsch, Eduardo Paolozzi and Austin Wright

1961

- 6th Congress of the International Union of Architects takes place on the South Bank; includes work by Kenneth and Mary Martin, Gillian Wise and Anthony Hill
- First *International Exhibition of Modern Jewellery* at Goldsmiths' Hall in association with the Victoria & Albert Museum. Sculptors including Elisabeth Frink and Bernard Meadows commissioned to make pieces
- Ian Hamilton Finlay founds the Wild Hawthorn Press
- Edward Bainbridge Copnall becomes president of the Royal Society of British Sculptors (1961–5)
- Jacob Epstein memorial exhibitions at Waverley Market, Edinburgh and the Tate Gallery, London
- Austin Wright awarded the Gregory Fellowship in Sculpture until 1964
- First English edition of Edward Trier's *Form and Space: The Sculpture of the Twentieth Century* and revised version of Carola Giedion-Welcker's 1937 *Modern Plastic Art* published as *Contemporary Sculpture: An Evolution in Volume and Space*
- Gustav Metzger stages a performance on the South Bank to demonstrate his manifesto of Auto-Destructive Art

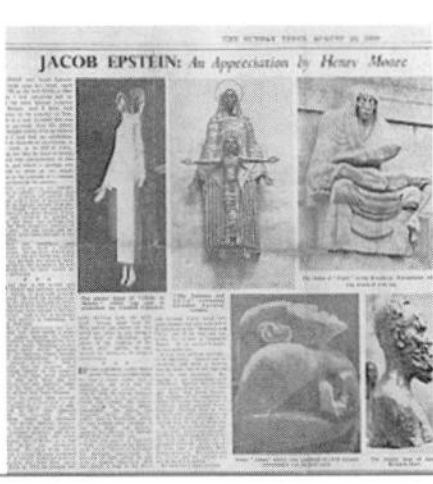
JACOB EPSTEIN: An Appreciation by Henry Moore

Obituary of Jacob Epstein written by Henry Moore

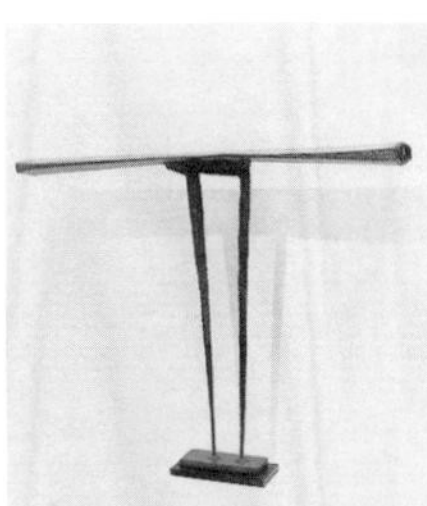

John Hoskin's 'Standing Figure'

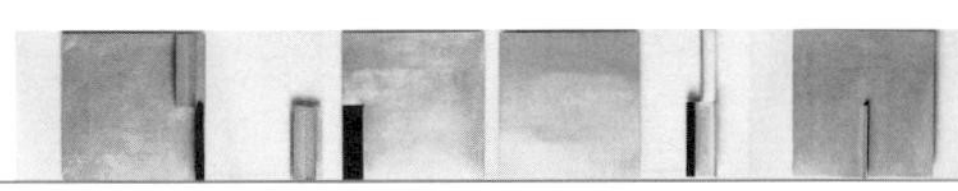

Anthony Hill's 'Maquette for the South Bank IUA Relief Mural'

1962

- Consecration of Coventry Cathedral with work by Jacob Epstein and Geoffrey Clarke
- Reg Butler's *Creative Development: Five Lectures to Art Students* published
- Peter Blake's first solo show at the Portal Gallery
- Ivan Meštrović dies in Indiana, USA
- *Alexander Calder: Sculpture, Mobiles* retrospective exhibition organised by the Arts Council at the Tate Gallery, London
- *Exhibition of New Art 1962* for the Festival of Labour held in the TUC building

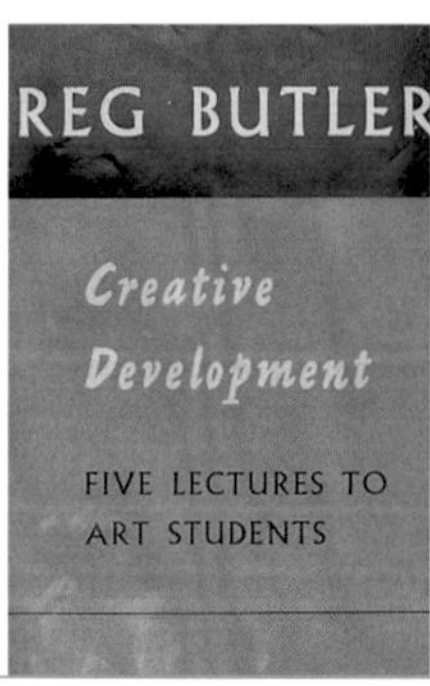

Reg Butler's book *Creative Development*

1963

- Michael Fried writes the introduction to the catalogue of *Anthony Caro: Sculpture 1960–63* exhibition at the Whitechapel, London
- *Construction England,* a touring exhibition curated by Alan Bowness for the Arts Council, is the first institutional recognition of the British Constructivist group
- Richard Buckle's *Epstein: An Autobiography* published
- Allen Jones' first solo exhibition at Arthur Tooth and Sons, London
- Rachel Whiteread, Anya Gallaccio and Michael Landy born

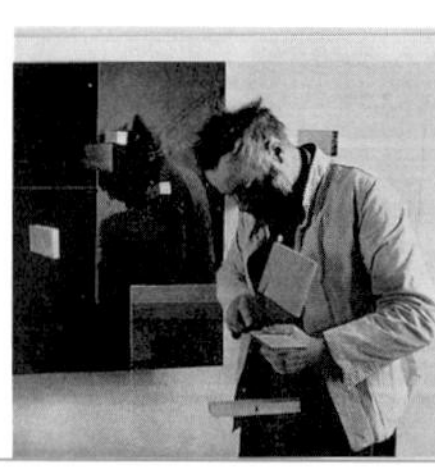

Photograph of Victor Pasmore from the *Construction England* exhibition catalogue

1964

- *Five British Sculptors* film (and book) directed by Warren Forma, featuring Kenneth Armitage, Reg Butler, Lynn Chadwick, Barbara Hepworth and Henry Moore
- Herbert Read's *Concise History of Modern Sculpture* published
- *Painting and Sculpture of a Decade: '54–'64* at the Tate Gallery, London
- Maurice Lambert dies
- Exhibition of the first eight Gregory Fellows in painting and sculpture: Reg Butler, Martin Froy, Kenneth Armitage, Terry Frost, Hubert Dalwood, Alan Davie, Trevor Bell, Austin Wright, organised by the Arts Council and touring the country

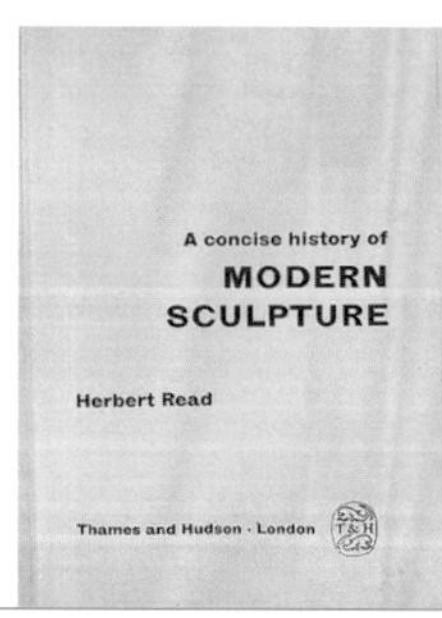

Title page to Herbert Read's *Concise History of Modern Sculpture*

1965

- *New Generation* exhibition at the Whitechapel Art Gallery, London
- *Private View,* a book by Bryan Robertson and John Russell, with photographs by Lord Snowdon, examines how London has become one of the world's three capitals of art, along with Paris and New York
- John Latham begins teaching at St Martin's School of Art
- *British Sculpture in the Sixties* exhibition organised by the Contemporary Art Society in association with the Peter Stuyvesant Foundation at the Tate Gallery, London
- Edward Carter Preston dies
- Alberto Giacometti retrospective exhibition at the Tate Gallery, London

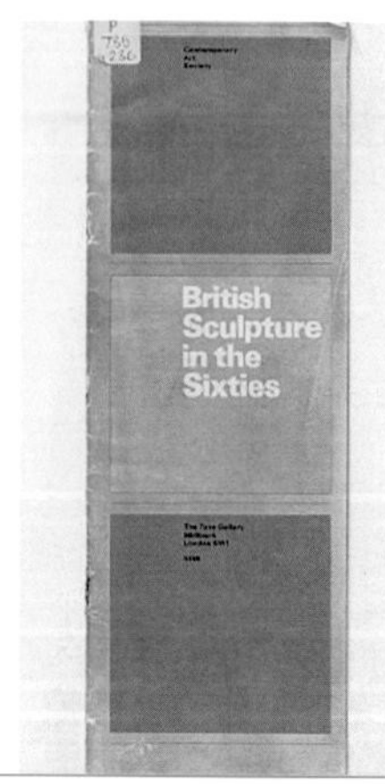

British Sculpture in the Sixties exhibition catalogue

1966

- Last *London Open-Air Sculpture* exhibition, criticised for putting sculpture in a landscape setting
- Anthony Caro represents Britain at the Venice Biennale; wins the David E. Bright Foundation Award
- Richard Long enrols at St Martin's School of Art and Bruce McLean leaves
- *The Almost Complete Works of Marcel Duchamp* exhibition at the Tate Gallery, London
- Robert Morris publishes his three-part essay 'Notes on Sculpture 1–3' in three issues of *Artforum*
- Naum Gabo is awarded honorary doctorate at the Royal College of Art

1967

- Gilbert & George meet at St Martin's School of Art
- John Latham and Barbara Stevini found the Art (later Artist) Placement Group to provide residencies for artists in industry
- Gertrude Hermes retrospective at the Whitechapel Art Gallery, London
- Stanley Cavell's essay 'A matter of meaning it' claims 'We no longer know what kind of object a piece of sculpture (grammatically) is', published in *Art, Mind and Religion* edited by W. H. Capitan and D. D. Merrill
- Sol LeWitt writes 'Paragraphs on conceptual art' in *Artforum*
- *Tim Scott; Sculpture 1961–67* exhibition at the Whitechapel Art Gallery, London, with a catalogue essay written by William Tucker
- Michael Fried publishes 'Art and objecthood' in *Artforum*
- *Sculpture 60–66 from the Arts Council Collection* showing thirty artists
- Selection of work from the Leicestershire Education Authority's collection, exhibited at the Whitechapel, London, in two consecutive exhibitions of sculpture and painting (1967–8)
- Roland Piché's first one-man exhibition of sculpture and drawings at Marlborough Fine Art, London

1968

- *Sunday Times* 'Sculpture Competition'
- The Hayward Gallery, London, opens, run by the Arts Council of Great Britain
- *Phillip King: Sculpture 1960–68* at the Whitechapel Art Gallery, London
- *Peter Peri 1899–1967: Memorial Exhibition: Sculptures and Graphic Work* at Central Library, Swiss Cottage, London, and opened by Sir Anthony Blunt
- *High Relief: The Autobiography of Sir Charles Wheeler, Sculptor* published
- Barbara Hepworth retrospective exhibition at the Tate Gallery, London

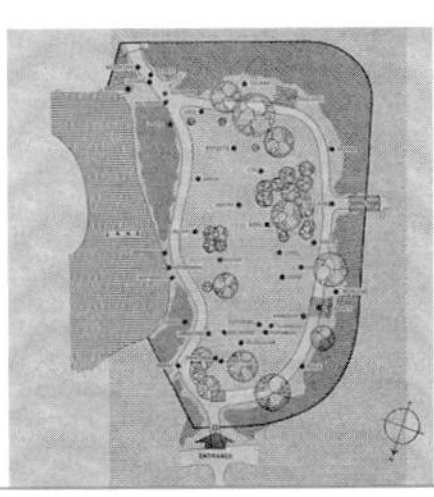

Plan of the exhibits at the *London Open Air Sculpture* at Battersea Park, London

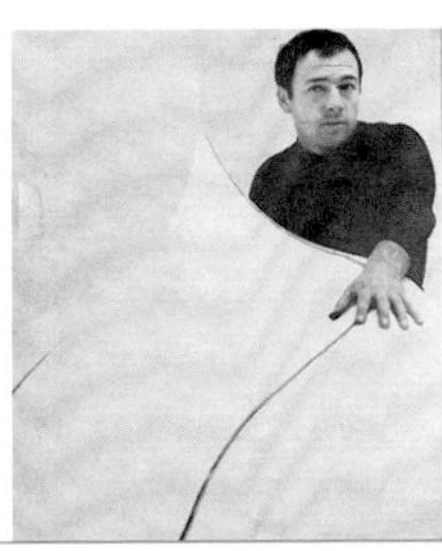

Photograph of Roland Piché from his exhibition catalogue, Marlborough Fine Art

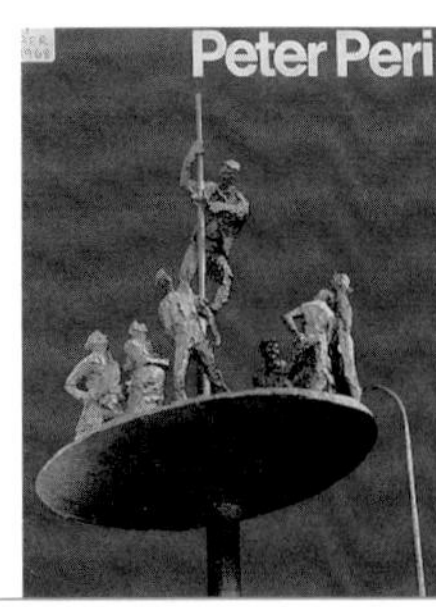

Peter Peri memorial catalogue

1969

- Kenneth Armitage made a CBE
- *When Attitudes Become Form* exhibition at the Institute of Contemporary Arts, London, curated by Charles Harrison
- Gilbert & George's *Our New Sculptures (Underneath the Arches)* first performed
- First *International Exhibition of Modern Sculpture*, at Hakone Open Air Museum, Japan
- Mary Martin is joint first prize winner (with Richard Hamilton), *John Moores 7*, at the Walker Art Gallery, Liverpool but dies this year
- *Art-Language* journal is published for the first time; in it Sol LeWitt writes a list of statements entitled 'Sentences on conceptual art'
- *Paul Neagu: Edinburgh Festival exhibition of new constructions*
- Competition for a sculpture for Darlington Civic Centre, won by John Hoskin

1970

- Victor Pasmore's Peterlee Pavilion completed
- Arts Council opens the Serpentine Gallery, London
- Joseph Beuys performs at the Edinburgh Festival
- Claes Oldenburg exhibition at the Tate Gallery, London
- Arthur Fleischmann produces first large-scale water sculpture, 'Harmony and Progress' for the British Pavilion at Expo 70, Osaka, Japan.
- *British Sculpture Out of the Sixties* exhibition at the Institute of Contemporary Arts, London

1971

- Eduardo Paolozzi and Victor Pasmore retrospectives at the Tate Gallery, London
- Kenneth Martin awarded OBE
- Hubert Dalwood and Hermon Cawthra die
- Robert Morris exhibition at Tate Gallery, London; part of it is deemed unsafe and is closed
- Alistair McAlpine gives sixty sculptures to the Tate Gallery of the work of David Annesley, Michael Bolus, Phillip King, Tim Scott, William Tucker, William Turnbull and Isaac Witkin
- *The British Avant-Garde* exhibition at the New York Cultural Center curated by Charles Harrison

1972

- *New Art* exhibition at the Hayward Gallery, London and *British Sculptors '72* exhibition at the Royal Academy of Arts
- Peter Stuyvesant City Sculpture Project which sited public sculptures in eight city centres
- *Eight Individuals: Sculpture and Drawings Chosen by Bryan Robertson for the Arts Council Collection*, a touring exhibition
- BBC film by John Read on Naum Gabo
- Keith Milow and Richard Oginz have an exhibition on their work as Gregory Fellows in Leeds City Art Gallery
- Bill Woodrow's first solo exhibition at the Whitechapel Art Gallery, London

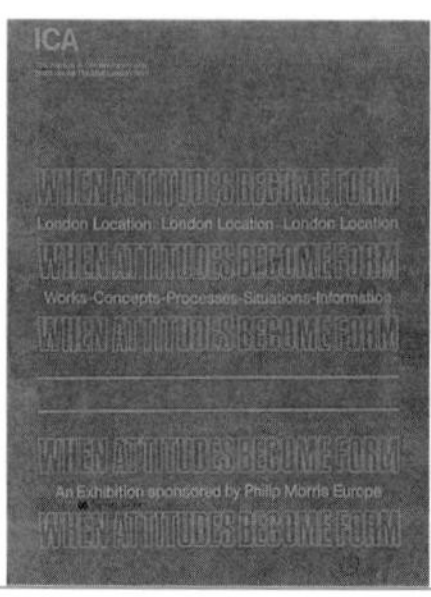

When Attitudes Become Form exhibition catalogue

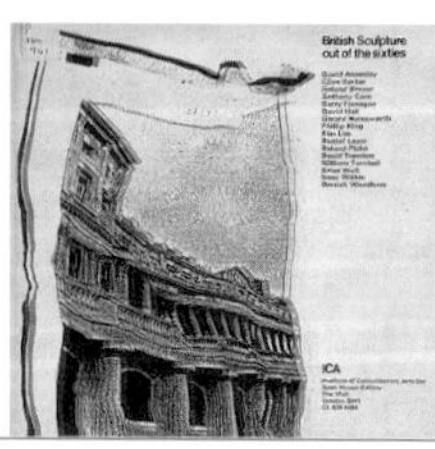

British Sculpture Out of the Sixties exhibition catalogue

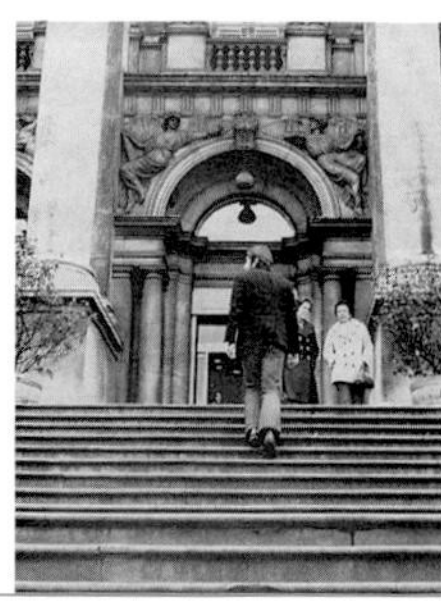

Keith Arnatt's 'I have decided to go to the Tate Gallery next Friday' shown at *The British Avant-Garde* exhibition

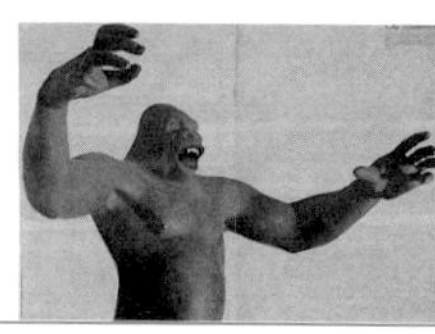

Pamphlet on the Peter Stuyvesant City Sculpture Project

1973

- William Turnbull retrospective at the Tate Gallery, London
- *Pioneers of Modern Sculpture* exhibition at the Hayward Gallery, London, curated by Albert Elsen
- Tony Cragg enrols at the Royal College of Art and Anish Kapoor enrols at Hornsey School of Art
- Harold J. Youngman, Jocelyn Horner and George Fullard die

1974

- William Tucker's *The Language of Sculpture* published, based on lectures given at the University of Leeds while a Gregory Fellow
- *Beyond Painting and Sculpture*, an Arts Council touring exhibition
- Michael Craig-Martin begins teaching at Goldsmiths' College
- Julia Busch's *A Decade of Sculpture: The New Media in the 1960s* published
- *Leon Underwood* by Christopher Neve published
- George Fullard memorial exhibition at the Serpentine Gallery

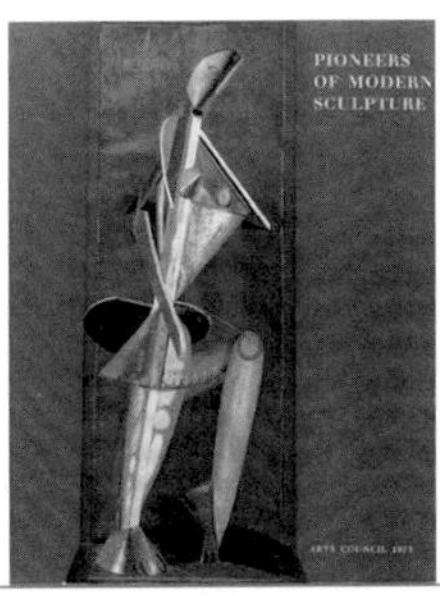

Front cover of *Pioneers of Modern Sculpture*

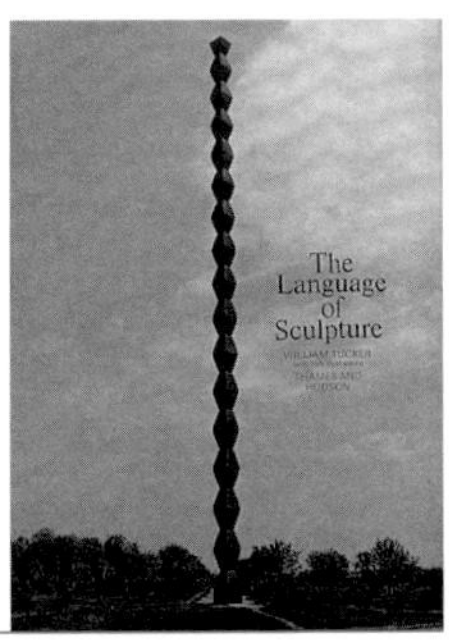

William Tucker's *The Language of Sculpture*

The identity of the sculptor 1950–75

What does it mean to ask about the identity of the British sculptor during the twenty-five years following 1950? Are we to analyse the range of possible identities represented by such a diverse group? Or should we seek to define a single 'British sculptor' identity that, despite that diversity, sets all such individuals apart from painters or, indeed, practitioners of any other line of work? Is there some essence that unites all British sculptors, male and female, English, Scottish, Welsh and Northern Irish, working-class and middle-class, black and white, feminist and misogynist, socialist and conservative? And, if there is, how does it differ from the essence of sculptors from beyond the United Kingdom? However we approach the question, we are bound to fail. We might consider the dominant public image of sculptors and the ways in which they were represented. We might, also, think about the ways in which they operated, the areas in which they moved and the constituencies they addressed. But perhaps the only thing uniting sculptors and setting them apart from all others is the fact that they made sculpture.

In the period under consideration, however, even that is problematic as the very definition of what constituted sculpture was thrown open to question during the 1960s. In 1950, modern sculpture was still dominated by the doctrine of direct carving exemplified by the work of Henry Moore and Barbara Hepworth. The subsequent decades saw a series of assaults upon this by sculptors seeking to redefine their practice. The major figures of the next generation chose to weld and cast metal rather than carve (practices adopted by Moore and Hepworth themselves). At the beginning of the 1960s, the mannered intensity of the work of Eduardo Paolozzi, Reg Butler and their generation was challenged by the austere, readymade components and bright colours of Anthony Caro's constructed sculptures. These were quickly followed by the overtly witty work, made mostly from new materials, of a new generation that was considerably wider and more varied in its output than those who showed in the 1965 Whitechapel *New Generation* exhibition.

Despite this formalist evolution, the successive sculptors were still people who made three-dimensional works of art with their hands and tools. In the second half of the 1960s and early 1970s, however, this basic distinction of the sculptor collapsed. A performative art had developed that replaced a manufactured object with the transient actions of the human body. Gilbert & George's first appearance as 'Singing Sculpture' (1969) may be the best known of these works, but Bruce McLean's series of poses on plinths (Fig. 1) exemplifies most

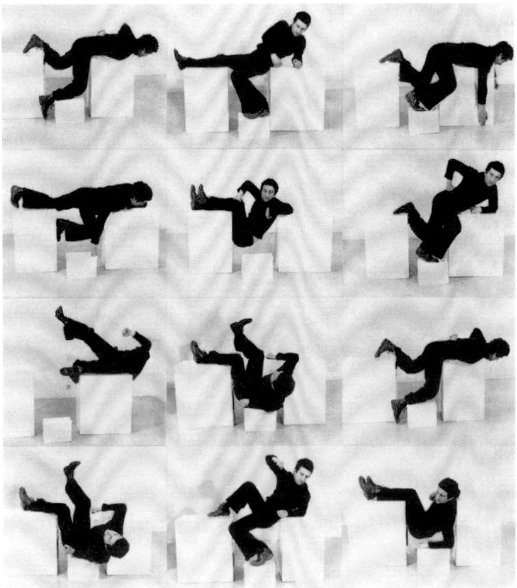

clearly the revolt against the traditional concept of sculpture as a solid mass elevated from the space of the everyday. In fact, the permanence of sculpture had been challenged almost ten years earlier with the emergence of an auto-destructive art, announced in Gustav Metzger's 1959 manifesto.[1] Similarly, the development of a kinetic art in Britain by such artists as David Medalla undermined the stasis hitherto basic to sculpture.

If the intrusion of the performative challenged the static nature of sculpture with the fourth element of time, the advent of a conceptual art dismantled its traditional imperative of manufacture. A seminal demonstration of this would be Michael Craig-Martin's 'An Oak Tree', 1973, which rehearsed the Duchampian notion that art is what the artist says it is. As Barry Flanagan wrote in an open letter to Caro, 'I might claim to be a sculptor and do everything else but sculpture'.[2]

It was around 1950 that sculpture secured a privileged position in British art. During the 1940s, Moore had established himself as, first, the leading contemporary artist in Britain and, then, as the leading British artist on the international scene. Ironically, this process had begun in earnest not with sculpture but with the wartime shelter drawings that were presented as speaking to and for a wider public than his pre-war avant-garde works. Writing for a government agency in 1950, Patrick Heron could claim that Moore was the first British artist 'without a rival in France' since the death of John Constable and J. M. W. Turner, if not longer.[3] Moore's success in New York in 1945 and triumph at the 1948 Venice Biennale encouraged the British Council to promote sculpture especially, despite the disappointing reception received by Hepworth in Venice in 1950. Throughout our twenty-five years, British sculpture seemed to dominate the officially promoted public face of British art abroad.

During the 1950s, Moore also dominated the realm of public sculpture at home. He was a lynchpin in the establishment of a series of open-air sculpture exhibitions, beginning in Battersea Park in 1948, which were part of the post-war Labour administration's policy to democratise access to art.[4] The clearly ideological motivations behind such events

1 Bruce McLean, 'Pose Work for Plinths I', 1971

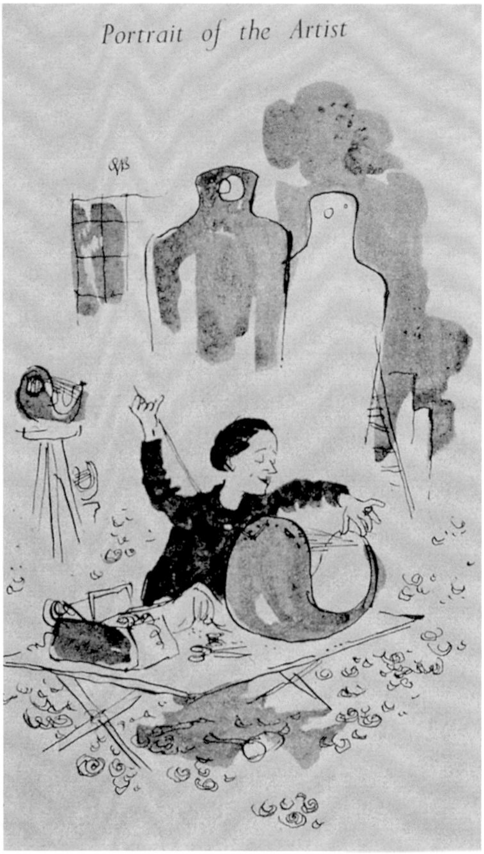

2 Punch cartoon of Barbara Hepworth, 1954

were echoed by the boom in public sculpture commissions that accompanied the process of urban reconstruction and the growth of the new towns, and that was exemplified by the incorporation of numerous commissioned sculptures into the South Bank site of the 1951 Festival of Britain. For many, the public image of the sculptor was as a professional contractor working alongside others in the realisation of an architectural scheme. These would, of course, include such high-profile buildings as Coventry Cathedral but also a host of state schools and other public facilities. It was in the nature of such commissions that they brought into the public realm not only the work of such modernists as Moore and Butler but also sculptors working in more traditional modes. For example, Peter Peri's commitment to social realism led him to produce, for a number of London's schools, a series of figurative sculptures depicting apparently recognisable figures engaging in everyday activities. The role of the artist in society had long been a source of concern for the modernists as much as for those, such as Peri and Raymond Mason, whose work reflected a commitment to reach a wider audience by depicting subjects recognisably relating to their own lives. Such works must surely have helped to temper the public's perception of modern sculptors, who were frequently lampooned when they stuck their head out into the wider public sphere. Such events as the Battersea Park exhibition, the Festival of Britain and the competition for a monument to the *Unknown Political Prisoner International Sculpture Competition* prompted cartoonists to ridicule the likes of Moore, Hepworth and Butler (Fig. 2).

The role of the artist in society, and the fusion of art and architecture, were issues at the heart of the Constructivist project. During the 1950s in Britain, the so-called Constructionists, such as Kenneth and Mary Martin, Anthony Hill and Victor Pasmore, developed those ideas alongside their search for a completely non-subjective art. They produced numerous works for public buildings. In 1956, the exhibition *This is Tomorrow*, in which twelve teams, each including artists and architects, presented a pavilion embodying their vision of a future built environment, was dominated by the Constructionists. If such events looked speculatively to a future shaped by such collaborations, Pasmore actually made the transition from one practice to another when, in 1955, he was appointed Consulting Director of Urban Design for the south-west quadrant of Peterlee new town in County Durham. The aesthetics and ideals that had determined his constructed reliefs were now brought to bear not only on the famous pavilion, an architectural/sculptural hybrid, but on the design and layout of the houses themselves as well as the landscaping of their environment. This really was bringing the sculptor into the public sphere of work and leisure.

In his 1954 Mellon lectures, Herbert Read set out to define 'an aesthetic of the art of sculpture'.[5] The resultant publication was largely made up of images from widely ranging historical periods and cultures. Echoing André Malraux's *Le Musée Imaginaire de la Sculpture Mondiale*, Read thus suggested a family of works united, regardless of time, place and cultural context, under the rubric of sculpture.[6] In so doing he implied a trans-historical community of practitioners, bringing his contemporaries (the book was dedicated to his friends Moore, Hepworth and Naum Gabo) together with the anonymous artists of medieval France, Ancient Egypt or pre-Columbian Mexico. Read saw the sculptor embedded in the social fabric, producing both 'the monument and the amulet', or something in between.[7] Like their ancient predecessors, Read suggested, contemporary sculptors were 'once again creating the symbols for our most profound spiritual experiences'.[8] Thus, the contemporary British sculptor could be seen as both the sub-contractor who produced monuments to new Britain's social democracy and a kind of seer producing numinous objects, almost a shaman. This is exemplified by the fascination among sculptors of the 1950s with the 'Venus of Willendorf', a tiny fertility symbol and one of the oldest sculptures known, casts of which several artists possessed, like talismans.

'A talisman' is how the critic David Sylvester described the significance of Sartre's 1948 essay on Alberto Giacometti, 'The search for the absolute', for the small group of British émigrés in post-war Paris that included sculptors Paolozzi and William Turnbull.[9] There Sartre described the sculptor's lonely struggle 'to prove that sculpture itself is possible'. The sculptor became the embodiment of existentialism's solitary individual, articulating his humanity in a godless world. This, too, was how Read represented the nine British sculptors shown at the 1952 Venice Biennale in a group whose work became known by his phrase 'the geometry of fear'. Ignoring the playful humour of some of

3 Henry Moore with carving, *c.*1928

4 Double-page spread showing Lynn Chadwick welding and at his home with his daughter, from *Private View*, 1965

the sculptures, he described this new generation as the articulators of the post-war world's nihilistic anxiety. Through his invocation of the tradition of amulets as well as monuments set within a framework of Jung's theory of a collective unconscious, Read was still able to locate this solitary activity at the heart of society. It was perhaps as a challenge to Sylvester and Read that John Berger claimed that George Fullard's tender observation of immediate, human details made him 'one of the few genuine existentialist artists of today'.[10]

In the Sylvester–Read view, the sculptor became individualised. The centrality of the artist's physical activity was reflected in the preference for pitted, evidently worked surfaces; as Sylvester wrote, 'roughness of surface is the symptom and symbol of a revolt against the anti-humanism of the streamlined surface, an assertion of the artist's humanity and of the value of the creative act'.[11] In contrast to the pre-war years, the 1950s was not a highly politicised period and this broad cultural tone was reflected amongst sculptors. Existentialism's concept of the studio as the site of heroic risk inevitably cast the artist in a masculine role. The manual labour of direct carving had already secured a macho image for the sculptor, epitomised by early depictions of Moore in a checked shirt – signifier of working-class labour (Fig. 3). A masculinised view of the sculptor was hardly dented by the shift from carving to processes more associated with industry, such as forging, welding and casting. This was especially powerfully communicated through photography, as sculptors such as Lynn Chadwick were represented in action, wielding their welding torches. The 1952 Biennale exhibition had been preceded by the Institute of Contemporary Arts' *Young Sculptors*; it is notable that of the artists in that show both of the two women were omitted from the selection for Venice. No wonder that female practitioners such as Hepworth and Elisabeth Frink struggled for equal respect. When the cartoonists at *Punch* lampooned Hepworth's work, they depicted her in a traditional female role, sewing a stringed sculpture (which ironically appears to be Moore's 'Bird Basket', 1939). The presumed identity of the sculptor was, unquestionably, male.

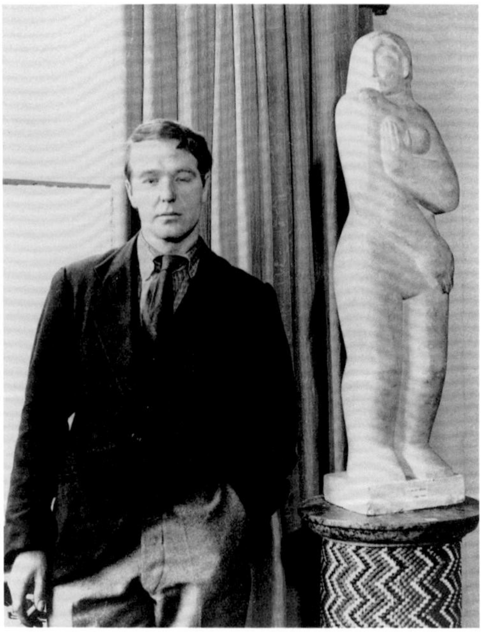

Snowdon's photographs in the celebrated book, *Private View* (1965), reveal, however, the beginnings of a shift in this macho image of the sculptor (Fig. 4). The setting of Brian Wall against the backdrop of a yard full of welded steel sculptures and scrap metal securely associated him with the world of heavy manual labour while William Tucker is show opposite 'assembling' a biomorphic, fibreglass piece.[12] But elsewhere in the book the reader finds a world of sculpture that is light, bright and playful. Caro's use of cut steel and such readymade industrial materials as I-beams may have kept the work of the sculptor in the world of the steel toecap but his use of strong colour relocated the finished work to another, more aestheticised space. It was this aspect that informed much of the work of the next generation, whose use of such new materials as fibreglass and plastics enabled them to achieve a whole new vocabulary of forms. The necessary change in studio practice undermined the sculptor's masculinised identity. While abandoning literally heavy materials, it also deliberately rejected the metaphorically heavy earnestness of 1950s sculpture. The titles of Phillip King's early works – 'Rosebud', 'Tra-La-La' and 'And the Birds Began to Sing' – signalled this new attitude, just as the twisted bubble-gum-pink form at the top of 'Tra-La-La' marked out his distance from the metal-workers of the preceding generation.

The materials and processes of sculpture had, until the mid-1960s, related it more to the world of engineering and construction than to the private realm. Nothing signalled a departure from this condition more starkly than Gilbert & George's piece, 'Singing Sculpture' (1969; Fig. 5). Apart from the obvious distinction between their performance

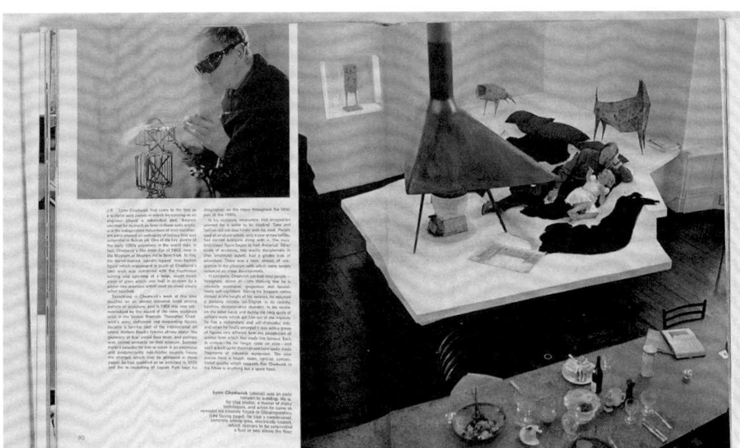

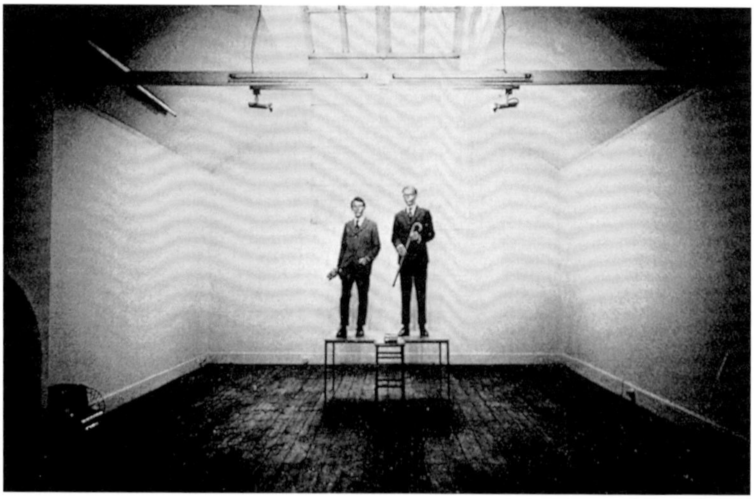

5 Gilbert & George, 'Singing Sculpture', performed at the Nigel Greenwood Gallery, 1970

and the understanding of sculpture as an object 'subject to gravity and revealed by light', as Tucker would later have it, their appearance at Nigel Greenwood's Gallery in matching dark suits and ties clearly distinguished them from the world of physical manufacture. In fact, the merging of the identity of the sculptor with that of the performer had been current throughout the 1960s. Metzger's earliest acid-on-nylon pieces (1961) mimicked painting, in that they involved the application of fluid to a fabric, but left a physical object that might claim to be akin to sculpture; nevertheless, the work was, essentially, a transient performance. The confused relationship between the theatre and the sculpture studio was even more apparent in the work of Bruce Lacey, who really did perform in theatres with such groups as The Alberts, and claimed to have begun making robotic figure sculptures in response to the need for a co-star. An even more dramatic precursor of Gilbert & George's performance was the series of events at the *Destruction in Art Symposium* (September 1966), which brought British artists like Metzger, Lacey and John Latham together with colleagues from abroad like Yoko Ono and Hermann Nitsch. In a series of interactive pieces, not only was the identity of the sculptor melded with that of the performer, but also the distinction between artist and viewer became blurred. In time, performance and sculpture would be seen as distinct, but in that period the boundary between the two was unclear, as suggested by Gilbert & George's self-description as 'living sculpture' and the deployment of constructed objects within interactive and performative pieces by such artists as Paul Neagu and Barry Martin.

By the late 1960s, then, the very notion of what constituted sculpture was the subject of urgent debate. Consequently, the identity of the sculptor was fundamentally revised. For the emergent conceptual artists, as they were dubbed, a sculpture was not necessarily a three-dimensional, massive object, though it might be. The sculptor was not, therefore, a manufacturer. Rather, they became performers or even quasi-academics as, for example, the Art and Language Group who recognised the necessary relationship between the two discourses of their name. The clearly stated dependence of sculptor/concrete poet Ian Hamilton-Finlay on others to fabricate his work made it clear that labour and craft need not be an essential part of sculptural practice. As the artwork dematerialised, so the coherence of the traditional identity of the sculptor was similarly dissolved. Indeed, in the work of McLean or Flanagan, for example, the craft-based, manual labour of traditional sculptural practice became the subject of their ironically humorous work.

It might be argued, however, that some of the other dominant tropes of sculptural identity persisted despite this problematisation of the idea of the sculptor. The notion of the sculptor as shaman was, if anything, enhanced. The arrival in Scotland and, later, London, of the German artist Josef Beuys offered an important model for many British artists able to experience first-hand the performances of a man who epitomised the idea of the artist as shaman. A predominant shamanic masculinity could certainly be discerned in the walk-based work of Richard Long and Hamish Fulton. Their work retained a sense of the artist as a solitary, heroic male, echoing the masculine world of exploration. One might equally argue that the stance they took towards the landscape was, despite any environmental concerns, that of the dominant, possessive male seeking to conquer mother nature.[13] Elsewhere in British sculptural practice the masculine tone was even more persistent, as a post-Caro tradition of constructed sculpture maintained the predominance of heavy labour and of works that aggressively occupied and encompassed space. More striking and less equivocal was the figurative work of such older artists as Butler and Ralph Brown, whose representations of woman were increasingly eroticised to the point that, to some, they seemed to draw near to pornography. It would only be in the last quarter of the 20th century that the identity of the sculptor might just as likely be female as male.

In 1975 the understanding of what sculpture was had fundamentally changed from that of 1950. The identity of the sculptor was equally altered. Rather than someone who carved or cast self-contained objects from stone, wood or metal, sculptors might now act out their work, or commission a fabricator to translate an idea into a physical object which might not, necessarily, be self-contained or even three-dimensional. At the same time, much remained the same. The figure of Moore still towered over British art. Sculptors still provided work to be incorporated into or sited alongside architecture and within urban spaces. By virtue of their public position and function, sculptors could still seem to have a shamanic and communitarian role that could rarely be claimed for the more private practice and product of the painter. Similarly, the world of sculpture remained a largely masculine realm and the sculptor generally male. In this, the identity of the sculptor was probably not far removed from the identity of most other professions in Britain.

Chris Stephens

Notes

1 G. Metzger, 'Manifesto: Auto-destructive art', 4 November 1959, published as *Cardboards Selected and Arranged by Gustav Metzger … Auto-Destructive Art*, London, 1960.

2 B. Flanagan, 'A letter and some submission', *Silence*, January 1965, no. 6, pp. 2–3.

3 P. Heron, 'Contemporary British sculpture', pamphlet produced by the Central Office of Information for the British Council, n.d. (written spring 1950), in M. Gooding (ed.), *Painter as Critic: Patrick Heron – Selected Writings*, London, Tate Gallery, 1998, p. 50.

4 R. Burstow, 'Modern public sculpture in "New Britain" 1945–53', unpublished PhD thesis, University of Leeds, 2000.

5 Published as H. Read, *The Art of Sculpture*, London, Faber and Faber, 1956.

6 A. Malraux, *Le Musée Imaginaire de la Sculpture Mondiale*, Paris, La Galerie de la Pléiade, 1952.

7 Read, *The Art of Sculpture*, p. 5. The phrase provides the heading for Chapter One.

8 Ibid., p. 120.

9 D. Sylvester, quoted in D. Mellor, 'Existentialism and post-war British art', in F. Morris (ed.), *Paris Post War: Art and Existentialism 1945–55*, London, Tate Gallery, 1993, p. 53.

10 J. Berger, 'George Fullard', in *Permanent Red*, London, Methuen, 1960. Second edition published by Writers and Readers Publishing Cooperative Society, London, 1979, p. 98.

11 D. Sylvester, 'End of the streamlined era in painting and sculpture', *The Times*, 2 August 1955, reprinted in D. Sylvester, *About Modern Art: Critical Essays 1948–96*, London, Chatto and Windus, 1996, pp. 50–1.

12 B. Robertson, J. Russell and Lord Snowdon, *Private View*, London, Thomas Nelson, 1965, pp. 254–5.

13 These points are made in A. Gruetzner Robins, '"Ain't going nowhere": Richard Long: global explorer', in S. Adams and A. Gruetzner Robins (eds), *Gendering Landscape Art*, Manchester, Manchester University Press, 2000, pp. 162–72.

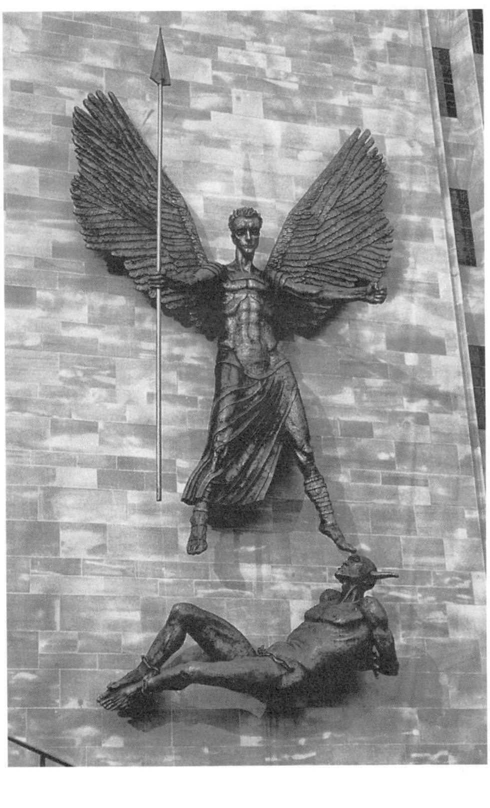

1 Jacob Epstein, 'St Michael and the Devil', on Coventry Cathedral, 1956–8

The critic Basil Taylor remarked in 1953 that 'the question of patronage has become an obsession'.[1] Patronage is part of the infrastructure, itself a broader concept grounded in social and political perceptions of culture and the place of the arts within that culture. Taylor was presumably referring to the plethora of organisations that emerged shortly after World War II, fuelled by the political conviction that the arts were a universal social benefit. The most prominent were the British Council, which played a politically oriented role, promoting British culture abroad, and the Arts Council, founded in 1945 as the cultural arm of the welfare state.[2] These were revenue-funded, though the rise in status of modern sculpture after 1950 coincided with an expansion of formal and informal structures, and critical and commercial responses. The infrastructure includes local authorities, universities, education authorities, private patrons, architects, art schools, dealers and galleries, publishing, critics and such artists' societies as the Royal Society of British Sculptors.[3] It extended to the powerful web of contacts within the metrocentric 'art establishment': a small number of people connected through their membership of committees. Their impact extended to small regional groups, so that Herbert Read, 'the Pope of modern art', was also the first president of the Penwith Society in St Ives, Cornwall.[4] Finally, though, the infrastructure is determined by social, economic and political factors outside the arts, not least maverick individuals.

If 1950–75 is an arbitrary temporal division, it coincides with real social change and shifts in the understanding of what might constitute a sculptural practice. While some aspects of the infrastructure recur throughout the 20th century, those years were distinguished by a developing dynamic between commercial and industrial patronage on the one hand and artist-led initiatives on the other. Both were deeply imbricated in the social fabric: one as the product of booming capitalism, the other the result of enhanced professional status and security. Between the commercial patron and artists' own organisations lies a swathe of reasons for supporting the arts, which include philanthropy, piety, prestige and self-interest. Our understanding of the infrastructure will depend on whether we approach it from the point of view of the artist or the receiver; how we interpret people's motives for patronage and, not least, our view of the sculpture that it helped to bring about. This is illustrated by considering a single aspect of the infrastructure: the conditions, requirements and purposes of the commissioning process that culminated in Henry Moore's 'Family Group' in Harlow New Town were significantly different from those that produced Jacob Epstein's 'St Michael' on the facade of Coventry Cathedral (Fig. 1).

The variety of sculpture produced between 1950 and 1975, from the academic peace memorial, 'Pax' (Fig. 2), made by the Austrian emigré Georg Ehrlich, to William Turnbull's 'Corrugations' (see Fig. 6 in Gillian Whiteley's essay 'Conditions of display: 1950–75') – painted galvanised sheets, displayed propped against walls or laid on the floor – was both a product of the infrastructure and a factor in its development. Yet broad as it was, the early post-war infrastructure was selective: immigrants, both those who fled from Nazi persecution and others who came later from the new Commonwealth, were often ignored. Siegfried Charoux, another Austrian emigré, found life harder than Ehrlich because of his pronounced left-wing politics. Similarly, despite the enthusiasm with which the Nigerian sculptor Ben Enwokwu was greeted in 1948 as 'an "Epstein" of west Africa',[5] he was rapidly forgotten. No critical, institutional or commercial support existed for artists outside the mainstream; even after the opening of the Commonwealth Institute in the early 1960s recognition for black and Asian artists owed more to black politicisation, the formation of Artists for Democracy in 1975 and the subsequent efforts of Rasheed Araeen.[6]

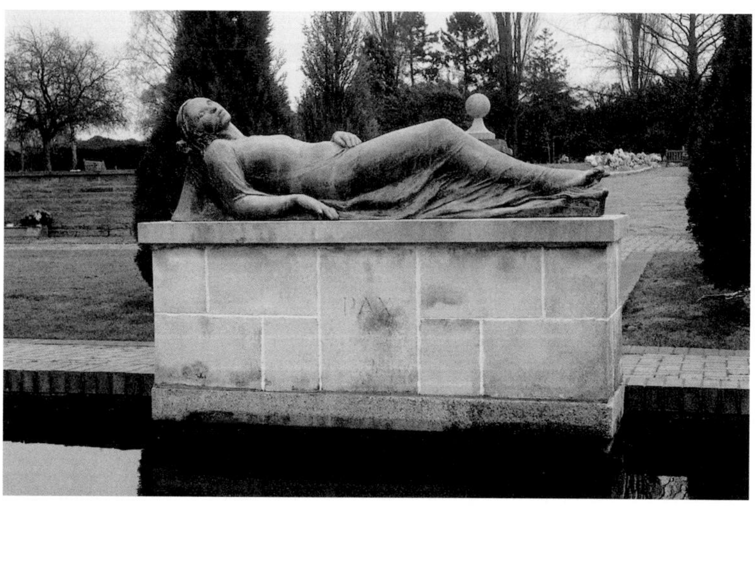

2 Georg Ehrlich, 'Pax', 1944–5

Early in the post-war years modernity emerged as central to the construction of a new, socialist society. Modernity dominated the negotiation 'between the public and the private spheres, between the state and the private sector and between social responsibility and individual freedom'.[7] The Festival of Britain provided a symbolic start to post-war modernity. In a far-sighted moment Philip James, the Arts Council's Director of Visual Art, was convinced that the event could also kick-start widespread commercial patronage by 'banks, hotels, churches, canteens, board rooms, showrooms and others',[8] though this was in fact delayed until the end of the decade. The dominant message of the South Bank exhibition, backed up by sculptures and murals, was that industry and technology were vibrant and viable, while the compulsion of scientists and the Labour Party to reconcile science and the arts – which was also central to the small circle that frequented the Institute of Contemporary Arts (ICA) – has also been identified within the Festival.[9] Consequently there was some encouragement for artists to disregard the limitations of specific media and to use new materials.

Yet even modernity was selective: a silence fell over non-professional artists and those whose work did not conform to a nature-based, 'organic' modernity. A considerable area of tolerance existed for the work of Barbara Hepworth, Denis Mitchell and John Milne, for instance, whereas the Constructivist artists of the early 1950s (Robert Adams, Anthony Hill, Kenneth and Mary Martin, Victor Pasmore, Adrian Heath) were obliged to exhibit in Heath's Fitzroy Street studio as no gallery would show their geometrically based work made with industrial materials.[10] The Arts Council's exhibition, *Construction England* (1963) was the first institutional recognition of the group.

In 1946 the Arts Council, seeking to revitalise private patronage, started a series of exhibitions of small sculptures, offering an eclectic range of work for sale.[11] The Council's exhibitions travelled so widely at this time that it was usually considered impractical to show sculpture. Instead, the Council offered discreet expert advice to the London County Council (LCC) on its commissioning programme and triennial *Sculpture in the Open Air* exhibitions which promoted sculpture to many people who might never have entered an art gallery.[12] Their success perhaps encouraged the Arts Council's series of survey exhibitions, *Some Contemporary British Sculpture*, held almost annually between 1956 and 1966. By the mid-1960s the Arts Council was able to address an unprecedentedly wide range of contemporary and foreign art while summer exhibitions at the Serpentine Gallery in the 1970s offered new exhibiting opportunities to young artists. The opening of the Hayward

3 Kenneth Armitage, 'Tower', 1963

4 Martin Naylor, 'A Young Girl Seated by her Window', 1973

Gallery in 1968 – leased by the Arts Council from the LCC – was probably more significant for a public newly enthused by the modern than for artists, since cutting-edge artists continued to see the Council as centrist and cautious, though this approach may well have been a sensitive response to the requirements of its majority public.[13]

The energy and enthusiasm of Lilian Somerville, head of the British Council's Fine Art Department, greatly enhanced the status of British sculpture abroad during the same period. While world-wide demand meant that Moore's work constituted the bulk of the Council's sculpture exhibitions through the 1960s, the work of younger artists offered a more compelling symbol of modernity.[14] Those who showed in *New Aspects of British Sculpture* at the 1952 Venice Biennale have, despite their diversity, become identified with the representation of an ideological moment, in Read's famous phrase, 'the geometry of fear'.[15] The career boost of the Venice exhibition was sustained by *An Exhibition of Sculpture and Drawings by Young British Sculptors* and the very similar *Young British Sculptors* that toured Germany and the USA and Canada respectively in 1955–6. Yet the culminating sculptural events of the 1950s, which established the dominance of a particular kind of contemporary sculpture, might be defined by Reg Butler's winning the Unknown Political Prisoner competition in 1953[16] and Lynn Chadwick's International Sculpture prize at the 1956 Venice Biennale. Council-sponsored sculptors continued to win prizes[17] but when, in 1969, a harsh if realistic critic noted 'the total avoidance of really experimental, avant-garde work',[18] he overlooked the incompatibility between a revenue-funded institution and the 'really experimental'.

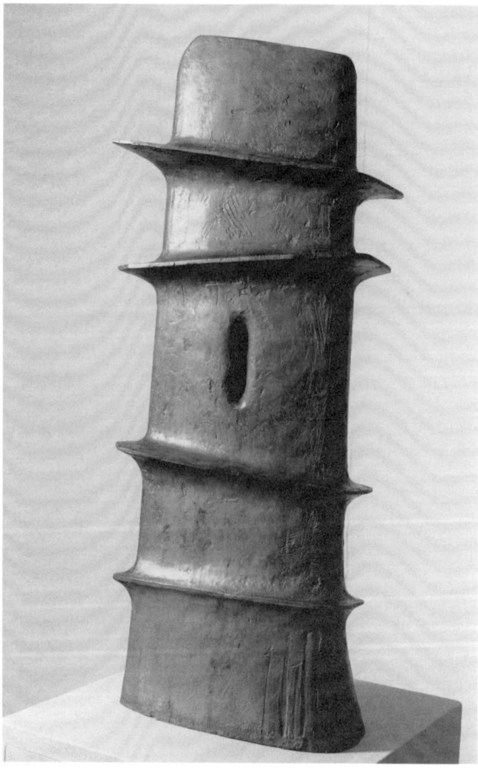

In the 1950s experiment was still an area for private patrons. Eric Gregory had been a founder of the ICA, within which the Independent Group soon established a collaborative relationship between sculptors, architects and painters, culminating in 1956 with the exhibition *This is Tomorrow*.[19] Gregory devised a new model of personal patronage, working through existing structures to extend the state system. He was a collector of contemporary art and managing director of the publishing firm Lund Humphries. It would be difficult to over-emphasise the indirect power that Gregory exerted through Lund Humphries. The first volumes of Moore's *catalogue raisonné*, published in the early 1950s, consolidated his international reputation and incidentally contributed to the creation of a hierarchy of English modernists. Today Gregory is best known for having founded the Gregory Fellowships at Leeds University. They provided three-year bursaries for a sculptor, a painter, a poet and a musician to extend their work without conditions or restrictions. Butler – who worked on his Unknown Political Prisoner entry – Kenneth Armitage (Fig. 3), William Tucker (see Fig. 4 in Robert Burstow's essay 'Aesthetics: forms and meanings 1950–75') and Martin Naylor (Fig. 4) were among the sculptor beneficiaries.[20]

Institutional structures began to change in the 1960s to accommodate artists' interventions in the infrastructure. Jennie Lee, who became the first minister with responsibility for the arts in February 1967, emphasised that 'in the field of the arts the initiative must come from individuals and from artists'.[21] The Art (later Artist) Placement Group was a maverick enterprise, supported until 1971 by the Arts Council, which was thus able to exercise some control over it. Founded by Barbara Steveni and John Latham in 1967 to foster relationships between art and industry, the APG arranged salaried residencies for

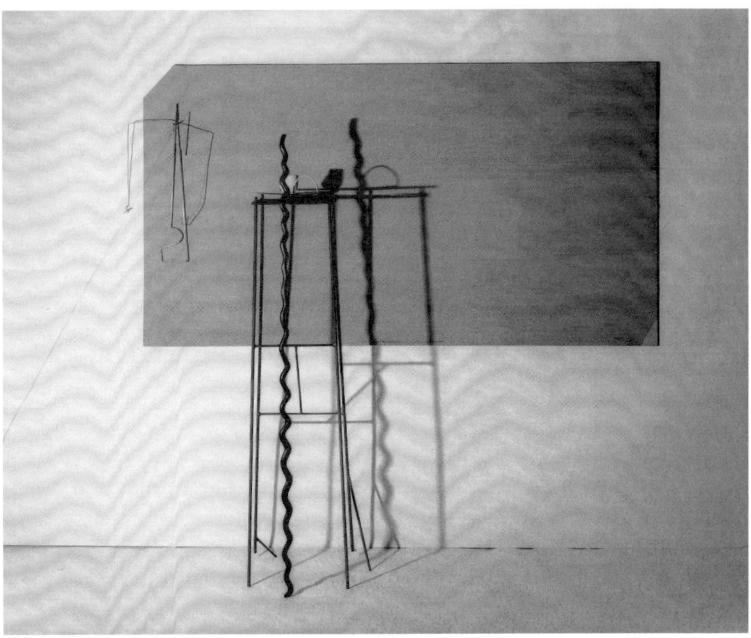

artists to work with 'new products and materials'[22] in order ultimately to influence industrial relations and, presumably, the future of capitalism. The sculptor Garth Evans was among the artists placed with companies that included British Steel, Hille (furniture), Esso and ICI.[23] Sculptural practice itself was reformulated by the Eventstructure Research Group, drawing on Latham's theories. The Group produced inflatable structures in order to demonstrate art's 'essential revolutionary function as a popular incitement to self-action and environmental transformation'.[24] Rhetoric notwithstanding, the APG contributed to the 1968 City of London Festival with 'Airground', a similar structure ('with a trampoline pneumatic floor'), in collaboration with Transatlantic Plastics.[25]

In contrast with the APG's efforts to incorporate commerce and industry into an intellectually sophisticated artistic agenda, the role of commercial galleries is straightforward. Given the problems of displaying large sculpture in small rooms, the steadfast support provided, for instance, by Gimpel Fils for Chadwick was rare in the 1950s. Erica Brausen, who ran the Hanover Gallery from 1947 to 1973, acted with the single-mindedness of a private patron, writing: 'this gallery has always been my baby'.[26] As well as exhibiting Butler and Moore, she provided unprecedented opportunities for English artists to absorb the work of foreign artists, notably Alberto Giacometti, Germaine Richier and César.

During the 1960s new galleries proliferated, run by 'small dealers who, in a different fiscal climate, would probably have remained collectors'.[27] They often found that aesthetic and commercial imperatives were in conflict. The Signals Gallery was founded in 1964 by Paul Keeler and the Filipino artist David Medalla. A locus for kinetic art and Brazilian artists, Signals exhibited the sculptors Sergio Camargo and Lygia Clark. The gallery closed prematurely in 1966, having provided Brazilian sculptors with invaluable exposure, though as Guy Brett commented, the closure underlined 'the lack of interest of the official London art world in maintaining the dialogue which has been opened'.[28] Few small galleries specialised in sculpture, though Axiom, which opened in 1966, was devoted to 'work of a Constructivist nature', showing some artists who had exhibited in Adrian Heath's studio fifteen years earlier.[29] The Rowan Gallery, opened in 1962, was an index of modernity; though painters predominated, its artists included Barry Flanagan (Fig. 5) and Michael Craig-Martin, who showed 'An Oak Tree' in 1974.

Art teaching, which expanded hugely after World War II, was as fundamental to the infrastructure as were commercial galleries. Since many artists were employed as teachers, they no longer had to

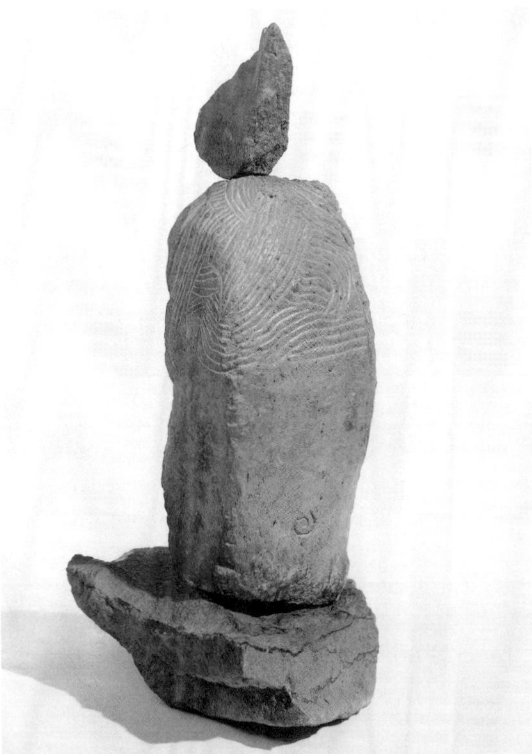

5 Barry Flanagan, 'Clay Figure', 1975

concentrate on making work to sell. The process of professionalisation was accelerated in 1960 with the publication of the Coldstream Report, which resulted in the replacement of the former National Diploma in Design (NDD) with a new qualification, the Diploma in Art and Design (Dip.AD), which was the equivalent of a first degree.[30] While the desire to raise the status of art education was related to wider post-war educational reforms, degree equivalence qualified students and their teachers respectively for statutory grants and university-level salaries.[31]

Not all art schools were immediately eligible for diploma status; those that were not continued to offer the older vocational courses, thus establishing a two-tier system which became a focus of controversy: 'Vocational students, like members of the Commonwealth, were the second-class citizens of the art schools.'[32] The Dip. AD demanded considerable restructuring of courses and their delivery, in which flexibility and teaching by critical advice rather than technical instruction became the new convention. Freed from the former centralised syllabus, foundation courses were introduced and students 'were encouraged to develop their own programmes and choose their own projects'.[33] While the Royal College of Art, adopted by Coldstream as a model of professionalism,[34] attained university status in 1966, less rarified establishments were also enabled to develop their own teaching methods. However, since the implications of Coldstream were ineluctably academic, demanding the General Certificate of Education as an entry qualification and allocating a proportion of every course to art history and complementary studies, some students were to dismiss their training as irrelevant, while some commentators regretted the new pedagogic orthodoxy that replaced the old skill-based approach.

On 28 May 1968, the students of Hornsey College of Art began the six-week occupation that has become famous as a grass-roots protest against the academic make-over of art teaching: 'In the Hornsey myth, the Dip. AD corresponded to the Norman invasion.'[35] When the College finally reopened in November 1968 after a Commission of Enquiry, no concessions were made to the students, while the part-time staff who had supported them were dismissed. Nevertheless, many of their demands have since become the orthodoxies of modern art schools.

The role of the exceptional vocational course run by Anthony Caro under Frank Martin at St Martin's School of Art has been widely discussed.[36] Far removed from the normal curriculum,[37] it had the allure of an intense, privileged coterie, so specialised that students learnt welding. In 1963 a partnership between Bryan Robertson, director of the Whitechapel Art Gallery, and the Peter Stuyvesant Corporation brought about the New Generation phenomenon, converting esoteric studio experiments into strong, eye-catching sculptural statements through a slick marketing operation.[38]

The relationship between corporate capital and the arts has been convincingly analysed by Chin-tao Wu, who concludes that corporate cultural interests are always grounded in self-interest and are to 'be seen as part of an overall strategy to bring together private economic power and public cultural authority'. Bourdieu's 'cultural capital' can 'be transformed into political power ... to serve business's own specific economic interests'.[39] This hints that certain kinds of art will be especially suitable for corporate patrons. The positive physical image projected by New Generation sculpture, with its concomitant lack of the kind of ideological baggage attached to the 'geometry of fear', apparently made it attractive to the Peter Stuyvesant Corporation and Alistair McAlpine, who purchased it extensively for his private collection.

The growth of commercial patronage at the end of the 1950s (after a spectacular if premature start in 1951 with Michael Rosenauer's Time-Life building in Bond Street) was a product of economic recovery and the property boom. This was in turn accelerated by the removal of controls on building materials in 1954,[40] and 'the scaling-back of national planning' by post-war conservative governments, which cleared the route to private sector development.[41] This in turn brought a demand for works of art to embellish new premises. Developers rapidly expanded into town centres, filling them with new offices, shopping malls and retail outlets that offered enticing opportunities for sculptors. A survey of work commissioned and purchased by new corporate patrons was published in *Patron: Industry Supports the Arts* in 1966.[42] Jennie Lee's preface carried a characteristically brisk message to rally potential patrons, noting that their support 'will increasingly come to be regarded as a form of enlightened self interest'.[43]

The property boom also caused a rise in land values and rentals, contributing to a severe shortage of affordable studios. To remedy this, SPACE (Space Provision [Artistic, Cultural, Educational] Ltd) and Stockwell Depot were founded in 1968 to take short-term leases on buildings scheduled for development and convert them into low-rent studios. Both were artist-led initiatives financially supported by the Arts Council and the GLC.[44] AIR (Artists Information Registry), a slide record of the work of recent graduates, was set up at the same time, supported by the Calouste Gulbenkian Foundation. Acme was established in 1972 by Jonathan Harvey and David Panton as an artists' housing association that included studios.

SPACE was founded by Bridget Riley and Peter Sedgley with Peter Townsend, editor of *Studio International*, while Stockwell Depot was independently colonised by artists from St Martin's, for whom the freedom to work on a very large scale was of primary importance. The sculptor Peter Hide wrote: 'The size of Stockwell gives me the freedom to make and exhibit a kind of sculpture which in the normal present-day circumstances I could not even consider.'[45] Studio exhibitions, which gave the opportunity to show such unsellable works as Roelof Louw's pyramid of 5,800 oranges,[46] were an integral feature of artist-led organisations, though the commercial sector remained the goal for many others.

During the quarter-century following World War II, numerous models of funding, organisation and self-help were tested, modified and discarded. Because both state and corporate support systems replicated old patterns in which artists played secondary, reactive roles, artists finally took the initiative in organising their own support structures, in one of the most radical shifts of this period. Concurrently, sculpture had become separated from its old commemorative functions by the 1960s, just as it had ceased to be a physical component of architecture;[47] the 'statue' gave way to the spatial experiences of abstract sculpture; bronze was replaced by painted steel and resin and, as Tucker lamented, 'the term "Sculpture" was used 'to describe a hole in the ground, a typewritten sheet, a music hall performance'.[48]

The years 1950–75 were an economic switchback, beginning in extreme austerity and passing into affluence in the 1960s, only to plunge into recession and high inflation a decade later. The sequence was visible in the pages of *Studio International*, where tinted papers and lavish colour gave way to monochrome uniformity and, finally, bi-monthly production in 1975. Some of the solutions to the recession – business intervention, self-help, art as a tool for regeneration – were pioneered before 1975, but it was only in the closing years of the 20th century that they came to dominate the infrastructure both organisationally and intellectually.

Margaret Garlake

Notes

1 BBC Third Programme, 'The prisoner on trial', discussion of the Unknown Political Prisoner competition, 24 June 1953. Transcript in the Kloman papers, Leeds Museums and Galleries (Henry Moore Institute Archive).

2 See Lord Keynes, 'The Arts Council: its policy and hopes', *The Listener*, 5 July 1945, vol. XXXIV, no. 860, pp. 3–4.

3 For fuller accounts of the infrastucture, including the two Councils, between 1945 and 1970, see M. Garlake, *New Art New World: British Art in Postwar Society*, London and New Haven,CT, Yale University Press, 1998, pp. 10–31, and 'Introduction', in M. Garlake (ed.), *Artists and Patrons in Post-War Britain*, Aldershot, Ashgate Publishing, 2001, pp. 1–14. For a survey of architects' commissions, see E. Rosenberg, *Architect's Choice: Art in Architecture in Great Britain Since 1945*, London, Thames and Hudson, 1992.

4 B. Read, unattributed quotation.

5 'An "Epstein" of West Africa: A modern Nigerian artist's work', *Illustrated London News*, 3 July 1948, vol. CCXIII, p. 25.

6 See R. Araeen, *The Other Story: Afro-Asian Artists in Post-war Britain* (exhibition catalogue), London, South Bank Centre, 1989.

7 See 'Introduction', in B. Conekin, F. Mort and C. Waters (eds), *Moments of Modernity: Reconstructing Britain 1945–1964*, London and New York, Rivers Oram Press, 1999, p. 15.

8 P. James, 'Patronage for painters: 60 paintings for '51', *Studio*, August 1951, vol. CXLII, no. 701, p. 47.

9 B. Conekin, '"Here is the modern world itself": The Festival of Britain's representations of the future', in Conekin, Mort and Waters (eds), *Moments of Modernity: Reconstructing Britain 1945–1964*, pp. 228–46.

10 See A. Grieve, 'Towards an art of environment: exhibitions and publications by a group of avant-garde abstract artists in London 1951–55', *The Burlington Magazine*, November, 1990, vol. CXXXII, no. 1052, pp. 773–81.

11 *Sculpture in the Home*, 1946, 1950, 1953, 1958.

12 See M. Garlake, '"A war of taste": the LCC as art patron 1948–1965', *The London Journal*, 1993, vol. 18, no. 1, pp. 45–65.

13 For the Hayward Gallery, see B. Taylor, *Art for the Nation: Exhibitions and the London Public 1747–2001*, Manchester, Manchester University Press, 1999, chapter 7.

[14] For the relationship between Moore and the British Council, see M. Garlake, 'Henry Moore as cold warrior', *Biuletyn Historii Sztuki*, 1999, vol. LXI, nos 3–4, pp. 337–50.

[15] H. Read, 'New aspects of British sculpture', in British Council, *The XXVI Venice Biennale, the British Pavilion*, London, Westminster Press, 1952; R. Burstow, '"The geometry of fear": Herbert Read and British modern sculpture after the Second World War', in B. Read and D. Thistlewood (eds), *Herbert Read: A British Vision of World Art* (exhibition catalogue), Leeds and London, Leeds City Art Galleries with the Henry Moore Foundation and Lund Humphries, 1993, pp. 119–32; *Henry Moore and the Geometry of Fear* (exhibition catalogue), London, James Hyman Fine Art, 2002.

[16] See R. Burstow, 'Butler's competition project for a monument to "The Unknown Political Prisoner": Abstraction and Cold War politics', *Art History*, December 1989, vol. XII, no. 4, pp. 472–96 and 'The limits of modernist art as a "weapon of the Cold War": Reassessing the unknown patron of the monument to the Unknown Political Prisoner', *The Oxford Art Journal*, 1997, vol. XX, I, pp. 68–80.

[17] See S. Bowness and C. Philpott (eds), *Britain at the Venice Biennale 1895–1995*, London, The British Council, 1995, pp. 108–12, 116.

[18] C. Spencer, 'Private view', *Art and Artists*, January 1969, vol. III, no. 10, p. 4.

[19] For the Independent Group, see D. Robbins (ed.), *The Independent Group: Postwar Britain and the Aesthetics of Plenty*, Cambridge, MA, and London, MIT Press, 1990; for *This is Tomorrow*, see A. Grieve, '"This is Tomorrow", a remarkable exhibition born from contention', *The Burlington Magazine*, April 1994, vol. CXXXVI, no. 1093, pp. 225–32.

[20] See M. Williams, 'A measure of leaven: the early Gregory Fellowships at the University of Leeds', in Garlake, *Artists and Patrons in Post-War Britain*, pp. 55–93.

[21] 'Talking to Jennie Lee', interview with Mario Amaya, *Art and Artists*, February 1968, vol. II, no. 11, p. 12.

[22] J. Latham and B. Stevini, *Art Placement Group*, London, private publication, 1966, pp. 1, 3.

[23] J. A. Walker, *John Latham: The Incidental Person – His Art and Ideas*, London, Middlesex University Press, 1995, p. 113.

[24] Jorge Glusberg, 'Air art. Two: concepts for an operational art', *Art and Artists*, January 1969, vol. III, no. 10, pp. 47–9.

[25] Ibid., p. 48.

[26] E. Brausen, letter to R. Butler, 31 March 1971, Butler archive.

[27] P. White, 'Hartnell & Eyre: A new gallery', *Art and Artists*, November 1968, vol. III, no. 8.

[28] G. Brett, 'Brazilian artists in Britain', in G. Brett and M. Garlake, *Britain and the São Paulo Bienal 1951–1991*, London, The British Council, 1991, p. 51.

[29] K. Coutts-Smith, 'London', *Art and Artists*, April 1966, vol. I, no. 1, p. 10.

[30] Ministry of Education, *First Report of the National Advisory Council on Art Education 1960*, London, HMSO (1960), 1961.

[31] Students and Staff of Hornsey College of Art, *The Hornsey Affair*, Harmondsworth, Penguin, 1969, pp. 78–9.

[32] Ibid., p. 94.

[33] C. Frayling, *The Royal College of Art: One Hundred and Fifty Years of Art and Design*, London, Barrie and Jenkins, 1987, p. 174.

34 Ibid., p. 174.

35 Students and Staff of Hornsey College of Art, *The Hornsey Affair*, p. 17.

36 See T. Marlow, 'The marketing and impact of New Generation sculpture', unpublished MA thesis, Courtauld Institute of Art, University of London, 1988; see also S. Faulkner, 'Art, cigarettes and visual culture in the sixties: the Peter Stuyvesant Foundation and the "New Generation" exhibitions, 1964–66', *Visual Culture in Britain*, 2000, vol. I, no. 1, pp. 65–87.

37 For the normative view of 'vocational course', see Ministry of Education, *Vocational Courses in Colleges and Schools of Art: Second Report of the National Advisory Council on Art Education*, London, HMSO, 1962, p. 1, para 3.

38 Marlow, 'The marketing and impact'; M. Yule, '"A place for living art": The Whitechapel Art Gallery 1952–1968', in Garlake, *Artists and Patrons in Post-War Britain*, pp. 94–124.

39 Chin-tao Wu, *Privatising Culture: Corporate Art Intervention Since the 1980s*, London and New York, Verso, 2002, p. 16. While this study focuses on the last twenty years of the 20th century, its findings apply to a much broader period.

40 E. Harwood, 'White light/white heat: rebuilding England's provincial towns and cities in the sixties', in E. Harwood and A. Powers (eds), *The Sixties: Life, Style, Architecture*, London, The Twentieth Century Society, 2002, pp. 57–70.

41 P. Mandler, 'New towns for old: the fate of the town centre', in Conekin, Mort and Waters (eds), *Moments of Modernity: Reconstructing Britain 1945–1964*, p. 216.

42 A. Osborne (ed.), *Patron: Industry Supports the Arts*, London, The Connoissuer, 1966, pp. 160–202.

43 Ibid., p. 5. Conversely, extensive socially oriented sculptural programmes were carried out during this period in the new towns, hospitals, churches, schools, old and new universities and numerous temporary festivals contributed to the proliferation of 'public art'. See Gillian Whiteley's essay 'Conditions of display: 1950–75' in this volume.

44 See *Studio International*, February 1969, vol. 177, no. 908, pp. 66–7.

45 'Sculptors at Stockwell', *Studio International*, January 1969, vol. 177, no. 907, pp. 34–7.

46 The diminution of the heap during the two-week exhibition through the removal of the oranges by visitors, who ate them, is recorded in 'Sculptors at Stockwell' (n. 45).

47 See J. Black, *The Sculpture of Eric Kennington*, Henry Moore Foundation with Lund Humphries, London, 2002, pp. 70, 85.

48 W. Tucker, 'What sculpture is', *Studio International*, December 1974, vol. 188, no. 972, p. 234.

The historiography of British sculpture between 1950 and 1975 is dominated by the expressionistic figuration of the 1950s, the abstractionist construction of the 1960s, and the experimental avant-gardism of the 1970s, when 'sculpture' variously redefined itself as conceptual, Performance, process or Land Art.[1] Other forms of modernist and traditionalist sculpture, notably the more overtly figurative work, remain marginalised and typically shoehorned into histories of pop art, assemblage, environments, realism and superrealism.[2] This short essay will not attempt to change this historical imbalance but, by limiting its focus to modernist and late modernist sculpture, will reflect renewed interest in the dominant tradition – witness several recent historical survey exhibitions and the emergence of British 'neo-conceptualist' and 'new formalist' sculpture.[3] Notwithstanding Charles Harrison's warning that analysis of a particular discipline within a single national tradition increases the risk of 'telling art history in a linear and hermetic manner',[4] my essay will, like Harrison's own, endeavour to situate the changing forms and meanings of this sculpture within broader shifts in the discourses of modernist art and criticism. In offering some account of contemporaneous critical interpretation, I hope to obviate another potential risk facing this analysis of sculptural aesthetics, that of slipping into purely formalistic description since this would be particularly inappropriate to a period when the adequacy of formalist criticism became a major issue.[5]

Figuration and humanism: Hepworth, Moore and the 'geometry of fear' sculptors

Among sculptors who had established reputations by 1950, Barbara Hepworth and Henry Moore were pre-eminent. In succeeding years they evolved more individual styles and themes, though they shared an overall tendency towards greater abstraction. For a brief period after World War II, however, the various primitivist, Surrealist and Constructivist strains in their work gave way to more overt figuration, in common with the postwar turn to 'modernist realism'.[6] At this time both sculptors showed more interest in social themes (often responding to public commissions), creating unprecedented numbers of grouped figures or forms. In the 1960s they both reverted to more abstract, massive, monumental and monolithic forms, and their divergence is plainer. As Moore pursued Surrealist metamorphic or biomorphic imagery, alluding to landscape and animal or human forms (Fig. 1), Hepworth increasingly returned to Constructivist geometry (becoming exemplary for younger 'constructionist' sculptors[7]). Their shared quest for sculpture 'in the round' progressed toward a fuller hollowing out

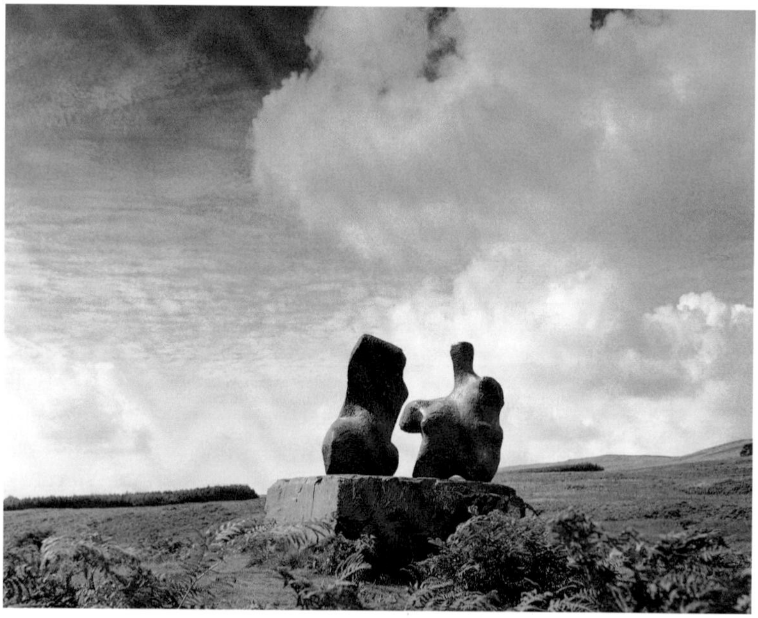

1 Henry Moore, 'Two Piece Reclining Figure No. 1', 1959, bronze, Glenkiln Estate, Shawhead

of the block, undermining distinctions between outside and inside. Although both continued to carve stone and wood, they abandoned rigid adherence to the doctrines of 'direct carving' and 'truth to material', increasingly using assistants and casting works in bronze. Moore retained his staple themes of mother and child, and standing and reclining female figures, but diversified into male figures and more abstract interlocking and multi-part works. Hepworth, meanwhile, abstracted from landscape and ancient standing stones (following her move to Cornwall), resulting in horizontally oriented sculptures as well as totemic figures and architectonic structures.

Hepworth's and Moore's privileging of the formal and tactile qualities of sculpture was endorsed by the most influential critic of the period and their greatest critical champion, Herbert Read, who described sculpture as 'an art … that gives satisfaction in the touching and handling of objects'.[8] Their shared belief in what Read called a 'world language of form' encouraged them to seek formal affinities between modern and prehistoric or 'primitive' sculpture. From an increasingly Jungian perspective, Read claimed that Hepworth's and Moore's work embodied archetypal forms which, like myths or dreams, retrieved fundamental human truths from the unconscious.[9] Yet despite their humanist ideology of universality and timelessness, Read's preference for Moore's declared aim of 'vitality' over Hepworth's of 'beauty' suggests the extent to which all three shared biologically based conceptions of gender.[10] Hepworth's standing also suffered in relation to Read's theorising of art and national identity: while he judged Moore's work consistent with ideas of Britishness (believing Surrealism originated in an essentially English tradition of romantic and fantastic art), he found Hepworth's interest in classical harmony and 'pure form' Mediterranean and alien. Read's interpretation and evaluation of both artists' work set the tone of postwar criticism, his predilection to psychologise and universalise increasing their popular appeal but reducing their social import. Recent reassessment has produced more critical and sometimes contradictory readings of Moore's work, presenting it as either the expression of a nationalistic conservatism – consolidating nationhood by uniting land and people, or exporting industrially scaled plaza art to international corporate capitalists – or of a progressive social-welfarism – promoting the nuclear family and open-air leisure among the masses of postwar Britain.[11] Contemporary reassessment of Hepworth's work has been inhibited by lack of access to her archive, but of late scholars have sought to distinguish her achievements from Moore's, examine the prejudices she encountered as a female artist, and open up psychoanalytical readings of her work.[12]

Of the younger British sculptors who emerged from Moore's shadow in the 1950s, eight have been associated as a group since their collective showing at the 1952 Venice Biennale – Robert Adams, Kenneth Armitage, Reg Butler, Lynn Chadwick, Geoffrey Clarke, Bernard Meadows, Eduardo Paolozzi and William Turnbull – though the grouping has often been extended to include many of their contemporaries, followers and students, such as Hubert Dalwood and Elisabeth Frink. Defying easy categorisation, their work ranges over and often synthesises aspects of expressionism (anatomical distortion and wrought surfaces), Surrealism (metamorphic imagery) and realism (psychological conviction). It owes a debt to contemporary Paris-based sculptors, especially Alberto Giacometti, Julio González, Pablo Picasso and Germaine Richier. Hepworth's and Moore's voluminous forms and polished surfaces were replaced by open, linear and planar forms, often with an emphatic frontality and rough facture. The materials and/or fabrication techniques were new to British sculpture, notably forged and welded iron, sectioned and jointed wood, and directly modelled, uncast plaster. Bronzes were often cast from plaster originals, and in Paolozzi's case embedded with machine parts (Fig. 2). These pitted and encrusted surfaces, and scarred and distressed patinas, evoked aged or worn human skin. Working directly with plaster, iron or wax accommodated notions of expressive spontaneity and Surrealist automatism, and was seen as appropriate to 'the tension and fugitiveness

2 Eduardo Paolozzi, 'Cyclops', 1957, bronze

of the twentieth century', while carving wood or stone was now seen to belong to a 'pastoral', 'leisured culture'.[13] However, the preferred subjects, like Hepworth's and Moore's, derived for the most part from the natural world, though their humans, animals, birds, crustaceans and insects often seemed to be scuttling, wounded or dying, resembling the imagery of contemporary, British realist painters, especially Francis Bacon, Lucian Freud and Graham Sutherland. But where Moore (and sometimes Hepworth) conflated body and landscape, the younger sculptors created hybrid 'personages' – man and animal, woman and bird and so on – or mutations of man and machine, or man and robot, coinciding with the Independent Group's anthropologically based comparisons of 'primitive' and modern culture. Typically these effigies stand, sentinel-like, tense and alert, singly rather than in groups, and are denied implied potential for movement or flight. They embody an ambiguous dialectic as creatures which are predatory, threatening and aggressive, but also vulnerable, anguished and frightened. Heads are diminutive and featureless, or reduced to a single eye, while limbs, wings, tails, beaks, claws and so on are reduced to spiky protuberances. Formally, the bulk of the body is usually raised on slender legs, or above a secondary base, or the whole figure may be precariously supported on rods, dramatising the relation between sculptural weight and spatial suspension. A sense of insubstantiality is sometimes heightened by massive, Giacometti-like, slab bases creating fictive and narrative space.

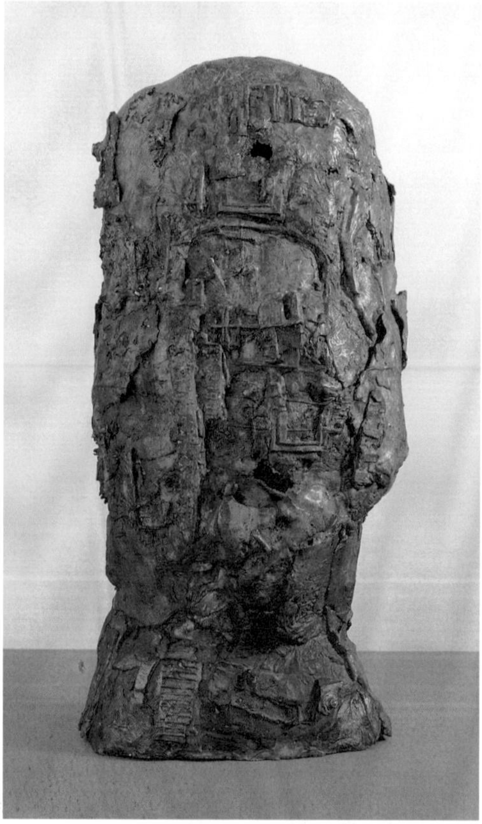

The attenuated forms and angry surfaces of this sculpture have long been compared with contemporary press images of the emaciated or charred bodies of the victims of the war, the Holocaust and the atom bomb.[14] Their humanistic pathos has most frequently been explained in terms of a general sense of postwar existential despair and foreboding, precipitated by the horrors of war and Cold War[15] (paralleling the proliferation of invading aliens and mutants in contemporary science-fiction literature and film). Existentialist philosophy was an attraction to many of these artists,[16] but the origin of their popular interpretation lies more particularly in Read's famous description of the sculptures: 'These new images belong to the iconography of despair, or of defiance; ... Here are images of flight, of ragged claws ... of excoriated flesh, frustrated sex, the geometry of fear.'[17] Read's view derived from an eclectic mix of cultural, psychological and political theory which combined his beliefs that geometric abstraction was characteristic of art produced in a hostile environment, that the world was living in a state of collective anxiety, and that man was alienated under capitalism.[18] Read's potent phrase has served for fifty years to define this metaphorical art but at the cost of more careful analysis, which might take as a starting point a recent observation that their 'imagery of metamorphosis ... speaks of the negation of identity, of selfhood'.[19]

Abstraction and formalism: Caro and the New Generation sculptors

A new aesthetic in British sculpture appeared in 1960 following increased awareness of American modernist art and criticism. Among the first to abandon expressionistic figuration were Anthony Caro, a former assistant of Moore's, and several of his students at St Martin's School of Art, London. One of them, Phillip King, claimed (erroneously) that in 1959 he destroyed 'everything' he had done, dismayed that contemporary European sculpture was 'dominated by a postwar feeling ... somehow terribly like scratching your own wounds – an international style with everyone showing the same neuroses'.[20] Caro's epiphany came after visiting the USA and meeting the influential critic Clement Greenberg and several of his protégés, including the sculptor David Smith. From early 1960 Caro followed Smith's example of working with metal – welding, bolting or riveting steel and aluminium plates, girders, bars and piping – to produce open, abstract, improvised compositions. But unlike Smith's lingering anthropomorphism, Caro's sculptures are laterally oriented, spreading across the floor or, in later pieces, the table-top. Severe orthogonal geometries are relieved by sweeping, irregular curves. Surfaces are without incident, unified by uniform flat colour which denies the utilitarian associations and physicality of the materials, and the expressive mark of the artist. Earlier modernist concerns with 'open-air' and 'in-the-round' sculpture were replaced by a preference for gallery display and privileged viewpoints (made explicit in the frontality of the 'table-pieces'). In 'Early One Morning' (1962; Fig. 3), for example, the combination of a low, heavy, lateral, orthogonal sub-structure and light, upwardly curving, non-structural rods creates a sequence of highly differentiated visual experiences. Abandoning the long tradition of the pedestal, Caro's

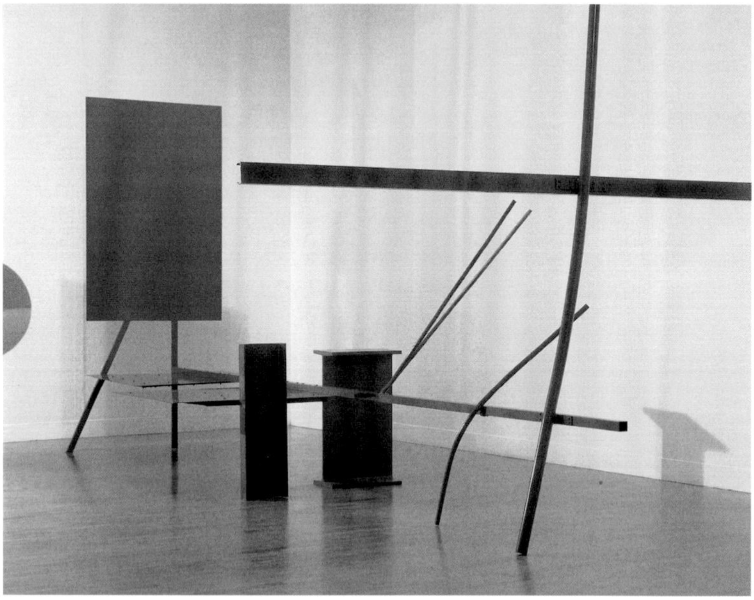

3 Anthony Caro, 'Early One Morning', 1962, steel and aluminium

sculptures stand directly on the floor in the same space as the spectator. Where the mood of 1950s sculpture had been anguished, Caro's sculpture was now exuberant.

Caro's sculptures mark the growing influence on British art of Greenberg's formalist criticism (and with it the demise of Read's and Moore's pre-eminence). Greenberg proposed that sculpture, like other modernist arts, was achieving purity and quality by confining itself to the unique and irreducible attributes of its medium; that through 'optical' rather than tactile or temporal effects sculpture offered transcendent experience; that 'figurative allusiveness' and 'pictoriality' were legitimate because three-dimensionality obviated the danger of illusionism (as long as it refrained from illusion of organic substance or texture); and that sculpture's autonomy made it 'the representative visual art of modernism'.[21] For Greenberg, modern sculpture's liberation from the 'monolith' and full engagement with the third dimension had been initiated by Cubism:

> The new construction-sculpture points back, almost insistently, to its origins in Cubist painting: by its linearism … openness and transparency and weightlessness, and by its preoccupation with surface as skin alone, which it expresses in blade- or sheet-like forms. Space is there to be shaped, divided, enclosed, but not filled or sealed in. The new sculpture tends to abandon stone, bronze and clay for industrial

materials like iron, steel, alloys, glass, plastics, celluloid, etc, etc, which are worked with the blacksmith's, the welder's and even the carpenter's tools. Unity of material and colour is no longer required, and applied colour is sanctioned. The distinction between carving and modeling becomes irrelevant: a work or its parts can be cast, wrought, cut or simply put together: the new sculpture is not so much sculpted as constructed, built, assembled, arranged.[22]

Greenberg's observations were based primarily on developments in American sculpture but might be read as a manifesto for Caro's post-1960 sculpture (which even dispensed with 'figurative allusiveness'). Greenberg and his associate, Michael Fried, agreed that Caro's sculpture represented a 'breakthrough' in the evolution of non-monolithic sculpture and hailed his importance as equal to Smith's. Indeed, Greenberg's contention that modernist sculpture sprang from the Cubists' escape 'into the non-pictorial, real space in front of the picture' might almost be illustrated by Caro's 'Early One Morning', which, when viewed from one end, invites its rectangular planes and curving rods to be seen 'pictorially' against the canvas-upon-easel-like component, evoking fragments of *papier-collé* and drawn lines.[23] Fried, however, argued that the expressive effects of Caro's 'syntax', bright colour and opticality should not be understood only in formal terms. Drawing on the phenomenological philosophy of Maurice Merleau-Ponty, Fried proposed that Caro's sculptures intimated profound emotion through the construction of abstract 'gesture' (i.e. prelingual expression), analogous to bodily movement and sensation: 'For all their abstraction one can imagine a gifted dancer dancing Caro's sculptures.'[24] Caro came to speak of his sculptures in similar terms, wishing them to be experienced temporally by being walked around, and physically by analogy with bodily feeling (lying, bending, stretching, etc.), underlining continuities with his earlier figurative work.[25]

Caro exerted unparalleled influence on British sculpture through his teaching on the Advanced Sculpture course at St Martin's. Like Moore, this was done not by establishing a 'school' of imitators but by his ambitious and inquiring example. Along with King, five other of his students, David Annesley, Michael Bolus, Tim Scott, William Tucker and Isaac Witkin, were given a collective identity by the Whitechapel's 1965 exhibition, *The New Generation.*[26] The catalogue announced 'a radically new and different concept of sculpture'.[27] Their sculptures are characterised by simple, geometric forms and brilliant, flat, primary or pastel, 'nursery' colours, applied or integral to the material, articulating structure and signalling optimism. The new sculptures were

4 William Tucker, 'Series A, No. 1', 1968–9, fibreglass

floor-based, of human proportion ('like working with another person opposite you'),[28] and used materials with industrial or manufacturing associations, not only metals but plastics, perspex, glass, acrylic sheet, and fibreglass and polyester-resin, fabricated by constructing, moulding or jointing. Their smooth, impersonal finishes were resolutely urban and non-organic. King's conical sculptures undermine the apparent weight of an 'earthbound' form by peeling, slicing or opening it, and by visually detaching its single, continuous, outer 'skin' from its internal 'core' through strong applied colour.[29] Following Greenberg's notion that modernist sculpture evolved from modernist painting, these sculptors looked to Kenneth Noland's target paintings, Henri Matisse's paper cut-outs, and the abstract canvases of British 'Situation' painters, several of them, like Richard Smith, colleagues at St Martin's.[30] Rejecting, however, the importance Greenberg and Caro attached to collage and expressivity brought new interests in volume, impersonal methods of assembly (stacking, laying or leaning) and a 'cool' aesthetic resembling US minimalist and post-minimalist works, similarly sanctioned ultimately by Constantin Brancusi. Instead of relational, syntactical, part-to-part composition, they are single, 'whole things' – 'specific objects' in Donald Judd's terms – or simple, unitary forms, configured by an apparent internal logic of repetition, alternation, inversion, reflection, variation or other sequential development. In Tucker's 'Series A (No. 1)' (1968–9; Fig. 4) the duplication of a comparatively simple, non-inflected form, with one laid on the floor and the other obliquely across it, is more like Judd's than Caro's sculpture, though despite the impersonal geometry there is a latent anthropomorphism.

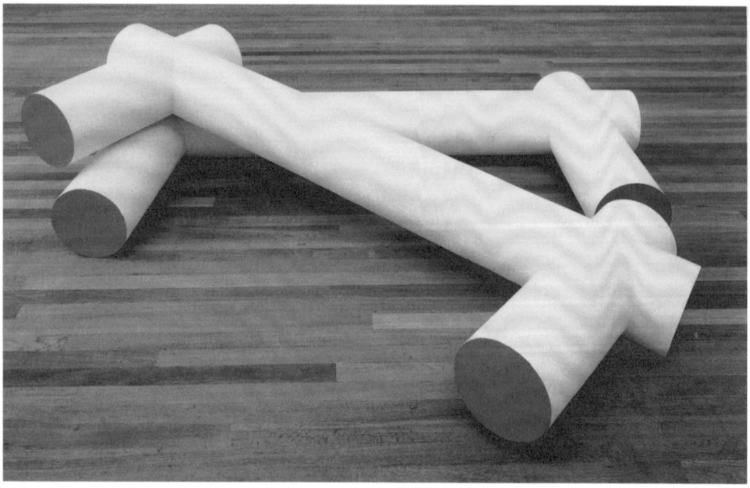

Tucker, the most theoretically minded of the New Generation sculptors, described himself as 'a formalist' yet elsewhere[31] acknowledged that sculpture's 'condition' was at least partly determined by the contingent and external. In doing so he signalled a move away from Greenberg's formalism and came closer to Fried (a frequent visitor to St Martin's in the 1960s). Though Fried came to oppose the 'theatricality' he identified with a nexus of phenomenological and existential understandings of sculpture,[32] Tucker and other New Generation sculptors embraced such concepts as they increasingly impinged on British aesthetics in the 1960s, especially through the writings of US minimalist sculptor Robert Morris and political philosopher Hannah Arendt, encouraging Tucker to conceive of sculpture metaphysically as 'thing' or 'presence'.[33] (Tucker now dismissed the influence of existentialism on 'geometry of fear' sculpture as superficial, denigrating its 'cheap and melodramatic imagery'.[34]) British abstract painting at the tellingly named *Place* and *Situation* exhibitions of 1959–63, involving several St Martin's painters, had already affirmed the phenomenological presumption of spectatorship as embodied, situated and conditional.[35] That King had absorbed similar ideas is apparent from his comment that 'The idea of space that interests me is always a physical space, it isn't an abstract or ideal notion of space, but a felt notion.'[36] The conflicted interests of New Generation sculptors – bridging formalism and phenomenology – gave them an ambiguous position in relation to Fried's efforts to police the boundaries between modernism and minimalism, or 'art and objecthood',[37] and may explain the comparative critical silence of both Greenberg and Fried.

Redefining sculpture: the St Martin's avant-garde

The St Martin's Advanced Sculpture course contributed vitally to the climate of artistic experiment which thrived in Britain between 1965 and 1975. British representation at the earliest international exhibitions and publications surveying 'the new art' was dominated by six of its former students, Barry Flanagan, Gilbert & George, Richard Long, Roelof Louw and Bruce McLean, and the part-time tutor, John Latham.[38] That the new 'British avant-garde'[39] was partly inspired by Caro's efforts to teach 'not a style or dogma, but a discipline of doubt and enquiry'[40] is confirmed by Flanagan's recollections of attending in 1960: 'The Friday evening classes at St Martin's … prompted the writing of poetry, a play, film scripts, songs, the purchase of cine equipment, and work on a means to translate movement and atmosphere into music.'[41] Yet, according to McLean, by the mid-1960s – when all six of the New Generation sculptors were on its teaching staff – teaching had rigidified into a narrow and dogmatic formalism: 'The St Martin's sculpture forum would avoid every broader issue, discussing the position of one piece of metal in relation to another for hours.'[42] McLean's 'pose works' (see Fig. 1 in Chris Stephen's essay 'Identity of the sculptor 1950–75' in this volume) lampoon the exaggeratedly contemplative attitudes adopted by his tutors in studio crits,[43] seemingly enacting their perception of sculpture's relation to the body. Dissatisfaction with the Greenbergian account of modernism was evidently shared by many students and some staff, as demonstrated in 1966 by the 'Still and Chew Event' in which Latham and several students (including Flanagan and Long) chemically dissolved the library copy of the American critic's influential collection of essays, *Art and Culture*, returning it in a phial wittily labelled 'Essence of Greenberg'. The desire to 'neutralise' Greenberg's essentialising theory accompanied scepticism toward his privileging of sculpture and painting as objects of aesthetic contemplation, his emphasis on retinal (rather than phenomenal) experience, and his presumption of art's detachment from social life. Greenberg's closures on modernist painting encouraged a belief in the 'precedence of sculpture over painting as an area for potential action'.[44] Commitment to 'sculpture' – or 'three-dimensional thinking' (Judd's terminology circumvented Greenberg's disciplinary boundaries) – distinguished St Martin's students from their UK-based conceptualist contemporaries whose more overtly political or philosophically oriented work more often utilised image-and-text or 'readymades'.[45] The recent 'rediscovery' of Duchamp, and greater knowledge of his US followers, such as John Cage, confirmed the fruitfulness of non-Greenbergian attitudes to modernism, revived the historical avant-garde's strategy of integrating 'art' and 'life', and encouraged a view that the artwork is 'completed' by the spectator.[46]

In keeping with a more phenomenologically based understanding of art as something apprehended by 'embodied consciousness' (Merleau-Ponty) and contingent upon its conditions of display, the new 'sculpture' explored duration and context, experimenting with time-based events and media (Jan Dibbets, David Dye, Hamish Fulton and John Hilliard taking 'sculptural thinking' into photography and film), and alternatives to the sanctified viewing conditions of the 'white cube'.[47] Unlike the carefully composed, rigid sculptures of their tutors, bearing associations with industrial manufacture and assumptions of formal permanence and autonomy, the new works might be transient, 'soft', and/or contingent upon environment or installation. In 'Floataway Sculpture' (1967), McLean threw pieces of chipboard and linoleum into a river and in 'Vertical Ice Sculpture' (1967) stood a sheet of ice on a frozen pond. Some of Flanagan's impermanent, 'self-forming' arrangements of mundane materials, such as rope, branches, flax sheets and hessian bags filled with sand, 'illustrated' basic verbs describing the manipulation of materials – folding, piling, stacking, propping, etc. – paralleling Richard Serra's 'anti-form' sculptures in the USA (Fig. 5).[48] Louw explored the 'interactive' relationship between sculptural works and their varied viewing conditions, often exhibiting in non-traditional spaces.[49] Gilbert & George and Long made 'sculpture' – never 'performance'[50] – from simple, inexpressive, ordinary actions, such as eating, drinking, walking, cycling, moving stones, etc., often monotonously and arduously repeated, and enacted outside the gallery. In their legendary 'Singing Sculpture' (see Fig. 5 in Chris Stephen's essay 'Identity of the sculptor 1950–75' in this volume), in which they mimed for hours on end to the music-hall song 'Underneath the Arches', they were elevated and metallicised like sculptures, while their robotic movements parodied expressionist gesture and perhaps, more specifically, Fried's notion of a dancer dancing Caro's sculptures. Long's linear or circular configurations in the landscape or gallery invited the spectator to take

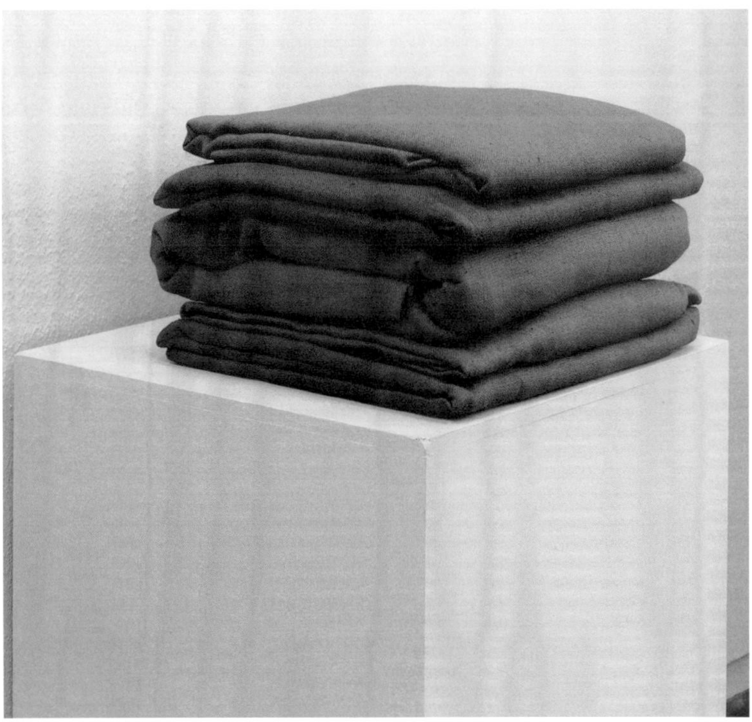

5 Barry Flanagan, 'Pile 3', 1968, hessian

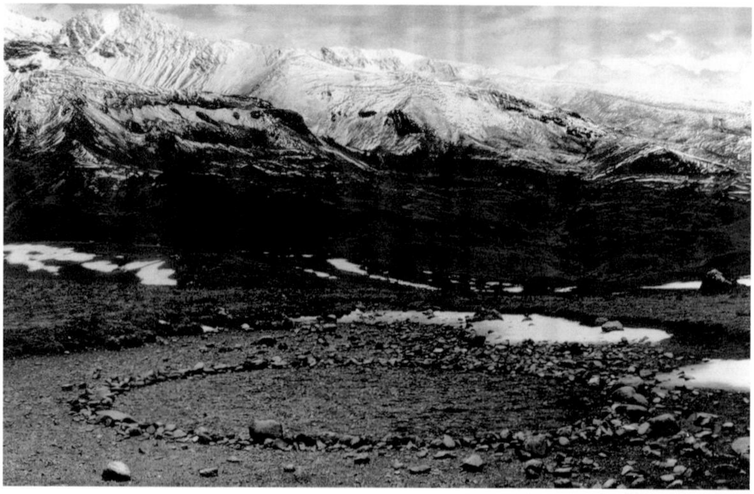

6 Richard Long, 'Circle in the Andes', 1972

a real or imaginative 'walk' along or around them, extending Caro's durational sense of sculptural experience (Fig. 6). But the 'timeless' and 'universal' forms of his sculptures and map routes were chosen to be non-expressive, avoiding 'personal unwanted aesthetic paraphernalia'.[51] Long's romanticism, however, leaves him unconcerned about the political specificities of landscape and susceptible to materialist and post-colonialist critiques.[52] Overall, the St Martin's avant-garde bears comparison with Italian *Arte Povera* and US post-minimalism, in its privileging of low-grade materials, formal repetition, chance and indeterminancy, process over product, and substance over form, as much as in its rejection of formal incident, expressive gesture and authorial personality.[53] By reinstating temporality and situatedness, these sculptors allied themselves with the 'theatricality' and self-reflexiveness Fried identified with minimalism, rather than modernism's supposed transcendence and liberation from self-awareness.[54]

The foremost 'ally and spokesman'[55] of this British avant-garde, and of the new St Martin's sculpture, was the critic Charles Harrison. Before becoming its principal historian, Harrison had written articles on this work for its chief organ, *Studio International* (of which he was also assistant editor), and curated two seminal exhibitions.[56] In his introduction to the initiatory *When Attitudes Become Form* (1969), Harrison presented the new 'three dimensional work' as an antidote to the autonomy and social exclusivity of modernist painting. Artistic experiment would be a model for social experiment; this 'radical art' would change 'human consciousness' and 'attitude to life', undermining the 'consensus view of the world'.[57] Though Harrison came to regret his extravagant avant-gardist claims,[58] he continues to argue that the new art's efforts to recover the traditional 'oppositional character' of modernism was an extension of the idealism and utopianism of 1960s 'counter-culture'.[59] Younger artists, according to him, felt 'relatively emancipated from that conviction of the authority of American art [and criticism]', because left-wing intellectuals, spurred on in an instinctive anti-Americanism by US involvement in Vietnam, had lost faith in modernism and virtually all claims for 'high art', recognising 'the implication of modernist theory in the cultural politics of the Cold War'.[60] But Harrison has had to admit, like others before him,[61] the failure of the avant-garde's efforts to resist institutional appropriation, assimilation to the market, and incorporation into the dominant cultural order.[62] (An early and striking example of this was MoMA's acquisition in 1970 of the paraphernalia used in Latham's 'Still and Chew Event'.) And, finally, just as Harrison notes modernism's implication in the politics of the Cold War, we may begin to discern the determining effects of the East–West ideological struggle on the forms and meanings of British modernist sculpture throughout this whole twenty-five-year period, as they underwent the most far-reaching transformation of any previous quarter-century, from the existential pathos of 1950s figuration, through the phenomenological individualism of 1960s abstraction, to the oppositional manoeuvring of 1970s disciplinary transgressions.

Robert Burstow

Notes

1 The key secondary sources are: S. Nairne and N. Serota (eds), *British Sculpture in the Twentieth Century*, London, Whitechapel Art Gallery, 1981; S. Compton (ed.), *British Art in the 20th Century*, London, Royal Academy of Arts, 1987; T. A. Neff (ed.), *A Quiet Revolution: British Sculpture Since 1965*, London, Thames and Hudson, 1987; I. Chambers and L. Cooke, *Starlit Waters: British Sculpture, An International Art 1968–1988*, Liverpool, Tate Gallery Liverpool, 1988; P. Curtis, *Modern British Sculpture From the Collection*, London, Tate Gallery, 1988; *Un Siècle de Sculpture Anglaise*, Paris, Galerie Nationale de Jeu de Paume, 1996; A. Causey, *Sculpture Since 1945*, Oxford, Oxford University Press, 1998.

2 For a rare exception, see T. Hyman, 'Figurative sculpture since 1960', in Nairne and Serota (eds), *British Sculpture in the Twentieth Century*, pp. 184–95.

3 Recent exhibitions include: *Colour Sculptures: Britain in the Sixties* (Waddington Galleries, London, 1999), *Live in Your Head: Concept and Experiment in Britain 1965–75* (Whitechapel Art Gallery, London, 2000), *Tra-La-La: British Sculpture in the Sixties*

(Tate Britain, London, 2002) and *Henry Moore and the Geometry of Fear* (James Hyman Fine Art, London, 2002). On the debt of neo-conceptualist young British artists (yBas) to their first-generation-conceptualist tutors at Goldsmiths', see M. Archer, 'Out of the studio', in C. Philpott and A. Tarsia (eds), *Live in Your Head*, London, Whitechapel Art Gallery, 2000, p. 29. On the debt of younger 'new formalists' to Anthony Caro and New Generation sculptors, see Whitechapel Art Gallery, London, *Early One Morning: British Art Now*, 2002 (including Shahin Afrassiabi, Claire Barclay, Jim Lambie, Eva Rothschild and Gary Webb). The exhibition title paid explicit homage to Caro [see Fig. 3]) and the catalogue made comparisons between the two groups of artists: see M. Horlock, 'Tra-la-la: British sculpture in the sixties', in *Early One Morning*, p. 39. The description 'new formalists' is used in J. J. Charlesworth, 'Not neo but new', *Art Monthly*, September 2002, no. 259, pp. 7–11.

4 C. Harrison, 'Sculpture's recent past', in Neff (ed.), *A Quiet Revolution: British Sculpture Since 1965*, p. 12.

5 At least one earlier essay has adopted this approach: J. Glaves-Smith, 'Sculpture in the 1940s and 1950s: the form and the language', in Nairne and Serota (eds), *British Sculpture in the Twentieth Century*, pp. 124–33.

6 See J. Hyman, *The Battle for Realism: Figurative Art in Britain During the Cold War 1945-1960*, New Haven, CT, and London, Yale University Press, 2001, pp. 11–35.

7 See A. Grieve, 'Constructivism after the Second World War', in Nairne and Serota (eds), *British Sculpture in the Twentieth Century*, pp. 154–65, and S. Gathercole, 'Welfare state constructionism', *Visual Culture in Britain*, 2002, vol. 3, no. 2, pp. 57–80.

8 H. Read, *The Art of Sculpture*, New York, Bollingen Foundation, 1956, p. 49. The book is based on his 1954 Andrew W. Mellon lectures in the Fine Arts, National Gallery of Art, Washington, which in turn were based on his 1953 ICA lectures, 'The aesthetics of sculpture'. For a fuller account of Read's aesthetics, see D. Thistlewood, *Herbert Read: Formlessness and Form – An Introduction to His Aesthetics*, London, Routledge and Kegan Paul, 1984.

9 See R. Burstow, '"The geometry of fear": Herbert Read and British modern sculpture after the Second World War', in B. Read and D. Thistlewood (eds), *Herbert Read: A British Vision of World Art*, Leeds and London, Leeds City Art Galleries with the Henry Moore Foundation and Lund Humphries, 1993, p. 122.

10 Read borrowed these terms from the artists' own statements; see H. Read, 'Introduction', in B. Hepworth, *Barbara Hepworth, Carvings and Drawings*, London, Lund Humphries, 1952, p. ix.

11 See, for example, A. Barnett, *England's Henry Moore*, Channel 4 TV, broadcast 21 September 1988; P. Overy, 'Lions and unicorns: the Britishness of postwar British sculpture', *Art in America* (New York), September 1991, no. 79, pp. 153; J. Stallabrass, 'The mother and child theme in the work of Henry Moore', in P. Cramer (ed.), *Henry Moore, Mother and Child*, Much Hadham, Henry Moore Foundation, 1992, pp. 13–36, and R. Burstow, 'Moore's "Open-air" sculpture: a modern, reforming aesthetic of sunlight and air', in J. Beckett and F. Russell (eds), *Henry Moore: Critical Essays: Place, Sculpture, Politics*, Aldershot, Ashgate with Henry Moore Foundation, 2003, pp. 143–72.

12 See D. Thistlewood (ed.), *Barbara Hepworth Reconsidered*, Liverpool, Liverpool University Press and Tate Gallery Liverpool, 1996.

13 R. Butler and B. Hepworth, 'Artists on art', BBC Third Programme, broadcast 26 August 1952; cited in L. Alloway, 'Britain's new iron age', *Art News* (New York), June–August 1953, vol. 52, no. 4, pp. 19–20.

14 For example, Causey, *Sculpture Since 1945*, p. 8.

15 For example, R. Cork, 'The emancipation of modern British sculpture', in Compton (ed.), *British Art in the 20th Century*, p. 40.

16 See D. Mellor, 'Existentialism and post-war British art', in F. Morris (ed.), *Paris Post War: Art and Existentialism 1945–55*, London, Tate Gallery, 1993, pp. 53–62.

17 H. Read, 'New aspects of British sculpture', in British Council, *The XXVI Venice Biennale: The British Pavilion*, London, Westminster Press, 1952, n.p.

18 For a fuller discussion, see Burstow, '"The geometry of fear": Herbert Read and British modern sculpture after the Second World War', pp. 123–5.

19 M. Garlake, 'Identifying the geometry of fear', in *Henry Moore and the Geometry of Fear*, London, James Hyman Fine Art, 2002, p. 5.

20 'British artists at Venice: 2. Phillip King talks about his sculpture', *Studio International*, June 1968, vol. 175, no. 901, p. 300.

21 'Sculpture in our time', *Arts Magazine* (USA), June 1958; reprinted in J. O'Brian (ed.), *Clement Greenberg: The Collected Essays and Criticism: Vol. 4: Modernism with a Vengeance, 1957–1969*, Chicago, University of Chicago Press, 1993, pp. 55–61. This is a heavily revised version of an earlier essay, 'The new sculpture', *Partisan Review*, June 1949, no. 16, pp. 637–42; reprinted in J. O'Brian (ed.), *Clement Greenberg: The Collected Essays and Criticism: Vol. 2: Arrogant Purpose, 1945–1949*, Chicago, University of Chicago Press, 1986, pp. 313–18.

22 'Sculpture in our time', p. 58.

23 C. Greenberg, 'The pasted-paper revolution', *Art News* (New York), September 1958, vol. LVII; reprinted in O'Brian (ed.), *Clement Greenberg: The Collected Essays and Criticism: Vol. 4*, pp. 61–6. According to Horlock, ever since it was exhibited at the Tate's exhibition, *British Sculpture of the Sixties* (1965), an allusion to the act of painting has been identified in the easel-like component ('Tra-la-la', in *Early One Morning*, p. 38); David Mellor refers to the 'allegorical easel at one end with the large rectangle standing in as a red monochrome canvas; a sign of painting.' (D. Mellor, *The Sixties Art Scene in London*, London, Phaidon with Barbican Art Gallery, 1993, p. 97); Rosalind Krauss has noted its relation to Greenbergian theory (R. Krauss, *Passages in Modern Sculpture*, Cambridge, MA, MIT, 1977, pp. 187–92); Charles Harrison refers to an illustration of this sculpture after quoting at length from Greenberg's 'Collage' essay (Harrison, 'Sculpture's recent past', p. 14).

24 M. Fried, 'Introduction', *Anthony Caro: Sculpture 1960–1963*, London, Whitechapel Art Gallery, 1963, pp. 1–5.

25 'Phyllis Tuchman: an interview with Anthony Caro', *Artforum* (New York), June and July 1972; reprinted in R. Whelan (ed.), *Anthony Caro*, Harmondsworth, Penguin, 1974, pp. 115–31.

26 The exhibition also included three sculptors from the RCA or the Slade who are not generally considered to be part of this group, while William Turnbull who did not exhibit usually is (see for example *The Alistair McAlpine Gift*, London, Tate Gallery, 1971). For more on the 'New Generation' exhibitions, see M. Yule, '"A place for living art": The Whitechapel Art Gallery, 1952–1968', in M. Garlake (ed.), *Artists and Patrons in Post-War Britain*, Aldershot, Ashgate, 2001, pp. 110–16.

27 B. Robertson, in *The New Generation*, London, Whitechapel Art Gallery, 1965, p. 8.

28 P. King quoted in R. Cork, *Phillip King: sculpturen*, Mannheim, Stadtische Kunsthalle, 1992; quoted in Horlock, 'Tra-la-la: British sculpture in the sixties', p. 46.

29 See 'British artists at Venice: 2', *Studio International*, June 1968, p. 301.

30 I. Dunlop, in *The New Generation*, London, Whitechapel Art Gallery, 1965, p. 25.

31 See 'Confessions of a formalist', unpublished transcript of a lecture given in the sculpture department at St Martin's, 12 March 1976, and 'Introduction', *The Condition of Sculpture*, London, Hayward Gallery, 1975, p. 7. For more on Tucker's increasingly phenomenological approach, see his 'What sculpture is' articles published in *Studio International*, 1974–5, and A. Sleeman, *William Tucker: The Language of a Sculptor*, Leeds, Henry Moore Institute, 1995, pp. 6–7.

32 M. Fried, 'Art and objecthood', *Artforum* (New York), June 1967, vol. 5, no. 10, pp. 12–23; reprinted in C. Harrison and P. Wood (eds), *Art in Theory, 1900–1990*, Oxford, Blackwell, 1992, pp. 822–34.

33 See R. Morris, 'Notes on sculpture', parts 1–4, and 'Some notes on the phenomenology of making', *Artforum* (New York), 1966–70; reprinted in R. Morris, *Continuous Project Altered Daily: The Writings of Robert Morris*, Cambridge, MA, MIT, 1994. Interest among US artists and critics was stimulated by Sartre's celebrated catalogue essay for Giacometti's 1948 exhibition at the Pierre Matisse Gallery in New York. Tucker valued Arendt's book, *The Human Condition* (1958), especially highly and circulated it at St Martin's. He quotes from it in his 'Essay on sculpture' (*Studio International*, January 1969, vol. 177, no. 907, p. 12). For more on the influence of existentialism and phenomenology on New Generation sculpture, see Mellor, *The Sixties Art Scene in London*, p. 94, and Causey, *Sculpture Since 1945*, p. 117.

34 W. Tucker, *The Language of Sculpture*, London, Thames and Hudson, 1974, p. 83.

35 On the *Place* exhibition, see T. Treves, 'Place', in Garlake (ed.), *Artists and Patrons in Post-War Britain*, pp. 154–82. In his review, Lawrence Alloway remarked that 'the pleasure-and-traps-of-the-spectator syndrome, [is] at present so characteristic of British aesthetics' (quoted in Treves, 'Place', p. 176).

36 'British artists at Venice: 2', *Studio International*, June 1968, pp. 303–4. On Arendt's influence on King, see T. Hilton, *The Sculpture of Phillip King*, London, Henry Moore Foundation with Lund Humphries, 1992, p. 40.

37 See M. Fried, 'Art and objecthood'. King, Scott and Tucker were included with US minimalists in *Primary Structures*, New York, Jewish Museum, 1966.

38 *Op Losse Schroeven (Square Pegs in Round Holes)* (Stedelijk Museum, Amsterdam, 1969) included Flanagan, Long, Louw and McLean; *When Attitudes Become Form* (Vereins Kunsthalle, Berne, Kaiser Wilhelm Museum, Krefeld and ICA, London, 1969) included Flanagan, Long (in Gary Schum's film, *Land Art*), Louw and McLean (Gilbert & George were not official participants but did an impromptu performance at the private view of the ICA showing; see A. Rorimer, *New Art in the 60s and 70s*, London, Thames and Hudson, 2001, pp. 142–3); *Information* (MoMA, New York, 1970) included Flanagan, Gilbert & George, Latham, Long and McLean; *The New Art* (Tate Gallery, London, 1972) included Flanagan, Gilbert & George and Long; L. Lippard, *Six Years: the Dematerialization of the Art Object from 1966–1972* (London, Studio Vista, 1973), included Flanagan, Gilbert & George, Latham, Long and McLean.

39 The term was used for the exhibition, *The British Avant-Garde* (New York Cultural Center, 1971), curated by Charles Harrison, which included several of the St Martin's graduates discussed here; the catalogue took the form of a special issue of *Studio International* (May 1971). Harrison claims that it formed the basis of *The New Art* (Tate Gallery, 1972).

40 N. Lynton, 'Latest developments in British sculpture', *Art and Literature*, Summer 1964, no. 2, p. 196.

41 B. Flanagan, letter to Caro, June 1963; published in *Silâns (Silence)*, a student magazine co-edited by Flanagan, 6 January 1965. Flanagan first attended the course for three months in 1960 before returning in 1964.

42 N. Dimitrijevic, *Bruce McLean*, London, Whitechapel Art Gallery, 1981; recited in *When Attitudes Became Form*, 1984, p. 64.

43 Archer, 'Out of the studio', in *Live in Your Head*, 2000, p. 29. In another work, 'There's a sculpture on my shoulder' (1970 and 2002), the artist is weighed down by New Generation sculpture (Horlock, 'Tra-la-la: British sculpture in the sixties', p. 47).

44 C. Harrison, 'Against precedents', in *When Attitudes Become Form*, London, ICA, 1969, n.p.; reprinted in *Studio International*, September 1969, vol. 178, no. 914, pp. 90–3.

45 Principally Victor Burgin and Michael Craig-Martin (both freshly out of Yale), and the Art and Language Group (centred on Coventry College of Art).

46 Duchamp's first UK exhibition was held in 1966, followed by his Tate retrospective in 1970. Flanagan's interest is demonstrated by his attendance at a performance of Merce Cunningham's dance company in 1964, which Cage also attended (L. Biggs, in *Barry Flanagan: A Visual Invitation, Sculpture 1967–1987*, Newcastle upon Tyne, Laing Art Gallery, 1987, p. 9).

47 The phrase was gaining currency in contemporary theoretical critiques of the gallery space; see, principally, Brian O'Doherty's three articles, 'Inside the white cube: the ideology of the gallery space', published in serial form in *Artforum* (New York) in 1976 (revised as *Inside the White Cube: The Ideology of the Gallery Space*, Berkeley and Los Angeles, University of California Press, 1999 [1986]).

48 See L. Biggs, in *Barry Flanagan: A Visual Invitation, Sculpture 1967–1987*, p. 13. On Serra's near contemporary sculptures derived from his 'verb list' compiled in 1967–8, see L. Rosenstock (ed.), *Richard Serra/Sculpture*, New York, MoMA, 1986, p.16.

49 See *Live in Your Head: Concept and Experiment in Britain 1965–75*, p. 125.

50 R. Long, interviewed by R. Cork, in *Richard Long: Walking in Circles*, London, Hayward Gallery, 1991, p. 248; Gilbert & George, letter, 17 April 1996, reproduced in *Un Siècle de Sculpture Anglaise*, pp. 256–7.

51 Interview with R. Cork, in *Richard Long: Walking in Circles*, p. 250.

52 Rasheed Araeen's *A Long Walk in the Wilderness* (1991) parodied Long's work (see M. Archer, *Art Since 1960*, London, Thames and Hudson, 1997, p. 200).

53 See especially R. Morris, 'Anti form', *Artforum* (New York), April 1968, vol. 6, no. 8, pp. 33–5; reprinted in R. Morris, *Continuous Project Altered Daily: the Writings of Robert Morris*, pp. 41–9.

54 Fried, 'Art and objecthood'.

55 Harrison's description of himself, in 'The late sixties in London and elsewhere', in *1965–1972: When Attitudes Became Form*, Cambridge, Kettle's Yard, 1984, p. 9.

56 For example, Harrison's 'Some recent sculpture in Britain' (*Studio International*, January 1969, vol. 177, no. 907, pp. 26–33) discussed all of these artists except Gilbert & George (on whom he has always been more reticent) and Latham. As curator of *When Attitudes Become Form* (for its London showing, ICA, 1969) and *The British Avant-Garde* (New York Cultural Center, 1971) Harrison, again, included in at least one of them all but Gilbert & George and Latham, though he later expressed regret for not including Latham in the ICA exhibition ('The late sixties in London and elsewhere', p. 10).

57 Harrison, 'Against precedents'.

58 Harrison, 'The late sixties in London and elsewhere'.

59 See Harrison, 'Sculpture's recent past', p. 27; C. Harrison, 'The suppression of the beholder: Sculpture and the later sixties', in Chambers and Cooke, *Starlit Waters: British*

Sculpture, An International Art 1968–1988, p. 40.

60 Harrison, 'Sculpture's recent past', p. 27.

61 For example, A. Seymour, 'Introduction', *The New Art*, London, Tate Gallery, 1972, p. 6.

62 Harrison, 'The late sixties in London and elsewhere', p. 14.

On common ground: sculpture and the viewing subject

The floor of the Whitechapel Gallery is on the same level as the street outside: you can get in or out very quickly. At least one psychological barrier between you and art has been removed. Similarly, in this exhibition, Caro's sculptures stand on the floor without the intervention of pedestals or bases. Their impact is direct and immediate .... (Bryan Robertson)[1]

At the first major exhibition of Anthony Caro's abstract work, held at the Whitechapel Gallery in 1963, the art objects inhabited the same space as the viewing public. Sculpture had, literally, been brought 'down to earth'. The relinquishing of plinths and pedestals had a particular significance which went beyond mere association with a modernist aesthetic. The act of 'grounding' the work implies a process of social levelling. In the exhibition catalogue, it is notable that Bryan Robertson alluded to the East End gallery's continuing commitment to removing barriers of social class and elitism. Traditionally, sculpture had been separated from its audience. Usually elevated on plinths or installed on buildings beyond human reach, sculpture was rarely in direct contact with ground, floor, pavement or people. Devoid of physical barriers, however, the unfettered object gave the viewing subject access to a more intimate and haptic encounter. Moreover, this closer relationship was powerfully symbolic of postwar political ideals of communal ownership and signifies the distinctly democratic nature of viewing in the period.

The trend was established with one of the earliest major postwar displays of sculpture – the South Bank site in the Festival of Britain.[2] Commissioned works, often misguidedly and unsuccessfully, vied for attention amongst 'the clamour and the crowds and the ice-cream cartons'.[3] However, for the viewing subject – the populace which thronged the pavilions, cafés and gardens – the interactive engagement with sculpture was not incidental. It was part of a constructed democratised experience prescribed by the organisers, who wanted to tell a single 'continuous interwoven story'.[4] At the heart of the prescribed narrative was the new Labour government's rebuilding of national identity – the remoulding of 'Britishness' – after the trauma of the war years.[5]

In 1985, Barry Curtis highlighted the programmatic nature of the Festival viewing experience as one which aimed to engender a positive sense of 'social democratic citizenship': '*Seeing* more closely and from more privileged positions, not previously afforded to the citizen-subject, is offered as a means of *participating.*'[6]

Curtis suggested that the 'participation' achieved by social and cultural practices such as art-viewing was superficial. Indeed, one might argue that the Reithian ethos of taking culture to the people enabled the mass consumption of the arts to act as a substitute for thorough going participatory democratic politics. Nevertheless, many subsequent sculpture exhibitions and displays did facilitate '*seeing* more closely'. They offered the viewer a more interactive experience. In addition to the physical grounding of sculpture, through the 1950s and 1960s viewers and objects increasingly shared what has been identified by Henri Lefebvre as 'social space'.[7] In particular, urban and industrial settings informed modes of sculpture production and display. Contemporary sculpture was incorporated into everyday social life as never before, becoming part of the 'situationist city'[8] as a lived-in working environment. The idea of 'common ground', therefore, offers a metaphor for reading narratives of display and examining the experience of viewing sculpture in the period.

Of course, the gallery continued to provide display space for British sculpture, both at home and abroad. In the early postwar years, one of the most influential shows was at the Venice Biennale in 1952, which, plinthbound and defined by nationality, did little to radicalise the viewing experience. On the domestic front, though, some galleries devised fresh approaches to showing sculpture. The Whitechapel, in particular, was at the forefront of many innovatory exhibitions: the 1951 show *Black Eyes and Lemonade*[9] featured sculptural kitsch; architecture and sculpture were integrated in *This is Tomorrow* in 1955; gaudy plastic and fibreglass forms hugged the floor at the *New Generation* show in 1965.

There is a general consensus that, in these postwar years, modernist aesthetics – underpinned by Greenbergian ideas – directly shaped the gallery context, including the curation and display of sculpture.[10] Of course, there were anomalies such as Gallery One in London, run by Victor Musgrave. The new Mayfair premises which Musgrave opened in May 1961 were reported in the press as 'expensively simple' with 'snow-white walls' and 'Cinderella-like splendour'.[11] Significantly, though, the majority of work which Musgrave showed did not fit into the modernist canon. In 1961, the gallery provided an elegant backdrop for George Fullard's assemblages made from bits of old furniture, wooden picture frames and bombsite finds. Later the same year, Musgrave showed a

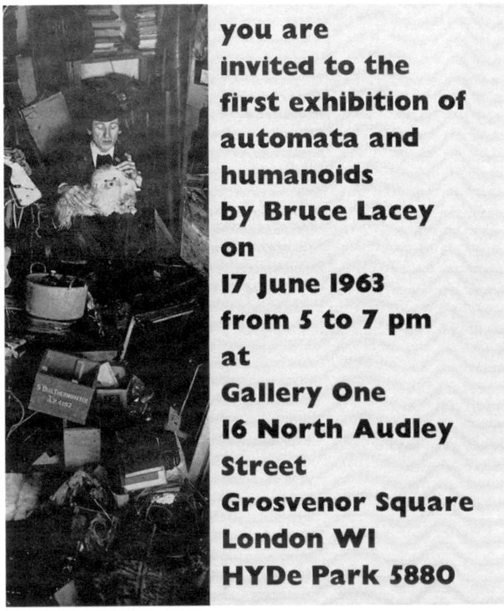

1 Cover of the catalogue for an exhibition of Bruce Lacey's work held at Gallery One, London, 1961

range of Bruce Lacey's 'humanoids' (Fig. 1), described by fellow artist Jeff Nuttall as 'sick, urinating, stuttering machines constructed of the debris of the century'.[12] Lacey's assemblages cluttered the gallery with junk and noise, creating an interactive comic spectacle which was more akin to theatre than to the kind of passive or contemplative experience associated with visiting a gallery.[13]

Elsewhere, however, modernist polemics did inform sculpture selection and display, as in William Tucker's exhibition, *The Condition of Sculpture*, staged at the Hayward in 1972. By the late 1960s, the modernist notion of 'the white cube' – the clean spacious gallery with 'the sanctity of the church, the formality of the courtroom'[14] – had permeated the thinking behind permanent collection displays in Britain. Norman Reid's article about a rehang at the Tate, published in *The Studio* in 1968, featuring the sparse results achieved in one of the rooms dedicated to sculpture,[15] reflected the modernist ethos perfectly.

Even the Royal Academy made its own bold effort at accommodating modernism with its exhibition of contemporary work, *Sculptors '72*. It helped counter accusations of conservatism, but the motley of work – and the form of display – failed to satisfy sculptors, critics or modernists.[16] Reviewing the exhibition for the *Guardian*, Caroline Tisdall described the result as 'uneven and safe': 'And what have we got after all this? Certainly not a shocking or bloody storming of the academic Bastille. Taken as a whole it's a pleasant ramble through a number of styles current in British sculpture over the past decade.'[17]

Despite the 'grounded objects', the radical initiatives and the modernism-inspired attempts to create neutral spaces and ahistorical environments, galleries generally continued to function ideologically, affirming institutional power and authority.[18] Overall, the gallery setting was a constant, largely providing an exclusive experience to the few and the initiated. In contrast, outside the gallery walls, and beyond the parameters of the London art circle,[19] there were alternative venues and sites – social, urban and industrial spaces – which facilitated the closer communion of viewers and objects. These new social, urban and industrial spaces demand closer examination here.

2 Peter Peri, seen here in 1965, working in situ in polyester resin on a free-standing figure of a flautist at Ernesford Grange Primary School, Foxton Road, Coventry. Alongside it on an exterior wall was a bas-relief in concrete which featured a girl singing.

3 Barbara Hepworth, 'Contrapuntal Forms', 1951, sited at Glebelands housing area in Harlow

Unexpectedly perhaps, the ordinary British household offered a new kind of social space. Temporary displays at the Festival of Britain – such as those in the 'Homes and Gardens' pavilion – reflected a willingness to locate objects influenced by contemporary sculptural forms in domestic environments. Modest but stylish lounges featured the occasional small sculpture amongst the Ernest Race furniture and Lucienne Day textiles. Furthermore, from 1946, the *Sculpture for the Home* exhibitions had travelled the provinces, promoting the idea that sculpture collecting and display need not be confined to the 'stately' home but could be happily accommodated – and afforded – by the 'least affluent' household.[20]

More importantly, a range of new locations for sculpture was provided as a direct result of the postwar social welfare programme. Instead of embodying Victorian notions of civic pride or deference to benevolent patrons, the sculpture on display in these new community spaces asserted itself as a public artform with contemporary social relevance.

The 'education for all' policy, for example, initiated programmes of school-building and a number of local authorities, notably Hertfordshire and Leicestershire, pioneered the commissioning and acquisition of contemporary sculpture throughout the 1950s and 1960s.[21] In Leicestershire, the Chief Education Officer Stuart Mason was personally involved in commissioning and selecting many of the large-scale sculptures and reliefs made for the twenty-five new schools which had been erected by 1957.[22] They included works such as Peter Peri's 'Boy with Globe and Book', a concrete figure which jutted out horizontally from the wall at Castle Donnington Community College.[23] In the case of Peri's various commissions, schoolchildren watched with fascination as the sculptor made his works in situ (see Fig. 2). This helped develop a strong sense of ownership on the part of the host community – an aspect noted by John Berger, an advocate for this kind of 'social' art in the 1950s: 'Sometimes the work is in the entrance hall (in the brick plinth of one of these is a cocoa tin inside which are the names of all the children who subscribed

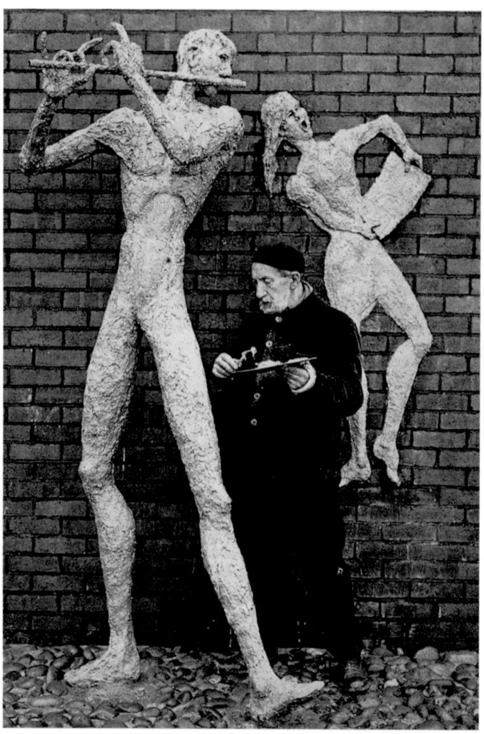

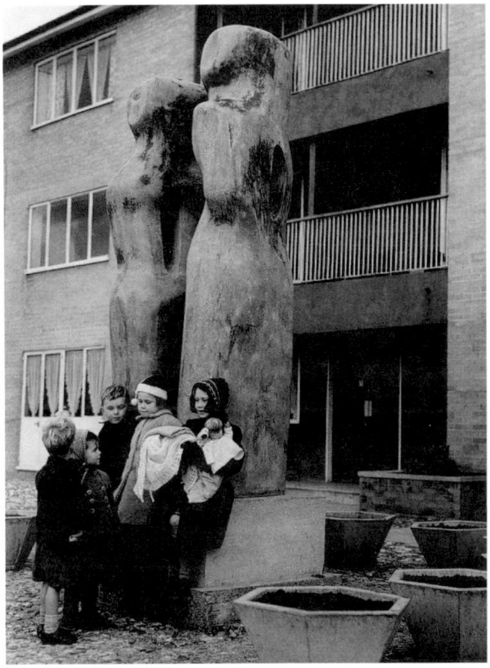

shillings or pennies towards the cost of it), sometimes outside on the forecourt in front of the playing fields, most often attached to the outside walls themselves.'[24]

In the 1950s, the London County Council supported a range of projects to site sculpture on housing estates, in playgrounds and community centres. In 1956, the Council assigned £20,000 per year for the provision of artworks in its 'Patronage of the Arts' scheme.[25] An early commission was Siegfried Charoux's iron group, 'The Neighbours', for the Quadrant Estate in Highbury. Two casts of Franta Belsky's 'The Lesson' were acquired, one of which was sited on the Avebury Estate in Bethnal Green. In 1961, the London County Council staff gazette featured extracts from an interview with local residents which had been broadcast on BBC radio just after the unveiling. Anecdotal evidence suggested that the working-class community was puzzled by the abstract style of the 'lady' though the younger residents seemed more interested in its play potential.[26]

New Towns such as Harlow and Stevenage also provided social sites for sculpture. The first sculpture commissioned by Harlow Art Trust was Mary Spencer Watson's 'Chiron', sited in the town's first neighbourhood shopping centre. Watson was committed to the idea that the piece should relate directly to the host community but was also wary of the pitfalls of producing 'social sculpture':

> I gave much thought to the idea which would be in keeping with the Community Centre – and to escape from the banal conception of community, which we have so often seen in the Communist and Fascist style of muscular young men and maidens, with implements of communal labour. I chose Chiron because he, in his wisdom as a teacher, incorporated all the activities embodied in a community centre.[27]

Watson spent a month in a caravan completing the carving on site in full view of the community.[28] By 1973, the Trust's policy of acquiring and commissioning works by contemporary sculptors had resulted in an extraordinary collection, including work by Henry Moore, Ralph

Brown, Lynn Chadwick, Antanas Brazdys and Gerda Rubinstein.[29] Sculpture was sited in shopping precincts, on housing estates, in health centres, outside sports centres and community rooms. The local population didn't always fully appreciate the form or location of the works, but residents expressed dismay at the suggestion that Hepworth's 'Contrapuntal Forms' (Fig. 3) might be removed from the Glebelands housing area to the central civic space in the town.[30]

Whilst Harlow and Stevenage acquired or commissioned works for communal areas, other New Towns took a very different approach. In particular, Peterlee and Glenrothes adopted the more radical policy of employing artists to work directly with architects and planners in developing new forms of creative environments.[31] Notably, Victor Pasmore was appointed at Peterlee in 1955, where he worked as a consultant to a team of architects and designers. In 1968, the Glenrothes Development Corporation appointed sculptor David Harding as Town Artist, to work with architects, bricklayers, engineers and other craftsmen and labourers, and in conjunction with the local community, on a wide range of projects.[32]

In sympathy with Fife's Communist traditions and 'a half-formed vision of the artist as artisan',[33] Harding moved into a Glenrothes council property and set up studio in the Direct Labour workshops, forging a strong creative collaboration within the community. His murals adorned underpasses, walkways, playgrounds, walls, bridges and houses. He also designed and built free-standing forms such as the 'Henge' (1970; Fig. 4), an environmental sculpture, comprising thirteen pre-cast concrete slabs in spiral form. Its obvious Celtic influence contrasted with surface elements inspired by 'world-figures of the 20th century – the Beatles, Bob Dylan, Bonhoeffer, Pele, Martin Luther King, Mother Theresa and many more'.[34] The Glenrothes project, in particular, offered a unique opportunity to integrate the viewing subject – in this case the whole community – with the sculpted environment.

Apart from permanent public sites for sculpture, towns and cities offered new locations for temporary displays. The creation of open-air galleries in urban spaces had been established in 1948 with the sculpture exhibition in Battersea Park. Subsequently, the London County Council and the Arts Council replicated their success with the triennial open-air exhibitions in London parks and a series of outdoor shows of contemporary sculpture which toured the country.

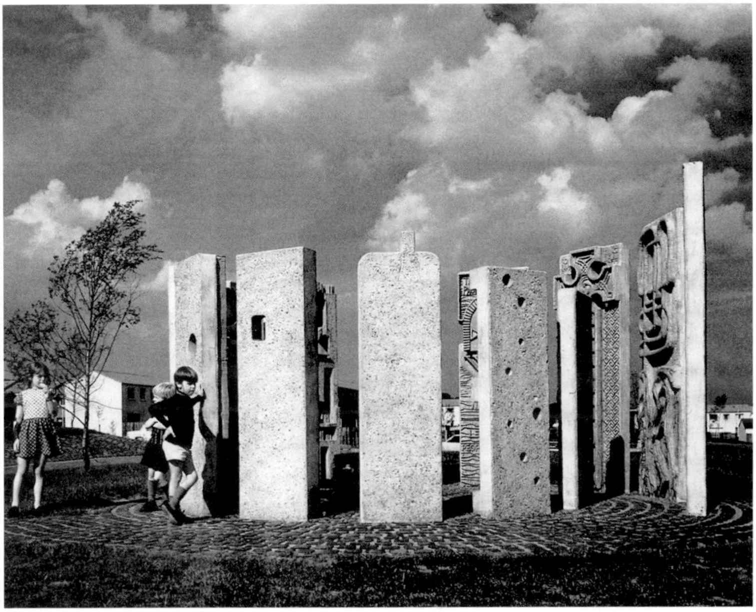

4 David Harding, 'Henge', 1970, pre-cast concrete, Glenrothes Development Corporation

The triennial shows ended in 1966 for a number of reasons; the complex problems of siting and displaying an increasingly diverse range of contemporary sculpture had undoubtedly become a contributory factor. At the 1963 show in Holland Park, a reviewer highlighted the incongruity of the exhibits with the surrounding landscape. Remarking on the muscular, mechanic, architectonic and untraditional character of much of the sculpture, Whittet argued that the setting of 'birds and greenery', remniniscent of the 'stately home', was entirely unsuitable. As an alternative, he suggested showing sculpture at Chelsea Hospital, along the South Bank or, more prophetically, maybe 'close one of the Thames bridges and mount the exhibition on its roadway'.[35]

At the end of the decade, it was precisely this kind of mundane cityscape – accentuated by a new celebratory sense of urbanism – that provided fresh contexts for open-air displays. Moreover, the most significant developments took place outside London. In particular, an outdoor show in Bristol in 1968 represented a pioneering attempt to integrate contemporary British sculpture with the busy built-up environment. Works by Garth Evans (Fig. 5), Brian Wall, Francis Morland and others were sited around the city streets.[36] For Evans, Bristol's footpaths and pavements not only complemented the sculpture but they also brought the audience closer to the work: 'I think that sculpture is the most public of the visual arts and I very much like to see it in places where people ordinarily go'.[37]

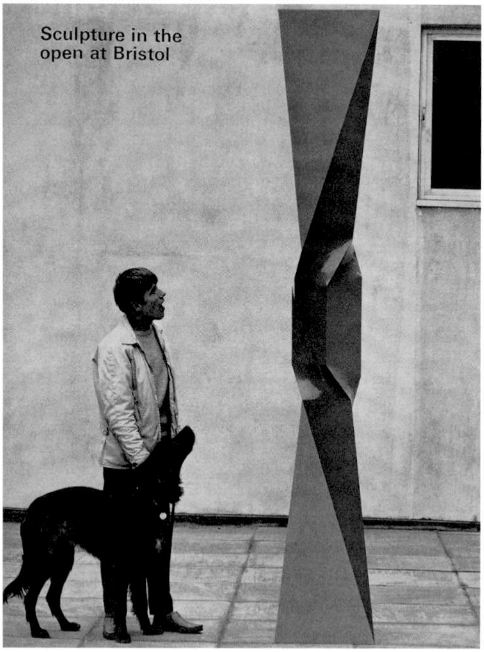

5 Garth Evans, 'Maid of Honour', 1966, reinforced polyster resin, at the open-air exhibition *New British Sculpture* in Bristol

Equally prescient was the major exhibition of British sculpture staged in Coventry, also in 1968. Unquestionably, since the war the city had demonstrated its commitment to revitalise sculpture as a public artform through various rebuilding projects and schemes.[38] Again, it is significant that this national sculpture exhibition – according to the organisers, the first of its kind for seventeen years – was outside the capital.[39] Although many exhibits were shown within the ruins of the old cathedral, once more the connection between the sculpture and the urban setting was emphasised: 'as all around sky and trees and a busy city are immediately in evidence. This is quite a unique event, where there is both containment, and open air, the interior and the exterior of architecture, as a setting for sculpture.'[40]

Held in conjunction with an international conference, 'People and Cities', the idealistic tenet of the show was that a display of sculpture could not only enrich human relations but could also help to break down the alienation and isolation experienced by city-dwellers. In the introduction to the catalogue, Stephen Verney summarised his view of the role of the sculptor: 'with the planner and the architect he forms an immediate team, within which he has the responsibility for summing up and expressing the meaning of the city, in buildings and networks, and the human life within it'.[41]

A few years later, in 1972, the Peter Stuyvesant City Sculpture Project attempted to embody these ideas – linking sculpture with a new urbanism in the most ambitious public display of contemporary sculpture in the period. The scheme involved sculptors designing work for specific public sites in eight cities: Birmingham, Cambridge, Cardiff, Liverpool, Newcastle, Plymouth, Sheffield and Southampton. Each city commissioned and sited two new works with the idea that, after six months of 'reasoned evaluation', the host community would be able to negotiate permanent acquisition. The organisers were determined to maximise the audience for sculpture: access was to be unlimited and there were to be no turnstiles.[42] The project was perceived as a failure in some quarters. Inevitably, media attention focused on the controversial and 'difficult' nature of some of the work and, by the end of the project, Birmingham was the only city to retain a sculptural work. Considerable efforts were made by some sculptors to make work which engaged with the cultural heritage of the sites. In Sheffield, Bernard Schottlander's huge steel structure, fabricated locally, evoked the crucible process of steel-making in the city. In contrast, Nigel Hall's light-piece projection high above council houses at Sky Edge, also in Sheffield, represented an innovative approach to the idea of 'public sculpture'.

The issue of siting and displaying sculpture was specifically addressed in the accompanying broadsheet. Statements and extracts from previously published writings situated the project alongside the experimental approaches taken by contemporaneous transatlantic and European avant-gardes. In 'One step towards social sculpture?', Lijn recounted the experience of making a kinetic sculpture for Plymouth. Regarding the project as a 'symbolic step in the right direction of the lifting of barriers', she explains how she found herself 'thinking of the city itself as a sculpture'. She closes with a clear call for the integration of the arts for the benefit of the whole urban community: 'I look forward to the day when architects become visionaries and poet-planners call these other artists, sculptors and painters into their ranks to outvote the supremacy of profit.'[43]

Equally revolutionary in tone was Otto Piene's statement, which condemned traditional gallery spaces as stilted and uninspiring: 'Ships, city halls, mines, TV stations, the sea, forests, farms, dairies, factories, homes, islands, airplanes, the sky and the moon seem better suited than most galleries and museums ... Like zoos they present only samples, not living organisms.'[44]

The commercial sponsorship of the project was important because it represented a final and significant aspect of the 'common ground' narrative being developed here – the engagement of sculpture with the field of industry and the culture of manufacture. Since its inception in 1963, the Stuyvesant Foundation had provided patronage to the arts through sponsoring exhibitions and its collections policy.[45] Although the Foundation's support for the Whitechapel shows ended in 1968, corporate connections with art flourished in the mid-1960s.[46] Other companies, such as John Moores, Pilkington Glass and British Aluminium, sponsored exhibitions and competitions. Apart from providing essential funds some companies handed over space for temporary exhibitions of sculpture. In 1972, the Guinness Brewery invited Bernard Schottlander to stage an open-air solo show of his

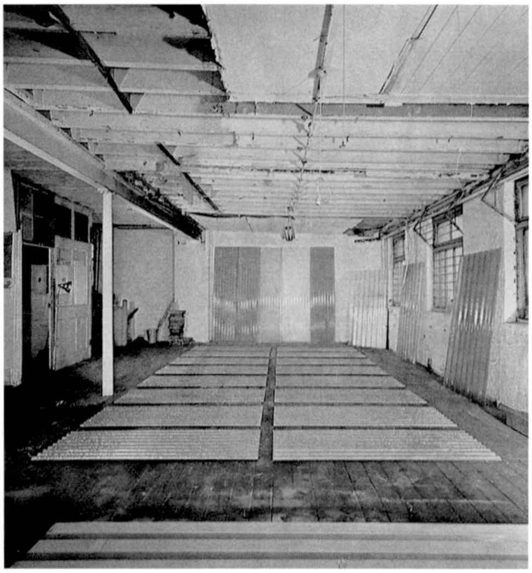

6 William Turnbull, 'Corrugations', 1967, galvanised sheets, as reproduced in *Studio International*, January 1969

enormous abstract sculptures on their land outside Park Royal Underground Station.[47]

The alignment of sculpture with manufacturing was further underlined by the contemporary appropriation of common industrial materials. In the 1950s, many sculptors turned to concrete as a cheap alternative to bronze. In the following decade, under the direct influence of David Smith and, in turn, Caro, many British sculptors worked with angle-iron, girders and rolled-steel joists. Paradoxically, though, whilst the 'white cube' provided the narrative for the display of sculpture inside the *New Generation* show at the Whitechapel in 1965, the cover of the exhibition catalogue allied art-making with factory-style metal construction. An image of William Turnbull's 'Corrugations' (1967; Fig. 6), reproduced in a special issue of *Studio International* devoted to contemporary sculpture, epitomises industrial chic. Turnbull wrote of his own preference for 'industrially produced raw materials (channel, angle, corrugation)' and an 'industrial finish' – the work fitted perfectly with the rundown factory surroundings, resembling raw materials waiting to be processed.[48]

The 'industrialisation' of display was widespread and many images in journals, exhibition catalogues and books of the time feature industrial and urban backdrops[49] – a trend which was reflected more generally in fashion photography of the day.

Indeed, sculpture was increasingly made and displayed in industrial settings from the 1960s.[50] Although affordability may have provided the impetus for initiatives such as Stockwell Depot, it was clear that many of the artists involved saw it as a conscious attempt to 'socialise' the work and move towards 'a more integrative situation … in line with modern trends in socio/political thinking.'[51] Sculptors were able to make an even more direct attempt to integrate art and industry through the activities of the Artists Placement Group (APG). In sympathy with an Althusserian emphasis on the idea that art could bring about social change – but with its own specific complex agenda – the APG placed a number of sculptors with nationalised industries in the 1960s and 1970s.[52] Garth Evans spent two years on a placement with the British Steel Corporation: describing it as a 'fascinating rich and scary experience', he faced a host of problems relating to the conflicting expectations and objectives of the various parties involved.[53] Eventually, Evans produced a major steel construction, 'Breakdown', which took up 500 sq. ft of floor space. Individual placements achieved different outcomes, and the extent to which artists integrated with the workforce and the workplace varied. Nevertheless, APG activities were an important part of a wider political dialogue which aimed to engage art more closely with industry at grassroots level.

The special issue of *Studio International* devoted to 'Art with a Social Purpose' makes it abundantly clear that, by 1976, 'common ground' had become contested ground.[54] Both artists and viewing subjects had become more demanding – cultural space was no longer a meeting place for discerning citizens coming together under the auspices of a benevolent, but possibly naïve, pluralism. Space was now recognised as political – it was for seizure and occupation. The notion of common ground which has framed this assessment of sculptural display was primarily consensual. New social, urban and industrial spaces had not only enabled '*seeing* more closely'; to an extent they had also engaged with issues of access and ownership in relation to sculpture-viewing.

By the early 1970s, however, another narrative of common ground was firmly established. This more sharply polemical narrative presented pluralism as a sham that served ultimately to mystify real relationships of power. Increasingly, the notion of 'display space' was interrogated, challenged and undermined not least by the increasing number of sculptors producing insubstantial or ephemeral work. Along with the sculptural object, space itself became destabilised, irreversibly deconstructed. Artists such as Victor Burgin demanded a 'moratorium on things',[55] Gilbert & George parodied the essentials of sculptural practice. Whilst others made kinetic art or worked with light, sound and air, sculpture became more concerned with space as a site of *possibility*. Contradictory narratives of display existed in tandem, initiating a dialogue which continued into the latter part of the 20th century. The May 1968 issue of *Studio International* exemplified the concurrent polysemic narratives of sculptural practice and display. Whilst it featured the geometric heavy metal sculpture seen on public display around the streets of Bristol, it also included an article on 'Air art' in which Willoughby Sharp declared that 'object art was over' and described static structures as anachronisms. He argued that a new durational conception of physical reality was leading to new forms of sculpture – kinetic, inflatable, immaterial, disposable – which explored the limitless potential of inner and outer space as both raw material and location. The notion that viewing sculpture was about the contemplation of a solid object in a fixed location was redundant:

> Kinetic sculpture is beginning to establish a subject–system dialectic capable of integrating us with the environment. We have reached the end of disinterestedness, impartiality and contemplation. We are embarking on a new phase of artistic awareness of which interest, partiality and participation are the chief characteristics.[56]

Gillian Whiteley

Notes

1 B. Robertson, 'Preface', *Anthony Caro: Sculpture 1960–1963* (exhibition catalogue), London, Whitechapel Art Gallery, September–October 1963.

2 See A. D. B. Sylvester, 'Festival sculpture', *Studio,* September 1951, vol. 142, no. 702, pp. 72–7. For recent reassessments, see R. Burstow, *Symbols for '51: the Royal Festival Hall, Skylon and Sculptures for the Festival of Britain* (exhibition catalogue), London, The Ballroom, Main Foyer, Royal Festival Hall, 2 March–21 April 1996 and R. Burstow, 'Modern sculpture in the South Bank townscape', *Twentieth Century Society Journal,* 2001, vol. 5.

3 Casson regretfully concluded that the hoped-for 'integration' of sculpture and surroundings was largely not achieved. Hugh Casson, 'South Bank sculpture', *Image: A Periodical of the Visual Arts,* Spring 1952, pp. 48–60.

4 The phrase taken from I. Cox, *Festival of Britain Guide,* London, HMSO, 1951 is identified in B. Curtis, 'One continuous interwoven story (The Festival of Britain)', *Block,* Issue 11, 1985/1986, in *The Block Reader in Visual Culture,* London and New York, Routledge, 1996.

5 See B. Conekin, *The Autobiography of a Nation: The 1951 Festival of Britain,* Manchester, Manchester University Press, 2003, for a comprehensive study of the Festival's construction of national, regional and local identities. Conekin reads the Festival as 'a tool of government used to act on an object of government, namely, national identity', p. 8.

6 Curtis, 'One continuous interwoven story (The Festival of Britain)', p. 214.

7 'Social space' might be defined as that which is inhabited, shared and used by people for everyday activities. See H. Lefebvre, *The Production of Space* (trans. D. Nicholson-Smith, first published 1974), Oxford, Blackwell, 1991. Lefebvre elaborated further in his 'Preface to the new edition', published in 1986.

8 For a discussion of situationist ideas of the city as open-ended, spontaneous and playful, see S. Sadler, *The Situationist City,* Cambridge, MA and London, MIT Press, 1998.

9 The London Commentary in *Studio,* November 1951, vol. 142, no. 704, p. 154, refers to the show as 'the first exhibition of its kind' – a 'gallimaufrey of objets trouvés from ships' figureheads to old Valentines … much of it in bad taste but executed with tremendous gusto'.

10 See, for example, F. Frascina, J. Harrison, C. Harrison and P. Wood, *Modernism in Dispute: Art Since the Forties*, New Haven, CT, Yale University and Open University, 1993, and James Hall, 'Clement Greenberg on English sculpture and Englishness', *The Sculpture Journal*, vol. IV, 2000, pp. 172–6.

11 Press cuttings from the Tate Gallery archive of Victor Musgrave and Gallery One (TGA 8714). Musgrave opened Gallery One in Litchfield Street, Soho in 1953, moving to D'Arblay Street in 1956 and to 16 North Audley Street, Mayfair in April 1961. Musgrave closed the gallery in 1963 to devote more time to writing poetry, organising Fluxus events and making films.

12 J. Nuttall, *Bomb Culture* [first published 1968], London, Paladin, 1970, p. 118. Lacey's assemblages featured in *sTigma*, a temporary environment created in 1965 in the basement of Better Books, a bookshop run by Bob Cobbing on Charing Cross Road. Nuttall's autobiographical account remains a valuable source of information on counter cultural art activities, events and performances that took place in alternative venues in the 1960s.

13 Victor Musgrave archive, Tate Gallery Archive, London. Also, author's interview with Bruce Lacey, *Artists' Lives*, National Life Story Collection, British Library, 2000.

14 B. O'Doherty, 'Notes on the gallery space' (orig. published in *Artforum* 1976), *Inside the White Cube: The Ideology of the Gallery Space*, Berkeley, University of California Press, 1999, p. 14.

15 Room 15, featured in the article, was transformed from being cluttered with sculpture on tall plinths, walls two-deep in paintings in August 1964, to a display of five or six sculptures resting on the floor. *Studio International*, January 1969, vol. 177, no. 907, pp. 38–9.

16 See, for example, Barry Martin's comments in 'The problem of British sculpture', *Studio International*, May 1972, vol. 183, no. 944, p. 187.

17 C. Tisdall, 'Stalking horses in Piccadilly', in the *Guardian*, 7 January 1972, p. 8.

18 A view expounded by Duncan and Wallach in their early Marxist critique of modern museum display in C. Duncan and A. Wallach, 'Museum of Modern Art as late capitalist ritual: an iconographic analysis', *Marxist Perspectives*, Winter 1978, vol. 1, no. 4.

19 During the mid-1960s *Studio International* started to include regular commentaries on exhibitions and projects around the country.

20 The first *Sculpture in the Home* exhibition, arranged by the Arts Council, was in 1946, with subsequent shows in 1950, 1953 and 1958. Although the 1958 catalogue suggested that new materials made sculpture cheaper, the small 'affordable' sculptures were largely bronzes – hardly an inexpensive option.

21 See M. Levy, 'Pioneering patronage for schools: British art in Leicestershire', *Studio*, September 1963, vol. 166, no. 845, pp. 92–7, and *British Sculpture and Painting in the Collection of the Leicestershire Education Authority* (exhibition catalogue), London, Whitechapel Gallery, December–January 1967/1968.

22 J. Berger, 'Artists and schools', *New Statesman*, 27 July 1957, pp. 108–9.

23 Peter Peri did a range of work for schools in Leicestershire, Derbyshire, Yorkshire and the West Midlands. See J. Kay and J. Lloyd, *Peter Peri 1899–1967: A Retrospective Exhibition of Sculpture, Prints and Drawings* (exhibition catalogue), Leicester, Leicestershire Museum and Art Gallery, 1991. For information on sculpture and schools, see G. Whiteley, 'Art for Social Spaces: Public Sculpture and Urban Regeneration in Postwar Britain', Design History Research Centre, University of Brighton, 2002 at www.designingbritain.org.uk.

24 Berger, 'Artists and schools', p. 109.

25 London County Council archive file, 'Works of Art for Housing Estates, 1957–1959'. Also see G. S. Sandilands, 'London County Council as art patron: II', *Studio*, February 1960, vol. 159, no. 802, p. 42–7.

26 Transcription of Leonard Parkin's interview for the BBC in 'The Lesson', *London County Council Gazette*, March 1961.

27 Letter, dated 2 March 1953, from Mary Spencer Watson to Frederick Gibberd, Harlow Art Trust archive.

28 Correspondence and papers, Harlow Art Trust archive.

29 *Sculpture in Harlow* (exhibition catalogue), Harlow Development Corporation, 1973.

30 Ibid.

31 Other towns which employed artists included Skelmersdale and Cumbernauld: the author is indebted to David Harding for advice and information about sculpture in new towns in the period.

32 Author's correspondence with David Harding, January 2003. See also David Harding, 'The art of building in Glenrothes', *Concrete Quarterly*, April–June 1974, no. 101, pp. 11–16.

33 Harding interviewed by Moira Roth in 'Art in community context', *High Performance*, Issue 33, 1986, p. 43.

34 *Glenrothes Town Artist David Harding*, Glenrothes Development Corporation, n.d., probably 1974.

35 G. S. Whittet, 'Battersea Power sculpture', *Studio*, August 1963, vol. 166, no. 844, p. 52.

36 The Arnolfini Gallery organised the show, which ran from 20 May to 29 June. Related events included a symposium on sculpture and an indoor exhibition of work by the older generation (including Henry Moore, F. E. McWilliam, Elisabeth Frink) at the City Art Gallery. *Studio International*, May 1968, vol. 175, no. 900, pp. 243–7.

37 *Studio International*, May 1968, vol. 175, no. 900, pp. 243–7. In the following year, the City of London Festival staged a similar outdoor show with work by fifty contemporary sculptors displayed in public areas around commercial office blocks and banks. *Studio International*, July/August 1968, vol. 176, no. 902, p. 41.

38 One scheme involved a continually changing display of free-standing sculpture in newly pedestrianised areas. See 'Public art in Coventry', *A Survey of Public Art in Coventry*, Herbert Art Gallery, 1980.

39 M. Amaya, 'Climate of freedom', *Exhibition of British Sculpture* (exhibition catalogue), Coventry Cathedral, June–August 1968.

40 F. Barraclough, *Exhibition of British Sculpture* (exhibition catalogue), p. 2.

41 Stephen Verney, 'Foreword', *Exhibition of British Sculpture* (exhibition catalogue).

42 Jeremy Rees, one of the organisers, makes these points in 'Introduction', *Peter Stuyvesant City Sculpture Project* (exhibition catalogue), 1972.

43 L. Lijn, 'One step towards social sculpture?', *Peter Stuyvesant City Sculpture Project* (exhibition catalogue).

44 O. Piene, extract from 'More Sky 1', reprinted in *Peter Stuyvesant City Sculpture Project* (exhibition catalogue).

45 Simon Faulkner maps the Stuyvesant Foundation's appropriation of art in 'Art, cigarettes and visual culture in the Sixties: the Peter Stuyvesant Foundation and the "New Generation exhibitions", 1964–66', *Visual Culture in Britain*, vol. 1, no. 1, pp. 65–87.

46 Faulkner suggests that the Whitechapel's serious financial problems were alleviated considerably by the Foundation's support – Robertson pledged publicity in exchange. Faulkner, 'Art, cigarettes and visual culture in the Sixties: the Peter Stuyvesant Foundation and the "New Generation" exhibitions, 1964–66', p. 73.

47 Papers of Bernard Schottlander, Leeds Museums and Galleries (Henry Moore Institute Archive).

48 See image of Turnbull's 'Corrugations' (1967), galvanized sheets 2 ft × 6 ft and accompanying statement, *Studio International*, January 1969, vol. 177, no. 907, p. 24.

49 See, for example, many of the photographs in *The Alistair McAlpine Gift* (exhibition catalogue), London, Tate Gallery, 30 June–22 August 1971.

50 Margaret Garlake discusses the setting up of artists' studios at Stockwell Depot and SPACE in her essay on 'Infrastructures: formation and networks 1950–75' in this volume. Also, see 'A proposal to provide studio workshops for artists', *Studio International*, February 1969, vol. 177, no. 908, pp. 65–7.

51 G. Richardson, *Studio International*, July/August 1968, vol. 176, no. 902, p. 36. Detailed statements from Stockwell sculptors were published in *Studio International*, January 1969, vol. 177, no. 907.

52 APG was set up in 1966 by John Latham, Barbara Severini, Barry Flanagan and Jeffrey Shaw. See J. A. Walker, 'APG: The individual and the organisation', *Studio International*, special issue on 'Art and Social Purpose', March/April 1976, vol. 191, no. 980, pp. 162–72 for artists' statements about various placements. Also see Garlake's comments on APG in her essay on 'Infrastructures: formation and networks 1950–75' in this volume.

53 Initially, Evans' placement was part of the BSC's established fellowship programme. Author's correspondence with Garth Evans, December 2002/January 2003.

54 *Studio International*, special issue on 'Art and Social Purpose', March/April 1976, vol. 191, no. 980.

55 Victor Burgin quoted in *1965–1972 – When Attitudes Became Form* (exhibition catalogue), Cambridge, Kettle's Yard Gallery, and Edinburgh, Fruitmarket Gallery, 1984, p. 34.

56 W. Sharp, 'Air art', *Studio International*, May 1968, vol. 175, no. 900, pp. 262–3.

Sculpture squared

Tracing the history of transformations in the gallery space, Brian O'Doherty discerned a white, box-like, cubic space, whose presence seemed to epitomise the modernist ideal. The white cube, a ubiquitous, ever-present and yet practically impossible space, was the ideal container for the auratic, unique, unreproducible work of art.[1]

And yet, the very site of the white cube's unmasking was another squarish space: the pages of the influential American art magazine *Artforum* (Fig. 1). And the means for the white cube's presentation in that space was through the reproductive media of photography. Indeed, O'Doherty went so far as to identify 'the installation shot, *sans* figures' – a photograph of a work of art in a white cube gallery space without the intrusion of any embodied viewers – as 'one of the icons of our visual culture'.[2] The only place it seemed where the unreproducible optical ideal of the perfect work in the perfect space could exist undisturbed was within the (squarish) frame of a photograph reproduced on the squarish page of an art catalogue, book or magazine. These squarish frames were no more or less ideal or conventional than the heavy, ornamental gold frames of a salon painting or a sculpture's plinth. The squarish frames of the photograph and the art magazine were conventions, institutions and spaces as rigid and as contested from without and from within as those of the salon, academy or gallery space they seemed to have escaped from. By the time O'Doherty published his now famous essay in 1976, a number of reproductive media – indeed the pages of *Artforum* magazine itself – had become both site and content of works of art, and of sculpture in particular.

Reproduction and publishing in the period 1950–75 are not only contexts for sculpture's replication and dissemination but also for sculpture's content, its subject and its material – both medium and message, in the terms of one of the most famous dictums of the mass media age.[3]

This era marked the establishment of the book as sculpture, the magazine article as sculpture, video recording or television broadcast as sculpture, photograph as sculpture and words – written and spoken – as sculpture. During this period it was demonstrated that any and every reproductive and publishing technology could be used in the production of sculpture as well as in its *re*production.

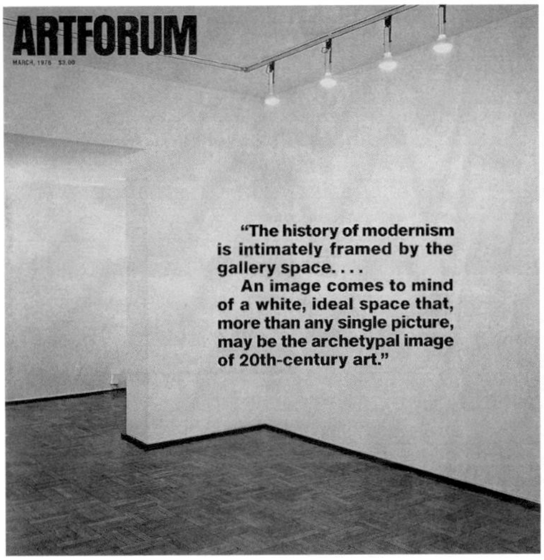

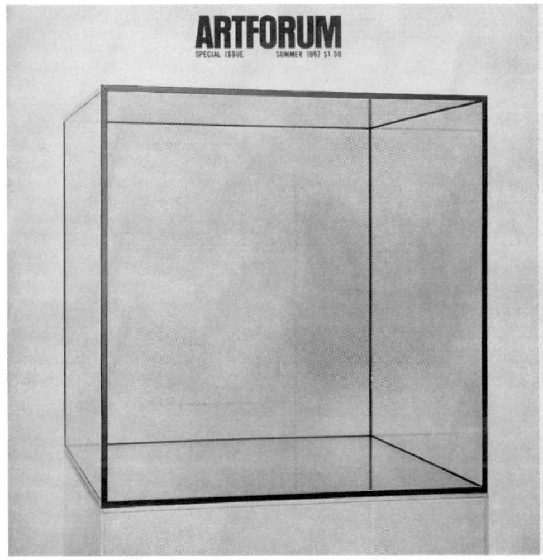

1 Cover of *Artforum*, March 1976

2 Cover of *Artforum*, summer 1967

Sculpture's repertoire of forms and techniques was dramatically extended and expanded through its interchange with the technologies of mass media. At the same time, through those self-same technologies all sculpture, but particularly those sculptural practices that utilised mass media forms directly, could reach a wider, international and potentially global audience.

The cover of one of the most cited and influential issues of *Artforum* magazine – published in the summer of 1967 – showed a photograph of a sculpted cube, framed by the distinctive square format of that magazine (Fig. 2): a complex overlay of square and squarish reproductive and sculptural forms.[4] The issue was devoted to a survey of American sculpture and it is a testament to his North American status that the work of the British sculptor Anthony Caro was included.[5] It is also an indication of the transatlantic dialogue between the USA and Britain that took place in the 1960s.

Caro provided a crucial link in this transatlantic exchange, particularly making links for his sculpture students at St Martin's School of Art in London. Michael Fried spent a term teaching at St Martin's in the late 1960s and subsequently commented that: 'The unique record of the sculpture department at St Martin's during more than a decade speaks for itself. In fact it is no exageration [*sic* Gresty] to say that the department is something of a legend wherever contemporary painting and sculpture are taken seriously.'[6]

Students at St Martin's were also well acquainted with debates in sculpture and art theory in the USA through the presence of books and magazines in the school's library. *Artforum* was available in St Martin's library from March 1966.[7] Writing in the thirtieth anniversary issue of *Artforum* magazine, Thomas McEvilley commented that:

> In the late-Modernist period (by which I mean more or less the '60s and some of the '70s) there was a keen sense of … the vibration of thick significance in what an art journal could do, and sometimes did. The feeling was based on an assumption understood at once vaguely and intensely by art world readers: that the art magazine is the entranceway to art history. … it is the magazines that stitch the history of their time in the most complete and seamless fabric. For an art history of the last thirty years, for example, one could do worse than read a full run of *Artforum*.[8]

This keen sense of what an art journal could do extended to the studios and seminar rooms of art schools in Britain, where student magazines were generated which ignited debate even if their actual run was brief. Examples from St Martin's include the publications *Silâns*[9] and *Potlatch*.[10] A number of such publications were included in the exhibition *Live in Your Head* at the Whitechapel Art Gallery, London in 2000. The exhibition presented the fascinating cross-currents of conceptual art, visual and concrete poetry and the burgeoning small and artists' presses in Britain during the years 1965–75. Its display was a testament to the status of such seemingly ephemeral material to now sit alongside and share something of the status of more conventionally sculptural or 'original' works of art.

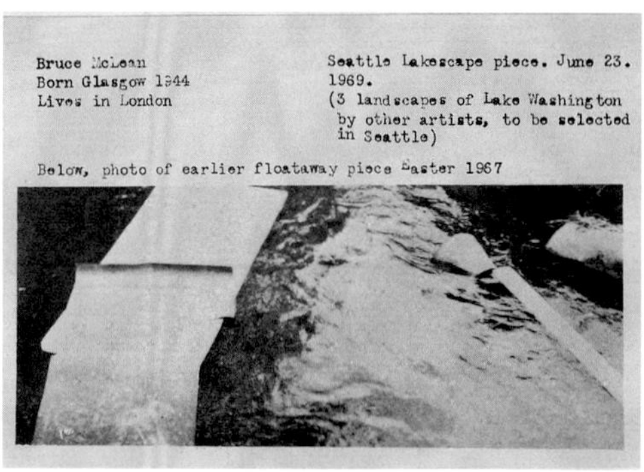

3 Index cards designed by Bruce McLean for the catalogue of *557,087: An Exhibition organised by Lucy Lippard at the Seattle Art Museum, 1969 and 955,000 at the Vancouver Art Gallery,* 1970. The participating artists all produced index cards based on questions sent by Lippard.

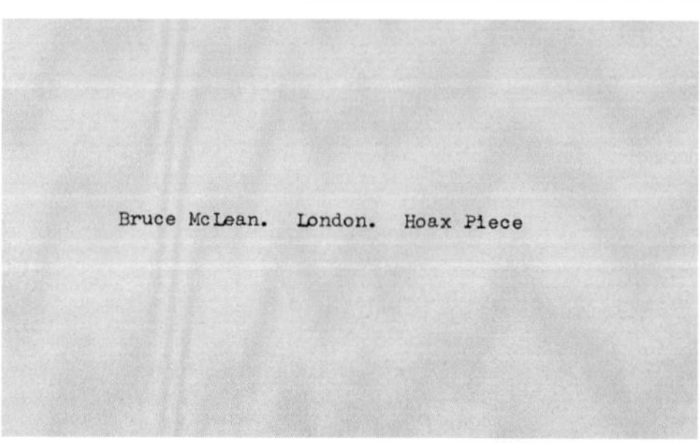

4 Index cards designed by Roelof Louw for the aforementioned Lucy Lippard exhibition

New reproductive technologies made possible the inexpensive and rapid production of artists' publications. Duplicating machines and photocopiers were rapidly assimilated to art production (Figs 3 and 4).[11]

In a move that the poet and sculptor Ian Hamilton Finlay has characterised as 'a crisis of syntax', words in concrete poetry took on materiality, solidity, 'being'. An evident reciprocity between sculpture and words had

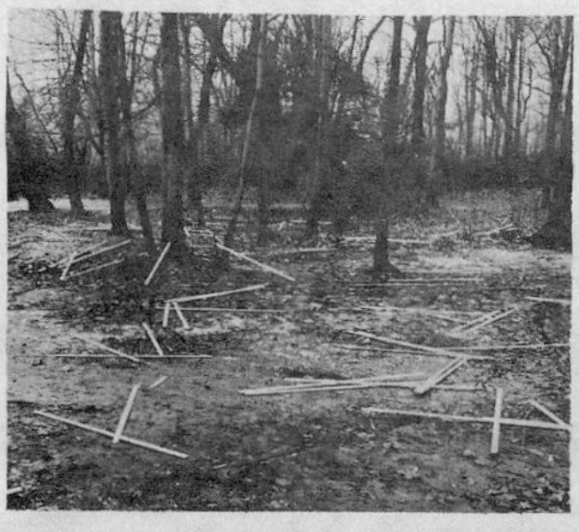

ROELOF LOUW BORN 17/2/36 RESIDENCE LONDON
WOOD PIECE/EXECUTED HOLLAND PARK/10'67
MATERIAL/A MIN OF 300(PREFERABLY MORE) APPROX. 3' x 1" x ¼" WOODEN SLATS SHOULD BE USED/THESE CAN BE PURCHASED FROM MOST TIMBER MERCHANTS (USED FOR PLASTER LATHING)
PROCEDURE FOR EXECUTION/THE SLATS SHOULD BE DROPPED (SCATTERED) AROUND TREES IN LOTS OF 2-6 PIECES AT IRREGULAR INTERVALS OVER AS EXTENSIVE AN AREA AS POSSIBLE WITHOUT THERE BEING A DEFINABLE PERIMETER

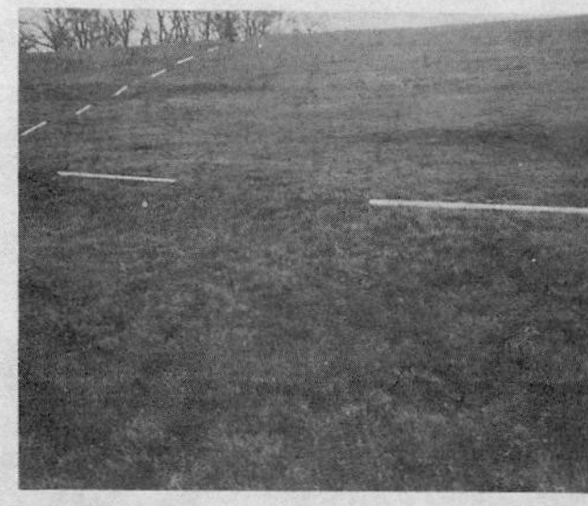

ROELOF LOUW BORN 17/2/36 RESIDENCE LONDON
HILL PIECE/EXECUTED HAMPSTEAD HEATH/ JULY '67/MATERIAL/2" DIAM x 10-12FT GALV STEEL POLES/QTY AS SITUATION REQUIRES/THESE CAN BE HIRED FROM ANY FIRM THAT SUPPLIES AND/OR ERECTS SCAFFOLDING (IF THE POLES ARE NOT NEW THEY SHOULD BE PAINTED MATT WHITE)
PROCEDURE FOR EXECUTION/THE POLES SHOULD BE PLACED AROUND A HILL NATURALLY FOLLOWING ANY CHOSEN CONTOUR(S) AT INTERVALS APPROX THE SAME LENGTH AS THE POLES
BOTH THE INCLUDED PIECES ARE IN ONE SENSE ACTS OF TAKING POSSESSION

a transforming effect on publications on and by sculptors. Michael Fried wrote about (Caro's) sculpture in terms of its syntax, whilst a range of sculptors made words into sculpture, from the writings of minimalist sculptors like Robert Morris and Sol LeWitt, through the work of Robert Smithson or Dan Graham – particularly their published magazine articles – to the visual poems of Carl Andre and the vast array of verbal practices characterised as 'conceptual art'. The outpouring of words by sculptors and words as sculpture was characterised by the critic and writer Craig Owens as 'an eruption of the verbal into the aesthetic field'.[12]

It might seem paradoxical to be asserting the physicality and material being of language at the same moment in which sculpture was shedding its historic ties to being material and object and becoming, in a term popularised at the time by Lucy Lippard and John Chandler, 'dematerialized'.[13] Lippard was soon forced to revise her term 'dematerialization' with the observation that 'a piece of paper or a photograph is as much an object, or as "material" as a ton of lead'.[14]

In 1964, the British art magazine formerly known as *The Studio* went international and became *Studio International*. In the years in which Charles Harrison was its assistant editor (1967–71), it also 'went conceptual', embracing the kinds of artworks and practices that made its pages artworks as much as they were pages about art. During that time the magazine doubled as the catalogue to an exhibition of *The*

British Avant-Garde (1971),[15] published Gilbert & George's 'magazine sculpture' (1970) and, in July/August 1970, became an exhibition space. This issue was curated by six invited international curators who were each given eight pages in which to present their chosen artist(s)' work.

Studio International also tackled the copyright, reproduction and authorship issues rendered problematic by artworks whose very material existence challenged traditional notions of reproduction, originality or uniqueness. The April 1971 issue carried a legal document on its cover and its pages (for easy reproduction). 'The artist's reserved rights transfer and sale agreement' was drafted by a New York lawyer in discussion with Seth Siegelaub. Siegelaub stated that '[t]he agreement has been designed to remedy some generally acknowledged inequities in the art world, particularly artists' lack of control over the use of their work and participation in its economics after they no longer own it'.[16] The fact that such an agreement was perceived as necessary also attests to a growing sense of artists' direct and continued involvement in the discourse that not only accompanied their work but increasingly came to constitute it. Reproduction of one's work, particularly in the leading art magazines of the day, held the key to artistic recognition. As a result, artists seemed unwilling to relinquish the interpretation and custodial care of their work to other professionals such as critics and curators. As Joseph Kosuth commented: 'The act of putting [the work of art/a proposition] into the world is empty unless an artist also fights for its meaning.'[17] Artists' statements and interviews with artists came into their own as a means for this continued engagement and involvement in the work. And again, new reproductive media both facilitated and prompted such possibilities. The development of audio recording from bulky tape-to-tape recorders to easily portable cassette recorders is one such development.

The means of reproduction became progressively invisible, a part of the unquestioned and unacknowledged process of exchange and reproduction. Transcripts of recorded interviews – or the very recordings themselves, for example in the case of *Audio Arts*, a magazine on audio tape – became a staple of art discourse.[18]

For her catalogue to the exhibition *The New Art* at the Hayward Gallery in 1972, Anne Seymour used interviews with the participating artists as a significant part of the information published. Some sculptors were particularly forthcoming: Gilbert & George demonstrating how they had already refined this particular form of exchange as a central aspect of their artistic practice. Others were more reticent. Neither Richard

5 Cover of *The New Generation* catalogue, Whitechapel Art Gallery, 1965

Long nor Hamish Fulton allowed any such material to be published in this context. Theirs was a silence given critical credence in Seymour's introduction to the catalogue where she defends their decision.[19]

If artists made increasingly 'noisy ... appeals for silence',[20] certain crucial artworld luminaries in Britain set themselves the task of using published words to promote and expand the audience and funding for the visual arts, and of sculpture in particular. Key amongst such figures was Bryan Robertson, particularly during his years as director of the Whitechapel Art Gallery in London. His ambitious programme of exhibitions aimed both to familiarise the British public with major figures in international art and to promote home-grown talent. But it was not just the content of these exhibitions but also their accompanying documentation that proved highly influential. In 1969, writing on Robertson's achievement at the Whitechapel, Maurice de Saumarez observed:

> Within two years of taking over at Whitechapel (1952), Robertson had launched his programme of comprehensive exhibitions of major international figures with the Mondrian exhibition, and had also introduced what soon became easily identifiable as 'Whitechapel-style' 9 × 8 in catalogues (which had a tonic effect on the prevailing standards of catalogue production in many of the smaller public galleries).[21]

Another publication in which Robertson had a guiding role now offers a vivid glimpse into the British artworld at a crucial, transformative moment. This was the book *Private View*, a glossy publication made in collaboration with Lord Snowdon and published in 1965. It aimed to record, publicise and attract funding for the artworld in London. The book concludes with the line: 'All that our artists need now is an increase in direct patronage, and adventurous commissions from public sources to match the vitality of their ideas.'[22]

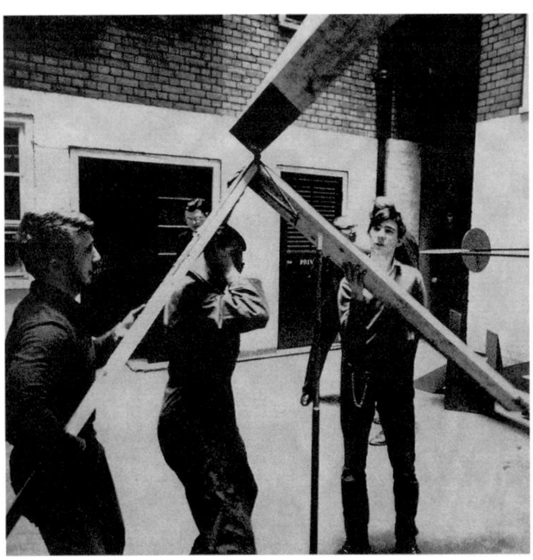

Publications such as *Private View* and some of Robertson's Whitechapel Gallery exhibition catalogues (particularly the now seminal *The New Generation* (1965; Fig. 5) gave unprecedented attention to the (photographic) image of the sculptor. The era under discussion here saw the development of the artist as media celebrity. Arguably Henry Moore was the first celebrity British artist in this sense. His work as official war artist, drawing people sheltering from air raids in the London Underground, made him a household name. Filmed documentaries of him in the Underground made him instantly recognisable.

The end of the 1960s witnessed the spectacle of Gilbert & George as living sculptures. Even the most determined assault on the visual by artists associated with conceptual art courted visibility through the person of the artist. In 1971 John Perrault imagined a photo-article on conceptual art, which in the absence of any visual 'works' would nevertheless have no shortage of visual material: 'Joe Kosuth at his typewriter, in the act of creation! The Art and Language group, conferring! Douglas Huebler loading his camera! Ian Wilson uttering! Mel Bochner measuring! Robert Barry thinking! Gilbert and George actually dancing! If Conceptual Art is not photogenic, certainly the artists themselves are.'[23]

Whether made from as immaterial a substance as breath or walking or as traditional a material as bronze, sculpture continued to need a space and a medium in which to exist in perpetuity and through which to become and remain a part of sculpture discourse. The written word, books, magazines, photographs, film and, as moving-image technologies developed, video recording, were all drawn into sculpture's material ambit.

In April 1969 a walk on Dartmoor became part of a historic exhibition that appeared in another squarish space – perhaps the most significant new media to develop during the period 1950–75 – the television. Although pioneering broadcasts had begun just prior to World War II and had resumed in 1946, many British homes first acquired a television set in order to watch one of the great British television events of the 20th century, the coronation of Queen Elizabeth II in 1953. 'Television has been a medium dependent upon a small, squarish picture',[24] and that format both shaped and contained its development. Long's contribution to the first broadcast television exhibition, *Land Art* – broadcast on national television in Germany on 15 April 1969 – was a ten-mile walk across Dartmoor, out and back, filming for six seconds every half mile. The resultant film interrogates the physical characteristics of television as a medium, using only the on and off controls on the camera as editing tools and only the television's 4 × 3 format smallish, squarish, screen as its purview.

Originally intended to exist only in the moment of its broadcast, the film has now become a video piece which can be shown repeatedly in a more conventional gallery space projected onto a wall or screen. Yet it retains the stigmata of its original format: the grainy quality of its image, the simplicity of its editing strategy.

The history of broadcasting devoted to sculpture on television deserves a longer and more detailed treatment than can be attempted here. It is however important to note the significance of the content of some of the earliest television programmes about art and artists, including the pioneering work of John Read, who made television programmes about Moore as early as 1951.

In 1971 Charles Harrison was rather cynical about 'Art on TV', commenting that: 'The general quality of involvement in art shown by television, certainly in this country, has been almost consistently abysmal. It has been characteristically second-hand and unprofessional; art as high-camp news, art as mystified by the art-critic-as-telegogue, art as panel game, art as snob culture, etc., etc.'[25]

John Berger's innovative and highly inventive use of television for presenting art, *Ways of Seeing*, had little space for sculpture. Despite confident assertions that Berger's series 'will almost certainly change the way you look at pictures', it perhaps did rather less for looking at sculptures, at least explicitly. The book that accompanied the series contains only three examples of sculptural work, only one of which was an authored piece of sculpture: Alberto Giacometti's 'Nude Standing Figure'.[26]

What seems most significant about television and sculpture is not the amount or presence of sculpture on television but its effect precisely on 'ways of seeing'. Television's increasingly unobtrusive filming strategies could mimic the movement of the embodied viewer. Through such dramatically increased mobility it could perambulate a sculpture in the round in much closer a way to the experience of it in real time and space. And yet despite this potential, television proved not so much a site for the presentation and dissemination of sculpture as an inspiration: through the content of its programmes and through the possibilities of it as a media for making sculpture. Indeed, even the television set became an element of sculpture, sometimes an object in its own right, whether explicitly as in Nam June Paik's work or, more ubiquitously and sometimes incidentally, placed sculptural object-like on a plinth in the gallery as part of an exhibition.

Some of the most effective televisual accounts of sculpture lie outside the time scale of this essay but the developments in the medium of television that make those so effective have their beginnings in this formative period in broadcasting history.

In July 1969 'about 600 million people, a little less than one-fifth of the world's population are estimated to have watched on television the American astronauts' walk on the moon.'[27] As perhaps a direct response to this event, David Medalla proposed 'Launching the Great Wall of China into orbit as a Satellite around the Moon (Cosmic Propulsion)' (1969).[28] Other sculptors were more dismissive in their response. Robert Smithson was outspokenly cynical, seeing the moon shot as a very expensive way of making artworks in a similar vein to the collections of geological material in his 'non-site' sculptures.[29] Much later, his widow, Nancy Holt, was to claim a far greater – if subliminal – influence on Smithson and his fellow artists. It 'was important', she said, 'because it was the first time that we saw the earth as a finite entity. Earth Art, of course,' she continued,'had already begun before the moon shot but the big sculptures, Bob's "Spiral Jetty" and Michael Heizer's "Double Negative" weren't done until after the moon shot'.[30]

The dramatic effect on perception wrought by space travel, characterised by such theories as 'The Overview Effect'[31] perhaps took some time to discern or measure. And perhaps the same might be said of the effects of television as a medium on the production, reception, reproduction and dissemination of sculpture.

Perhaps today we might not think the idea of McLuhan's 'Global Village' or Malraux's 'imaginary museum' ('that the arts of all nations and cultures could be simultaneously brought together before the mind's eye by photographs and reproductions') as 'preposterous an illusion' as Brandon Taylor did in 1977.[32] Even Berger's claim in *Ways of Seeing* that the 'boards … on which [adults and children] pin pieces of paper: letters, snapshots, reproductions of paintings, newspaper cuttings, original drawings, postcards' should 'logically … replace museums' – designed to prompt the viewer/reader to question notions of ownership and property – seems less shocking a proposition now than it did in 1972.[33]

O'Doherty's essay on the White Cube opens with a vivid image of the space age: 'the earth withdrawing from the spacecraft until it becomes a horizon, a beachball, a grapefruit, a golf ball, a star'.[34] Change of perspective can radically alter our view of the history of any medium.

Sculpture is no exception. Expansions in mass media forms of technological reproduction and dissemination have dramatised the phenomenological and experiential aspects of viewing. In 1967 Fried railed against the theatrical in art (although he made an exception for the movies as escaping from theatricality). Now theatricality is the accepted currency of a vast amount of sculptural activity, with its increased importance of the viewer, the viewer's interaction and particularly the viewer's body, which in the white cube was an encumbrance. In the context of today's so-called 'black box' installation conventions, sculpture can just as well be what you experience when you sit down in front of a video monitor or projection.

Mass media forms of reproductive technology such as audio and video recording and television hold the potential for the vast expansion of sculpture's presence. This is a process begun by photography; as Walter Benjamin observed, photography is 'the first truly revolutionary means of reproduction'.[35] Art's 'antagonist', photography, also proved its indispensable ally: not only for recording and documenting art but also as the artwork itself. The period from 1950 to 1975 saw the photograph change from something that recorded or documented sculpture through something that could be an equivalent to sculpture to a situation where the photograph itself could be claimed as sculpture.

The moving image – and television in particular – does not just add movement to pictures but represents a dramatic escalation of photography's terms and potential. Through moving-image technology we witness the spectacle of sculpture not only 'squared' but also multiplied to the 'nth' power.

Benjamin's essay dwells on the question of the auratic: a sense perceptible in a work of art of its authenticity and separateness from the everyday world. The use of reproductive and reprographic technologies in the era in question here saw a shift in the location of the auratic from something only to be found in the 'original' work of art to something with which any number of reproductions could be invested. One can detect the auratic in many of the squarish forms under discussion here. The auratic in sculpture is no longer exclusively the domain of the unique but multiple: possessed and intuited in and by the many.

Joy Sleeman

Notes

1 B. O'Doherty, *Inside the White Cube: The Ideology of the Gallery Space*, London, University of California Press, 1999. The essays originally appeared in *Artforum* magazine in four parts: parts 1–3 in 1976, part 4 in 1986.

2 O'Doherty, *Inside the White Cube: The Ideology of the Gallery Space*, p. 15.

3 Marshall McLuhan's ubiquitous observation that 'the medium is the message'; see M. McLuhan, 'Introduction' from *Understanding Media*, in C. Harrison and P. Wood (eds), *Art in Theory*, Oxford, Blackwell, 1992, pp. 738–40.

4 The sculpture in question is Larry Bell, 'Memories of Mike', metal and glass, 24 in. square, 1966–7.

5 P. Leider, 'American sculpture at the Los Angeles County Museum', *Artforum*, Summer 1967, pp. 6–11.

6 M. Fried, letter to Frank Martin (head of sculpture at St Martin's), 10.8.71, quoted in H. Gresty, 'From the New Generation 1965 to the New Art 1972' (retitled 'Sculpture in Britain in the early '70s'), M.Phil. dissertation, Courtauld Institute of Art, London, 1984, p. 11.

7 Gresty states that *Artforum* was available in the St Martin's library from March 1966. Gresty, 'From the New Generation 1965 to the New Art 1972', note 6 to chapter on John Hilliard.

8 T. McEvilley, 'Sweet thoughts', *Artforum*, September 1993, p. 179.

9 *Silâns* was the magazine of the St Martin's Vocational Sculpture course. It was edited by Barry Flanagan, Alastair Jackson and Rudy Leenders, 16 issues, September 1964–June 1965. It was produced on very low-grade paper using a spirit duplicator. The title is sometimes given in the magazine as 'Silence' rather than 'Silâns'.

10 Edited by Glynn Foulkes and Roger Bates, London, St Martin's School of Art, 1968.

11 An exhibition and accompanying publication demonstrating some of the vast range of artists' books was presented at the Henry Moore Institute in 1997: S. Cutts, E. Van Horn and J. Janssen (eds), *The Space of the Page*, Leeds, Henry Moore Institute, 1997.

12 C. Owens, 'Earthwords' (1979), in S. S. Bryson (ed.), *Beyond Recognition*, Berkeley, Los Angeles and London, University of California Press, 1992, p. 45.

13 Lippard and Chandler's essay 'The dematerialization of art' was written in 1967 and published in *Art International*, February 1968, vol. 12, no. 2. It is reprinted (in edited form) in A. Alberro and B. Stimson (eds), *Conceptual Art: A Critical Anthology*, Cambridge, MA and London, MIT Press, 1999, pp. 46–50.

14 L. Lippard, *Six Years: The Dematerialization of the Art Object from 1966 to 1972*, Berkeley, Los Angeles and London, University of California Press, 1997, p. 5.

15 The May 1971 issue of *Studio International* doubled as the catalogue to the exhibition of that name held at the New York Cultural Center in 1971, curated by Harrison. This exhibition showed works by: Keith Arnatt, Sue Arrowsmith, Terry Atkinson, David Bainbridge, Michael Baldwin, Victor Burgin, Colin Crumplin, Andrew Dipper, David Dye, Barry Flanagan, Gilbert & George, Harold Hurrell, Richard Long, Roelof Louw, Bruce McLean, Gerald Newman and David Tremlett.

16 *Studio International*, April 1971, vol. 181, no. 932, p. 142.

17 J. Kosuth, 'Intention(s)', in A. Alberro and B. Stimson (eds), *Conceptual Art: A Critical Anthology*, p. 463.

18 *Audio Arts* was the invention of two artists, William Furlong and Barry Barker. It began publication in 1973 as the first art magazine to be published on audio cassette. For more information about the magazine, see W. Furlong, *Audio Arts: Discourse and Practice in Contemporary Art*, London, Academy, 1994.

19 A. Seymour, 'Introduction' to *The New Art*, Hayward Gallery, London, Arts Council of Great Britain, 1972, pp. 5–7. The exhibition ran from 17 August to 24 September.

20 S. Sontag, 'The aesthetics of silence' (1967), in S. Sontag, *Styles of Radical Will*, London, Vintage, 1994, p. 12.

21 'Bryan Robertson's achievement at the Whitechapel', *Studio International*, February 1969, p. 58.

22 B. Robertson, J. Russell and C. R. Armstrong-Jones, 1st Earl of Snowdon, *Private View*, London, Nelson, 1965, p. 295.

23 J. Perrault, 'It's only words', *The Village Voice*, 20 May 1971, reprinted in G. Battcock (ed.), *Idea Art*, New York, Dutton, 1973, p. 138.

24 A. Smith, 'Introduction', *Television: An International History*, 2nd edn, Oxford, Oxford University Press, 1998, p. 5.

25 C. Harrison, 'Art on TV', *Studio International*, January 1971, p. 30.

26 The other two are an 11th-century Indian temple carving and a piece of Peruvian pottery.

27 *The Times*, July 1969, reprinted for the 30th anniversary of the moon landing, 1999, p. 4.

28 Illustrated in the catalogue to *Live in Your Head*, Whitechapel Art Gallery, London, 2000, p. 128.

29 In interview with Bruce Kurtz in 1972, Smithson said 'I described the moon shot once as a very expensive non-site.' J. Flam (ed.), *Robert Smithson: The Collected Writings*, Berkeley and LA, University of California Press, 1996, p. 268.

30 A. Newman, *Challenging Art: Artforum 1962–1974*, New York, Soho Press, 2000, p. 251.

31 F. White, *The Overview Effect: Space Exploration and Human Evolution*, Reston, VA, American Institute of Aeronautics and Astronautics, 1998.

32 B. Taylor, review of 'Simultaneity. Paris. World. 1910. 1914', *Art Monthly*, February 1977, no. 4, p. 23.

33 J. Berger, *Ways of Seeing*, London, Penguin, 1972, p. 30.

34 O'Doherty, *Inside the White Cube: the Ideology of the Gallery Space*, p. 13.

35 W. Benjamin, 'The work of art in the age of mechanical reproduction' (1936), reprinted in H. Arendt (ed.), *Illuminations*, London, Fontana, 1973, p. 218.

Sculpture in 20th-century Britain **1975–2000**

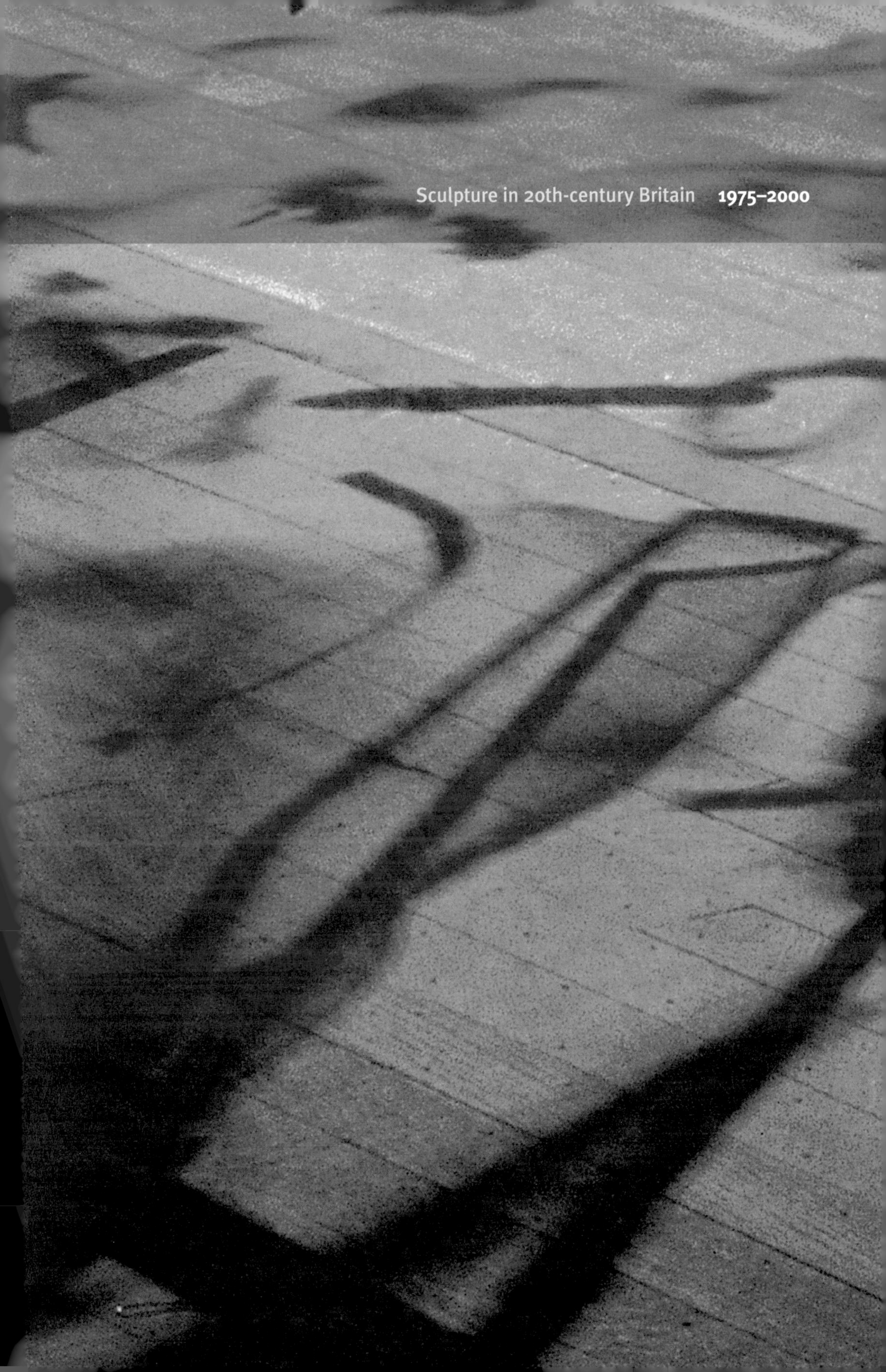

1975

■ Barbara Hepworth dies
■ Coracle Press, a small printing press in London, is set up to publish the work of artists and writers
■ William Tucker selects recent sculpture by younger British and foreign artists for *The Condition of Sculpture*, an Arts Council exhibition at the Hayward Gallery, London
■ Anthony Caro retrospective exhibition at MoMA, New York and Museum of Fine Arts, Boston
■ AIR Gallery opens on Shaftesbury Avenue, London

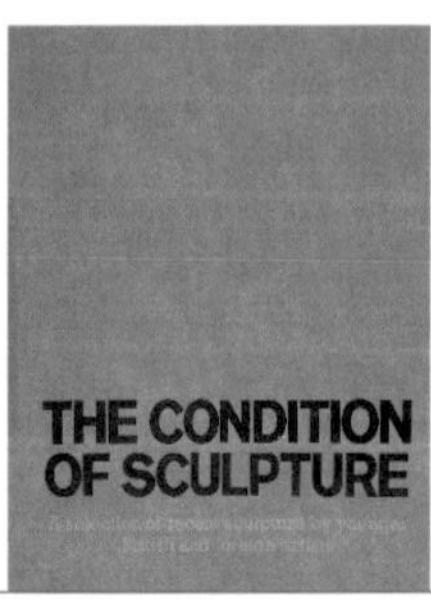

Front cover of the exhibition catalogue *The Condition of Sculpture*, London

1976

■ Controversy about Carl Andre's 'bricks' when the sculpture 'Equivalent VIII' is exhibited at the Tate Gallery, London
■ *Art Monthly* and *Artscribe* begin publication
■ Richard Long exhibits his work at the British Pavilion, Venice Biennale
■ Acme Gallery opens on Shelton Street, London

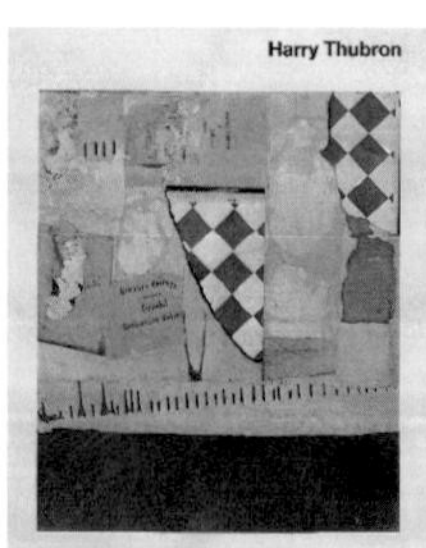

Front cover of the exhibition catalogue, *Harry Thubron*, Serpentine Gallery, London

1977

■ Henry Moore Foundation established by Henry Moore
■ Yorkshire Sculpture Park opens to provide an outdoor site for displaying sculpture
■ Grizedale Sculpture Project established in the Lake District to use Grizedale Forest as a working environment for sculptors
■ For the Silver Jubilee celebrations an exhibition of contemporary British sculpture is held at Battersea Park, London
■ *Passages in Modern Sculpture* by Rosalind E. Krauss is published and acclaimed as one of the few books on the theory of sculpture

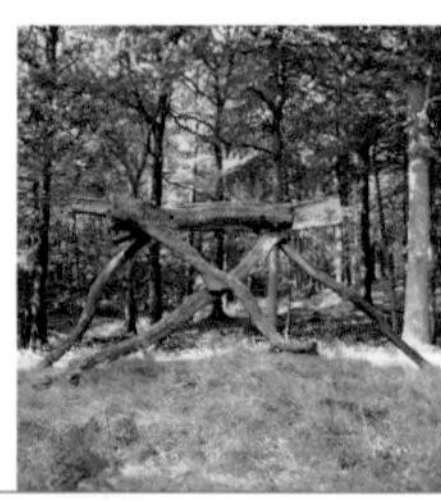

David Nash, 'Running Table', at Grizedale

1978

■ Scottish Sculpture Trust set up for the promotion and presentation of modern sculpture on public sites in Scotland
■ *Constructive Context*, an Arts Council Collection exhibition, begins its UK tour
■ *Objects and Constructions: Selected Contemporary Scottish Sculpture*, a Scottish Arts Council exhibition, shown in Edinburgh
■ As part of Henry Moore's 80th birthday celebrations the Tate Gallery exhibits Moore's recent gift of sculpture and drawing to the Gallery's collection

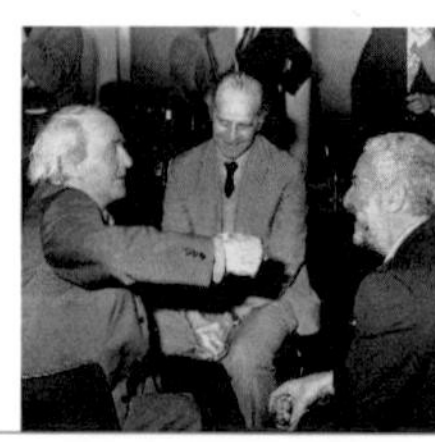

Henry Moore, Phillip King (centre and Anthony Caro at the private v of his *Eightieth Birthday Exhibiti* at Cartwright Hall, Bradford

1979

- Peter Randall-Page works on conservation of 13th-century sculpture at Wells Cathedral
- Robin Klassnik opens Matt's Gallery in his studio at London Fields
- AIR Gallery re-established in new premises on Roseberry Avenue, London

1980

- Barbara Hepworth Museum and Sculpture Garden opens in St Ives
- *Pier+Ocean: Construction in the Art of the Seventies*, an Arts Council exhibition at the Hayward Gallery, London
- *Nature as Material*, an Arts Council Collection touring exhibition of sculpture and photography
- Nicholas Pope exhibits his work at the British Pavilion, Venice Biennale
- The eight-part BBC television series *The Shock of the New* by Robert Hughes brings the history of modern art to public attention
- *British Art Now: An American Perspective*, exhibition at the Guggenheim Museum, New York includes work by Keith Milow, David Nash and Nicholas Pope

1981

- *Objects and Sculpture*, an exhibition at the Institute of Contemporary Arts, London and the Arnolfini, Bristol
- *British Sculpture in the Twentieth Century* exhibition at the Whitechapel Gallery, London
- *New Sculpture* exhibition at the Midland Group Gallery, Nottingham
- *Sculpture for the Blind* exhibition at the Tate Gallery, London for the International Year of Disabled People
- Austin Wright retrospective exhibition at the Yorkshire Sculpture Park to celebrate his 70th birthday
- Welsh Sculpture Trust set up to expand the accessibility of sculpture to the people of Wales

1982

- Henry Moore Centre for the Study of Sculpture established in Leeds
- HM The Queen opens new sculpture galleries at Leeds City Art Gallery
- *Sculpture in the Garden*, exhibition at Camden Arts Centre, London
- *Making Sculpture*, an exhibition at the Tate Gallery, London introduces the materials and methods of sculpture
- Anish Kapoor is artist in residence at the Walker Art Gallery, Liverpool

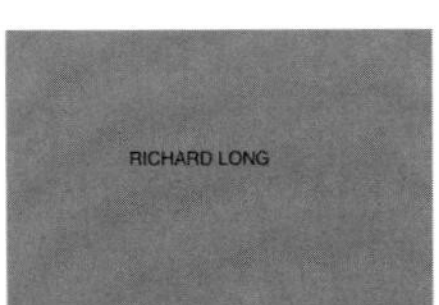

Front cover of *Richard Long*, Van Abbemuseum, Eindhoven

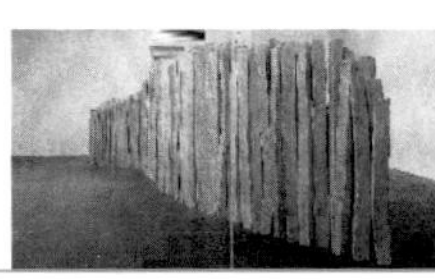

Front and back covers of the exhibition catalogue *Nicholas Pope: British Pavilion, Venice Biennale 1980*

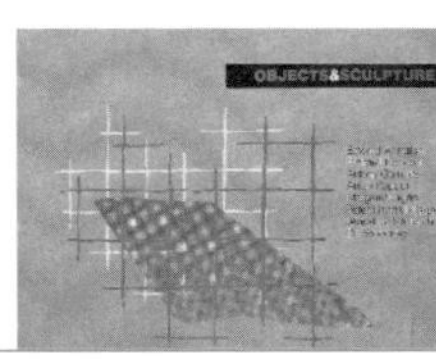

Front cover of the exhibition catalogue *Objects and Sculpture*

1983

- The Showroom opens, a lettable exhibition space
- Welsh Sculpture Trust opens sculpture park at Margam, West Glamorgan
- International Sculpture Symposium hosted by the Yorkshire Sculpture Park, the first International Sculpture Center event to be hosted outside the USA
- *Figures and Objects*, John Hansard Gallery, University of Southampton
- *The Sculpture Show* at the Hayward and the Serpentine Galleries, London
- A man dies setting fire to David Mach's sculpture 'Polaris', a submarine constructed of lorry tyres, at the South Bank, London
- Elisabeth Frink retrospective exhibition at the Yorkshire Sculpture Park
- *Transformations: New Sculpture from Britain* presented by the British Council at the São Paulo Bienal

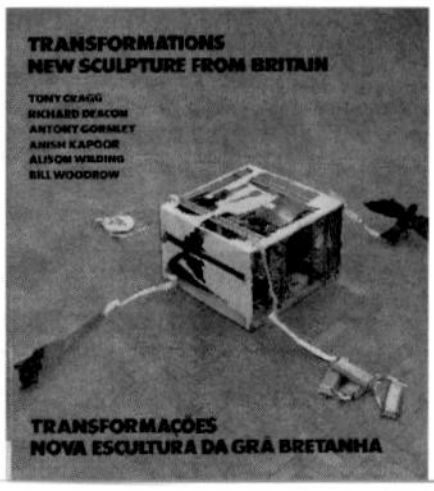

Front cover of the exhibition catalogue *Transformations: New Sculpture from Britain*

1984

- Maureen Paley establishes Interim Arts on Beck Road, London
- Richard Deacon, Gilbert & George and Richard Long are shortlisted for the new Turner Prize, founded by the Patrons of New Art
- Sculpture is a feature of the Liverpool International Garden Festival
- *1965 to 1972: When Attitudes Became Form*, exhibition at Kettle's Yard, Cambridge and Fruitmarket Gallery, Edinburgh
- *Catalogue raisonné* of Elisabeth Frink's sculpture is published
- Young artists inspired by the human figure show *Have You Seen Sculpture From the Body?* on the lawn of the Tate Gallery, London

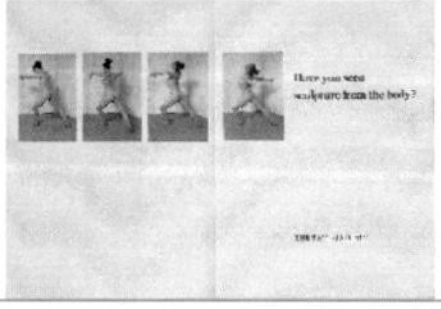

Title page of the exhibition catalogue *Have You Seen Sculpture From the Body?*

1985

- *A Noise in Your Eye*, an international exhibition of sound-producing sculptures and installations is held at the Arnolfini, Bristol
- *The Poetic Object*, an exhibition of the work of Richard Deacon, Shirazeh Houshiary and Anish Kapoor, at the Douglas Hyde Gallery, Dublin
- Artangel founded by Roger Took to commission and support new public artworks in unusual locations

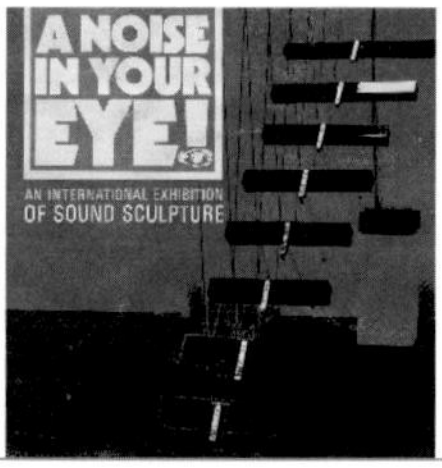

Front cover of the exhibition catalogue *A Noise in Your Eye*

1986

- First phase of the Forest of Dean Sculpture Project opens, with complementary exhibitions at the Arnolfini, Bristol
- Henry Moore dies
- Complete catalogue of Jacob Epstein's sculpture by Evelyn Silber is published by Phaidon Press
- *The Artist Publisher*, a survey exhibition of artists' books by Coracle Press, is held at the Crafts Council Gallery, London
- *Feeling Through Form*, an exhibition organised by the Windhorse Trust is held on the roof of the Barbican Centre, London
- Gilbert & George win the Turner Prize
- Eduardo Paolozzi is made 'Her Majesty's Sculptor in Ordinary for Scotland'

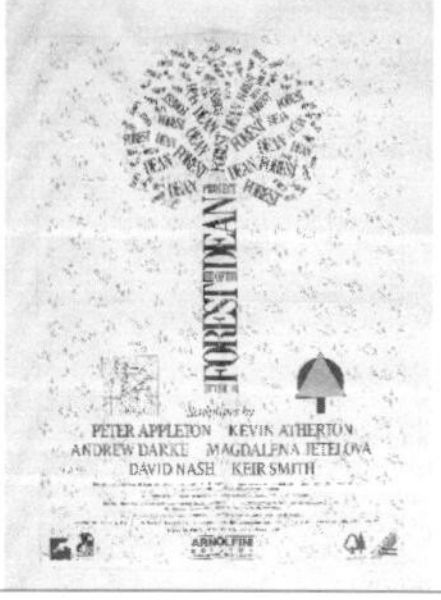

Forest of Dean Sculpture Project poster

1987

- Hampshire Sculpture Trust is launched in Winchester
- Andy Goldsworthy is artist in residence at the Yorkshire Sculpture Park
- *Casting an Eye*, an exhibition of sculpture selected by Richard Deacon and Alison Wilding at the Cornerhouse, Manchester
- David Mach exhibits his work at the São Paulo Bienal
- *A Quiet Revolution: British Sculpture Since 1965*, an exhibition of work by Tony Cragg, Richard Deacon, Barry Flanagan, Richard Long, David Nash and Bill Woodrow tours the USA
- Richard Deacon wins the Turner Prize

1988

- Damien Hirst, a student at Goldsmiths' College, organises *Freeze*, an exhibition of student work in a disused building in the London Docklands
- *Starlit Waters: British Sculpture, An International Art*, the first exhibition at the new Tate Gallery, Liverpool
- Henry Moore Sculpture Trust founded in Leeds to develop public knowledge and appreciation of sculpture
- Installation is integrated in the gardens and landscaping of the Glasgow Garden Festival
- 550 sculptors respond to the advertisements for the open submission exhibition *Grey Matter: New Sculpture 88* and six selected to show at the Ikon Gallery, Birmingham
- International Conference on Sculpture held at Trinity College, Dublin, organised by the Sculptors' Society of Ireland
- Tony Cragg wins the Turner Prize

1989

- *3D '89*, National Open Sculpture Exhibition at Watermans Art Centre, Brentford and Small Mansion Arts Centre, London
- Edward Allington wins the John Moores Liverpool Exhibition Prize
- Henry Moore Sculpture Trust Studio opens at Dean Clough, Halifax
- Richard Long wins the Turner Prize for the enduring influence and importance of his sculpture, both internationally and in Britain

1990

- Artist-run gallery City Racing established in a former betting shop at the Oval, south London
- Museum of Installation opens in Deptford, south-east London
- Anish Kapoor exhibits his work at the British Pavilion, Venice Biennale
- Edward Allington becomes Gregory Fellow in Sculpture at the University of Leeds
- *Catalogue raisonné* of the sculpture of Anthony Caro is published in a set of nine volumes
- Turner Prize suspended when its sponsorship is discontinued

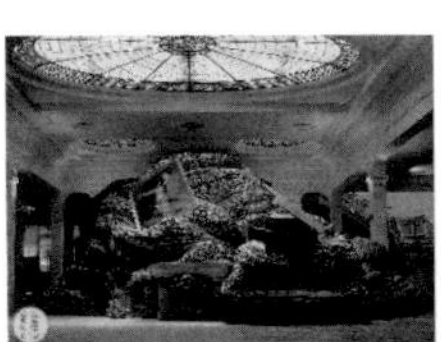

Front cover of the exhibition catalogue *David Mach: 19 Bienal de São Paulo*

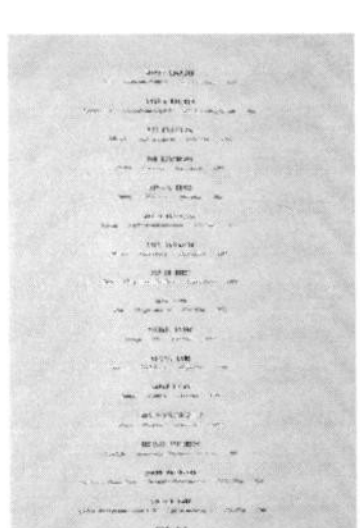

List of artists and exhibits from the exhibition catalogue *Freeze*

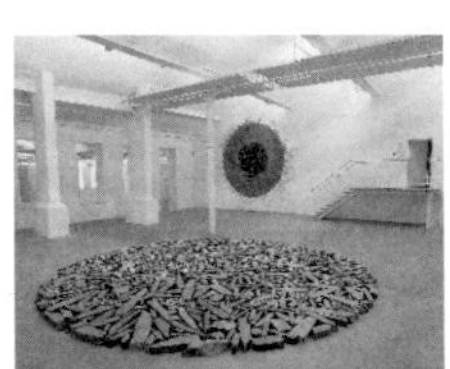

The first exhibition at The Henry Moore Sculpture Trust Studio, 'Halifax Circle' by Richard Long

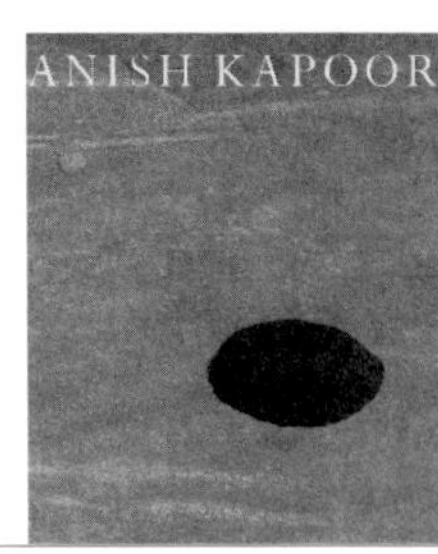

Front cover of the exhibition catalogue *Anish Kapoor: British Pavilion, XLIV Venice Biennale, May–September 1990*

1991

■ Channel 4 becomes main sponsor of the Turner Prize and prize money is doubled to £20,000
■ Public Monuments and Sculpture Association founded to encourage the study and conservation of public sculpture in Britain
■ *Broken English*, exhibition of work by young English artists at the Serpentine Gallery, London
■ *Frieze* magazine launched
■ *Virtue and Vision: Sculpture and Scotland 1540–1990*, exhibition in Edinburgh
■ Anish Kapoor wins the Turner Prize

1992

■ Sculpture at Goodwood founded to commission and promote British sculpture
■ Millfield School in Somerset opens a new Fine Arts Centre and holds an exhibition of British sculpture on the campus, a designated sculpture park
■ *Young British Artists 1*, the first of a series of exhibitions at the Saatchi Gallery, London attracts unprecedented media attention
■ Damien Hirst exhibits 'Mother and Child, Divided', a bisected cow and calf in tanks of formaldehyde, at the Venice Biennale
■ Grenville Davey wins the Turner Prize

1993

■ Henry Moore Institute, a centre for the study of sculpture, opens in Leeds
■ Jay Jopling opens the White Cube Gallery in London
■ Tate St Ives opens
■ New Art Sculpture Park and Gallery founded at Roche Court in Wiltshire
■ First issue of *Untitled*, a quarterly review of contemporary art, published in London
■ Tracey Emin and Sarah Lucas set up 'The Shop' in east London
■ Locus+ is established to work with artists on projects for non-gallery locations
■ Rachel Whiteread is the first woman to win the Turner Prize. She then wins the K Foundation prize of £40,000 for the worst artist of the year

1994

■ Rachel Whiteread's 'House', an Artangel project in east London, is demolished
■ *Some Went Mad, Some Ran Away*, a touring exhibition, opened at the Serpentine Gallery, London
■ Damien Hirst's sculpture 'Away From the Flock' is vandalised by a visitor to the Serpentine Gallery, London
■ Sculpture at Goodwood opens its grounds in West Sussex to the public
■ Eduardo Paolozzi's 70th birthday exhibition at the Yorkshire Sculpture Park
■ A critical forum accompanies the Barbara Hepworth retrospective exhibition at Tate Gallery Liverpool
■ Antony Gormley wins the Turner Prize

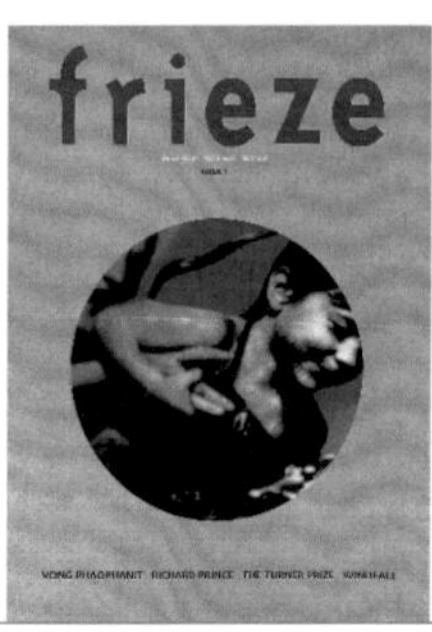

Front cover of *frieze*, Issue 1

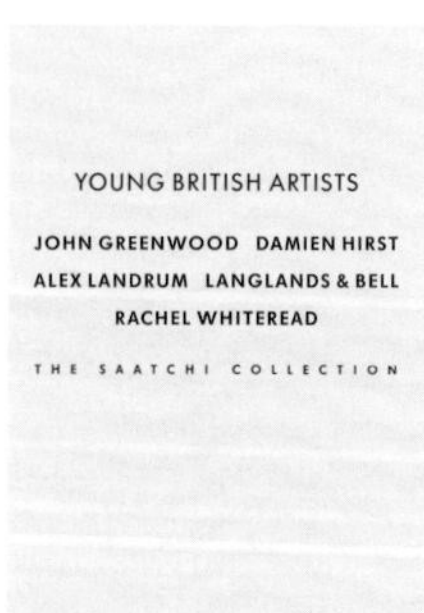

Front cover of *Young British Artists*, Saatchi Gallery, London

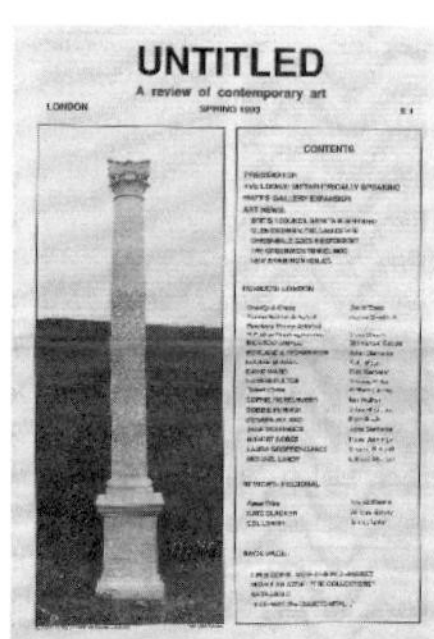

Front cover of *Untitled*, with a photo of Ian Hamilton Finlay's 'Saint Just Column' by John Stathatos

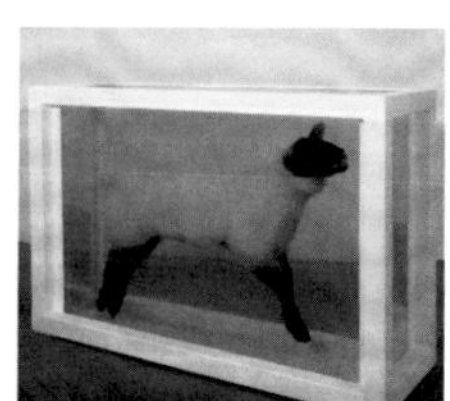

Damien Hirst, 'Away From the Flock'

1995

- The Serpentine Gallery celebrates its 25th anniversary with *Here and Now*, an exhibition of work by the sculptors who had exhibited there
- *Minky Manky* exhibition at the South London Gallery, curated by Carl Freedman
- Tracey Emin Museum opens at Waterloo, London
- *The Maybe*, an exhibition by Cornelia Parker in collaboration with the actress Tilda Swinton, at the Serpentine Gallery, London
- Damien Hirst wins the Turner Prize for his curatorship of and contribution to *Some Went Mad, Some Ran Away*

1996

- Year of the Visual Arts in the North of England doubles visitor figures at northern art venues
- *Barbara Hepworth Reconsidered* published as a result of a conference held in conjunction with the 1994 Hepworth retrospective at Tate Gallery Liverpool
- *'Brilliant!' New Art from London*, exhibition at the Walker Art Center, Minneapolis and the Contemporary Art Museum, Houston
- *Un Siécle de Sculpture Anglaise*, exhibition at Galerie Nationale du Jeu de Paume, Paris

1997

- A memorial exhibition for Austin Wright is held at the Yorkshire Sculpture Park
- *Public Sculpture of Liverpool* is published, the culmination of the pilot project of the Public Monuments and Sculpture Association's National Recording Project
- *Sensation: Young British Artists From the Saatchi Collection*, an exhibition at the Royal Academy, London hits the news headlines
- *The Sculpture Journal* begins publication
- Claude Heath is a prize-winner, John Moores Liverpool Exhibition, Walker Art Gallery
- Rachel Whiteread is the first woman to be the single representative artist at the British Pavilion, Venice Biennale

1998

- Building work starts on converting the Baltic Flour Mills into a new international centre for contemporary art on the banks of the river Tyne at Gateshead
- Antony Gormley's 'Angel of the North', the largest sculpture in Britain, is erected at Gateshead
- Christie's Contemporary hold an exhibition of works from the Saatchi Collection in a Clerkenwell warehouse and raise £1.6m for art students at London colleges
- *Artranspennine98*, international exhibition of contemporary visual art from Hull to Liverpool

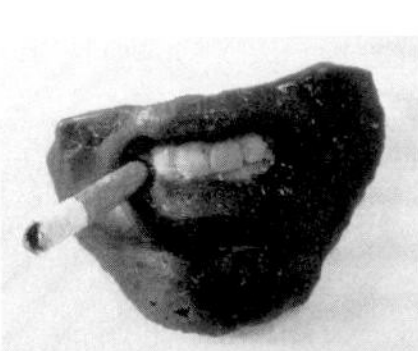

Sarah Lucas, 'Where Does It All End', one of the sculptures shown in the exhibition *Minky Manky*

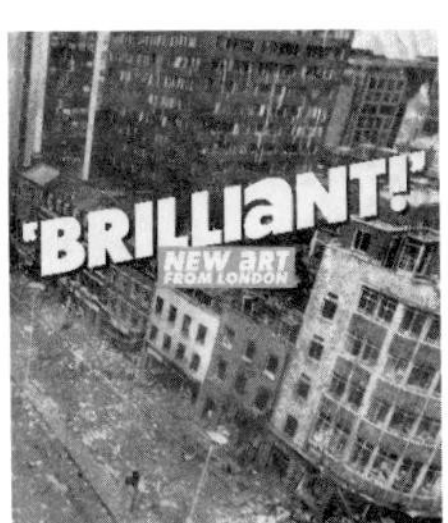

Front cover of exhibition catalogue *'Brilliant!': New Art from London*

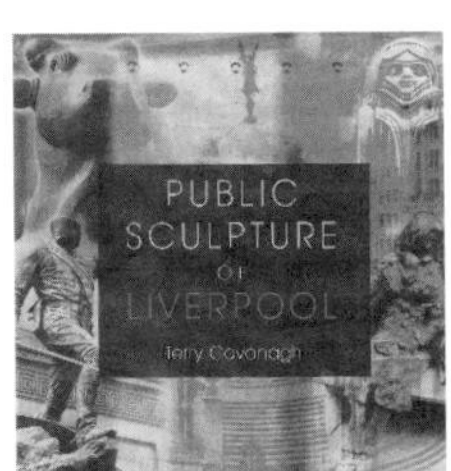

Terry Cavanagh, *Public Sculpture of Liverpool*, Liverpool University Press

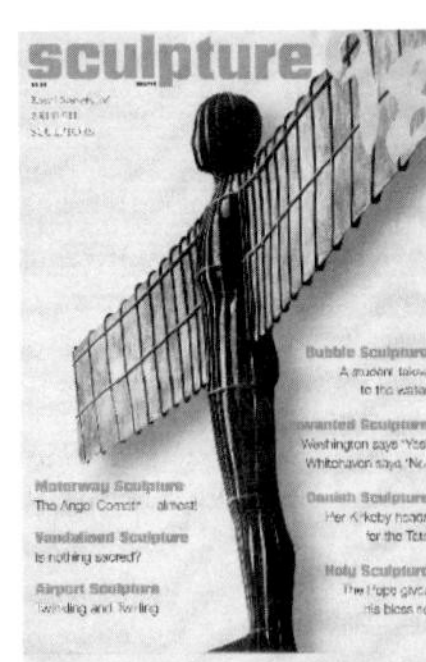

Royal Society of British Sculptors, *Sculpture '98*, with 'Angel of the North' by Antony Gormley

1999

■ *Trace*, the first Liverpool Biennial of international contemporary art
■ Charles Saatchi donates 100 works by 63 artists to the Arts Council Collection
■ Phillip King becomes president of the Royal Academy of Arts
■ Tracey Emin's unmade bed, 'My Bed', hits the headlines when exhibited at the Tate Gallery, London
■ National Galleries of Scotland open the Dean Gallery for the permanent display of work by Eduardo Paolozzi
■ Mark Wallinger's 'Ecce Homo' is the first in a series of sculptures to be installed on the empty plinth in Trafalgar Square, London

2000

■ Bill Woodrow's sculpture 'Regardless of History' is installed on the empty plinth in Trafalgar Square, London
■ Tate Modern opens at Bankside, London
■ Jerwood Sculpture Park opens at Witley Court in Worcestershire
■ *Intelligence: New British Art*, the first in a new series of contemporary art exhibitions at Tate Britain, Millbank, London
■ *Bronze: Contemporary British Sculpture at Holland Park*, a millennium exhibition
■ Sculpture is part of the New Millennium Experience at the Dome, London

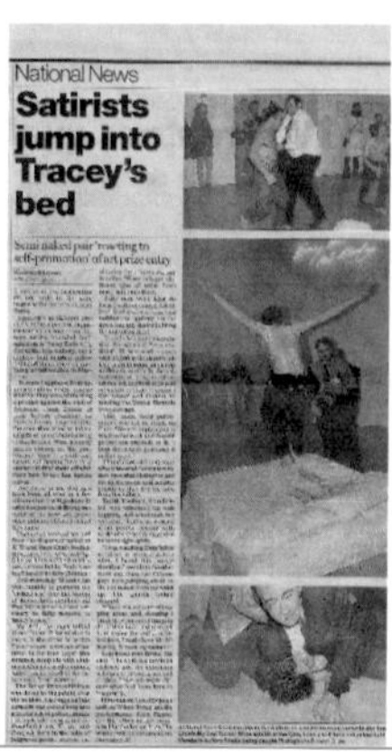
National News

Satirists jump into Tracey's bed

Fiachra Gibbons, 'Satarists jump into Tracey's bed', *Guardian*, 25 October

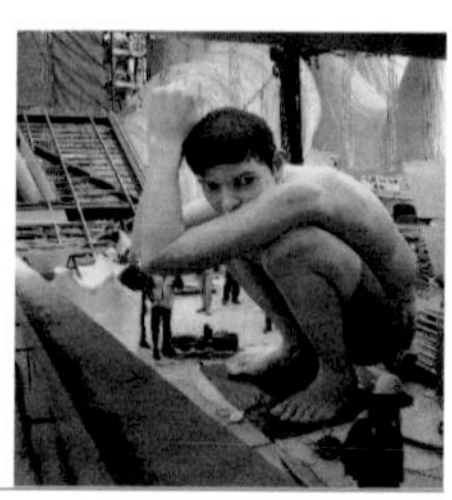

Ron Mueck, 'Boy', 1999, at the Millennium Dome

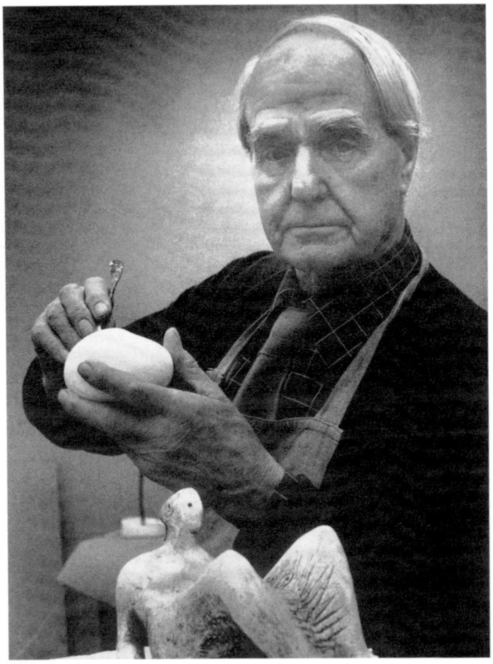

'Identity?' said Jack, comfortably pouring out more coffee. 'Is not identity something you are born with?'

'The identity I am thinking of is something that hovers between a man and the rest of the world: a mid-point between his view of himself and theirs of him – for each of course, affects the other continually. A reciprocal fluxion, sir. There is nothing absolute about this identity of mine.'[1]

When I first worked in an art college it had a traditional tripartite departmental division of painting, sculpture and printmaking. The sculptors looked down on the painters as wimps, the painters looked down on the printmakers as being mere craftspeople, the printmakers got on with their work – which both painters and sculptors saw as antiquated. The painters saw the sculptors as less intellectual than themselves, and certainly they were physically stronger. The sculptors and printmakers would go drinking at the end of the day, or at lunchtime – having built up more of a sweat than the painters. If you needed to move anything heavy, or get something mended, you would ask a sculpture student to do it because they were tougher and more practical than the others – they were jacks of all trades.

There is a paradox here, for whilst the sculptors may have been less overtly 'intellectual', the literature around sculpture – or certainly the theoretical element of that literature – was intellectually so much more challenging. Did this change between the years 1975 and 2000? How did sculptors' perceptions of themselves change and how did others' perceptions of them change too?

In 1979 a book of photographic portraits of artists was published.[2] Henry Moore comes first (Fig. 1). He stands with his eyes fixed on the viewer. He wears a work apron; in his left hand is a rounded stone, in his right a small chisel. In the foreground is a model of a reclining figure. This is a classic image of the artist that bears comparison with self-portraits of Renaissance artists. It portrays the commitment to and vocation for his profession. His expression betrays high seriousness, his hands convey pride in the tools of his trade. His face and posture

1 Portrait of Henry Moore by Walia

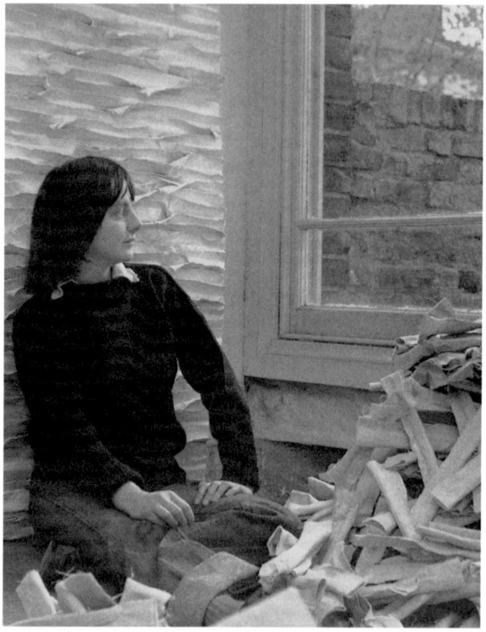

have the same dignified mien as those of Gianlorenzo Bernini, Nicolas Poussin or Diego Velázquez. Subsequent photographs in the book of the sculptors of a (then) middle generation give variants of this sort of image. Reg Butler, Willi Soukop and Phillip King look at or fondle their sculptures like lovers. Bernard Meadows and F. E. McWilliam look at their sculptures as if they were Rubik cubes: puzzles to be solved. Tim Scott and Roland Piché look at the fragmented elements of their work as if they were gangers inspecting a wrecked car. These are not just postures or poses but embodied metaphors of what a sculptor is or should be – a serious intellectual, but committed to the material forms of sculpture. These images now – from the perspective of 2003 – seem curiously old-fashioned. The two that perhaps do not, are those of Phyllida Barlow (Fig. 2) and Barry Flanagan (Fig. 3). Barlow is surrounded by a clutter of stuff but looks away from it through a window to a world outside.[3] Flanagan seems more like a prospective employer or professor about to interview someone. He is behind a desk. Beside him is a sculpture somewhat like a template for a corset. One expects the first question to be 'and what do you think this is?' In short, there is a shift from the vocational to the interrogatory, or to an identification with the world outside taking precedence over an *a priori* sense of identity as a sculptor.

For comparison, consider how in 1995 Jane and Louise Wilson posed for *Time Out* as fashion models (Fig. 4): Louise wore a snakeskin-look Joseph suit, Jane a Paul Smith jacket. They seemed to simultaneously parody the image of artist and of model. In the accompanying blurb they jest: 'Have you ever bought a bespoke suit?' 'Never, but I wore a giant chicken for the school play', says Louise. They are at ease with the camera and the media, free to spoof it. Indeed, such a spoof could be seen as part of their work. The comedy, irony and posture had become part of their work. They have eschewed *gravitas* in favour of a playful involvement with the media. Consider also the picture of Richard Deacon and Bill Woodrow seated together on a sofa both playing guitar. The microphone they are playing into is a globe. It was on the front of the invitation card to the preview on 18 May 1993 of their exhibition *Only the Lonely and Other Shared Sculptures* at the

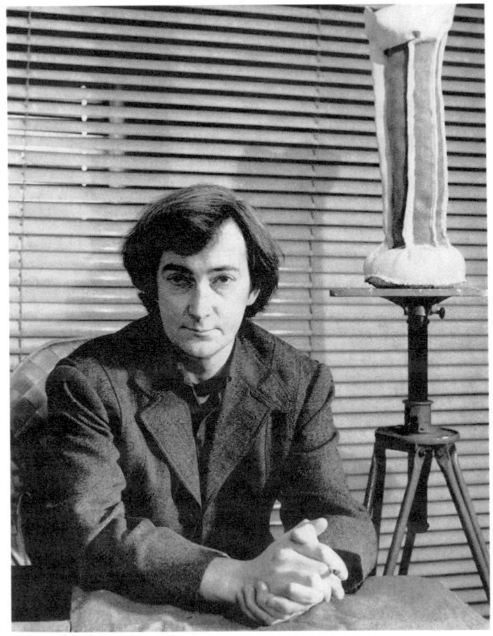

Chisenhale Gallery (Fig. 5). On the card the picture is set in an unseasonal frame of Christmas decoration. These are not typical photographs but are indicative of tendencies: sculptors have come out of the studio: there is a shift from self-presentation in terms of professional expertise to self-presentation in the 'real' world. The emphasis in the two photographs on play, companionship and other media (fashion, music) is telling. Underlying identity is identification: who or what do you associate yourself with?

Identity is an individual thing – my identity, your identity – but it has no meaning save in the context of others. I am English but that means nothing unless there are other English people and there is a history of being English. We calibrate our identity in relation to others and to what has happened in the past. To be a sculptor means to be doing something that some other people are doing as well (companionship and competition) it also means having a relationship to what has been done in the past. Traditions are, in a sense, languages: we 'speak' in their forms and manipulate and develop those forms.

The very word 'identity' is fraught in this period. The 1980s may be seen subsequently as the decade of identity politics.[4] The right to be different from the mainstream was fought for by women, gay people and ethnic minorities. Art was obviously a site for these struggles. The increased number of 'coloured' sculptors emerging in this period dictates that we consider this aspect of identity. Indeed, the term 'identity of the sculptor' may seem quaint when people are concerned with their identity as lesbians, blacks, Muslims, disabled, etc.

One obvious example is Shirazeh Houshiary, who has, since first showing in Britain in 1979, consistently used the poetry of the Persian mystic Rumi as source and inspiration and in one extended body of work adapted Parsee letter forms into sculptural shapes. The early trajectory of Houshiary's career is telling: having studied literature in Tehran and initially intending to be a writer, she moved to Chelsea School of Art but while a student concentrated initially on making light installations. As she said subsequently in 1989, 'I've never really been faithful to any

2 Portrait of Phyllida Barlow by Walia

3 Portrait of Barry Flanagan by Walia

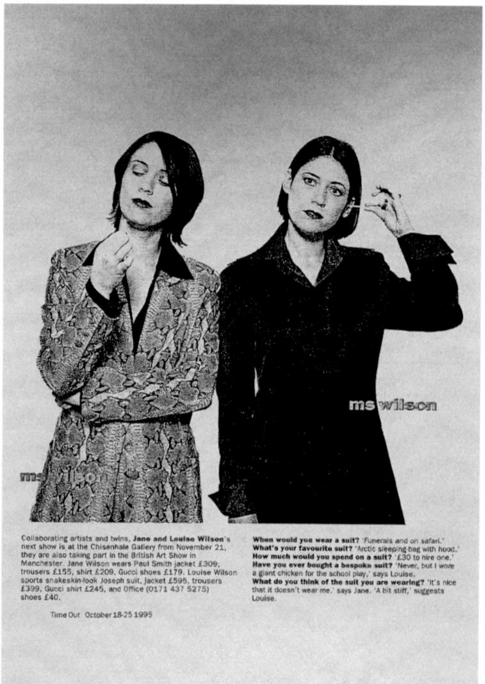

ms wilson

Collaborating artists and twins, **Jane and Louise Wilson**'s next show is at the Chisenhale Gallery from November 21, they are also taking part in the British Art Show in Manchester. Jane Wilson wears Paul Smith jacket £309, trousers £155, shirt £209, Gucci shoes £179. Louise Wilson sports snakeskin-look Joseph suit, jacket £595, trousers £399, Gucci shirt £245, and Office (0171 437 5275) shoes £40.

Time Out October 18-25 1995

When would you wear a suit? 'Funerals and on safari.' **What's your favourite suit?** 'Arctic sleeping-bag with hood.' **How much would you spend on a suit?** '£30 to hire one.' **Have you ever bought a bespoke suit?** 'Never, but I wore a giant chicken for the school play,' says Louise. **What do you think of the suit you are wearing?** 'It's nice that it doesn't wear me,' says Jane. 'A bit stiff,' suggests Louise.

form or material; they are only tools, passages that the thought or idea can move through.'[5] Her 'identity' is not then dependent on the British sculptural tradition but based firstly on her own Persian literary tradition, secondly on the other Lisson Gallery sculptors with whom she has consistently shown her work, and thirdly on what she emphasises is the universality of mystical experience: the sort of mystic experiences Rumi speaks of are remarkably similar to those described by St John of the Cross. A fourth[6] strand of her identity as a sculptor is her use of a non-traditional paragon: poetry. She has commented that for her sculpture is closer to poetry than painting since in her view paint is necessarily descriptive and not a real thing in itself.

Likewise Anish Kapoor, Houshiary's compatriot at Chelsea School of Art, was to draw on non-western sources: mounds of coloured spices in the markets of his native India and oriental carpets. This was not a matter of adding a *soupçon* of exoticism to British sculpture; it was part of a wider way of looking at things: 'I don't wish to make sculpture about form … I wish to make sculpture about belief, or about passion, about experience, that is outside of material concern.'[7] Also he was engaging more with the *raison d'être* of painting than of sculpture: the key influence was Yves Klein who had used pigmented pictures and objects to create a sense of dematerialisation and the void. Kapoor made objects and covered them with disembodying pigment. He was, in short, using sculpture rather than making it. Sculpture provided the set or scenery for the *mise-en-scéne.* The effect was more important than the tool. One recalls James Turrell's abjuration of Mark Rothko: as a student he had been enormously impressed by slides of Rothko's work, which gave him the sense of floating shapes, but was disappointed by the real paintings when he eventually saw them; he was in subsequent light installations to attempt to recreate that original and incorrect sensation.

A number of other artists of ethnic backgrounds used their heritages or situations to create amalgams: Zadok Ben-David, the goldsmithing tradition of Yemen; Veronica Ryan, Caribbean plant forms; Mona

4 Jane and Louise Wilson, *Time Out*, 16–25 October 1995

5 Bill Woodrow and Richard Deacon, *Only the Lonely*, 1993

Hatoum, the nature of exile itself. Generally, these works were pictorial and this mirrored the shift most especially on the continent to image making that paralleled developments in painting in the 1980s.[8] Indeed, identity politics became increasingly seen as simplistic or essentialist as the period developed. Allegiance to 'black' positions gave way to more sophisticated, even ironic positions of hybridity or the Creole or subaltern. Artists such as those mentioned above both enriched and challenged the tradition by bringing in other associations or cultural allegiances – from high or low. The very word 'identity' ended up as painfully problematic in this period in that it becomes so specifically associated with gender and race. Perhaps we should consider whether in fact, and if so how, artists develop *hybrid* identities where allegiances or identifications are multiform and being a sculptor or even a British sculptor is only one among many identity positions.

At the same time as the definition of sculpture expands and arguably dissipates, the notion of a sculptor's identity is disturbed. Houshiary and Kapoor *et al.* demonstrated a shift away from British identity to

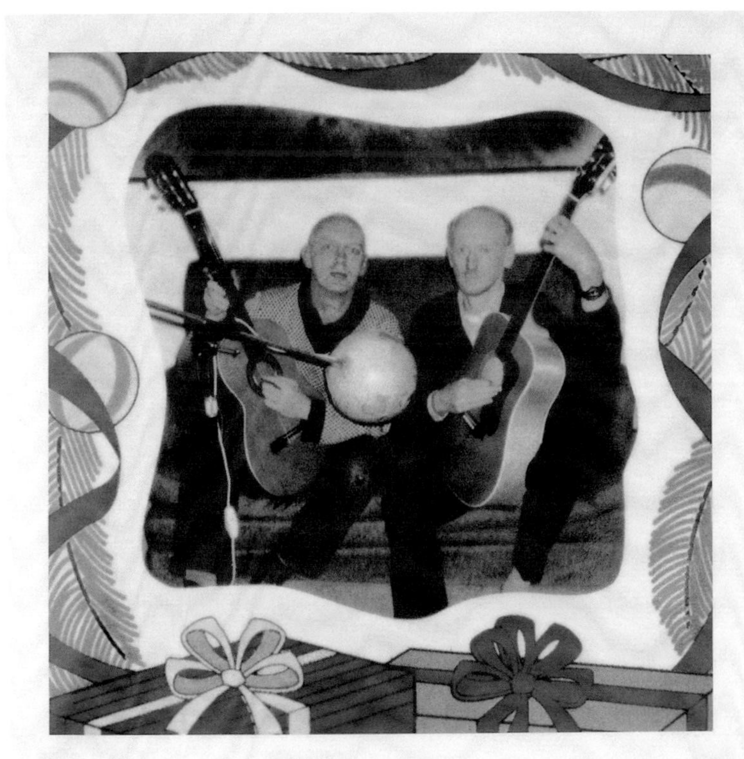

something more global, but in their search for this there seems to be a much deeper paradigm shift where sculptors – or artists who make sculpture – consider themselves very differently.

At the start of the 1980s this can be seen most clearly in the types of metaphor that were being used for sculptors or sculpture-making: magus or *passeur*, cultural critic, poet, *bricoleur*. Although a relatively clear sense of sculptural identity is given by the publications supporting the many exhibitions of British sculpture organised abroad by the British Council, the best picture of the diaspora of sculptural intentions, metaphors and hence identities is given in *The Sculpture Show* at the Hayward and the Serpentine in 1983.

In a discussion with the selectors, Bryan Robertson protests that students no longer go to the British Museum to look at past sculptures. He sees the lack of a historical knowledge as being disastrous. Paul de Monchaux's measured response is that what takes the place of a native tradition of sculpture has been the involvement of sculptors in teaching since about 1950.[9] Kate Blacker, another of the selectors, makes a familiar claim: 'sculpture has widened its doors, and if you are a sculptor and your work develops through philosophy, through the use of poetry or prose, I believe that in sentiment you are still a sculptor.'[10] It is Blacker in the personal introduction to the section she chose who elucidates the crux of recent changes:

> the artists move back into the centre of contemporary life. One of their shared characteristics is a search for totality of vision, applied to history *and* the present. This is quite different from the idea of the artist who (in England, at least) believes in the tenets of modernist abstraction – a search for perfection *within* art terms. Instead, newer artists tend to seek perfection in sculpture as a way of life, or rather, sculpture as a manifestation of the search for perfection and truths within the terms of daily life.[11]

Perfection seems a curious, rather than apposite, word in a period when such pragmatic terms as appropriate or contingent were more common. The only artist who showed a real commitment to the ideal was Edward Allington in his ideal form sculptures, and that was to critique the very concept. Allington trained as a ceramicist and this alternative background has presumably helped him enunciate different paradigms for sculpture: furniture, mass-produced kitsch, baroque architecture. What matters here is, firstly, how he can act as a critic of things in the world and how they are mutated and, secondly, the lack of a signature style – indeed style appears in his work always within quotation marks (rococo scrolls or classical pastiche). With the peripheralisation of direct carving identity is no longer expressed through a signature style.[12]

Tony Cragg too functions as a critic of society and its artefacts. Early readings of his work emphasised its political content.[13] If *Nouveau Réalisme* or neo-dada took the notion of the readymade and turned it into a sort of sociological collecting, they amassed and bore witness to the artefacts of their time.[14] Cragg may be described as a sort of artistic *nouveau réaliste.* In searching for an identity as a sculptor, artists looked to other areas: society, science, spirituality, natural history.[15] Cragg looked to some degree to science, much as Allington had looked at history. Cornelia Parker, one could argue, adopted archaeology as a paradigm; Richard Deacon, Alison Wilding and Houshiary the paradigm or metaphor of the poet.

It was to Woodrow that the most far-reaching alternative metaphor was applied: the *bricoleur*, a term used in France for the odd job man who mends your plumbing with whatever he has to hand. The term was sanctified by Claude Lévi-Strauss' use of it to describe how 'primitive' man constructs beliefs. This was an artist available in response, travelling light: 'generally all my tools are contained in that small canvas bag over there and I can jump on a plane and get straight to work whenever I land'.[16] Wit, ingenuity and appropriateness defined his style. Cultural criticism was at the heart – certainly as others saw it – of what he did. The role of cultural critic was to become more explicit in his work as it became more allegorical.

It would be too easy to see Antony Gormley as spiritual teacher or magus, but in fact his work is especially interesting in that he takes the identification/identity issue as a theme in itself. It is this that has made him a current rather than *retardataire* figure.

It is important to bear in mind that there are still some artists who place themselves in a specifically sculptural tradition although they may be considered peripheral to the avant-garde of the moment, for example, Peter Randall-Page, whose career has always been dominated by a commitment to carving and the natural world. As he was quoted in the catalogue for the exhibition *Objects and Sculpture*:

I'm drawn to its [stone's] age and beauty. The fact that it has been around long before human beings … It can comfort us with a sense of our own existence in a way that something that is second-hand or manmade cannot. I enjoy the feeling of the material not having been touched. … My primary interest in sculpture lies in its potential as a vehicle for what I can best describe as the celebration of a direct response to the world.[17]

But even here his allegiance is to world sculpture, not British sculpture: world sculpture that includes the Willendorf Venus and Egyptian art as much as – or more than – Caro. Indicatively, he did his student thesis on Isamu Noguchi, that archetype of east and west conjoined. Stephen Cox's 'world tour' of sculptural materials and methods from Renaissance Italy to Egypt to Mahlibalipuramis is also more to do with a totalising vision of sculpture than of local colour.

The notion of identity is no longer concerned with doing but thinking, not a professional identity but a problematised ontological one. Not what do I do but why am I doing it and for whom? It is this that unifies all serious sculpture of the 1980s: that sculpture should be made with links to the past but querying itself.

The emergence of the Young British Artist (yBa) subsequent to the *Freeze* exhibition in 1988 was when artists first defined themselves as artists rather than painters or sculptors. Partly this was because artists had a base in conceptual art as a medium (or more properly an approach), because an artist such as Bruce Nauman, whose work spread across many media was a widely acknowledged model, and because installation was being discussed as a form in itself.[18] *Freeze* artists such as Anya Gallaccio, Michael Landy and Abigail Lane were discussed in terms of site specificity or conceptual stratagems, not how they extended or responded to sculpture. Of the four artists who may be seen as representing the 1990s generation of English sculptors (Grenville Davey, Cathy de Monchaux, Julian Opie and Rachel Whiteread), it was only the last who exhibited regularly as a sculptor per se.

Identity as sculptor: is this a vocation or an option taken up during the foundation year at art school? Has the very term 'sculptor' lost its resonance? Was the renaming of the 1997 Münster sculpture exhibition indicative of the way sculpture has been subsumed into a wider and less easily defined way of thinking and working? In 1977 the first exhibition was entitled *Skulptur Ausstellung in Münster* (Sculpture Exhibition in Münster) the second in 1987 *Skulptur Projekte in Münster* (Sculpture Projects in Munster) and the third in 1997 *Skulptur. Projekte in Münster* (Sculpture. Projects in Münster). The most extreme of the projects was Bethan Huws', which was a tour of a wooded area. There was no evidence of the tour in that wood, no object, nor any text – only the place. It was truly a search for identity in the place itself.

Although the sculpture schools continued to function, and although artists such as Randall-Page and David Nash continued to work as self-professed sculptors, the 1990s were oriented rather to installations, neo-conceptualism, projects and video. The press was abnormally interested in novelty and in the personality cults formed round some younger artists.[19] It was only in the first years of the 21st century that there seemed to be a real re-engagement with the notion of sculpture and the taking on of the vocation of 'sculptor' and with it a sense that it is again possible to reconnect with the generational dynamic of British sculpture.[20]

Tony Godfrey

Notes

1 P. O'Brien, *Master and Commander,* London, Collins, 1970, p. 249–50

2 C. Parry-Crooke (ed.), *Contemporary British Artists,* with photographs by Walia, London, Bergstrom and Boyle, 1979.

3 It is interesting to note that Barlow's work moved very much into the category of installation art.

4 The epitome of this in Britain was *The Other Story: Afro-Asian Artists in Post-War Britain* at the Hayward Gallery in 1989 and globally the Whitney Biennial of 1993.

5 In interview with Anne Morgan, *Art Papers,* vol. 13 no. 6, November–December 1989, pp 14–17.

6 There is no significance to the order: the issue is the plurality of identity.

7 Quoted in *Objects and Sculpture* (exhibition catalogue), ICA, London/Arnolfini Gallery, Bristol, 1981, p. 20.

8 There is no equivalent in Britain for the number of painters in continental Europe making sculpture: Georg Baselitz, Anselm Kiefer, Mimmo Paladino, Miquel Barcelo, etc.

9 *The Sculpture Show* (exhibition catalogue), London Hayward Gallery and Serpentine Gallery, 1983, p. 9.

10 *The Sculpture Show,* p. 10. It should also be mentioned that in his review of the exhibition the most prominent critic of the pluralisation of sculpture, Peter Fuller, castigated the ageing trendies he saw as responsible and called for a return to *real* sculpture, 'the science of the bump and hollow'. Above all he called for a return to training or apprenticeship based on the 'mastery of the particular skills and traditions of sculpture'. He renounces Blacker's view as reprehensible and most especially lambasts Norbert Lynton for having written in a guide to the exhibition that 'sculpture is what sculptors do. No other definitions fit.' It was clear to Fuller that sculpture meant carving and modelling and anyone who claimed to be a sculptor and did anything else was an impostor.

[11] *The Sculpture Show*, p. 92.

[12] Although one could argue that the syntax and wit of Anthony Caro's welded counterpoint is a signature style equivalent to direct carving.

[13] See for example early articles by John Roberts on Cragg's work.

[14] It could be argued that this is much what Haim Steinbach and Jeff Koons did in the USA in the 1980s, though no British artists worked quite in that way.

[15] Witness the use of the title *Wonderful Life* for the 1994 exhibition at the Lisson Gallery. The title originates with the Hollywood movie but more significantly here refers to Stephen Jay Gould's book of the same title about pre-Cambrian life forms.

[16] Bill Woodrow interviewed by Peter Hill, *Art Monthly*, December 1986, pp. 12–15.

[17] Quoted in *Objects and Sculpture* (exhibition catalogue), ICA, London/Arnolfini Gallery, Bristol, 1981, p. 18.

[18] There is an argument that the two most influential practitioners of installation from an earlier generation, Cornelia Parker and Richard Wilson, were very much sculptors.

[19] The most obvious being Tracey Emin, Damien Hirst and Sam Taylor-Wood.

[20] I am thinking here of such exhibitions as *Early One Morning* at the Whitechapel Art Gallery in 2002.

A revolution in the gallery: from the Arts Council to the artist

By the early 1970s, the Arts Council had developed two core models for the support and presentation of the contemporary visual arts in Britain. First, its own exhibitions established temporary exhibiting as the curatorial currency for contemporary visual arts. Second, it developed the network of regional galleries that was to become the backbone of the infrastructure and to define visual arts patronage in the late 20th century. These models had been developed for two-dimensional artworks and that presented particular problems for sculptors. However, by the end of the century artists had changed the gallery and the exhibition beyond recognition. In a direct challenge to the Arts Council's gallery network, artists created new models for gallery exhibition, such as commissioning and site-specific installation, that have revolutionised curatorial discourse within even the largest institutions, such as Tate Modern and Baltic.

The Arts Council's gallery network

When the Arts Council was founded in 1946, it decided not to fund the existing network of collections-based galleries and museums but rather to establish an alternative infrastructure based on temporary exhibitions. Initially this took the form of providing touring exhibitions. Later this transformed into support for a different group of venues: the *Kunsthallen* or exhibition galleries. The initial policy decision not to assume responsibility for funding the collections-based infrastructure was largely expedient. Local authorities had been providing revenue funding for collections-based art galleries since the 19th century, often within library complexes, due to a belief in the civilising and educative potential of visual arts. The Arts Council's statutory responsibilities included the stimulation of patronage by other bodies, and therefore it preferred to add value to local authority investment in the buildings and staff by providing a programme of touring exhibitions using these spaces.[1]

With a dramatic increase in funding and a new policy emphasis on the living artist,[2] the Arts Council created a group of funded galleries including the Whitechapel Art Gallery, the Institute of Contemporary Arts (ICA), Arnolfini, Bristol, Ikon Gallery, Birmingham, MoMA Oxford, the Midland Group, Nottingham, the Penwith Society, Cornwall and Kettle's Yard Gallery, Cambridge during the late 1960s. Through conditions attached to its funding, the Arts Council shaped these galleries into a network, each generating their own exhibitions,

1 Ron Haselden, 'Working 12 Days at The Acme Gallery', 1978

but also touring to the other galleries. According to Alan Bowness, a leading member of the Arts Council's advisory Art Panel, the vision for the gallery network was modelled on Whitechapel Art Gallery, which at this time was showing contemporary British artists within a programme of innovative foreign art.[3] The Arts Council added two new London venues to this infrastructure, the Hayward and Serpentine Galleries, both of which it was to administer directly until 1986. The Hayward Gallery was purpose-built in 1968 for international touring exhibitions of modernist and historic art, in partnership with the London County Council. The Serpentine Gallery was opened in 1970 in a former tea pavilion in Hyde Park to provide a programme of contemporary group exhibitions, providing a platform for younger artists to have their first exhibition in London.

By the 1970s many artists had become dissatisfied with exhibition as a platform for their work. The development of post-object sculptural practices further exacerbated this problem.[4] Artists such as Barry Flanagan, Richard Long, Bruce McLean and Stephen Willats were creating sculpture which involved complex installation, time-based elements and interaction with the viewer. Often these works were created specifically for a particular space or place, or in response to a particular opportunity to show them. As the catalogues of exhibitions from this period demonstrate, the programmes of publicly funded galleries in the late 1960s and early 1970s reflect a very partial view of the types of sculpture being made with programmes at venues such as the Serpentine being dominated by a more object-centred form of sculpture. It was in this context in the mid- to late 1970s that a new generation of galleries emerged, providing opportunities for artists who were not necessarily producing objects for display.

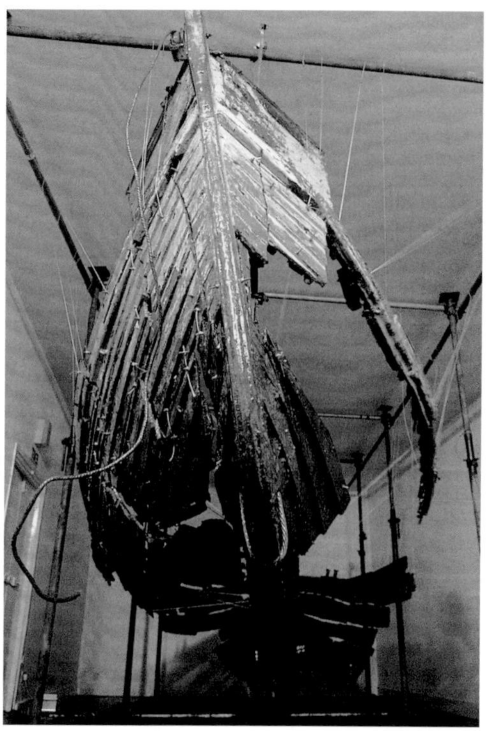

Artist-led spaces of the 1970s and early 1980s

Writing about his project *Radical Attitudes Towards the Gallery*, a group exhibition held at Art Net Gallery, London in 1977, Tony Rickaby claimed that 'the role of the gallery has been a major concern of much recent art'.[5] Rickaby asked artists and arts professionals to respond to the question of what should be the attitude of the politically committed artist to 'the gallery' in no more than 500 words. Surveying his respondents, Rickaby concluded there were three broad 'solutions':

> 1. Reject galleries and use other formats such as film, video, books, murals, magazines, performance, the land, etc.
>
> 2. Start alternative galleries, either on existing models (but aimed at different audiences and run by different people) or a completely new model.
>
> 3. Use existing galleries but change the type of work shown in them (make it more radical, accessible, etc.).[6]

During the 1970s, a number of artists and artists' organisations pursued Rickaby's second option: starting new galleries. Some, like AIR (Art Information Registry) Gallery, which was run by Art Services Grants Ltd (1975–89), were largely based on existing models, changing the range of artists they profiled rather than the model itself. Others, such as Acme Gallery and Matt's Gallery, offered artists a radically different model of operating which was to be profoundly influential on the later generation of galleries (such as Café Gallery, Chisenhale Gallery, The Showroom, Milch, BANK), which underpinned London's gallery infrastructure in the later 1980s and 1990s. For example, AIR showed around 200 artists in its first two years, providing an alternative platform for exhibiting. By contrast, the emphasis at Matt's was on a qualitative approach and the aim was 'not to increase the visibility of the work, but to create a space for the experience of art'.[7]

Sandy Nairne's article, 'The institutionalisation of dissent', on the development of alternative spaces by women and black artists in the USA makes brief reference to the British scene.[8] Nairne characterises two features of experimental galleries in the late 1960s, 'the making of new and complex works of art and of new forms of interaction with an audience', which resulted in new models taking the form of the laboratory or the studio.[9] British examples of the laboratory model, cited by Nairne, include the short-lived Arts Lab in Drury Lane and the ICA. Matt's Gallery and Acme Gallery are the other key examples of this new model of exhibition.

Acme Gallery

Acme Studios Housing Association was founded in 1972 to provide residential and work space for a small group of young artists in London. Acme's role in supporting artists through provision of work and living space is the subject of unpublished research by Alison Raftery and an article by Michael Archer.[10] In 2000 Acme began its own wider and ongoing research into artists in east London 1960–2000, but the role of the gallery space it ran from 1976 until 1981 in Shelton Street, Covent Garden requires particular mention in the history of the gallery infrastructure in Britain.

Directed by Jonathan Harvey, the Acme Gallery provided an important forum for large-scale sculpture, installation and performance work at a time when few other galleries were showing this kind of work. The gallery programme was eclectic, ranging from a painter such as John Bellany through to the pyrotechnic sculptor Stephen Cripps.[11] Seeking to offer an 'alternative' to the programmes of the larger public and commercial spaces, the gallery policy was to exhibit a wide range of practice – performance, video, experimental film work and installation. However, by virtue of its willingness to accommodate practice which had so few other outlets, the gallery became particularly associated with these areas, for example hosting the 'Live Work' element of *New Contemporaries* in 1976 and 1977. The gallery also developed particular relationships with certain artists, showing their work repeatedly, for example Stuart Brisley and Ron Haselden (1978; Fig. 1). Artists were selected for a programme of mainly solo exhibitions on the basis of their ability to take on what was usually the biggest challenge of their career to date.

A 1977 Acme Gallery brochure outlines an exhibition policy that sought to create opportunities which were responsive to the needs of artists:

> Accepting the limitations of the building itself, we see the space as being entirely flexible. We want artists to feel that the gallery is here for them to use and alter to suit their own requirements, not only in terms of the space, but also in the broader sense of how exhibitions are presented and publicised. In this way we hope that artists will be directly involved in the dialogue of what a gallery can and should be.[12]

The 'limitations of the building itself' could also be challenged, as architectural modifications by artists such as Darrell Viner, Kerry Trengove and Brisley highlighted. The two gallery spaces (one upstairs, one downstairs) had, by the time the gallery closed in 1981, been thoroughly modified, undermined and occupied in spectacular ways, and artists making new work for the space became increasingly engaged in an ongoing dialogue with a space that had a history of particular installations and events.

2 Kerry Trengove, 'An Eight Day Passage', 1977

Kerry Trengove's 'An Eight Day Passage' (1977; Fig. 2) involved the artist being walled up inside a brick structure in the lower gallery and then digging his way out to escape into the basement. For the duration of the performance the artist was walled up inside the gallery, which was open twenty-four hours a day to visitors who could see and talk to him via a video link to the upper gallery space. Visitors talked to the artist about the experience, his progress and his ideas, prompted by a sound installation in the upper gallery with political prisoners recounting their stories providing a political context for the performance. Considerable public interest was created, not least when the District Surveyor became concerned about the legal status of the construction and building work, a situation which was resolved with advice from art lawyer Henry Lydiate.[13]

Viner's 'Who Manipulates Who' (1981) was a kinetic sculpture which extended through the upper gallery into the lower space. On entering the lower gallery, the visitor saw a large wooden beam structure, suspended on ropes, pitching and listing erratically and apparently without cause (Fig. 3). On reaching the upper gallery the mechanics were revealed (Fig. 4): an identical beam structure (supporting its mirror image below and pivoted on a metal tripod) was caused to move, in threatening and apparently unpredictable ways, by the effect of small electric motors with tiny rotating arms attached to each corner. The fractional variation in motor speeds shifted the beam's balance through a cycle, at times swaying gently, at others moving close to, but never reaching, self-destruction.

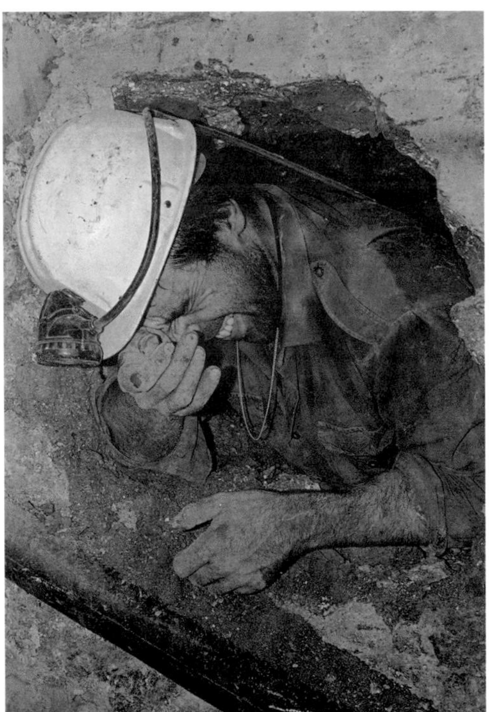

Acme Gallery closed in 1981 when its lease expired, having served its purpose. Other galleries were now beginning to show more experimental work. Acme continues as a provider of studios and has also provided premises for a number of other galleries, including Interim Art (established in 1984 by Maureen Paley, originally at Beck Road), The Showroom (opened in 1983 as a lettable exhibition space and later, in 1988, let to David Thorp to run as a public gallery), and Matt's Gallery (since 1992).

3 Darrell Viner, 'Who Manipulates Who' 1981

4 Darrell Viner, 'Who Manipulates Who' 1981

5 Richard Wilson, 'She Came in Through the Bathroom Window, 1989

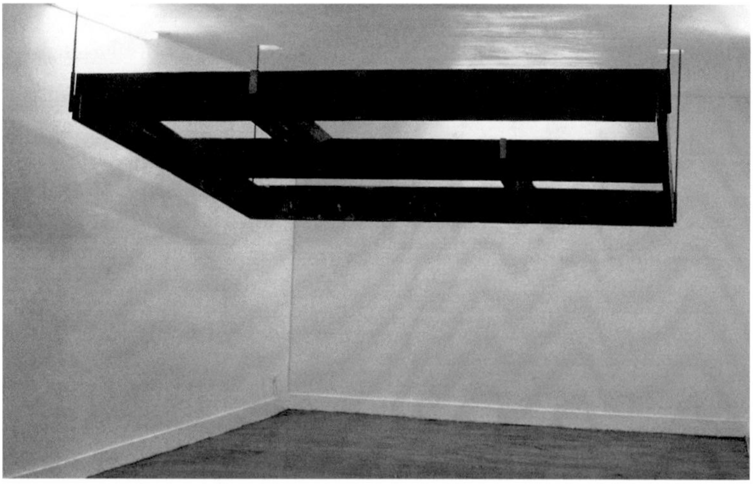

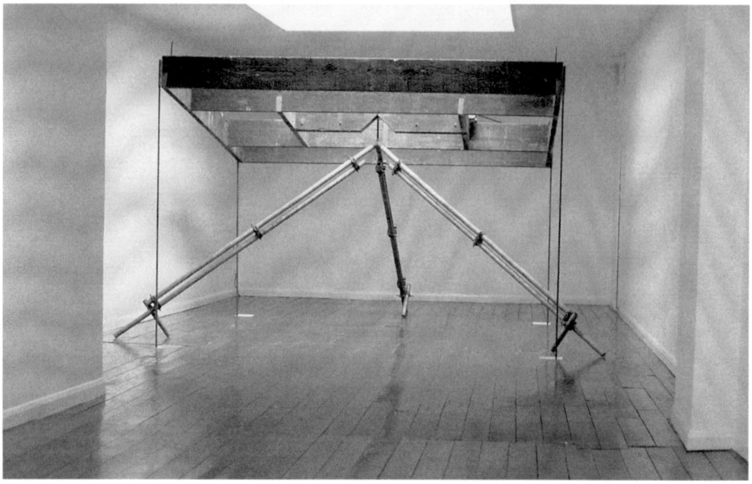

Matt's Gallery

The exhibition guide to *Backspace* – an exhibition marking the 20th anniversary of Matt's Gallery – outlines the origins and objectives of this unique institution. Founded, and still led, by Robin Klassnik, Matt's Gallery opened in 1979. Originally Klassnik's own studio space in Martello Street (in a studio complex managed by SPACE, part of the umbrella organisation Art Services Grants Ltd) was used as a location for other artists to make and present new work. Matt's Gallery moved in 1992 to its current location in Copperfield Road, where it continues 'to provide artists with the space and time to develop new ideas and possibly new ways of working while making a new work for the space'.[14] This approach, Klassnik believes, is the most effective way to support artists in showing their work, adding that timing is a key consideration, 'to allow for the fine tuning for which there is often not enough time at other galleries'.[15] Matt's Gallery often works with younger and less-established artists but also 'established artists who find the need for an open approach that they cannot find elsewhere'.[16]

As an artist, Klassnik had worked with the Polish artist Jaroslaw Kozlowski at his Galerie Akumulatory 2 in 1975 and cites this example as a model for the approach developed at Matt's. Akumulatory 2 converted a students' union building in Poznan into an exhibition space for exhibitions of international artists which ran for only a few days, attracting a dedicated audience of peers. It was this focus on engaged communication that appears to have particularly impressed Klassnik.[17]

Richard Wilson's exhibitions at Matt's Gallery, such as '20:50' (1987) and 'She Came in Through the Bathroom Window' (1989) are recognised as canonical works within the history of sculpture and installation. Requiring considerable architectural modifications to the building, these works reveal the lengths to which the gallery is prepared to go to accommodate artists' ideas and works. For 'She Came in Through the Bathroom Window' (Fig. 5) the industrial-size windows stretching the length of the gallery's exterior wall were taken out and reconstructed at a different angle, jutting into the gallery space.

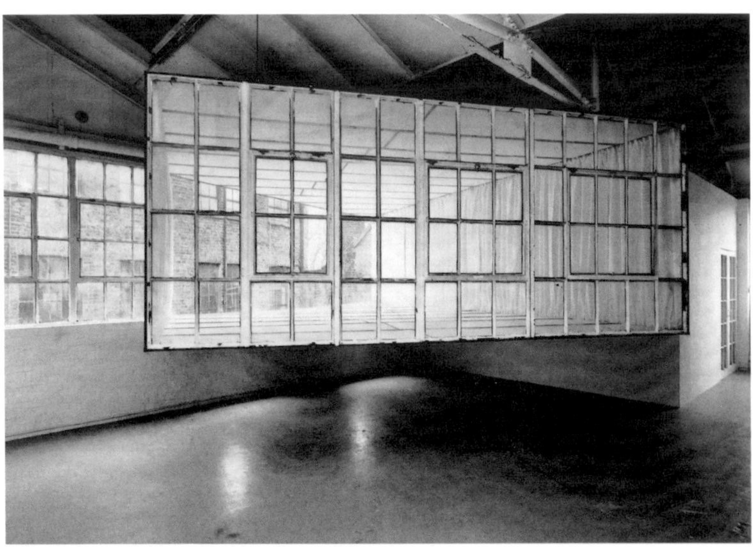

New gallery models

Acme Gallery and Matt's, through focusing above all else on the requirements of the artist, were able to support an extraordinary range of ambitious projects which have been pivotal within individual artists' artistic and professional development. These galleries have equally had significant impact on the models of curating practised throughout the wider gallery infrastructure. An emphasis on solo exhibitions and relationships between artists and the gallery over a period of time characterise both spaces. Also striking is the prevalence of process-based work, whether Trengove's work at Acme or Susan Hiller's 'Work in Progress' (1980) and more recently Hayley Newman's 'The Daily Hayley' (2001) at Matt's, which offer the viewer an opportunity to observe and even engage with the artist during the realisation of the work.

Outside the gallery

Curatorial developments outside the gallery, including organisations such as Artangel and Locus+ as well as one-off initiatives such as artranspennine98, have equally built on this legacy of artist-centred production. After Acme Gallery closed in 1981, Jonathan Harvey became involved with the TWSA 3D[18] project, along with James Lingwood (who has been co-director of Artangel from 1992), which in some ways can be seen as a precursor to the temporary public commissioning that was to become an important aspect of sculptural practice in the 1990s. Artangel enables artists to produce ambitious works which engage with sites and audiences in new and challenging ways; for example, for Michael Landy's 'Break Down' (2001) the artist and a team of assistants disassembled all his possessions on an inverted production-line installed in the former C&A Oxford Street flagship store.[19] Rachel Whiteread's 'House' (1993–4) is perhaps Artangel's most celebrated project. A temporary public sculpture created through casting the internal space of a Victorian terraced house on Grove Road in east London, 'House' typifies Artangel's approach to commissioning at its most successful. Attracting many tens of thousands of visitors during its short life, and stimulating debate within the press about sculpture and social issues (such as regeneration and homelessness), the sculpture also offered the young artist an unparalleled opportunity to develop her practice and her profile.

2000: the new art factories

Tate Modern opened in May 2000, Baltic a year later. These two institutions comprise the latest additions to the gallery infrastructure in Britain.

The impact of the artist-led commissioning practice is evident not only in Tate's collections (for example, Cornelia Parker's 'Cold Dark Matter: An Exploded View' (1991), an installation created through blowing up a shed with the aid of the army, originally created for Chisenhale Gallery), its exhibitions (with artist-led spaces featuring in the London section of the exhibition *Century City* in 2001), but most importantly in its programme of commissions in the Turbine Hall. This programme of commissioning work specifically for the space has its origins in the new approaches to working with artists developed in venues such as Matt's and Acme during the 1970s and early 1980s, and later at spaces such as The Showroom, Café Gallery and Chisenhale.

At Baltic this curatorial tendency finds its most recent and highly developed outlet through the replacement of the gallery with an 'Arts Factory' model.[20] These large institutions may not be able to offer the same degree of experimental opportunity to artists as smaller spaces but – as was witnessed during the installation of Anish Kapoor's 'Marsyas' at Tate Modern in 2002 (Fig. 6), and from the viewing platform above one of the main exhibition galleries at Baltic (from where visitors can see into the main gallery during installation) – they can offer new ways for visitors to experience sculpture, opening up the processes of production and installation.

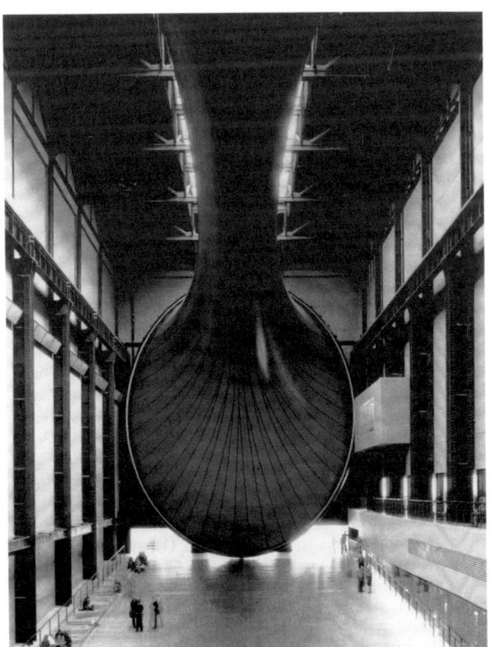

6 Anish Kapoor, 'Marsyas', 2002

Areas for further research

The ongoing impact on artists and audiences of the Arts Council's policy for the visual arts infrastructure demands further study; however, the importance of artist-centred galleries such as Matt's Gallery and Acme Gallery in developing exhibition practice is clear.[21] Acme Gallery no longer exists and there is little published information available regarding the gallery infrastructure in the

1970s and 1980s, although Acme's research programme and web site are beginning to address this need.[22] Archive materials, although not catalogued or conserved in any systematic way, do exist and interviews with key individuals have informed this writing. Considering the important role these galleries played in how artists and curators work today, the lack of research and publishing in this area, and the need to preserve and study the archives of these organisations, stands out as a pressing priority for the future study of sculpture at the beginning of the 21st century.

Claire Glossop

Notes

I would particularly like to acknowledge the valuable advice of Alison Raftery, whose MPhil is an important source of information on this subject and Sir Alan Bowness, the late Joanna Drew, Jonathan Harvey and Robin Klassnik who were interviewed as part of my research.

1 The Arts Council's position on the funding of local authority galleries is discussed in the Arts Council of Great Britain, *Annual Report and Audited Accounts*, London, The Arts Council of Great Britain, 1954/55, pp. 10–11. The following year's *Annual Report* relays communication between the chair of the Arts Council (Kenneth Clark) and the Board of Education (the government ministry which funded the Arts Council at this point) for clarification of its responsibilities for art collections. It was determined that the Museums' Association retained responsibility for art collections and art museums.

2 The prioritisation of the living artist was a central theme of the government's first arts policy; Her Majesty's Government, *A Policy for the Arts: the Arts; the First Steps*, Cmnd 4676, London, HMSO, 1965.

3 It should be noted, however, that a number of regional galleries (particularly York, Wakefield and Leeds) developed their own exceptional programmes of sculpture during the 1940s and 1950s, as detailed in R. Calvocoressi, 'Public sculpture in the 1950s', in S. Nairne and N. Serota (eds), *British Sculpture in the Twentieth Century* (exhibition catalogue), London, Whitechapel Art Gallery, 1981, pp. 135–54.

4 'Post-object art' is one of the many terms used to embrace the diverse manifestations of conceptual, installation, performative and non-formalist practice in which the process of making the work is more important than any object finally produced. It entered mainstream usage following its employment in Donald Karshan's essay 'The seventies: post-object art', written for the exhibition *Conceptual Art and Conceptual Aspects* held at the New York Cultural Center in 1970 and published as an article in *Studio International* (D. Karshan, 'The seventies: post-object art', *Studio International,* September 1970, vol.180, no.925, pp. 69–70). As a term, it is particularly relevant to discussions of sculpture as it neatly conveys the distinction between these divergent and expansive practices of post-object artists and the essentialism of the formalist object sculptors.

5 T. Rickaby, 'Radical attitudes towards the gallery', in R. Cork (ed.), *Studio International*, special issue, 'Art Galleries and Alternative Spaces', 1980, vol. 195, no. 990, p. 20.

6 Rickaby, 'Radical attitudes towards the gallery', p. 21.

7 R. Klassnik, 'The galleries talk', *Flash Art News*, 1987, no. 1.

8 Nairne, 'The institutionalization of dissent', in R. Greenberg, B. W. Ferguson and S. Nairne (eds), *Thinking About Exhibitions*, London, Routledge, 1996, pp. 387–410.

9 S. Nairne, 'The institutionalization of dissent', p. 391.

10 A. Raftery, 'surviving the decade: the alternative in context – the fate of the alternative visual arts organisation in the Thatcher decade', unpublished MA thesis, City University, London, 1994; M. Archer, 'Oranges and lemons, oranges and bananas', in *Artists in East London (1960–2000)*, research project bulletin, London, Acme, 2001; and www.artistsineastlondon.org.

11 For further details, see J. Harvey (ed.), *Stephen Cripps: Pyrotechnic Sculptor*, London, Acme and Stephen Cripps Trust, 1992.

12 Acme, *The Acme Gallery*, (brochure), (London, Acme Housing Association Ltd, 1977).

13 Henry Lydiate, 'Self expression and the law', *Art Monthly*, 1977, issue 13, p. 34. The collected published 'Art Law' series of articles is available at www.artquest.org.uk/artlaw.

14 Matt's Gallery, *Backspace* (exhibition catalogue), London, Matt's Gallery, 1999.

15 Ibid.

16 Ibid.

17 '[The audience] came there because they wanted to see a piece of work, come and meet the artist, come and have some form of communication and discuss things', Robin Klassnik interview with Alison Raftery, cited in Raftery, 'Surviving the decade', p. 60.

18 Television South West developed arts programming and projects in the early 1980s, including the Four Cities Project and TWSA 3D, which involved siting sculpture in public spaces. See D. Petherbridge, 'Conference: Making space – art projects beyond the gallery', *Art Monthly*, April 1988, no. 115, pp. 27–9, and J. Lingwood (ed.), *TSWA Four Cities Project: New Works for Different Places*, Bristol, TSWA, 1990.

19 A catalogue of Artangel's projects to the current day is available at www.artangel.org.uk.

20 S. Nordgren and S. Martin (eds), *New Sites – New Art* (first BALTIC international seminar), Newcastle, University of Newcastle and BALTIC, 2000, p. 9.

21 The development of the Arts Council's exhibition policy and its impact for artists and audiences is addressed at length in C. Glossop, 'Exhibition and the reception and practice of sculpture in Britain 1945–2000', unpublished PhD thesis, University of Leeds, 2001. This research focuses mainly on the role of the Arts Council and the major galleries because information regarding the smaller galleries, and particularly those such as AIR, Arts Lab and Acme, which no longer exist, was very difficult to locate and access.

22 AIR Gallery archives are held by Art Services Grants Ltd and the organisation has plans to make these accessible in its new Triangle building in Hackney, although the collection is not catalogued. Matt's Gallery has its own archive comprising installation photography and materials relating to the programme. Neither organisation employs an archivist or has the resources to provide public access to their collections. Acme has begun a research project into artists in east London, material from which is available publicly online at www.artistsineastlondon.org.

Impure objects

Over the past twenty-five years art has extended its boundaries exponentially. Three-dimensional artworks are frequently hybrid productions, more installation than sculpture. Artists increasingly resemble latter-day hunter-gatherers, accumulating objects, images, ideas and co-opting institutions and environments. Given the range of possibilities for sculpture in this expanding landscape, it is interesting that in Britain some of the most memorable works made since the mid-1970s have had a particular *gestalt*, a certain formal resonance that marks them out as sculptural objects. That this appears to be the case suggests that there is a continuing possibility for sculpture as specifically constructed entity, whether solid or mutable, site-based or translatable.

In a review of British sculpture since 1975 outstanding works are: Tony Cragg's 'Stack' works, minimal accretions of discarded rubbish, the metropolitan equivalents of geological sections, and his later arrangements of plastic or glass assemblages; David Mach's submarine constructed from lorry tyres, 'Polaris' (1983), beached on the South Bank; Richard Wilson's glutinous and aromatic lake of sump oil '20:50' first installed at Matt's Gallery in 1987; Damien Hirst's Surrealistically titled shark, 'The Physical Impossibility of Death in the Mind of Someone Living' (1991; Fig. 1), and 'Pharmacy' (1992), a clinical and ambivalent temple to the drugs industry; Michael Landy's 'Scrapheap Services' (1995); Rachel Whiteread's 'House' (1993–4); Antony Gormley's community-planted ongoing 'Field' project. The obverse of such

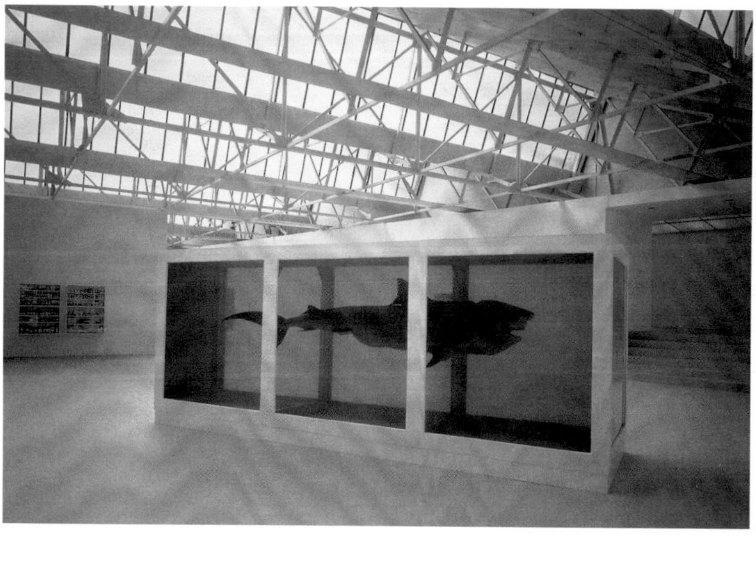

1 Damien Hirst, 'The Physical Impossibility of Death in the Mind of Someone Living', 1991

affirmative accumulation has been Landy's 'Break Down' – the ultimate act of deconstruction and divestment – an extreme critique of the consumer society, where everything the artist owned was dismantled and ultimately destroyed over a two-week period in an Oxford Street store in 2001.[1]

In the early 1970s the serial, environmental and experiential work of the American minimalists had brought audiences into a new spatial and perceptual congruence with sculptural objects. In London young artists like Richard Long, Hamish Fulton, Barry Flanagan and Gilbert & George had expanded the conceptual possibilities of sculpture post-plinth by taking their work beyond the studio, into the 'real' world of natural and political systems, time and decay. In the less utopian environment of the later 1960s, artists could again admit the quotidian, but whether the artistic practice involved becoming a 'Singing Sculpture' (Gilbert & George) or walking in the landscape (Fulton/Long), the retrieved evidence – stone circle, photograph and text or live performance – still generally relied upon a white cube in the best traditions of 1960s abstraction.[2]

A difference has been that while since their student days, artists like Long and Fulton, Roger Ackling and David Nash have needed to escape the city to make their work, Gilbert & George have remained consistently urban. In the late 1960s these *soi-disant* 'living sculptures' began living their art by genre, as still-lifes and portraits, against the raw landscape of London's East End. They have remained provocative and transgressive, appearing as subjects in large photographic monuments to urban life. In these, Gilbert & George have addressed the fundamental themes (life, sex, death) shaped by complex, sometimes ambiguous references to multicultural urban Britain, to national stereotypes and taboos, and to their own sexuality and bodily functions. Their multi-panelled set pieces, such as 'Death Hope Life Fear' (1984), intensely coloured and perfectly printed, coalesce into something both disturbing and glamorous, resembling profane stained-glass windows. Such works give context to Hirst's ambitious engagement with the shocking and the sublime ('The horrible things in life make the beautiful things possible and more beautiful')[3] and have established a landscape of topography for a younger and equally street-wise generation.[4]

In 1980, Flanagan, whose elegant and understated eccentricity, in works like the tottering soft towers of 'Four Casb 2 '67' (1967) had seemed closer to the aesthetic of *Arte Povera*, exhibited a gilded hare at the Waddington Galleries. This animal, shown in full sprint, balanced upon a pyramid of red wooden battens, was the first of many (1981; Fig. 2). The artist observed that:

> the conventions of the cartoon and the investment of human attributes into the animal world is a very well practised device, in literature and film etc, and is really quite poignant, and on a practical level, if you consider what conveys situation and meaning and feeling in a human figure, the range of expression is in fact far more limited than the device of investing an animal – a hare especially – with the expressive attributes of a human being.[5]

Apart from its zoomorphic possibilities, the hare reflected Flanagan's interest in country lore and literature and suggests the sort of mystical associations invoked in Joseph Beuys' 1960s performance 'How to Explain Paintings to a Dead Hare'. It also seems to connect with later politicised taxidermic works of the 1990s.[6]

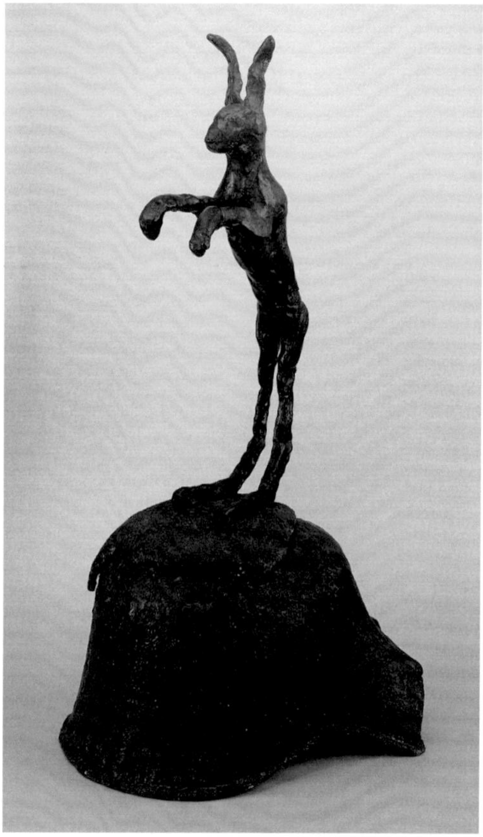

2 Barry Flanagan, 'Hare and Helmet II', 1981

Despite an international drift towards figuration, especially in painting, and the beginnings of a Eurocentric challenge to American dominance,[7] British sculpture in the early 1980s remained independently heterodox. The catalogue introduction to the signal *Objects and Sculpture* exhibition of 1981, which included work by Richard Deacon, Bill Woodrow, Anish Kapoor, Edward Allington and Gormley, amongst others, identified as a defining characteristic that the work appeared to be 'impure' in that it combined 'either base or rejected materials … with the frequent incorporation of actual real objects or images of real objects'. The work's strong 'human' connotations were also remarked upon and the fact that it was not directly connected with the environment in which it was seen.[8] What struck a home audience, following the rigours of conceptual art, was a new variety, expressed in an almost profligate approach, which mirrored the image appropriation and spontaneity, if not the expressionist aspect, of 'new' European painting.[9] Despite the selectors' assertion that 'the work expressed a rejection of space and form as areas of pure exploration',[10] the new sculpture was materially robust.

Other artists who, like Woodrow, were using discarded material and effecting pictorial transformations upon it were Cragg and Mach. They had in common the fact that their 'host' materials (plastic shards, pieces of wood, domestic appliances, unsold publications) were not hidden, so that the content of their work did not rest solely within its formal configurations. The material recycled had an additional symbolic and metaphoric potential, deriving from its original purpose, a history that was enriched or inflected by the work's construction. There were also significant differences between the artists: Cragg's arrangements of discarded man-made materials could be seen at the time as an act of recycling, an urban response to Long's arrangements from nature. He remarked of his scavenging for his sculpture 'Axehead' (1982): 'It is not a religion that I should actually find the objects ... if something is missing and I need it, then I will buy it' and described the parameters of his work as 'the material, the object and the image': 'one prequalification for me to be interested in making a work is that it has to be visually interesting. One can use an object or an image in the way philosophy has used words to describe things, to express ideas. I think this is a function of art.'[11]

Around the same time, Woodrow was unravelling more solid items, peeling back the skin of mute household objects to make new images. In works that use the discarded relics of western consumerism to reference the erosion of cultures and the ecology, he has customised the mass-produced. His works are thus twice commodified, as indispensable domestic items and as 'original' artworks. In the 1980s, Deacon, like Woodrow, also used familiar domestic materials, but built up his structures from laminates, linoleum and corrugated metal, to make sculptures that half-resembled everyday objects but were metonymic hybrids, influenced and qualified by their titles, drawn from the poetry of Rainer Maria Rilke.

During this period political messages, for example allusions to built-in obsolescence, were conveyed with ironic humour. Woodrow's resolutely domestic works such as 'Twin Tub and Guitar' (1981) were followed by more overtly political statements, such as 'English Heritage – Humpty Fucking Dumpty' (1987; Fig. 3), made nearly ten years into Margaret Thatcher's premiership. Made from of a vaulting box, this work suggests accumulated layers of history from, at the bottom, the plough, to the book, the clocking-in machine of the Industrial Revolution and finally a radiation hazard sign.[12] Surmounting all this, the unfortunate Humpty adds to the precariousness of the installation. Here Woodrow was giving a specifically English slant to his critique of a now prevalent

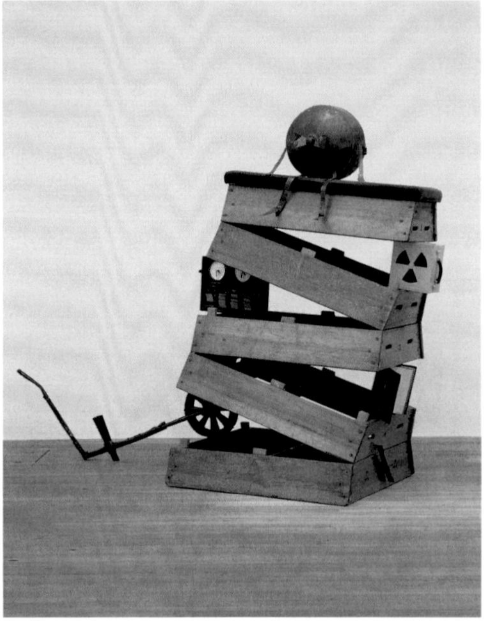

vision of 'heritage' as displacement or distraction. At the same time, Cragg's contemporary comment on the state of the nation was to up-end the map in 'Britain Seen From the North' (1981), part of his response to a period of inner-city riots and in the artist's words 'the superficial hysterical enthusiasm generated by such an irrelevant event as a royal wedding'.[13] Mach's 'Thinking of England' (1983) consisting of 1,800 HP Sauce bottles arranged to suggest a union flag and a spread-eagled woman, mocked the ubiquitous sauce with its Houses of Parliament label and, by extension, the national edifice. Mach, who at that time also worked with magazines and other objects surplus to requirements, was also implicitly criticising western over-production and over-consumption.

Gormley's concern with nature and culture has centred on his exploration of the body in space, connecting man to nature, inside to outside, originally with lead-wrapped casts of his own body. His sarcophagus-like work, 'Bed' (1980), was built from sliced bread that he hollowed by eating it. His activities now also encompass the body politic as he increasingly works collaboratively, and his work has involved a particularly intense personal physical emersion and endurance, suggesting some sort of expiation or attrition as a means of achieving transcendence. This links his practice to the performative works of artists like Beuys and in London the Romanian artist Paul Neagu. Kapoor, whose work is also strongly linked to the body, has addressed desire and difference by means of inviting yet unstable surfaces and 'exotic,' organic shapes. In the 1980s his intensely coloured forms, covered in unstable layers of raw pigment, were a pleasurable shock after some years of linearity, and conceptual black and white. They alluded to spiritual and sexual sources and graduated from a canon of simple shapes. Later work has been metaphysically aligned, exploring exterior and interior spaces and culminating in his recent gigantic visceral installation, 'Marsyas' (2002) at Tate Modern.

3 Bill Woodrow, 'English Heritage – Humpty Fucking Dumpty', 1987

Also in the 1980s, Stephen Cox, who with Kapoor and Gormley stands slightly apart from the more openly political concerns of his peers, was reading the critical writings of Adrian Stokes and Vasari's *The Lives of the Artists*. From a study of the forms and iconography of the Mediterranean basin, he has since moved on to explore other sculptural conventions, such as South Indian religious stone-carving and the sculpture of Ancient Egypt. Cox is a traditional sculptor in that he goes to the sources of his materials and works with assistants in situ.

In the early 1990s, great excitement greeted the emergence of a new and provocative British school of art. This predominantly urban phenomenon, nurtured in the hothouses of London's art schools, and sometimes curated by the artists themselves in industrial or domestic spaces, was heavily promoted and bought by a new generation of art patrons. The new 'Brit Art' combined some of the strategies of the concept- and systems-driven art of the 1960s with an upfront accessibility and street humour that seemed nearer to pop art. This connection was further endorsed by a relaxed, even consumerist approach to art history on the part of the artists after a period in the late 1980s when it had appeared that the practice of strategic image appropriation had backed artists into a corner.[14]

Influential for the new generation were Michael Craig-Martin, Jon Thompson and Richard Wentworth, who taught at Goldsmiths', and Stuart Brisley and Susan Hiller at the Slade. All these artists had explored the powerful combination of word and image, their researches deriving from various philosophical, sociological and art-historical roots. Craig-Martin, for example, was influenced by Wittgenstein's exploration of the transforming power of language.[15] In 1973 Craig-Martin had reassigned an ordinary glass of water placed on a small glass shelf as 'An Oak Tree'. In a series of printed questions and answers the artist argued that 'the actual oak tree is physically present but in the form of the glass of water'. His later wall works, resembling flat sculptures, which recycle in different configurations a refined taxonomy of objects as a way of naming them, find resonance also in the work of Julian Opie, whose computer-generated object and image works, whether flat, electronic or three-dimensional, have oscillated between the virtual and the real, the specific and the general.

Hiller appropriates the content of her work in a stealthy and sophisticated way, again in a range of media. Her works explore the relationship between language and meaning, the familiar and the overlooked. She has selected material across cultures, objects and ideas at the margins: 'valueless' objects, personal memories, paranormal phenomena, for example 'Witness' (2000), a forest of suspended recordings, simultaneously broadcast polyglot accounts of UFO sightings, amongst which her audience can graze. In the earlier poetic but anti-heroic installation 'Monument' (1980–1), the viewer sits on a park bench to listen to the artist's ruminations on memory, death and representation, triggered by reproductions of a set of ceramic plaques commemorating acts of working-class heroism in Victorian London that Hiller discovered in a City of London park. Her device of layering sound over object, subjective commentary over documentary evidence, finds echoes in the work of artists like Mona Hatoum and Tacita Dean.

Another model for sculpture in the 1990s has been the work of Bruce Nauman, who has consistently reinvented himself, giving up painting early on in favour of performance, installation, film, video, photography, neon word-play and sculpture. Like Nauman, the new young artists were making work that was variously controlling, ironic, humorous and confrontational. Sarah Lucas' body-part sculptures and punning titles seem to echo Nauman's aesthetic and his allusions to life as a tragic–comic treadmill of consumption and production. Nauman's casts taken of the spaces under chairs or beneath shelves, that expand sculpture into displaced space as well as creating form, anticipate Whiteread. His darker preoccupations, for example the latent humour combined with the violence of his animal casts, link him to the work of Hirst.

In 1994, echoing Gilbert & George, Mark Wallinger created his own sentient artwork, 'A Real Work of Art' (Fig. 4), the chestnut filly he raced

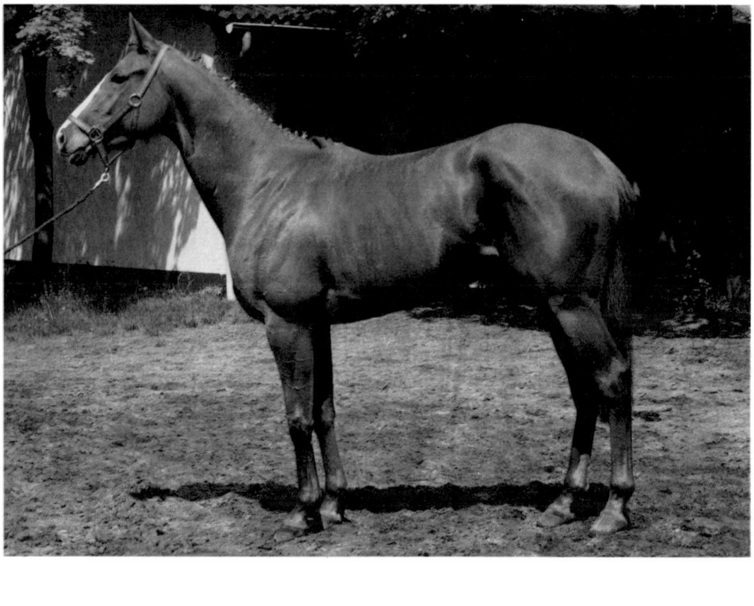

4 Mark Wallinger, 'A Real Work of Art', 1994

briefly with a syndicate in 1994. This living sculpture, the ultimate aestheticised object, further extended Wallinger's investigation of the politics of representation, using the paradigm of horse racing and breeding. As a racing enthusiast, Wallinger was a (knowingly) compromised critic but set out to expose aspects of this big business run for pleasure. When he registered his colours with the Jockey Club he subversively took the suffragette colours, green, violet and white, in memory of Emily Davidson, who threw herself in front of the king's horse at the 1913 Derby.

Predictably, in the lead-up to the millennium, the fragility of the human condition became a recurrent theme as art became simultaneously darker and more playful. Hirst's shark (Fig. 1), though disempowered, was a threatening presence and, like 'Pharmacy', suggested a modern *memento mori.* These represent only two examples of Hirst's ongoing address to the systems of life and death and to his own mortality. He has continued to use vitrines or cages[16] as systematised framing devices. In Wallinger's slow-motion film 'Threshold to the Kingdom' (2000), the afterlife becomes an airport arrivals lounge, his audience manipulated by an emotive soundtrack. Whiteread's mattresses and bath casts resemble sarcophaguses, catafalques or mortuary slabs. Equally commemorative, in that they suggest absence, have been Lucas' metonymic still-lifes such as 'Au Naturel' (1994). Like Lucas but more directly, Tracey Emin reclaimed and commemorated a fragment of autobiography in her little tent, 'Everyone I Have Ever Slept With 1963–1995' (1995) and in her abject and much-publicised 'My Bed' (1999). Part of the same tendency – their work elicits extreme responses and deals with violence and voyeurism – are the set pieces of Jake and Dinos Chapman, for example their three-dimensional Goya etching 'Great Deeds Against the Dead' (1994). Quieter but no less voyeuristic and extreme is Hatoum's interiorising and invasive 'Corps d'Etranger' (1994), a tubular room within which individual viewers may watch a video projected at their feet, charting the penetration and examination of the artist's body by means of medical cameras.

Whiteread's concrete 'House' (1993) has come to stand for her inverted retrieval processes, the casting and thereby objectification of the space around her selected subjects, showing the inside outside. Like Cragg and Hiller, she retrieves the overlooked and makes it real. Her work is anthropomorphic in its implication of now-absent human presences. Her sculptures have the subliminal shimmer of culturally embedded artefacts, but 'House', which provoked debates in parliament, related to her first-hand experience of the deprivation of east London.

Whiteread reminds us not only of a culture of consumption and obsolescence, but also of the neglected owners of the objects and places she use. In contrast to her usual sites, for the temporary occupation of the fourth plinth in Trafalgar Square, she made an untitled, up-ended plinth upon a plinth where Woodrow and Wallinger had previously shown. Wallinger's 'Ecce Homo' (1999) was a vulnerable-looking, modern, life-sized Christ that challenged the scale of its site. At the opposite end of the scale stands Gormley's commanding 'Angel of the North' (1998) at Gateshead.

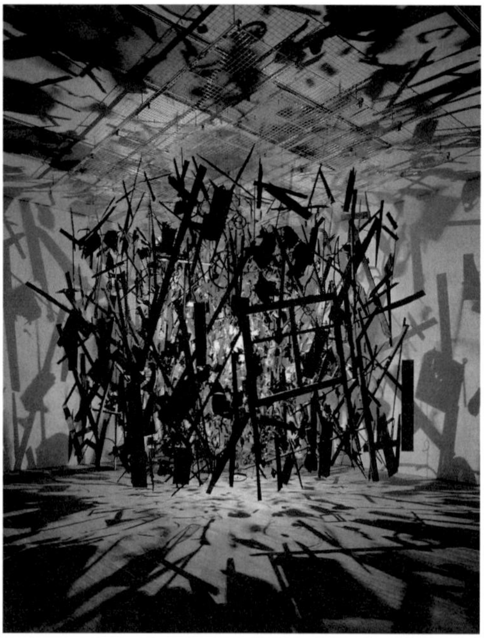

Like Hiller and Whiteread, Cornelia Parker uses history as raw material. Her Serpentine installation, 'The Maybe' (1995), included a live exhibit, the actress Tilda Swinton as a sleeping princess surrounded by a landscape of significant historic objects. In Parker's fragmented installations, suspended in delicate grid formations, traditionally heavy items achieve a particular lightness. These have been flattened silver artefacts, as in 'Thirty Pieces of Silver' (1988) or, in 'Cold Dark Matter: An Exploded View' (1991; Fig. 5), an exploded garden shed. In reassembling the items she effects a transformation upon them, suggesting an extended symbolic life and history after dramatic intervention or change.

Although this essay has been chiefly confined to a discussion of three-dimensional works, it is worth mentioning the 'sculptural' films of artists like Dean and Steve McQueen, the former fusing real and imaginary time and place in intimate poetic narratives, the latter providing a more sculptural and psychologically charged experience of space. There are also the 'word sculptures' of Emma Kay or Fiona Banner to consider, and those artists who, extending the strategies of conceptual art in the 1960s and 1970s, deal with political geographical and psychological space in manipulated maps, for example Layla Curtis, Simon Patterson and Kathy Prendergast. Stephen Willats' installation 'Macro to Micro' (1998–2000) takes the form of a rich and complex patchwork of images and sounds where the artist has indicated that understanding of place comes through the reception and editing of fragmented, simultaneous, and often contradictory signals.

5 Cornelia Parker, 'Cold Dark Matter: An Exploded View', 1991

One of the most radical shifts in attitudes and practice is habitually tracked to the mid-1960s' debates around the structural integrity, internal logic and display requirements of autonomous abstract sculpture. Today, works like Phillip King's Sino-baroque 'Ghengis Khan' (1963) may be considered alongside a Zobop vinyl-tape floor installation by Jim Lambie, so that where John Latham's 'Art and Culture' (1966–9)[17] might once have seemed some sort of Pandora's box, locking away the rules of abstraction, the inevitable conflations of history have again given young sculptors a refreshed space. Tim Scott's observation in 1967 that sculpture 'acts by displacement' – that it is about the *state* of being, of feeling, of experience, of physical awareness, of sensation and of confrontation by physical phenomena[18] – seems much closer to the 21st century than it did to 1975.

Catherine Kinley

Notes

1 For an account of Landy's projects, see S. Rainbird, *Are We as a Society Going to Carry on Treating People This Way? Michael Landy's Scrapheap Services 1995*, Patrons Papers 2, Tate, 2002.

2 For a discussion of this period, see *1965–1972: When Attitudes Became Form* (exhibition catalogue), Cambridge, Kettle's Yard and Edinburgh, Fruitmarket, 1984.

3 Damien Hirst, in *Damien Hirst* (exhibition catalogue), London ICA, 1991.

4 For example, Tracey Emin, Sarah Lucas, Gillian Wearing, all ex-Goldsmiths' College.

5 In *Barry Flanagan: Sculpture*, London British Council, 1982, p. 93.

6 For example, Maurizio Cattelan.

7 In exhibitions in 1981–2 like *Westkunst: A New Spirit in Painting, Zeitgesit* and *Documenta 7*.

8 L. Biggs *et al.*, *Objects and Sculpture* (exhibition catalogue), London, ICA/Bristol, Arnolfini, 1981, n.p.

9 For example, the *Neue Wilden* in Germany and *Transavanguardia* in Italy.

10 *Objects and Sculpture*, 1981.

11 Tony Cragg, quoted in *Tate Illustrated Catalogue of Acquisitions 1982–4*, pp. 130–1.

12 This referred to the Chernobyl disaster of 1986.

13 *Tate Illustrated Catalogue of Acquistions 1980–2*, p. 74.

14 Taken to its limits in the work of Jeff Koons, Heim Steinbach and Sherrie Levine. Levine in particular had challenged the authority of the model by perfect acts of simulation.

15 See Virginia Button in conversation with Michael Craig-Martin in *Inhale/Exhale* (exhibition catalogue), Manchester Art Gallery, 2002.

[16] Devices that suggest the work of Louise Bourgeois and Stuart Brisley.

[17] *Art and Culture: Critical Essays,* Boston, Beacon Press, 1961, a book of the collected essays of Clement Greenberg chewed and distilled by Latham with the help of sculpture students from St Martin's School of Art, now in the collection of the Museum of Modern Art, New York.

[18] In *Tim Scott: Sculpture 1961–67,* London, Whitechapel Art Gallery, 1967.

In a few short years in the 1960s, sculpture came off its plinth, onto the floor and left the gallery altogether. Artists' radical reformulations of sculptural possibility not only dissolved its physical barriers but, in part as a consequence and sometimes as a condition of the work itself, sought out a plethora of alternative venues that ranged from the printed page to remote rural locations. In the years that ensued, such practices generated a crisis which, contrary to artists' hopes and expectations, in part turned back on the art itself rather than outwards towards the art systems that it had hoped to prise open.

As Lynne Cooke has argued in 'British sculpture in the eighties', the ontological and epistemological issues raised by the multiple forms of artistic experimentation in the 1960s had, as the 1970s progressed, been 'increasingly reduced to questions relating to subject matter and form'.[1] The extent to which any definition of expanded sculpture had failed to take root in Britain was, on the one hand, made clear by the Hayward Annual of 1975, an exhibition selected by William Tucker and somewhat optimistically titled *The Condition of Sculpture.* A reflection of Tucker's own concerns, the show advocated a Greenbergian formalism and sculptural essentialism, in direct line of descent from New Generation sculpture, which was perceived by many as academic in the wake of the experimentation that had preceded it: 'The Arts Council should not have invested so much money in a project that allowed a particular artist to perpetrate his manifestly inadequate understanding of the condition of sculpture.'[2] At the other end of the spectrum, critical debate had increasingly come to read the work of artists who sited their practice in landscape – such as Hamish Fulton, Richard Long and David Tremlett – in a romantic tradition that imbued nature with notions of truth, authenticity and, ultimately, transcendence. In either of these debates, the gallery re-established itself as a neutral frame and mediator, a place of communion with the simultaneously internal and universalising conditions of the stable and 'recognisable' object of art.

The 'New British Sculpture' that emerged in the late 1970s and early 1980s marked a return to objecthood after the deconstructive impulse of sculpture in the 1960s and 1970s. This was not the formalist sculpture of New Generation artists, however, but one that embraced the plurality of materials and emphasis on process that had typified the 1960s and 1970s. These strategies were now synthesised in an image-based sculpture that posited the idea of sculpture as a sign, or as an unstable object that pointed beyond its physicality for its meanings. This was partly achieved through the choice of materials used, salvaged from the scrap-heap and imbued with a distinctly post-industrial, urban flavour. Such materials were not elevated onto a plinth or simply transferred into the gallery in a Duchampian, Warholian or even minimalist gesture, but manipulated and transformed in a way that connected art more readily to life beyond the gallery, in doing so rendering manifest the processes through which the 'real' may become filtered and transformed into art. If this was true of artists such as Tony Cragg, Jean-Luc Vilmouth and Bill Woodrow, others like Richard Deacon, Shirazeh Houshiary or Anish Kapoor, created more elliptical works that none-the-less made explicit references to the body or to other cultures respectively. Such works sought to create a dynamic relation between the gallery and the wider world, rather than setting up a more straightforward opposition between the two:

> The artists have little reason to see their work as consciously avant-garde any more, and the self-confidence that this affords has allowed them to make work which can connect in a variety of more interesting ways with other parts of the world. The thunder clouds of an over-self-conscious avant-garde in sculpture have rolled away to reveal a clearer sky.[3]

The extent to which artists were working in this way was gradually refined in a number of solo and group exhibitions that took place between the late 1970s and mid-1980s. Initially, the connection to a sphere beyond the purely aesthetic was understood exclusively on the level of subject matter through an emphasis on materials alone. Cragg's presentation of 'New Stones – Newton's Tones' in 1978 (Fig. 1) has come to be regarded as one of the formative moments in the genesis of the New Generation. The work, which consisted of coloured plastic shards arranged in a square directly on the floor, drew comparisons with Long's installations and was pitched, in its perceived gritty urban realism, against what was seen as the romanticising landscape tropes of some British sculpture in the 1970s. This reading of materials as subject was also true of Woodrow's 1978 ICA exhibition. This included works such as 'The Long Aspirator', a vacuum cleaner partly embedded in cement which was seen to suggest an archaeology of contemporary living in sharp contrast to the works of Long and others. Cragg's solo exhibition at the Whitechapel early in 1981 contributed to re-formulating the debate in slightly more complex terms. With works such as 'Britain Seen From the North', it became clear that his interest was in revealing the historic and culturally specific definitions of both the rural and the urban environment. The six works included in the show, furthermore, were all wall-mounted, and signalled a shift away from earlier geometric compositions towards image-based works.

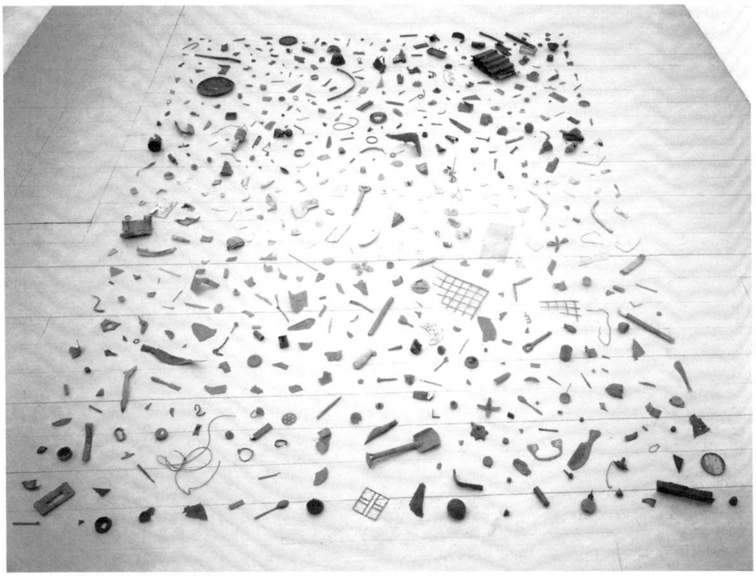

1 Tony Cragg, 'New Stones – Newton's Tones', 1978

Objects and Sculpture, held in 1981, was the first group exhibition that sought to place individual practices within a broader contemporary context. The exhibition emphasised associativeness as one of the defining conditions of the work included, more specifically the relationship between material, process and form in generating associative readings. *Figures and Objects*, held in 1983, further refined these readings by firmly placing the emphasis on the image-based nature of the work exhibited. The shift represented in the titles of the two shows – from sculptures to figures – is emblematic of the extent to which critical debate had shifted its focus from the materials used to their relationship with compositional strategies adopted as a locus for the meaning of this work. The trajectory was temporarily completed in the British Council's exhibition for the São Paulo Bieniale, also held in 1983, appropriately titled *Transformations*.

Strategies such as these relied on the gallery as a discursive frame, and the new British sculptors found a strong institutional network capable of supporting their practices. The Arts Council's policy of opening, or funding existing non-collection-based venues across the UK had generated a number of galleries devoted to the presentation of contemporary art. The ICA collaborated with the Arnolfini in Bristol on the presentation of *Objects and Sculpture*, while *Figures and Objects* was held at the John Hansard Gallery in Southampton, which had opened only a year previously. The British Council's exhibition in São Paulo similarly spoke of an institutional ability and willingness to support

British art abroad, as well as of the extent to which British artists were viewed both in the UK and abroad as participating in an international dialogue. In London, the Whitechapel Art Gallery re-emerged under Nicholas Serota as an important venue for the early presentation of contemporary developments. Besides Cragg, Boyd Webb and Antony Gormley also received their first large-scale solo exhibitions there, respectively in 1978 and 1981 (Woodrow had shown soon after graduating in 1972), while the 1983 *Whitechapel Open* included the work of Edward Allington, Richard Wentworth and Alison Wilding among others.[4]

In 1983, Bryan Robertson proposed to the Arts Council that that year's Hayward Annual should focus on sculpture. The result was *The Sculpture Show*, selected by Kate Blacker, Fenella Crichton and Paul de Monchaux along personal, and often diverging, lines. Much broader in scope than previous exhibitions, the show extended beyond the Hayward to include the Serpentine Gallery, and featured a number of public artworks that were sited along the South Bank and in Kensington Gardens. The show was perhaps most successful in highlighting the range of contemporary practices, and in making a case for a broader definition of sculpture with the selection, by Blacker, of Audio Arts and Stephen Willats, amongst others.

The generation of artists that came to prominence in the late 1980s and 1990s reflected this openness of sculptural possibility. Some are more conventionally sculptural – David Batchelor, Grenville Davey, Marc Quinn, Gavin Turk and Rachel Whiteread, for example – while many others worked in the expanded idiom of installation which, in Britain as elsewhere, became prevalent throughout the 1990s. Such installations were concerned with a variety of approaches – phenomenal, discursive, theatrical – that created more holistic environments which drew the exhibition space and the viewer into the work itself. This broadening of definitions of sculptural practice was met by the proliferation of alternative, artist-run or independent spaces that presented work in less 'neutral' environments than those of conventional gallery settings. The functions of such spaces were varied, foremost among them a drive towards creating support networks and exhibiting opportunities that by-passed the often limited official networks. Whether one-off exhibitions, longer-term projects or connected to studio facilities, they embraced the experimental, a plurality of viewpoints and working practices, and provided a curatorial terrain that shifted between the democratic and the highly idiosyncratic. In opening these spaces, artists often took on or parodied

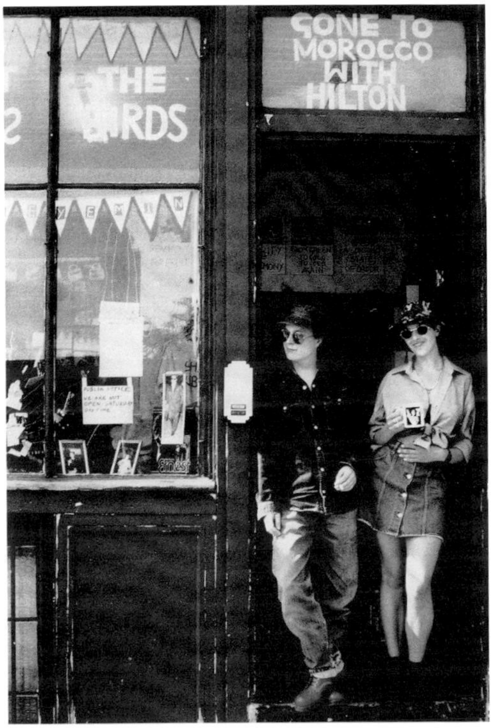

2 Tracey Emin and Sarah Lucas, 'The Shop', 1993

traditional roles. Tracey Emin and Sarah Lucas set up 'The Shop' in 1993, in east London, effectively a gallery for the sale of their and other artists' limited editions (Fig. 2). Christine Borland and Cornelia Parker amongst others turned to a form of creative ethnography, while at least two artists, Emin over a period of about a year in 1995 and Ross Sinclair with his 1994 installation, 'Museum of Despair', set up their own museums. Emin's, which opened in a former mini-cab office in south London, was funded with the issue of Mini (£50) and Major (£500) Emin Bonds. As the artists involved in City Racing have recently written, 'Out on the pavement, you realise that you are surrounded by your own scene. There is only so much room inside, but the good thing is that outside the space is unlimited.'[5]

While the New British Sculptors of the early 1980s were often defined as *bricoleurs* for their use of discarded materials, this generation developed into small-scale entrepreneurs who made use of vacated domestic and industrial buildings to exhibit, market and sell their own work. The use of warehouses as artist-run exhibiting spaces stretches at least as far back as St Catherine's Docks and Stockwell Depot in the 1960s, as well as studio initiatives such as SPACE and Acme. A more recent precedent was the opening of Matt's Gallery in 1979, originally in Robin Klassnik's studio in London Fields and later in Mile End. Under Klassnik's directorship, Matt's emerged out of the expanded sculptural field of the late 1960s, consistently focusing on the gallery as a site of production and as a showcase for less well-known and emerging artists. Providing the coordinates of the space alone as the starting point for any exhibition, Matt's has in its twenty-five-year history generated exhibitions in a variety of media, notable among them a series of installations that stretch from David Troostwyk's 'Supreme Object' (1979), to Richard Wilson's '20:50' (1987) and Mike Nelson's 'The Coral Reef' (2000). These not only provided a working model since widely adopted and reflected in specific programmes such as Tate's Art Now and the Henry Moore Sculpture Trust Studio at Dean Clough, Halifax, but also act as forerunners to some of the architectural and site-specific strategies that came, in part, to define the 1990s.

Wilson's '20:50' was bought and permanently installed in another venue that provided an altogether different model of warehouse exhibition space: the Saatchi Gallery. Opened in 1985 with an exhibition that included a 1,200 ft sculpture by Donald Judd, it introduced what many at the time referred to as an 'American scale and approach' to both collecting and displaying contemporary art.[6] Initially focused on American and European artists, including the first exhibitions of Robert Gober and Jeff Koons among others (later contextualised in the ICA's 1990 *Sculpture Show*), Saatchi switched the focus of his collection in the early 1990s, and the gallery became one of the primary 'institutional' spaces for the presentation of work by young British artists.

The example set by the Saatchi Gallery was undoubtedly influential to Damien Hirst and his fellow Goldsmiths' BA students in the mounting of their seminal *Freeze* exhibition in London's Docklands in 1988, officially canonised as the founding moment of the Young British Artists phenomenon. The former paint factory which housed the Saatchi Gallery on Boundary Road, however, had been redeveloped into a series of pristine, dazzling, almost spectacularly white spaces, while the organisers of *Freeze* allowed the grunge and incidental visual objects and imagery indigenous to the space to remain, and indeed to participate in the overall effect of the exhibition. The emergence of a new generation, already announced by the strategies adopted, was in this way also communicated as an overall aesthetic experience, as important as individual works themselves. This sense of dramatic staging was matched in later exhibitions organised by Hirst, Carl Freedman and Billie Sellman at Building One in 1990, *Modern Medicine* and *Gambler*, but perhaps most explicitly in a series of shows mounted by the collective BANK. These took on the quality of veritable tableaux that the viewer stepped into and around: 'BANK, The Charge of the Light Brigade' (1995), a history painting made flesh in cardboard and tin foil and hung upside down from the ceiling; 'BANK, GOD' (1997), where the viewer had once again to look up, this time at wooden sculptures of the artists crucified in a darkened space; and 'Cocaine Orgasm' (1995; Fig. 3) which, amongst other elements, surrounded videos by Janette Paris and Rebecca Warren in a flurry of crumpled polystyrene, lit in a flash of mirrors and neon. Such notions of the exhibition as an experiential encounter, often visually mapped out in the curatorial strategies adopted, has become one of the primary conditions of exhibition making over the last few decades. Whether through installations or more 'conventionally' sculptural works, many artists in this period sought to activate and create a more dynamic

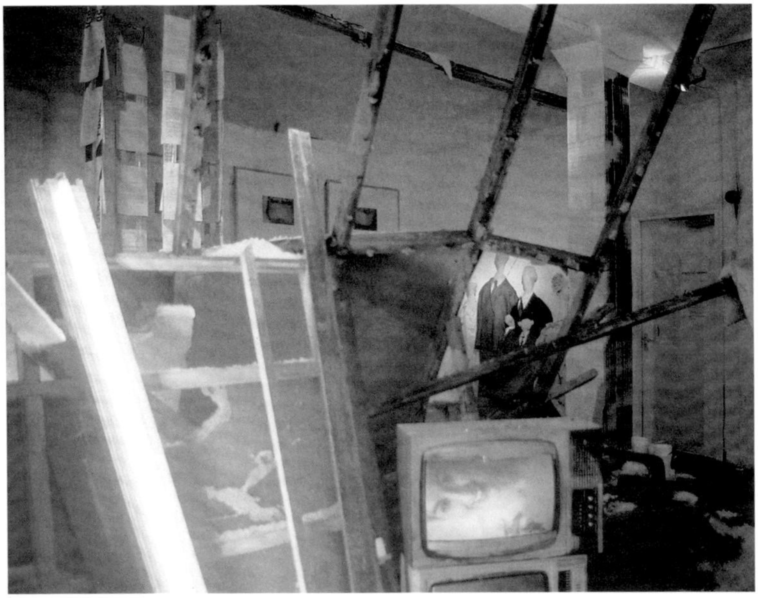

3 BANK, 'Cocaine Orgasm' (detail; video by Rebecca Warren) 1995

relationship between their work and the space that it inhabited, one that similarly engaged the viewer on a more phenomenal level. This finds a more discursive articulation in the works of artists such as Angela Bulloch or Liam Gillick; a perceptual register in that of Mark Wallinger; psychic and existential in Whiteread; architectural in Wilson; organic and sensual in Anya Gallaccio.

Other projects which flourished in abandoned warehouses include Beaconsfield, Gasworks, Milch, the Tannery, Tramway, Underwood Street and the Chisenhale Gallery among many others. The last, a former factory for Spitfire propellers and complex of artists' studios, was intermittently used as an exhibition space until fully opened in 1985 by David Thorp. In the early 1990s, under the direction of Jonathan Watkins, it commissioned and mounted a series of solo exhibitions that alternated between major sculptures and installations, capturing a range of artistic approaches. Notable among them are Whiteread's 'Ghost' (1990) and Parker's installation 'Cold Dark Matter: an Exploded View' (1991), both of which drew particular strength from the gallery's pragmatic architecture; Rose Finn-Kelcey's untitled installation of 1992 and Woodrow and Deacon's 'conversation', *Only The Lonely and Other Shared Sculptures* (1993).

Perhaps the best-known gallery housed in a domestic property was City Racing in south London, opened in 1988 in a squatted building

4 City Racing, South London, 1988

5 Michael Landy, 'Market', 1992

that included a betting shop at street level – from which the gallery derived its name – and which occupied modest premises split over two floors (Fig. 4). The gallery was opened by John Burgess, Keith Coventry, Matt Hale, Paul Noble and Pete Owen, the majority of whom came from a sculptural background, and included in its programme a significant number of sculpture or installation-based shows. These brought together different generations of artists that included Barry Flanagan, Gustav Metzger and Tim Mapston (organised by Andrew Wilson); their own work alongside that of Gavin Brown, Adam Chodzko, Lucas, Giorgio Sadotti, Sinclair and Kerry Stewart among others; as well as younger artists like Brian Griffiths and Mark Titchner. The history of domestic spaces in art is, of course, a long one, stretching back to the private palaces of wealthy collectors that gave rise to the museum in the late 18th and 19th centuries. While the conditions could not be more startlingly divergent, the two are none-the-less linked by a sense of the personal passions and visions that shape particular endeavours, by an approach more closely linked to the informed amateurism which gave rise to artistic connoisseurship than to the professionalised entrepreneurial spirit demonstrated elsewhere. Aesthetically, this translated into a DIY or Lo-Fi approach that privileged poor materials and methods of construction or assembly, and in exhibitions that moved between minimal hangs and salon-style installations. Today, it would appear that it is this approach that has influenced the most recent generation of British

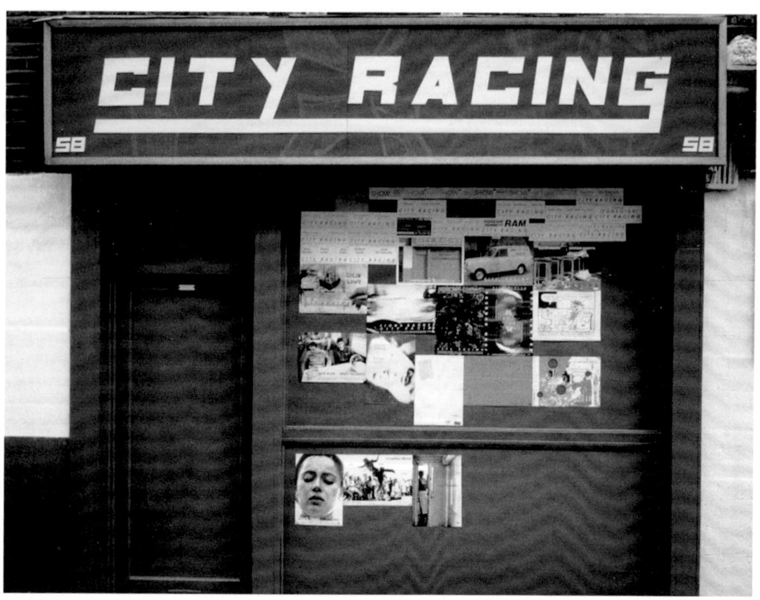

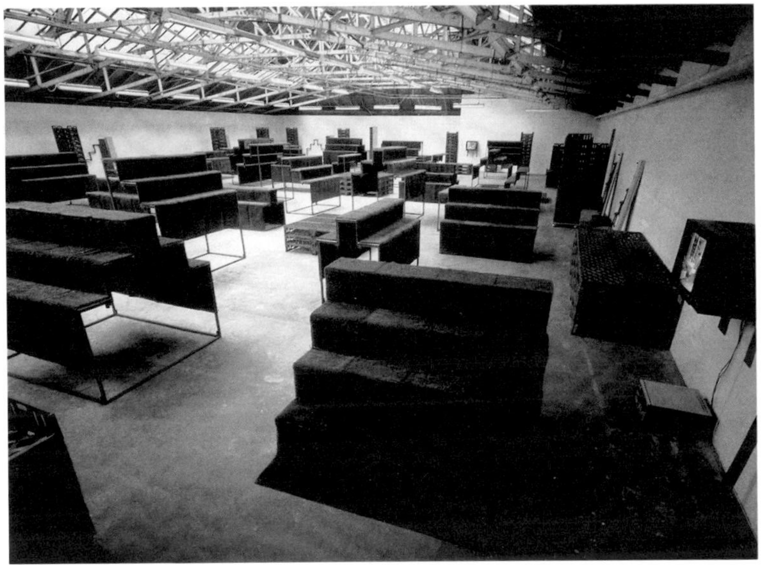

sculptors, the exhibitions – such as *Heart and Soul* – that first brought them to attention and some of the galleries, among them The Approach and Vilma Gold, who represent them.

If the impetus behind City Racing and the exhibitions it mounted was partly to explore 'the relationship between the artist and the gallery, between public and private space and between Gombrich culture and "real" culture',[7] the limitations and contradictions of this approach were soon apparent. In writing about *Show 28*, which featured Sadotti and Brown, the City Racing artists point out how both works in the exhibition inevitably reflected back on the gallery as a frame that mediates our relationship to art. Sadotti's '1…2' consisted of drums, guitars, microphones and amps, plugged in and ready to use; 'Like a car with the keys left in, or a cash till left open', it was there to be played. 'Looking was not enough. *1…2* was a lesson in participation over voyeurism. *1…2* kicked against the typically exclusive notion that art is only for the "talented" and the genius.'[8] Brown's installation, on the other hand, consisted of furniture and other objects from his parents' home, as well as photographs of two architecturally identical flats, rendered different and distinctive 'by the belongings that make a place home'.[9] Yet the 'realism' of Sadotti's installation was only achieved through the careful arrangement and lighting of the objects on display, while Brown's translation of domestic objects into the space of the gallery only served to remove their functionality and transform them into cultural signs.

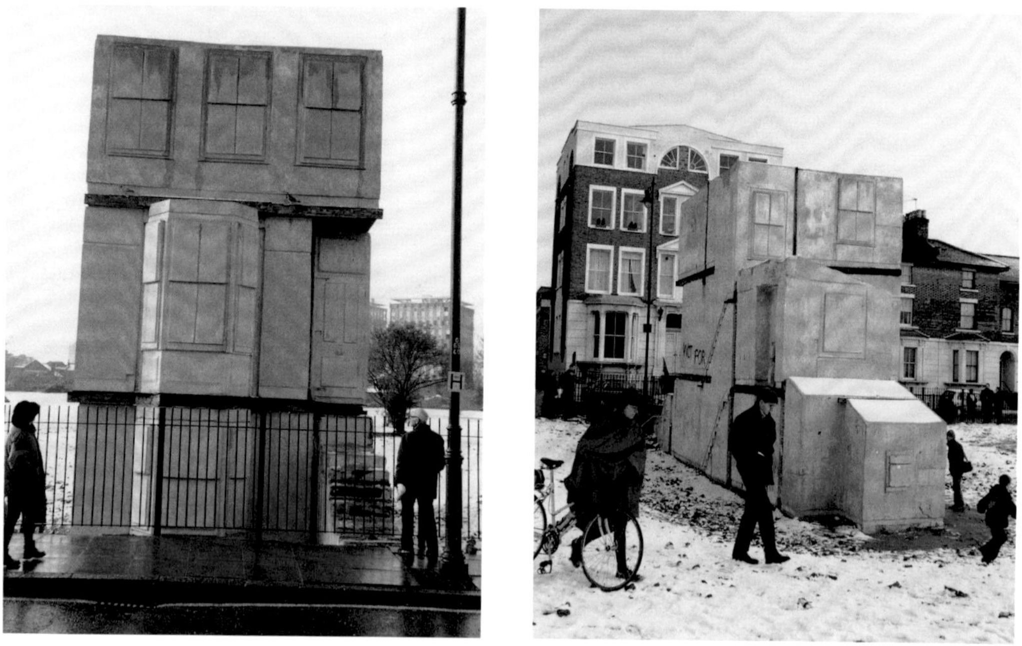

6 Rachel Whiteread, 'House', 1993

As Lisa Panting has succinctly argued, 'the story of this period is largely one of property, for without the vacant buildings – and the legal rights of squatters – many of the achievements would never have been realised'.[10] Large empty warehouses represented the ghosts of an industrial past, the last vestiges of which had been dismantled during the Thatcherist decade, while the availability of domestic housing arose from the deep recession that hit Britain in the early 1990s. The work of two artists stands as a poignant comment on this history: Michael Landy's rows of empty market stalls, 'Market' (1992; Fig. 5) and Whiteread's cast of a terraced home in east London, 'House' (1993; Fig. 6). Both works exploit and give voice to the gaps between reality and its representation, conveying a negative space that is, however, charged with meaning.

Andrea Tarsia

Notes

1 L. Cooke, 'British sculpture in the eighties: questioning cultural myths, confirming artistic conventions', *British Sculpture 1960–1988* (exhibition catalogue), Antwerp, Museum van Hedendaagse Kunst, 1989, p. 57.

2 P. Fuller, 'The condition of sculpture', *Connoisser*, August 1975, vol. 189, no. 762, p. 27.

3 L. Biggs, I. Blazwick and S. Nairne, 'Introduction', in *Objects and Sculpture* (exhibition catalogue), London, ICA and Bristol, Arnolfini, 1981, p. 6.

4 The expansion of the public sector was not reflected in a burgeoning commercial sector. Many galleries which had promoted minimalism and conceptualism in the 1960s and 1970s had either closed or shifted focus towards painting by the late 1970s and early 1980s. Almost alone among them, Nicholas Logsdail's Lisson Gallery was quick to recognise the emergent group and by 1983 represented Cragg, Deacon, Houshiary, Kapoor, Opie, Wentworth and Woodrow.

5 J. Burgess, K. Coventry, M. Hale, P. Noble and P. Owen, *City Racing: The Life and Times of an Artist-Run Gallery*, London, Black Dog Publishing, 2002, p. 1.

6 Cf. for example P. Overy, 'What makes Saatchi run?', *The Journal of Art*, October 1990, vol. 3, no. 1, p. 26.

7 Burgess, K. Coventry, M. Hale, P. Noble and P. Owen, *City Racing: The Life and Times of an Artist-Run Gallery*, p. 13.

8 Ibid.

9 Ibid.

10 L. Panting, 'Changing Topography', *Contemporary Visual Arts*, issue 24, 1999, p. 45.

'Send for the men in white coats'

Throughout the last quarter of the 20th century, it was sculpture in its various forms that dominated public debate on the meaning, function and status of art in Britain. The tone of this debate was established in 1976 with the controversy surrounding the Tate Gallery's purchase of Carl Andre's 'bricks' (Fig. 1) and it continued unabated up to at least 2001 with the controversy over Martin Creed's Turner Prize-winning installation 'The Lights Going On and Off' (Fig. 2). In 1976, however, few would have guessed that artists would eventually be utilised as the avant-garde of urban regeneration schemes and that contemporary art would play a key role in an emerging financial sector (eventually labelled 'the creative industries').[1] Tabloid journalists and conservative critics continued with their statements that 'a child of six could do it' and carried on complaining about the waste of 'taxpayers' money', but this had little negative effect on the reputation of the artists and institutions they sought to discredit. Art controversies ignited by the tabloid press were quickly followed by sympathetic feature or profile articles in the broadsheet newspapers.[2] The combined weight of such coverage invariably led to coverage on television and radio and in the specialist art magazines and eventually in art-historical accounts such as this essay. This was agenda-setting in the age of celebrity and art's visibility increasingly relied upon its talent for scandal.

Sculpture proved to be particularly suitable in this respect because it existed in real time and place and often outside of the sanitising white

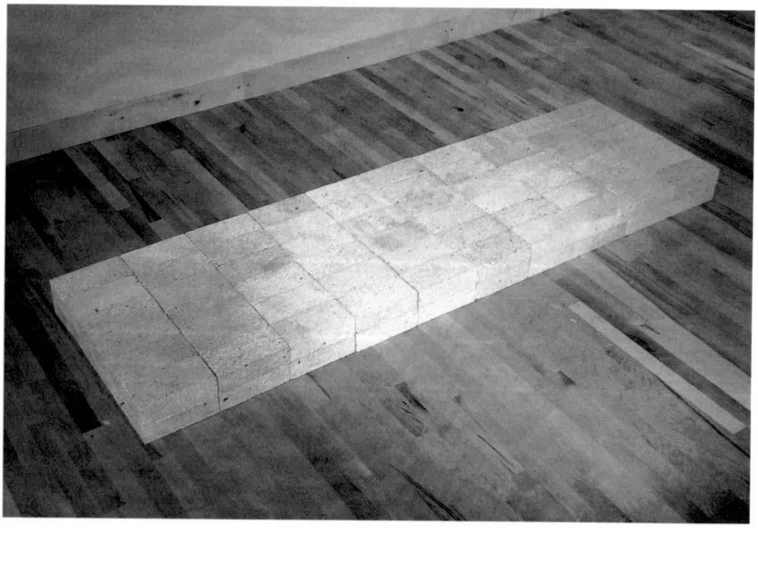

1 Carl Andre, 'Equivalent VIII', 1966

2 Maggie Stratton, 'Minimalist Creed pays off as empty space takes Britain's top art prize', newspaper cutting from the *Yorkshire Post*, 10 December 2001

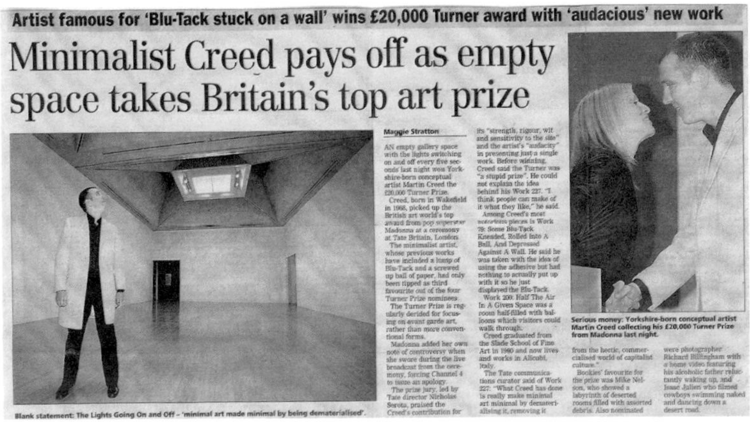

Artist famous for 'Blu-Tack stuck on a wall' wins £20,000 Turner award with 'audacious' new work

Minimalist Creed pays off as empty space takes Britain's top art prize

Blank statement: The Lights Going On and Off – 'minimal art made minimal by being dematerialised'.

Maggie Stratton

AN empty gallery space with the lights switching on and off every five seconds last night won Yorkshire-born conceptual artist Martin Creed the £20,000 Turner Prize.

Creed, born in Wakefield in 1968, picked up the British art world's top award from pop superstar Madonna at a ceremony at Tate Britain, London.

The minimalist artist, whose previous works have included a lump of Blu-Tack and a screwed up ball of paper, had only been tipped as third favourite out of the four Turner Prize nominees.

The Turner Prize is regularly derided for focusing on avant garde art, rather than more conventional forms.

Madonna added her own note of controversy when she swore during the live broadcast from the ceremony, forcing Channel 4 to issue an apology.

The prize jury, led by Tate director Nicholas Serota, praised the Creed's contribution for its "strength, rigour, wit and sensitivity to the site" and the artist's "audacity" in presenting just a single work. Before winning, Creed said the Turner was "a stupid prize". He could not explain the idea behind his Work 227. "I think people can make of it what they like," he said.

Among Creed's most notorious pieces is Work 79: Some Blu-Tack Kneaded, Rolled Into A Ball, And Depressed Against A Wall. He said he was taken with the idea of using the adhesive but had nothing to actually put up with it so he just displayed the Blu-Tack.

Work 200: Half The Air In A Given Space was a room half-filled with balloons which visitors could walk through.

Creed graduated from the Slade School of Fine Art in 1990 and now lives and works in Alicubi, Italy.

The Tate communications curator said of Work 227: "What Creed has done is really make minimal art minimal by dematerialising it, removing it from the hectic, commercialised world of capitalist culture."

Bookies' favourite for the prize was Mike Nelson, who showed a labyrinth of deserted rooms filled with assorted debris. Also nominated were photographer Richard Billingham with a home video featuring his alcoholic father reluctantly waking up, and Isaac Julien who filmed cowboys swimming naked and dancing down a desert road.

Serious money: Yorkshire-born conceptual artist Martin Creed collecting his £20,000 Turner Prize from Madonna last night.

space of the art gallery. Sometimes its non-traditional material proved enough of a provocation (for example, sharks, kebabs, slept-in beds, blood, urine, rubber tyres, chocolate, body parts, nappies and used tampons). Traditional sculptural materials such as marble, bronze and wood – and traditional techniques such as casting, carving and modelling – were still employed but notions of the 'classical' or 'ideal form' were supplanted by attention to the 'everyday' and the blurring of distinction between high and low cultural subject-matter. Sculpture also lent itself to the photo-opportunity, and true to the viral nature of our media-dominated age, through mass reproduction some sculpture even acquired a powerfully iconic status (for example, Carl Andre's 'Equivalent VIII', Rachel Whiteread's 'House' and Antony Gormley's 'Angel of the North'), becoming as instantly recognisable as the most popular of brands.

Interestingly, however, it was not until the 1990s that the full potential of this type of exposure became a conscious strategy on the part of some artists and their advisers. The gallerist Jay Jopling traced the origin of this brave new world to a think-tank set up by Nicholas Serota at the Tate Gallery in 1991. Serota, according to Jopling, was looking for a way to encourage newspapers to take contemporary art more seriously, but Jopling had other plans:

[I]t seemed to me that if the tabloid press was only interested in ridiculing contemporary art, then get them to ridicule it properly, so that people actually take notice. … So we got the *Daily Star* to take a bag of chips to one of Damien's fish in formaldehyde pieces which was then on show at the Serpentine and photograph it as the most expensive fish and chips in the world. Stunts like that forced people to know about the art and if they know about it, then that encouraged them to go and see it, and then they were forced to take a view. It certainly was a way of getting art into the public arena.[3]

Jopling's clear aim was to use the tabloid press to generate publicity for his artists, however derogatory. He realised that past art controversies had been poorly managed and that artists had subsequently been unable to take advantage of the exposure they provided. This was clearly the case back in February 1976 when Andre's 'bricks' controversy began, first with an article in the business pages of the *Sunday Times*[4] and then the next day by a front-page article in the *Daily Mirror*, with the headline 'What a load of rubbish: how the Tate dropped 120 bricks'.[5]

The controversy centred on the Tate Gallery buying (in 1972) and exhibiting (in 1976) Andre's 'Equivalent VIII' (1966), a sculpture made of 120 bricks arranged to form a double-layered rectangle.[6] Other newspapers quickly picked up on the story and delighted in its humorous possibilities, with a typical stunt being to interview and photograph 'real' brickies building their own brick sculptures.[7] The implication was that the Tate curators had been 'conned' into buying a work of art that anybody could produce using the same materials. The case against contemporary art quickly settled into a soon familiar litany of assertions:

[F]ind the link between a row of bricks, a lavatory chain, a heap of stones and a plastic mac adorned with two rusty screws … they have all been elevated, labelled ART, and put on show at one or other of London's most prestigious galleries. … [T]hey try and shove all this rubbish under our innocent noses because they claim that art can be stretched to a potty point. Well, it cannot and it must not. Contrary to what they say, art can be defined with precision. Visual art is about shape and colour and the use of space. And the first step in bringing back to their senses those who confuse it with refuse, is to scrap their taxpayer's subsidy.[8]

Such statements spelt out clearly what was at stake: they (the contemporary art establishment) must not be allowed to elevate 'rubbish' to the exulted status of 'art'; chaos and madness would result from such an inversion of an established hierarchy; art was definable only within the terms of a strict formalism; and most importantly, discipline should be exacted through economic sanction, specifically through the withdrawal of state subsidy. The difference from later controversies, as manufactured by the likes of Jopling, became readily apparent when

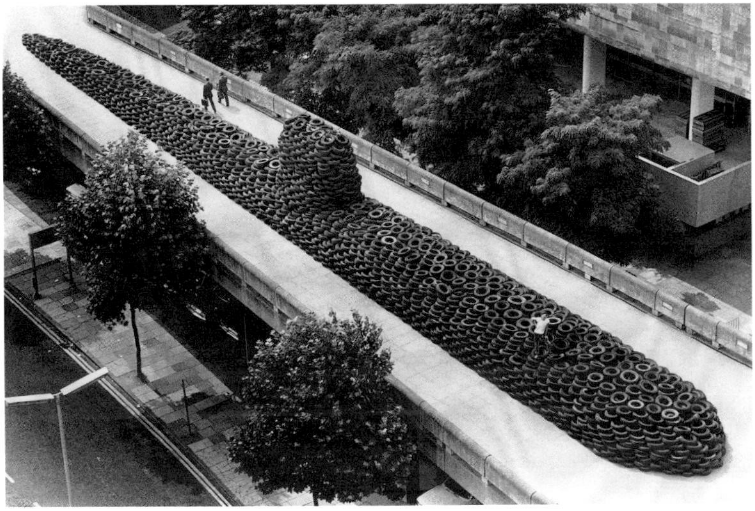

3 David Mach, 'Polaris'; exhibition, *The Sculpture Show*, Hayward Gallery, London 1983

examining Andre's reaction: 'Mass media exposure like that is absolutely no use to an artist. It doesn't even help commercially. You don't have 100,000 brick pieces in a warehouse, like a rock and roll group's albums.'[9] Obviously by the 1990s the potential for leveraging celebrity to increase cultural capital was a much better-understood concept.

During the 1980s and early 1990s, sculpture continued to ignite controversy. In August 1983 a man died while trying to set fire to David Mach's sculpture 'Polaris', a submarine made from rubber tyres (Fig. 3).[10] Four years later, in December 1987, in an exhibition entitled *Animal* at the Young Unknowns Gallery, Rick Gibson exhibited 'Human Earrings' (1985), human foetuses made into earrings and placed on a mannequin. Along with Peter Sylveire, the gallery director, he was later prosecuted and found guilty of 'outraging public decency'.[11] In October 1993 Whiteread's 'House' became a *cause célèbre*, exciting the interest of a wide range of commentators, from tabloid journalists and cartoonists to the art press and even locally based activists.[12] In November Whiteread won both the Turner Prize and the K Foundation's Worst Artist prize, but despite these awards and a forceful campaign by the broadsheet press, nothing could stop the sculpture being demolished, as planned, by the local council in January 1994.

As was often the case, such acts of destruction, iconoclasm or vandalism added to a sculpture's newsworthiness. A few months later, in May 1994 at the Serpentine Gallery, Mark Bridger poured black ink into Damien Hirst's 'Away From The Flock' (1994) – a dead lamb in a glass tank filled with formaldehyde – and changed the title to 'Black

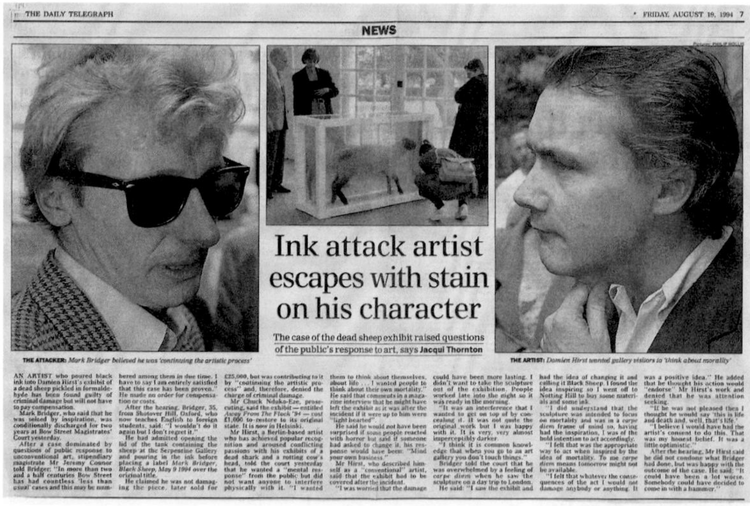

THE DAILY TELEGRAPH FRIDAY, AUGUST 19, 1994 7

NEWS

Ink attack artist escapes with stain on his character

The case of the dead sheep exhibit raised questions of the public's response to art, says **Jacqui Thornton**

THE ATTACKER: *Mark Bridger believed he was 'continuing the artistic process'*

THE ARTIST: *Damien Hirst wanted gallery visitors to 'think about morality'*

AN ARTIST who poured black ink into Damien Hirst's exhibit of a dead sheep pickled in formaldehyde has been found guilty of criminal damage but will not have to pay compensation.

Mark Bridger, who said that he was seized by inspiration, was conditionally discharged for two years at Bow Street Magistrates' Court yesterday.

After a case dominated by questions of public response to unconventional art, stipendiary magistrate Mr Jeremy Connor told Bridger: "In more than two and a half centuries Bow Street has had countless 'less than usual' cases and this may be numbered among them in due time. I have to say I am entirely satisfied that this case has been proven." He made no order for compensation or costs.

After the hearing, Bridger, 35, from Shotover Hill, Oxford, who now teaches English to foreign students, said: "I wouldn't do it again but I don't regret it."

He had admitted opening the lid of the tank containing the sheep at the Serpentine Gallery and pouring in the ink before placing a label *Mark Bridger, Black Sheep, May 9 1994* over the original title.

He claimed he was not damaging the piece, later sold for £25,000, but was contributing to it by "continuing the artistic process" and, therefore, denied the charge of criminal damage.

Mr Chuck Nduko-Eze, prosecuting, said the exhibit — entitled *Away From The Flock '94* — cost £1,000 to restore to its original state. It is now in Helsinki.

Mr Hirst, a Berlin-based artist who has achieved popular recognition and aroused conflicting passions with his exhibits of a dead shark and a rotting cow's head, told the court yesterday that he wanted a "mental response" from the public but did not want anyone to interfere physically with it. "I wanted them to think about themselves, about life . . . I wanted people to think about their own mortality."

He said that comments in a magazine interview that he might have left the exhibit as it was after the incident if it were up to him were "light hearted".

He said he would not have been surprised if some people reacted with horror but said if someone had asked to change it, his response would have been: "Mind your own business."

Mr Hirst, who described himself as a "conventional" artist, said that the exhibit had to be covered after the incident.

"I was worried that the damage could have been more lasting. I didn't want to take the sculpture out of the exhibition. People worked late into the night so it was ready in the morning.

"It was an interference that I wanted to get on top of by concealing it. It was not quite the original work but I was happy with it. It is very, very almost imperceptibly darker.

"I think it is common knowledge that when you go to an art gallery you don't touch things."

Bridger told the court that he was overwhelmed by a feeling of *carpe diem* when he saw the sculpture on a day trip to London.

He said: "I saw the exhibit and had the idea of changing it and calling it Black Sheep. I found the idea inspiring so I went off to Notting Hill to buy some materials and some ink.

"I did understand that the sculpture was intended to focus on mortality and was in a *carpe diem* frame of mind so, having had the inspiration, I was of the bold intention to act accordingly.

"I felt that was the appropriate way to act when inspired by the idea of mortality. To me *carpe diem* means tomorrow might not be available.

"I felt that whatever the consequences of the act I would not damage anybody or anything. It was a positive idea." He added that he thought his action would "endorse" Mr Hirst's work and denied that he was attention seeking.

"If he was not pleased then I thought he would say 'this is life and death and, well, that's life.'

"I believe I would have had the artist's consent to do this. That was my honest belief. It was a little optimistic."

After the hearing, Mr Hirst said he did not condone what Bridger had done, but was happy with the outcome of the case. He said: "It could have been a lot worse. Somebody could have decided to come in with a hammer."

4 Jacqui Thornton, 'Ink attack artist escapes with stain on his character', newspaper cutting from *Daily Telegraph,* 19 August 1994

5 A selection of periodicals from the Henry Moore Institute Library: *Artscribe* 42, August 1983; *Frieze*, November/December 1993; *Art Monthly* 194, March 1996; *Modern Painters*, Winter 1997. Covers showing work by Bill Woodrow, Gavin Turk, Damien Hirst and Gilbert & George respectively

Sheep' (Fig. 4).[13] The Serpentine also hit the headlines in the following year with Cornelia Parker's 'The Maybe' (1995), which starred the actress Tilda Swinton asleep in a glass case alongside a collection of 'relics' relating to various famous dead people. The press attention inevitably led to increased viewing figures with up to 3,000 people visiting the show each day.[14]

A key event and soon a regular fixture of the artworld calendar during this period was the Turner Prize. The Prize started relatively quietly in 1984 but this changed in 1991 when the Tate Gallery doubled the prize money to £20,000, reduced the short-list from six to four artists and introduced an age limit (under-fifties only). Most importantly Channel 4 became the main sponsor and immediately boosted the prize's media profile and created a focus for public debate on contemporary art. Over the years a disproportionate number of sculptors won the Turner Prize, including Richard Deacon (1987), Tony Cragg (1988), Richard Long (1989), Anish Kapoor (1991), Grenville Davey (1992), Whiteread (1993), Gormley (1994), Hirst (1995) and Creed (2001).

The Turner Prize was paradigmatic of the increasingly competitive environment within which artists now operated. To gain attention, some took to making art that was bigger, more spectacular and more expensive than that of their rivals. During the early 1990s nobody did this better than Hirst and Charles Saatchi, an artist–patron relationship that resulted in such works as 'The Physical Impossibility of Death in the Mind of Someone Living' (1991), a 14-ft tiger shark preserved in formaldehyde.[15] But competition led inevitably to an 'arms race' within the artworld and with it an escalation of costs. By the year 2000 Hirst was making a 10-ton, 20-ft-high bronze sculpture entitled 'Hymn' (in fact a scaled up version of a 14-in.-high Humbrol science toy).[16] Other examples of sculpture as spectacle were provided by *The Unilever Series* situated in Tate Modern's giant Turbine Hall, first with Louise Bourgeois' 'Maman' (2000), then Juan Muñoz's 'Double Bind' (2001) and most recently Kapoor's 'Marsyas' (2002).

As the name of this series reveals, the funding necessary to realise these projects increasingly depended on partnerships between the public and private sector. Again this was to a degree unimaginable back in 1976. While in 1973 arts sponsorship stood at £250,000 per year, by 1976 (when the Association for Business Sponsorship of the Arts was founded) the figure had crept up to an estimated £500,000 per year. By 1980 that figure had risen dramatically to £5 million.[17] But even this figure pales into insignificance when compared to the £114.4 million spent on art sponsorship during the financial year 2000/2001.[18] The strings attached to these finances tied artists and art institutions ever closer to the marketing agendas of big business. The target audience came broadly from the social groups ABC1, but more specifically the notoriously difficult-to-reach 'opinion formers'. An important element of any sponsorship deal was therefore the recruitment of a media partner (see for example *Time Out*'s support for the exhibition *Sensation* at the Royal Academy in 1997). Collaborations like this pushed art further in the direction of lifestyle culture and opened up space in the new youth style magazines, including *The Face* (1980–), *i-D* (1980–) and *Dazed and Confused* (1994–), as well as their older rivals *Vogue* (1925–) and *Harpers and Queen* (1970–). The increasing popularity of art as a leisure pursuit had a knock-on effect in the publishing industry, with a 117 per cent increase in the sale of art books over the period 1993–7. In 1997 alone a staggering 3,507 art-related titles were published.[19] Art magazines and journals also flourished, with many new titles appearing, including *Art Monthly* (1976–), *Artscribe* (1976–90), *Third Text* (1987–), *Modern Painters* (1988–), *Frieze* (1991–), *The Sculpture Journal* (1997–) and *British Art Journal* (1999–) (Fig. 5).

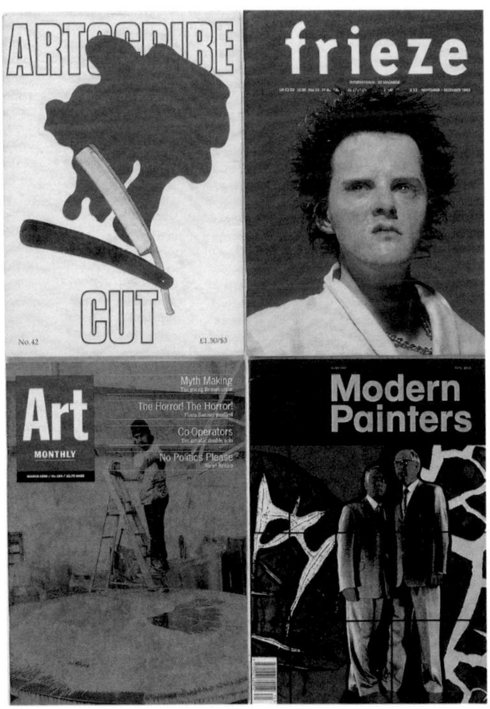

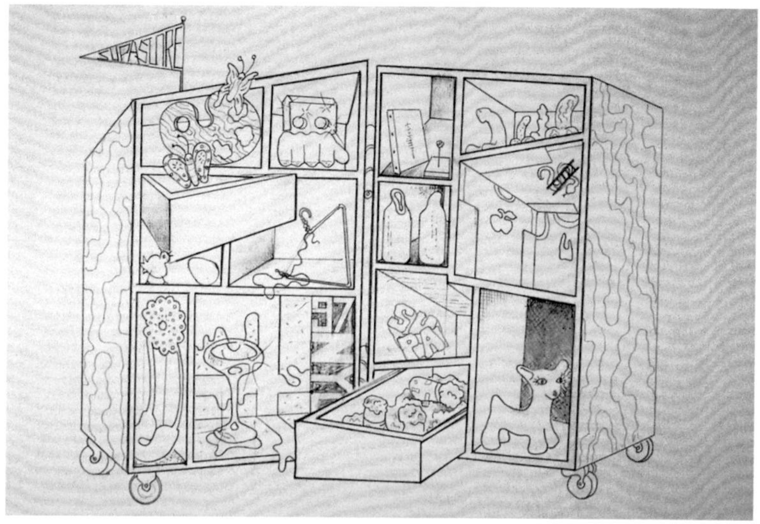

6 Sarah Staton, drawing of the Supastore – Kunst Kammer Kiosk at UP & Co., NYC, 1997, showing works by Tord Bontje, Christina Mackie, Simon Periton, Jane Simpson and Sarah Staton

Alongside publishing, the retail sector soon realised the cachet involved in working with artists and invited some to produce 'affordable' sculptural works suitable for domestic settings.[20] Three recent examples included Whiteread's day bed for SCP available in 'anthracite, blue, tan and stone' for £3,020, Kapoor's 'Form', a co-production with glass producers Salviati available through Vessel, and Tracey Emin's tea towels available from Modern Art Oxford.[21] Such work formed the rarefied end of a genre known as multiples (artworks made in variously sized editions). The best of these drew on the example of the radical artists and art movements of the 1950s and 1960s, including Piero Manzoni and the Fluxus artists.[22] 'Sarah Staton's Supastore' (1993–8; Fig. 6) provided a mobile distribution centre for just such editioned works with shows at various venues including Poster Studio in 1993 and the Cornerhouse in 1998. An institutionalised manifestation of this trend was the ICA's *Glass Shelf Show* where you could buy Creed's 'Work no. 88' (1994) for £5 (an A4 sheet of screwed-up paper), Anya Gallaccio's 'Preserved Rose Petals' for £35, and Bob and Roberta Smith's 'Concrete Aeroplane', an unlimited edition for £40.[23] But a fine line existed between multiples and the new forms of merchandising available in gallery shops accompanying most institutional exhibitions.[24]

All of these developments indicate that during the years 1975–2000, the production, dissemination and reception of sculpture were structurally transformed along with the rest of the artworld and the wider economy. In particular, trends such as increasing commercialism, lifestyle marketing, the cult of the celebrity and the emphasis on spectacle profoundly affected the public perception and understanding of art and artists. During this period of radical political and social upheaval, the mainstream media refined their skills in the technology of co-option and often edited out those oppositional tendencies within the artworld that critiqued the growing neo-liberal/conservative consensus. Like the Hollywood movies that many spectacular works of art sought to emulate, 'critical' attention settled into a blandly affirmative tone, always at pains to shift attention away from the material conditions of a work's production towards the 'spontaneous' creativity of the celebrity artist. But what of those that refused to play this game? What could they expect from the society of the spectacle? In a book on the media's reaction to the murder of his friend Gérard Lebovici in 1984, Guy Debord described the emergence of a new capital offence: 'He who does not, of his own free will, make himself as visible as possible in the spectacle, lives in fact in secrecy, since all current communication in society passes through this mediation. He who lives in secrecy is a clandestine person. A clandestine person will be more and more likely to be considered a terrorist.'[25]

Simon Ford

Notes

1 According to a recent report the creative industries were London's third-largest source of jobs in 2000, accounting for one in every five of its new jobs since 1995, and in 2000 the sector contributed £21 billion to the output of the UK. See the October 2002 report by the Greater London Authority, *Creativity: London's Core Business*, at http://www.london.gov.uk/approot/gla/publications/economy.jsp.

2 See, for example, S. Hattenstone, 'From house to holocaust: interview: controversial sculptor Rachel Whiteread talks to Simon Hattenstone', *Guardian*, 31 May 1997.

3 R. Aidan, 'Brit art's square dealer', *The Observer*, 22 September 2002.

4 C. Simpson, 'Tate drops a costly brick', *Sunday Times*, 15 February 1976.

5 P. Mellor, 'What a load of rubbish: how the Tate dropped 120 bricks', *Daily Mirror*, 16 February 1976.

6 Also known by its Tate inventory number as T. 1534 because the original 'Equivalent VIII' was destroyed by Andre in 1966 after its original display. The Tate reconstruction was bought from the John Weber Gallery, New York. For the Tate's defence of the purchase, see R. Morphet, 'Carl Andre's bricks', *Burlington Magazine*, vol. CXVIII, no. 884, November 1976, pp. 762–7.

7 The press reaction has been collected by the Tate Archive. See TGA, Exhibitions 1976–1981. Carl Andre's Bricks. Press Cuttings.

8 Editorial, 'Send for the men in white coats', *Evening News*, 15 October 1976.

9 P. Fuller, 'An interview with Carl Andre', in P. Fuller, *Beyond the Crisis in Art*, London, Writers and Readers Publishing Co-operative Ltd, 1980, p. 110. First published in *Art Monthly*, May/June 1978, nos 16 and 17.

10 The work was exhibited on the walkway near the Royal Festival Hall as part of *The Sculpture Show*. For more information on this and other art controversies of the period, see J. A. Walker, *Art and Outrage: Provocation, Controversy, and the Visual Arts*, London, Pluto Press, 1999.

11 At the Old Bailey in February 1989 Gibson was fined £500 and Sylveire £350. Channel 4 dramatised the trial in 'Art on Trial' as part of its *Signals* strand (broadcast 22 February 1989). In a similar case in March 1998 at Southwark Crown Court, Anthony-Noel Kelly was found guilty of stealing body parts for his sculptures. The most recent 'body-parts' scandal involved Professor Gunther Von Hagens and his exhibition *Body Worlds* and the public autopsy on 20 November 2002, both of which took place at the Atlantic Gallery on Brick Lane, London.

12 A selection of the press coverage can be found in J. Lingwood (ed.), *House*, London, Phaidon Press and Artangel, 1995. See also 'Housey! Housey!', *London Psychogeographical Association Newsletter*, 1994, no. 5.

13 The sculpture was part of the Hirst-curated show *Some Went Mad, Some Ran Away*, and had already featured in the press after it was sold for £25,000 to Charles Saatchi.

14 R. Fowler, 'A load of ****', *The Sunday Times*, 10 September 1995.

15 A £45,000 commission, according to G. Burn, 'The knives are out', *Guardian*, 10 April 2000.

16 Hirst's investment in the production costs of the work paid off immediately when Charles Saatchi bought the work for a reported £1 million. See G. Burn, 'The godfather', *Guardian*, 14 April 2000.

17 Figures from D. Petherbridge, 'Patronage and sponsorship', *Art Monthly*, July–August 1980, no. 38, p. 9. With the grant to the Arts Council in 1981–2 standing at £80 million and local authority expenditure at £65 million over the same period, the size of the figure, although significant, still only represented a small percentage of overall arts subsidy. (Figures from F. F. Ridley, 'Tradition, change and crisis in Great Britain', in M. C. Cummings, Jr. and R. S. Katz (eds), *The Patron State: Government and the Arts in Europe, North America, and Japan*, Oxford, Oxford University Press, 1987, p. 229.)

18 Figures from an Arts & Business report dated 12 April 2002. Press release available at: http://www.aandb.org.uk/content/news/article_45.shtml. For an overview of art sponsorship in Britain and the USA, see C. Wu, *Privatising Culture: Corporate Art Intervention Since the 1980s*, London, Verso, 2002.

19 Figures from Policy Studies Institute, *Cultural Trends*, 1998, no. 29.

20 For more on this subject, see C. Painter (ed.), *Contemporary Art and the Home*, Oxford, Berg, 2002.

21 All illustrated in L. Siegle, 'Take three Turner Prize homemakers', *The Observer Magazine*, 17 November 2002, p. 82.

22 Many examples of which are illustrated in S. Bury, *Artists' Multiples 1935–2000*, Aldershot, Ashgate, 2001.

23 Full title: *Glass Shelf Show: Artists' Multiples and Editions*, London, ICA, 4 November–23 December 1995.

[24] Just one example of this was Hirst's 'Relationships' (1991), produced in conjunction with the ICA in an edition of 125 and consisting of a glass and ping-pong ball in a cardboard tube plus a signed diagram.

[25] G. Debord, *Considerations on the Assassination of Gérard Lebovici*, Los Angeles, Tam Tam Books, 2001, p. 47. Translated by Robert Greene.

This bibliography covers the main publications on sculpture in 20th-century Britain that have been published since 1981. Previous publications are covered by the bibliography in the Whitechapel exhibition catalogue *British Sculpture in the Twentieth Century.*

Publications are listed by year of publication. 'Sculpture' has been the main criterion for selection but it is acknowledged, first, that many other publications on art will include sculpture and, second, that sculpture as an art form has been increasingly difficult to define since 1981. Therefore the bibliography is by no means exhaustive, but rather an indication of publishing activity in the subject area over these years.

1981

S. Nairne and N. Serota (eds), *British Sculpture in the Twentieth Century*, London, Whitechapel Art Gallery

1982

Coloured Constructions, Birmingham, Ikon Gallery

M. Kunz (ed.), *Englische Plastik Heute*, Luzern, Kunstmuseum Luzern

Making Sculpture: Materials and Methods, London, Tate Gallery Publications

D. Graham-Campbell, *Scotland's Story in her Monuments*, London, Robert Hale

S. Hourahane, *Sculpture at Margam: Maquettes for Public Sculpture*, Cardiff, Welsh Sculpture Trust

The Sculpture Show: Fifty Sculptors at the Serpentine and the South Bank, London, Arts Council of Great Britain

B. Read, *Victorian Sculpture*, London, Yale University Press, (Studies in British Art)

1983

K. Blacker, *Figures and Objects: Recent Developments in British Sculpture*, Southampton, John Hansard Gallery

Sculpture by Women, Birmingham, Ikon Gallery

Welsh Sculpture Trust, *Sculpture in a Country Park: An Outdoor Exhibition in the Grounds of Margam*, West Sculpture Trust/West Glamorgan County Council

S. Beattie, *The New Sculpture*, London, Yale University Press, (Studies in British Art)

M. Harrison (ed.), *Three Little Books About Sculpture: 1 Flesh and Stone*, London, Arts Council of Great Britain

M. Harrison (ed.), *Three Little Books About Sculpture: 2 Mind Over Matter*, London, Arts Council of Great Britain

Transformations: New Sculpture from Britain, London, British Council

1984

D. S. James, *A Century of Statues: A History of the Morris Singer Foundry*, Basingstoke, Morris Singer Foundry

A Noise in Your Eye: An International Exhibition of Sound Sculpture, Bristol, Arnolfini

P. Davies and T. Knipe (eds), *A Sense of Place: Sculpture in Landscape*, Sunderland, Ceolfrith Press

B. Robertson, *English Contrasts: Peintres et Sculpteurs Anglais 1950–1960*, Paris, Artcurial

From the Figure, Birmingham, Ikon Gallery

V. Knight and A. Gouk, *Have You Seen Sculpture From the Body?*, London, Tate Gallery Publications

G. Dunlop, *Just What Is It?* (video recording), London, Arts Council of England

H. Gresty, C. Harrison and V. Burgin, *1965 to 1972 – When Attitudes Became Form*, Cambridge, Kettle's Yard Gallery/Edinburgh, Fruitmarket Gallery

W. J. Strachan, *Open Air Sculpture in Britain: A Comprehensive Guide*, London, Zwemmer in association with Tate Gallery Publications

Royal Society of British Sculptors Anniversary Journal 1904–1984, London, Royal Society of British Sculptors

N. Konstam, *Sculpture: The Art and the Practice*, London, Collins

The Tate Gallery Collections: British Painting, Modern Painting and Sculpture, 8th edition, London, Tate Gallery Publications

M. Harrison (ed.), *Three Little Books About Sculpture: 3 Sculpture's Dance*, London, Arts Council of Great Britain

1985

Beyond Appearance: Sculpture for the Visually Handicapped and Sighted to Share, London, Arts Council of Great Britain

1986

Entre el Objeto y la Imagen: Escultura Britanica Contemporanea, London, British Council

Feeling Through Form, London, Windhorse Trust

M. Whybrow, *Forms and Faces: Sculptors in SW Cornwall*, St Ives, St Ives Printing and Publishing Company

N. Serota and R. Kirby (eds), *In Tandem: The Painter–Sculptor in the Twentieth Century*, London, Whitechapel Art Gallery

Aberdeen International Youth Festival, *Mobil Young Sculptors Competition*, Lumsden, Scottish Sculpture Workshop

B. Read and P. Skipwith, *Sculpture in Britain Between the Wars*, London, Fine Art Society

D. Briers, *Seven Sculptors Working in Wales*, Swansea, Glynn Vivian Art Gallery and Museum

D. O'Connell, *Two Generations of Northern Irish Sculptors: A Series of Interviews*, Derry, Orchard Gallery

1987

T. A. Neff (ed.), *A Quiet Revolution: British Sculpture Since 1965*, London, Thames and Hudson

R. Valorinta (ed.), *Britannia: Paintings and Sculptures from the 1980's*, Tampere, Sara Hildén Art Museum

R. Deacon and A. Wilding, *Casting an Eye*, Manchester, Cornerhouse

Current Affairs: British Painting and Sculpture in the 1980s, Oxford, Museum of Modern Art

Revelation for the Hands, Leeds, Henry Moore Centre for the Study of Sculpture

E. Silber, *Sculpture in Birmingham Museum and Art Gallery: A Summary Catalogue*, Birmingham Museum and Art Gallery

A. C. Papadakis (ed.), 'Sculpture today', *Art and Design*, December 1987, vol. 3, no. 11/12

P. Overy, 'The Britishness of sculpture', *Studio International*, November, vol. 200, no. 1018, pp. 8–13

S. Cutts, *The Unpainted Landscape*, London, Coracle Press/Edinburgh, Graeme Murray Gallery/Edinburgh, Scottish Arts Council,

1988

About Sculpture, London, Anthony d'Offay Gallery

D. Boorman, *At the Going Down of the Sun: British First World War Memorials*, York, Ebor Press

Britannica: Trente Ans de Sculpture, Le Havre, Musée des Beaux-Arts André Malraux

S. Grant Marchand, *British Now: Sculpture et Autres Dessins*, Montreal, Musée d'Art Contemporain de Montréal

A. Payne, *Grey Matter: New Sculpture 88*, Birmingham, Ikon Gallery

P. Curtis, *Modern British Sculpture: From the Collection*, Liverpool, Tate Gallery Liverpool

P. Curtis, *Sculpture on Merseyside*, Liverpool, Tate Gallery Liverpool

Starlit Waters: British Sculpture, An International Art 1968–1988, Liverpool, Tate Gallery Liverpool

P. Randall-Page, *Stone Carving* (video recording and booklet), Brighton, Brighton Polytechnic

1989

M. Livingstone (ed.), *British Object Sculptors of the '80s I*, Kyoto, Kyoto Shoin International

M. Livingstone (ed.), *British Object Sculptors of the '80s II*, Kyoto, Kyoto Shoin International

C. Grenier, F. Cohen and L. Cooke, *Britse Sculptuur 1960/1980*, Antwerp, Museum van Hedendaagse Kusnt

P. Curtis (ed.), *Patronage and Practice: Sculpture on Merseyside*, Liverpool, Tate Gallery Liverpool

Sculpture in Stone: An Inaugural Exhibition of Contemporary Sculpture to Celebrate the Opening of the National Stone Centre 1989, Loughborough, East Midlands Art/Wirksworth, National Stone Centre

3D '89: National Open Sculpture Exhibition, Brentford, Watermans Arts Centre/London, The Small Mansion Arts Centre

1990

J. W. Mills, *Encyclopaedia of Sculpture Techniques*, London, Batsford

R. Martin, *The Sculpted Forest: Sculptures in the Forest of Dean*, Bristol, Redcliffe Press

J. W. Mills, *The Technique of Casting for Sculpture*, revised edition, London, Batsford

1991

J. Marrow (ed.), *A Sculpture Trail for Norton Priory*, Runcorn, Norton Priory Museum Trust

Broken English, London, Serpentine Gallery

P. Overy, 'Lions and unicorns: The Britishness of post-war British sculpture', *Art in America*, September, vol. 79, no. 9, pp. 104–11, 153–5

B. Read and J. Barnes (eds), *Pre-Raphaelite Sculpture: Nature and Imagination in British Sculpture 1848–1914*, London, Henry Moore Foundation in association with Lund Humphries

R. Hughes and M. Rowe, *The Colouring, Bronzing and Patination of Metals: A Manual for Fine Metalworkers, Sculptors and Designers*, London, Thames and Hudson, (originally published 1982)

B. Grant and P. Harris (eds), *The Grizedale Experience: Sculpture, Arts and Theatre in a Lakeland Forest*, Edinburgh, Canongate Press

J. Darke, *The Monument Guide to England and Wales: A National Portrait in Bronze and Stone*, London, Macdonald

Tout Quarry: Isle of Portland, Dorset (video recording), London, Portland Sculpture Trust

F. Pearson (ed.), *Virtue and Vision: Sculpture and Scotland 1540–1990*, Edinburgh, National Galleries of Scotland

1992

I. Jenkins, *Archaeologists and Aesthetes in the Sculpture Galleries of the British Museum, 1800–1939*, London, British Museum Press

H. F. Senie, *Contemporary Public Sculpture: Tradition, Transformation and Controversy*, Oxford, Oxford University Press

Gibson to Gilbert: British Sculpture 1840–1914, London, Fine Art Society

I. Gregory, *Sculptural Ceramics*, London, A&C Black

C. Renfrew, *Sculpture in the Close: Jesus College Cambridge*, Cambridge, Jesus College

Sculpture on the Campus, Canterbury, University of Kent

1993

Chelsea Harbour Sculpture 93, London, Royal Society of British Sculptors

T. Friedman, *Four Centuries of Sculptors' Drawings from the Collection of Leeds City Art Galleries*, Leeds, Henry Moore Centre for the Study of Sculpture

In Site: New British Sculpture (two video compilations), London, British Council

A. Benjamin (ed.), *Installation Art*, London, Academy Editions, (Art and Design Profile 30; published as part of *Art and Design*, March–April 1993, vol. 8, no. 5/6)

Yorkshire Sculpture Park, *Putting Art in its Place: Galleries Without Walls* (video recording), London, Arts Council of Great Britain

Recent British Sculpture From the Arts Council Collection: A National Touring Exhibition From the South Bank Centre, London Arts Council

Sculpture at Margam: Welsh Open Sculpture Exhibition 1993, Port Talbot, Sculpture at Margam

P. Rockwell, *The Art of Stoneworking: A Reference Guide*, Cambridge, Cambridge University Press

The Henry Moore Sculpture Trust Studio at Dean Clough, Halifax, 1989–1993, Leeds, Henry Moore Sculpture Trust

N. Penny, *The Materials of Sculpture*, London, Yale University Press

The Raw and the Cooked: New Work in Clay in Britain, Oxford, Museum of Modern Art

1994

A Changing World: Fifty Years of Sculpture From the British Council Collection, London, British Council

N. de Oliveira, N. Oxley and M. Petry, *Installation Art*, London, Thames and Hudson

Into the Elements: Sculpture From the Landscape, Aberystwyth, Aberystwyth Arts Centre

M. Macdonald, *Nine Sculptors in Scotland*, Edinburgh, Edinburgh College of Art

Scandex XV 94: An Exhibition of Scottish Contemporary Sculpture, Huntly, Scottish Sculpture Workshop

S. Kent, *Shark Infested Waters: The Saatchi Collection of British Art in the 90s*, London, Zwemmer

1995

S. Bowness and C. Phillpot (eds), *Britain at the Venice Biennale, 1895–1995*, London, British Council

Escultura Britanica Contemporanea: de Henry Moore a los Anos 90, Porto, Fundacao de Serralves

D. Boorman, *For Your Tomorrow: British Second World War Memorials*, York, Ebor Press

J. Heuman, *From Marble to Chocolate: The Conservation of Modern Sculpture*, London, Archetype

S. Kent, *Here and Now*, London, Serpentine Gallery

Minky Manky, London, South London Gallery

Sculpture at Goodwood 1, Goodwood, Hat Hill Sculpture Foundation

1996

Walker Arts Center (Minneapolis), *Brilliant: New Art from London*, New York, Distributed Art Publishers

P. Curtis and T. Friedman (eds), *Leeds' Sculpture Collections Illustrated Concise Catalogue*, Leeds, Henry Moore Institute

L. Greene, *On the Beaten Track: Care and Maintenance for Sculpture Commissions in a Working Forest – The Forest of Dean Sculpture Trail*, Exeter, Public Art South West

Private view: A Temporary Exhibition of Contemporary British and German Art, Leeds, Henry Moore Institute

Sculpture at Goodwood: British Contemporary Sculpture 96/97, Goodwood, Hat Hill Sculpture Foundation

R. Burstow, *Symbols for '51: The Royal Festival Hall, Skylon and Sculptures on the South Bank for the Festival of Britain*, London, Royal Festival Hall

The Colour of Sculpture 1840–1910, Zwolle, Waanders Uitgevers

Un Siécle de Sculpture Anglaise, Paris, Galerie Nationale du Jeu de Paume, 1996

1997

A Guide to North Lanarkshire's Public Art Works, North Lanarkshire Council

R. Hitchcock, *A Sculpture Walk on the Streatham Campus*, University of Exeter Fine Art and Exhibition Advisory Group

C. Marshall (ed.), *Breaking the Mould: British Art of the 1980s and 1990s – The Weltkunst Collection*, London. Lund Humphries

P. Curtis, *Follow Me, British Art at the Lower Elbe: British Sculptures of the Post-War Period from Leeds*, Stade, Schwedenspeicher Museum

Four Seasons: A Gateshead Sculpture Project, Portcullis Press/Gateshead Libraries and Arts Service

M. Archer and G. Hilty, *Material Culture: The Object in British Art of the 1980s and '90s*, London, Hayward Gallery

T. Cavanagh, *Public Sculpture of Liverpool*, Liverpool, Liverpool University Press, (Public Sculpture in Britain 1)

E. Ranfft and A. Hughes (eds), *Sculpture and Its Reproductions*, London, Reaktion

Sculpture at Goodwood: British Contemporary Sculpture 97/98, Goodwood, Sculpture at Goodwood

P. Lindley (ed.), *Sculpture Conservation: Preservation or Interference?*, Aldershot, Scolar

Sensation: Young British Artists From the Saatchi Collection, London, Thames and Hudson in association with the Royal Academy of Arts

P. Curtis (ed.), *The Sculpture Business: Documents From the Archive*, Leeds, Henry Moore Institute

V. Button, *The Turner Prize*, London, Tate Gallery Publishing

1998

Here to Stay: Arts Council Collection Purchases of the 1990s, London, Hayward Gallery Publishing

S. Michalski, *Public Monuments: Art in Political Bondage 1870–1997*, London, Reaktion Books, (Essays in Art and Culture)

G. Noszlopy, *Public Sculpture of Birmingham* (including Sutton Coldfield), Liverpool, Liverpool University Press, (Public Sculpture in Britain 2)

G. A. Johnson (ed.), *Sculpture and Photography: Envisioning the Third Dimension*, Cambridge, Cambridge University Press, (Cambridge Studies in New Art History and Criticism)

Sculpture at Goodwood: British Contemporary Sculpture 98/99, Goodwood, Sculpture at Goodwood

Sculpture at Goodwood: Drawings and Models 94/98, Goodwood, Sculpture at Goodwood

R. Blandford and Z. Dobson, *Sculpture for Winchester*, Winchester, Hampshire Sculpture Trust

A. Causey, *Sculpture Since 1945*, Oxford, Oxford University Press, (Oxford History of Art)

1999

A. Clay, E. Morris, S. Penketh and T. Stevens, *British Sculpture in the Lady Lever Art Gallery*, Liverpool, National Museums and Galleries on Merseyside

Colour Sculptures: Britain in the Sixties, London, Waddington Galleries

A. Patrizio, *Contemporary Sculpture in Scotland*, Sydney, Craftsman House

A. Guest and R. McKenzie (eds), *Dangerous Ground: Sculpture in the City*, Edinburgh, Scottish Sculpture Trust

B. Robertson, *'45–99: A Personal View of British Painting and Sculpture*, Cambridge, Kettle's Yard Gallery

R. Hopper and G. Worthington, *Here and Now: Experiences in Sculpture*, Leeds, Henry Moore Foundation External Programmes

N. Barley (ed.), *Leaving Tracks: Artranspennine98 –An International Contemporary Visual Art Exhibition Recorded*, Manchester, August Media in association with Artranspennine

D. Taylor (ed.), *Leeds' Sculpture Collections: Works on Paper – Concise Catalogue*, Leeds, Henry Moore Institute

J. Heuman (ed.), *Material Matters: The Conservation of Modern Sculpture*, London, Tate Gallery Publishing

A. Dawson, *Portrait Sculpture: A Catalogue of the British Museum Collection, c.1675–1975*, London, British Museum Press

Sculpture at Goodwood: British Contemporary Sculpture 99/00, Goodwood, Sculpture at Goodwood

R. McKenzie, *Sculpture in Glasgow: An Illustrated Handbook*, Foulis Archive Press with Neil Baxter Associates

P. Curtis, *Sculpture 1900–1945: After Rodin*, Oxford, Oxford University Press, (Oxford History of Art)

J. Hall, *The World As Sculpture: The Changing Status of Sculpture from the Renaissance to the Present Day*, London, Chatto and Windus

A. Bond, *Trace: 1st Liverpool Biennial of International Contemporary Art*, Liverpool, Liverpool Biennial of Contemporary Art in association with Tate Gallery Liverpool

Young British Art: The Saatchi Decade, London, Booth-Clibborn Editions

2000

A. Dyer (ed.), *Bronze: Contemporary British Sculpture, Holland Park*, London, Royal Borough of Kensington and Chelsea

V. Button and C. Esche, *Intelligence: New British Art 2000*, London, Tate Publishing

C. Phillpot and A. Tarsia, *Live in Your Head: Concept and Experiment in Britain, 1965–75*, London, Whitechapel Art Gallery

T. Cavanagh, *Public Sculpture of Leicestershire and Rutland*, Liverpool, Liverpool University Press, (Public Sculpture in Britain 4)

P. Usherwood, J. Beach and C. Morris, *Public Sculpture of North-East England*, Liverpool, Liverpool University Press, (Public Sculpture in Britain 3)

P. Curtis, P. Funnell and N. Kalinsky, *Return to Life: A New Look at the Portrait Bust*, Leeds, Henry Moore Institute

Sculpture, an Abbey and a Cathedral (Malmesbury Abbey, Gloucester Cathedral)

Sculpture at Goodwood: British Contemporary Sculpture 00/01, Goodwood, Sculpture at Goodwood

V. De Circasia, *The Concealed Space: British Sculpture*, Torino, Provincia di Torino

A. Potts, *The Sculptural Imagination: Figurative, Modernist, Minimalist*, London, Yale University Press

2001

P. Davies, *After Trewyn: St Ives Sculptors Since Hepworth*, Abertillery, Old Bakehouse Publications

I. Jenkins, *Cleaning and Controversy: The Parthenon Sculptures 1811–1939*, London, British Museum, (British Museum Occasional Paper 146)

R. McKenzie, *Public Sculpture of Glasgow*, Liverpool, Liverpool University Press, (Public Sculpture in Britain 5)

P. Ward-Jackson, *Public Sculpture of the City of London*, Liverpool, Liverpool University Press, (Public Sculpture in Britain 7)

G. T. Noszlopy, *Public Sculpture of Warwickshire, Coventry and Solihull*, Liverpool, Liverpool University Press, (Public Sculpture in Britain 6)

K. Mey (ed.), *Sculpsit: Contemporary Artists on Sculpture and Beyond*, Manchester, Manchester University Press in association with Transcript

C. Ledwith (ed.), *Tailsliding*, London, British Council

2002

Kunstmuseum Wolfsburg, *Blast to Freeze: British Art in the 20th Century*, Ostfildern-Ruit, Hatje Cantz

D. Bilbey and M. Trusted, *British Sculpture 1470 to 2000: A Concise Catalogue of the Collection at the Victoria & Albert Museum*, London, V&A Publications

Close Encounters: The Sculptor's Studio in the Age of the Camera, Leeds, Henry Moore Institute

M. Baker, *Discovering London Statues and Monuments*, 5th edition, Princes Risborough, Shire Publications

I. Blazwick and A. Tarsia, *Early One Morning: British Art Now*, London, Whitechapel Art Gallery

International 2002: Liverpool Biennial, Liverpool Biennial of Contemporary Art

S. Gartside, *Model Forms: Sculpture/Architecture in 50s and 60s Britain*, Leeds, Henry Moore Institute

D. Merritt, *Sculpture in Bristol*, Bristol, Redcliffe Press

J. Wood, *Shine: Sculpture and Surface in the 1920s and 1930s*, Leeds, Henry Moore Institute

2003

M. Withey, *A Fine Tomorrow: Sculpture and Socialism in Mid-Century Britain*, Leeds, Henry Moore Institute

Jonathan Blackwood is a lecturer in cultural studies at the University of Glamorgan. His PhD, completed at the Courtauld Institute of Art, was on aspects of the 'primitive' in 20th-century English sculpture. He is currently working on a monograph of the Scots painter Edward Baird. Contact: School of Humanities and Social Sciences, University of Glamorgan, Trefforest, RCT, Cymru CF37 1DL

Robert Burstow's research specialism is the history and theory of British postwar sculpture. His recent publications include 'Henry Moore's "open-air" sculpture', in *Henry Moore: Critical Essays* (2003) and 'Modern sculpture in the South Bank townscape', in *The Festival of Britain*, special issue of the *Journal of the Twentieth Century Society*, 2001. He is currently a postdoctoral fellow at the Paul Mellon Centre for Studies in British Art. Contact: University of Derby, Division of Arts, School of Art and Design, Britannia Mill, Mackworth Street, Derby DE22 3BL

Ann Compton is preparing a monograph on Charles Sargeant Jagger for the Henry Moore Foundation and is also doing more general research on the study, practice and context of sculpture in the early 20th century. Her publications include: 'Charles Sargeant Jagger: War and peace sculpture' (1985), 'Edward Halliday: Art for life 1925–39' (1997), and 'Edward Carter Preston, 1885–1965: Sculptor, painter, medallist' (1999). Contact: acompton@liv.ac.uk

Sarah Crellin writes on aspects of figurative sculpture, including artists' contributions to facial masking and reconstructive surgery in World War I. A monograph on the sculpture of Charles Wheeler for the Henry Moore Foundation/Lund Humphries British Sculptors Series is planned. Contact: screllin@lineone.net

Martina Droth's research interests include 19th-century sculpture, decorative objects and material culture, particularly British and French. She is currently preparing a book on the relationship between ornament and sculpture in late 19th-century Britain and France. She is research coordinator at the Henry Moore Institute. Contact: martina@henry-moore.ac.uk

Simon Ford is a freelance writer. His books include *The Realization and Suppression of the Situationist International* (1995), *Wreckers of Civilisation* (1999), *Hip Priest: The Story of Mark E. Smith and The Fall* (2003), and, as editor, *Information Sources in Art, Art History and Design* (2001). He writes regularly for *Art Monthly, Texte zur Kunst*, the *Wire* and *Mute*. Contact: sford@metamute.com

Margaret Garlake writes on mid-20th-century British art. Publications include *New Art, New World: British Art in Postwar Society* (1998) and *The Drawings of Peter Lanyon* (forthcoming). She is currently the editor of the *Sculpture Journal*. Contact: MGARLAKE@aol.com

David J. Getsy is the Andrew W. Mellon Postdoctoral Fellow at the Leslie Center for the Humanities, Dartmouth College, USA, and specialises in the history and theory of sculpture in the 19th and 20th centuries. He is editor of the forthcoming anthology *Sculpture and the Pursuit of a Modern Ideal in Britain, c.1880–1930* and is completing a book titled *Body Doubles: Sculpture in Britain 1877–1905*.
Contact: david.getsy@dartmouth.edu

Claire Glossop works for Arts Council London, where she is responsible for visual arts policy and development. In 2001 she completed her Ph.D. at the University of Leeds on 'The importance of exhibition for the reception and practice of sculpture in Britain'.
Contact: Arts Council England, London Office, 2 Pear Tree Court, London EC1R 0DS

Tony Godfrey is programme director of the MA (contemporary art) at Sotheby's Institute. He writes regularly for the *Burlington Magazine* and his most recent book was *Conceptual Art.*
Contact: tony_godfrey@hotmail.com

Nigel Halliday is a freelance art historian. He is the author of *More Than a Bookshop: Zwemmer's and Art in the 20th Century* (1991). His doctorate from the Courtauld Institute of Art focused on British art critics between World Wars I and II.
Contact: nigelhal@waitrose.com

Valerie Holman holds a three-year Leverhulme postdoctoral research fellowship in book history at the University of Reading to study English publishing from 1938 to 1949. She co-edited *France at War in the Twentieth Century: Propaganda, Myth and Metaphor* (2000) and *Humour as a Strategy in War* (special issue of the *Journal of European Studies*, 2001), and recently contributed to *The Rise of the Image* (2003).

Catherine Kinley studied fine art at St Martin's School of Art, 1963–7, and at the Royal College of Art, 1967–70. She joined Tate's staff in 1978, where her work has been chiefly allied to Tate's permanent collection. She currently heads the team responsible for the acquisition of art post-1960 and she has curated a number of exhibitions for Tate.
Contact: catherine.kinley@tate.org.uk

Sue Malvern lectures in history of art at the University of Reading. She has published widely on art and war. She curated the exhibition *Eric Kennington's War God and Other Works* for the Henry Moore Institute in 2001. She is completing a book, *Witnessing, Testimony and Remembrance: Modern Art, Britain and the Great War.*
Contact: s.b.malvern@reading.ac.uk

Joy Sleeman is senior lecturer in the history and theory of art at the Slade School of Fine Art, University College London. Her research has focused on landscape and Land Art in Britain, and she has also published on British sculpture. She curated an exhibition of the early work of Richard Long at the Henry Moore Institute in 1997 and is now preparing a book on William Tucker.
Contact: alison.sleeman@ucl.ac.uk

Chris Stephens has published widely on the artists of St Ives and on British sculpture, including books on Hubert Dalwood (1999), Peter Lanyon (2000) and Barbara Hepworth (with Matthew Gale, 1998). He is curator of *Barbara Hepworth: Centenary* for Tate St Ives in 2003 and is writing a critical history of St Ives.
Contact: Senior Curator at Tate Britain, Millbank, London SW1P 4RG

Andrew Stephenson teaches in the Art, Design and Film History Department at the University of East London. He has published articles on British art of the late 19th and 20th centuries, most recently 'Anxious performances: aestheticism, the art gallery and the ambulatory geographies of late nineteenth-century London', *Victorian Studies* (2001), and 'Staging authenticity: tourist spaces and artistic inscription in inter-war British Art', *Visual Culture in Britain* (2002). He is co-editor with Amelia Jones of *Performing the Body/Performing the Text* (1999) and is currently working on a study of British modernism 1920–40 and *Patrilenes: Masculine Self-Fashioning and Artistic Performance in Britain 1850–1910.*
Contact: A.P.Stephenson@uel.ac.uk

Andrea Tarsia is a curator and writer based in London. He has worked on a variety of exhibitions, including *From Figure to Object: A Century of Sculptors' Drawings* at the Karsten Schubert Gallery, London, and more recently *Alighiero Boetti, Live in Your Head* and *Early One Morning* at the Whitechapel Art Gallery, London, where he is currently head of exhibitions and projects.
Contact: AndreaTarsia@whitechapel.org

Anne M. Wagner is an art historian whose interests are focused on sculpture, gender and modernity in the 19th and 20th centuries. Since 1988 she has been a professor at the University of California, Berkeley, where she is a member of the *Representations* editorial board.
Contact: awagner@socrates.Berkeley.EDU

Gillian Whiteley is a freelance researcher, editor and writer, and lectures at the University of Leeds and Loughborough University School of Art and Design. Publications include essays, journal articles and reviews, exhibition catalogues and online web-based material on 20th-century and contemporary sculpture. Her monograph *Assembling the Absurd: The Sculpture of George Fullard 1923–1973* was published in 1998.
Contact: whiteleybright@ntlworld.com

Matthew Withey is based at the Henry Moore Institute in Leeds, where he is assistant curator of the sculpture collection of Leeds Museums and Galleries. A former researcher for the Public Monuments and Sculpture Association's cataloguing project in Glasgow, he has written on various aspects of sculptural and architectural history.
Contact: matthew@henry-moore.ac.uk

Roman numerals refer to timeline column.

LEEDS MUSEUMS AND GALLERIES (LEEDS CITY ART GALLERY)
3i, 3iii, 5i–iii, 6iv, 7ii, 17, 68iv, 69i, 72iv, 73ii, 76iii, 109, 114, 115, 119, 140iv, 141ii, 141iii, 158, 159, 161

LEEDS MUSEUMS AND GALLERIES (HENRY MOORE INSTITUTE ARCHIVE)
2i, 2iii, 2iv, 3ii, 3iv, 4i, 4ii, 4iv, 6iii, 7i, 7iv, 8i, 8ii, 15, 16, 33, 35, 37, 39, 40, 68i, 69iii, 71iv, 73iv, 74iv, 75i, 75iv, 76i, 88, 90, 91, 105, 118, 138i-iii, 140i, 141i, 144iv, 148, 150, 155, 188

HENRY MOORE INSTITUTE LIBRARY
2ii, 4iii, 6ii, 7iii, 69ii, 69iv, 70ii–iv, 71ii, 72ii, 74i–iii, 75ii, 108, 127, 131, 132, 139i, 139ii, 140ii, 140iii, 142i–iv, 143i–iv, 144i–iii, 145ii, 187, 192, 194, 201, 202, 205, 214i, 215ii, 215iii, 216i–iv, 217i, 217ii, 217iv, 218iii, 219ii–iv, 220i, 221, 222, 223, 268, 269

HENRY MOORE FOUNDATION
107, 117, 121, 168, 214iv, 217iii

PHOTOGRAPHIC CREDITS
Grizedale: 214iii; Gautier Deblonde: 220ii; Jerry Hardman-Jones: 3i, 3iii, 5i–iii, 6iv, 7i, 7ii, 7iv, 69i, 69iii, 72iv, 73ii, 76iii, 109, 114, 115; G.W. Harvey: 191; Philip Hollis: 268; Peter Hollings: 217iii; Errol Jackson: 168; Paul Laib: 105; Barry Lewis: 266; Richard Littlewood: 2ii, 3ii, 4iv, 6ii, 7iii, 8i, 11, 68iv, 69ii, 69ii, 69iv, 70ii–iv, 71ii, 71iv, 72ii, 73iv, 74i–iv, 75i, 75ii, 75iv, 76i, 119, 148, 187, 214i, 215ii, 215iii, 216i–iv, 217i, 217ii, 217iv, 218iii, 219ii–iv, 220i; Ray McKenzie: 36; John Vincent: 262

The publishers wish to thank the following individuals and organisations for permission to reproduce copyright material:

Acme Gallery: 232, 235, 236; Carl Andre/VAGA, New York/DACS, London, Tate London: 264; Anthony Caro/Tate London (presented to the Tate by the Contemporary Art Society): 172; Arts Council Collection, Hayward Gallery: 255; Bank: 259; Brotherton Collection at Leeds University Library: 51; Chisenhale Gallery: 225; City Racing: 260; Conway Library/Courtauld Institute: 10; *Coventry Evening Telegraph*, as reproduced in Peter Peri Memorial Exhibition Catalogue: 188; Sarah Crellin/W. D. and H. O. Wills: 94, 97; Barry Flanagan/ Tate London: 177; Margaret Garlake: 156; Gilbert & George: 152; Gjon Mili: 121; *Guardian*: 220i; David Harding: 191; Harlow Art Trust collection, Museum of Harlow, Harlow Council: 189; Valerie Holman: 127, 131, 132; Jay Jopling/White Cube, London: 218iv, 242; Michael Landy: 261; Lisson Gallery on behalf of Jane and Louise Wilson: 224; London Library: 50; Matt's Gallery: 237; Richard Long/Anthony d'Offay Gallery: 178; Sarah Lucas/Sadie Coles HQ: 219i; Sadie Coles HQ: 257;

David Mach: 266; Bruce McLean/Tate London: 147; Musée Rodin, Paris: 45; Eduardo Paolozzi/DACS/Tate London: 170; Prudence Cuming Associates/ Royal Academy of Arts: 44; Reading University Library: 49; Roger-Viollet: 47; Scottish National Gallery of Modern Art: 38; Selfridges: 92; Lord Snowdon: 151, 205; Special Press: 16; Sarah Staton: 270; Andrew Stephenson: 109, 111, 112; Tate Liverpool: 11; Tate London: 9, 11, 12, 239, 244, 246, 250; William Tucker/ Tate London (presented to the Tate by A. McAlpine): 174; Mark Wallinger/ Anthony Reynolds Gallery: 247; *Yorkshire Post*: 265